*Portrait of Joanna Southcott drawn by Edgar Player in 1926 from an engraving*

# Joanna Southcott's Box of Sealed Prophecies

Frances Brown

The Lutterworth Press

**The Lutterworth Press**
**P.O. Box 60**
**Cambridge**
**CB1 2NT**

**www.lutterworth.com**
**publishing@lutterworth.com**

ISBN 0 7188 3041 5

*British Library Cataloguing in Publication Data*
A catalogue record is available from the British Library





First Published in 2003





Printed in the United Kingdom by
Athenaeum Press Ltd, Gateshead, Tyne and Wear

# Contents

# List of Illustrations

# Acknowledgements

In researching this book I have received invaluable help from David McLynn who shared with me his intimate knowledge of the Panacea Society Archives in Bedford and made available their unrivalled collection of pamphlets, books, newspaper cuttings and letters to and from Southcottians. He has generously supplied most of the illustrations and the book would not have been possible without his assistance in tracing relevant documents. I also wish to record my gratitude to Ruth Klein and John Coghill for being so patient with my queries and forthcoming in their information and reminiscences.

I am indebted to the British Library; the London Metropolitan Archive; the Guildhall Library; the Harry Price Library, University of London; and public libraries at Bradford, Bridgwater, Bristol, Burnham-on-Sea, Dudley, Exeter, Leeds, Morecambe, Plymouth, Rochdale, Stourbridge and Taunton. I am also grateful to the staffs of the Public Record Office and the Record Offices of Devon, Gloucestershire, Somerset, Surrey, Wiltshire and Worcestershire. The Surrey History Centre in Woking and Blockley Antiquarian Society were particularly helpful when replying to queries, and Mrs Eileen Shaw, Town Clerk of Burnham-on-Sea & Highbridge Town Council, was generous in her assistance.

I should also like to thank Gordon Allan, Mr and Mrs J. Baxendale, David Bromwich, Jake Budden, Professor J. D. M. Derrett, Frank P. Jowett, Ian Maxted, Hudson John Powell, Dieter Rader and Shelley Tobin for all their help.

Finally, I wish to thank my husband, Henry Brown, who has (as always) been unstinting in his support and encouragement.

## Illustrations

The illustrations used in this book are courtesy of the Panacea Society, Bedford, apart from the following:

Author: 28, 60, 133, 160

David McLynn: 73, 86, 223, 228, 257, 260, 261, 262

Taunton Local Studies: 119

Burnham-on-Sea & Highbridge Town Council: 163

Devon Library & Information Services: 23

# Foreword

## by the Rev. Dr Jane Shaw

On a number of occasions over the past few years, when I have mentioned the name Joanna Southcott in a lecture on British history or a sermon on prophecy, inevitably, at the end, an older member of the audience or congregation has come up to tell me that they remember the advertisements in the British press calling for the bishops to open Southcott's Box of prophecies. They were each referring, of course, to the box of prophecies sealed up by Southcott, to be opened by 24 bishops of the Church of England (echoing the 24 elders of the Book of Revelation) in a time of 'grave, national danger'. As Frances Brown notes early on in her book, it is this "famous Box of sealed prophecies with which the name of Joanna Southcott has . . . become synonymous." In fact, Joanna Southcott's Box is a part of our national memory, almost something of an institution. But how and why did this Box become famous?

Frances Brown offers us, in this meticulously researched book, the history of the Box, telling us where it has been, and who has cared for it for over two hundred years. The story of the nineteenth century, after Southcott's death in 1814, is not that of a 'public' Box: rather, it is the story of faithful Southcottian families, such as the Foleys and the Jowetts, safeguarding the Box in their homes, but feeling little need to promote its importance to the general public. There is no history of letters to and from bishops in this period, no widespread advertising campaign. All this changed in the early twentieth century when the Box emerged as a 'public' object, albeit kept in a secret location. This emergence was fuelled by a new impetus given to Southcottian life and study, the spread of which needs to be understood, at least in part, in the context of the horrors of the First World War.

It was Alice Seymour, headmistress of a girls' school in Plymouth and a believer from an old Southcottian family, who first promoted a new interest in Joanna Southcott in the early twentieth Century. She began to publish, and in some cases re-publish, Southcott's writings primarily through a monthly publication called *The Express Leaflets* (which ran to 42 editions and was then re-titled, firstly as *The Two Witnesses* , then as *The Southcott Despatch,* both of which incidentally also ran to 42 editions), and in her ambitious project of re-publishing what has become known today as the sixty-five books. Seymour was also astute in targeting her literature: she and others sent it to those considered influential in the land, including Anglican clergy and even rabbis. The result was a wave of new believers, many of them women, most of them disillusioned members of the Church of England. That so many women were involved is not surprising: Southcottianism had always attracted women – giving them a special role in the theology of the redemption of the world, and active roles in the leadership and running of the movement. With the outbreak of war many thought that this was the time of 'grave, national danger' and thus the moment for the bishops to do their duty and open the Box. As Frances Brown documents here, articles began to appear in the national press about the Box, causing many older Southcottian families to be nervous about both the publicity and the zeal of new converts. A campaign to get the bishops to open the Box was initiated, and its fame as a national and public phenomenon began.

But 1914 did not only see the beginning of The Great War. Within the Southcottian world, for some an event of extreme importance occurred. Mabel Barltrop, a forty-eight year old Church of England vicar's widow, read a Southcottian pamphlet in her local library in Bedford. From that moment on her world was to change forever as she began her own personal campaign to get the bishops to open the Box. Well-educated in theology, she maintained a vigorous correspondence not only with bishops and their chaplains but also with many other clergy. She began to correspond with others who had a connection to the Southcottian world, such as Rachel Fox, a descendant of George Fox, the founder of the Quaker movement. Gradually Mrs Barltrop began to gather around her in Bedford interested Southcottian women, and in 1919, they recognised her as both the incarnation of 'Shiloh' – Southcott's soul child born in 1814 – and the eighth English prophet. Henceforth she would be referred to, amongst her followers, simply as Octavia. This group, first known as the Community of the Holy Ghost, and subsequently as the Panacea Society, grew at its height to about seventy resident members at its headquarters in Bedford, with a somewhat greater number who chose to remain resident elsewhere.

In its early manifestation, the campaign to make not only the bishops but also other members of the Establishment and the general public aware of the Box even managed to reach the eyes and ears of King George V, through the efforts of Princess Louise, his aunt, and Lady Paget, both of whom were encouraged by the determination of Mrs Fox and her cousin Lady Portsmouth. As World War 1 drew to a close in the autumn of 1918, these four women – and gradually many others – believed that England's fate was sealed in the prophecies placed in the Box over a century ago. Surely it was now only a matter of time before 24 bishops consented to its opening?

It was largely through the Panacea Society's efforts in advertising and in the organisation of petitions in the 1920s and 1930s that the campaign to get 24 bishops to open the Box became so visible in the public eye. The photographs in this book illustrating this campaign give evidence of their work and impact. The Panacea believers even prepared one of their houses to accommodate the bishops during the expected opening of the Box, so sure were they that this event would occur imminently. They and Alice Seymour did not, however, always see eye to eye, and Frances Brown ably documents the tensions in their relations and the resulting disagreements about the fate of this item of great mutual interest. Undoubtedly, however, without the work of the Panacea Society, the Box would not have become so well-known in the twentieth century. Interestingly, it was only in 1957 that the Society acquired the Box and became its custodian, some twenty years after Octavia's death. Before that, in the first half of the twentieth century it had primarily been in the quiet safekeeping of an old Southcottian family, the Jowetts, who had played no part in the national campaign for its opening. After acquiring the Box the Society continued to place their advertisements in the national press twice a year for much of the second half of the century, but as Mrs Brown points out, by then their approach had become more low-key.

Frances Brown offers us here the story of this extraordinary Box and its sealed prophecies (and the fake boxes which have emerged over the years). The story she tells is one of individuals and communities of faith and strong religious belief. The Southcottian movement stands in a broad tradition of millennial beliefs in Britain and so, as Mrs Brown reminds us, the Box has for many believers promised answers to the troubles of this life. Hence, there has been a great desire to ensure its security, and the concern that, should it ever be opened, exact conditions pertaining to this long awaited event be adhered to. Such conditions have been of paramount importance to all its custodians. By tracing the provenance of the Box so carefully, and examining the debates between different Southcottian believers, Mrs Brown provides us with an historically accurate account of an object which has been seen by very few, but which nevertheless has been (and remains) the focus of religious hope, whilst also capturing the public's imagination.

Jane Shaw,<br>Dean of Divinity,<br>New College,<br>Oxford.

# Introduction

> 'The secret things belong unto the Lord our God: but those things which are revealed belong unto us and to our children for ever, that we may do all the words of this law.' *Deuteronomy 29:29*

If the name of Joanna Southcott strikes a chord today, it is usually in connection with her famous Box of Sealed Prophecies. But, if asked what that Box is, some will assure you that it contains the secrets of the universe, while others say that it holds nothing more significant than a woman's lacy night cap and a pistol. As to where the Box is now, some repeat that it was opened in 1927 in Westminster Hall and that it is now housed in the Harry Price Library in London. Others have suggested that its contents are in the British Library, while the Box itself languishes in a cellar of the British Museum. Still others maintain that the Box no longer exists – if, indeed, it ever did. The truth is far simpler, yet in some ways more mysterious. The Box does still exist. The author has seen and examined it. There has been an unbroken chain of custodians from Joanna's day to this, and the present guardians of the Box take their responsibilities every bit as seriously as their predecessors. Moreover, all the evidence suggests that Joanna Southcott's Box has not been opened for at least a hundred and fifty years and that it contains prophecies which have been kept with their seals intact ever since her death.

Joanna Southcott was born in 1750 in Ottery St Mary, Devon, the daughter of a struggling tenant farmer and, growing up in a typical rural environment of the time, her life was changed in 1792 when she heard the 'still, small voice' that would inform and guide her for the rest of her days. Her claim that it was the voice of God speaking through her was rejected by church leaders, yet her prophecies of the Second Coming and her 'sealing' of believers against harm brought her many thousands of followers. The climax of her mission came when, at the age of sixty-four and still a virgin, she announced that she was about to give birth to a new Messiah whose name was Shiloh. After more than a dozen doctors confirmed that she was pregnant, feverish interest in Joanna swept the country. Newspapers issued bulletins on her health. A prestigious house near Manchester Square, London, was taken for her lying-in. She was inundated with magnificent gifts for Shiloh and she held court to distinguished visitors, such as the Russian ambassador and the Emperor's chief aide.

When she died in 1814 Joanna Southcott left a legacy of sixty-five published works as well as various manuscripts and letters. However, her inner voice had commanded her to keep some of her writings secret. These had been sealed and locked away in a box which was only to be opened under certain strict conditions, that it must be requested by twenty-four bishops of the Church of England 'in a time of grave national danger', for example. This is the origin of the famous Box of Sealed Prophecies with which the name of Joanna Southcott has since become synonymous.

The mystique of a sealed box is the stuff of myth and legend. In ancient Egypt, Isis wandered bereft over the face of the land in search of the locked, nailed and sealed box that contained her husband, Osiris. In Greece, Pandora's Box, when injudiciously opened, allowed all the afflictions of mankind to fly into the world, apart from Hope, which alone remained. Early Christian art represented Noah's Ark as a large box from which emerged a figure with arms outstretched in a posture signifying openness to God. In medieval romance the dream that haunted people's imagination was that somewhere on earth there was a certain object, often identified as the Grail, but according to Robert de Borron, it was the Ark of the New Covenant; the visible pledge of God's good will toward mankind. As a physical object this Ark enshrined God's promise to humanity that, despite the apparent cruelty and indifference of the world, there was a divine plan that – in God's own time – would be realised. The nature of the quest was discovering how to approach the sacred object, and in Wolfram von Eschenbach's *Parzival* the knight might approach the Grail castle but still be denied access, if he failed to ask the key question.

If all these allusions seem far removed from Joanna Southcott's Box, yet there are congruities. Firstly, Joanna's Box has always been elusive, its whereabouts kept a closely guarded secret by a succession of custodians. Moreover, all attempts to bring forward its opening have failed, because the exact conditions (the right question) have never been met. As a result, the world is left with a conundrum. Many would love to know what is in the Box, but will find out only if twenty-four bishops of the Church of England meet the specified conditions. To do this, the bishops would have to take the matter seriously, but this they will not do without first being convinced that the contents of the Box merit their interest. However, the contents of the Box are unknown and must remain so until the bishops take the matter seriously.

The reputation of Joanna Southcott has gone through many vicissitudes since her death. The *Dictionary of National Biography* dubbed her an 'English religious fanatic'. Sharp's engraving of her in the National Portrait Gallery was labelled 'Religious Impostor' until in 1913, at the behest of her followers, the wording was changed to 'Prophetess'. Then, in 1927, Harry Price perpetrated a hoax which, although exposed at the time, has lived on in popular imagination and is still regularly cited as evidence that Joanna Southcott's Box has already been opened and found to contain only trivia. It is as if 'Piltdown Man', discovered in 1912 and exposed as a forgery in 1953, was still being hailed as the 'missing link'.

It is not difficult to understand why there is so much confusion about the fate of Joanna Southcott's Box of Sealed Prophecies. Over the years Custodians opted for obscurity as their best defence against dramatic attempts to steal the Box from them, for there have been people who were prepared to go to extraordinary lengths to gain possession of the object they called the 'Sacred Treasure'; 'the Spiritual Ark', or 'The Ark of the New Covenant'. For Custodians it was (and is) a terrifying prospect that the Box might fall into the hands of curious or over-enthusiastic people who would want to open it without delay and would break the seals without first making sure that the exact conditions were met.

Again, there are echoes of legend and myth. Modern life is fraught with dangers – ecological, economic, social and political – just as the Grail Castle was surrounded by the Waste Land which could be redeemed only by someone who, by asking the right question, shows that he holds the key. In the popular subconscious there is the image of Arthur surrounded by his knights sleeping in a cave, and Drake lying five fathoms down, all awaiting their nation's urgent call. In contrast, Joanna Southcott's Box is a physical object that has been preserved for two hundred years and still exists today, waiting to be opened 'in a time of grave national danger'. In July 2001 a picture of it appeared in the *Independent* newspaper, the first photograph of Joanna's Box to be published for over a hundred years. This marked a change in attitude of the Custodians who, with the advent of a new Millennium, decided that it was time to remind people of the Box's existence and to clear away some of the confusion of the past. This book, by establishing the provenance of the Box, aims to dispel the falsehoods that have blurred its history. The simple fact is that Joanna Southcott's Box of Sealed Prophecies exists. It is locked, nailed and corded, its contents still awaiting examination. Doubtless when the time is right, the truth will be revealed.

# 1

# Nailed up in a Box, 1798-1802

On 16 November, 1802, Joanna Southcott wrote to the Reverend Nicholas Bull, Vicar of Saffron Walden,

> After being visited by the Lord by day and by night in 1792, of what was coming on the whole earth, I was ordered to leave my work and write it down, but not to keep it in my own possession, and my writings were to be sealed up every year.

There is no mention at this date of any particular box being the repository of Joanna's Communications, but in a manuscript dated 12 May, 1798, she mentions putting her sealed writings together and, in obedience to instructions given by the Spirit a year before, nailing them up 'in a box':

> While I was putting my writings together the weather was cloudy with some rain but the afternoon was sunshine and when I had put them into the Box I was answered to open my Bible it was at the 47 ch of Ezekiel of the Vision of the Holy Waters. . . .
>
> Mark thou this day the 1st of May (old style)
> Or else the 12th appears
> In order every thing does lie
> And all may now see clear
> What days are come and hastening on
> If they the Seals behold
> Remember now the Box is come
> Last year to thee was told
> I'll jest no more the time is o'er
> For it must be nailed up
> Unless that man to thee appears
> Before that May is up
> And tell thee plain that they do mean
> To stop thy heavy hand.[1]

Joanna had been writing down her Communications since 1792 when she had first started taking instruction from the Spirit of Truth, but she admitted that, since her handwriting was barely legible, when she showed them to the Reverend Joseph Pomeroy in 1800,

*Joanna Southcott, 'drawn and engraved from life' by William Sharp, 7 January 1812, with the Bible in her hands open at the last two chapters of Isaiah. A print of this engraving in the National Portrait Gallery, London, was labelled 'Religious Impostor' until 1913, when, at the behest of her followers, the wording was changed to 'Prophetess'.*

> He bade me get the writings of 1792 copied out, as he could not set the originals before ministers, who would not attend to manuscripts which they could not read: and they would not trust to what I should read to them. Therefore, he bade me open the seals on the writings of 1792, and send them with the fair copy; and if the ministers he consulted should judge them to be of God, I might have 12 or 14 afterwards.

So, Joanna opened the seals on her writings before witnesses, who marked and then copied them out for her, and these, together with the originals, were sent to Pomeroy. A week later she repeated the process when Pomeroy asked her to open the Seals set in 1794 and 1795 and send these as well. He was then allowed three weeks 'to examine, to consult ministers, and to judge whether the writings were of God, or not.[2] Whilst waiting for Pomeroy's response Joanna wrote to three other Anglican ministers, asking them to respond within seven days:

> The century is ended; the seals are cut open in the presence of six witnesses (what was written in 1792) and marked, and copied out. What was written in 1794, till 1795 and 1797, and nailed up in a box, is broken open in the presence of twelve witnesses; and they have signed their names to all the writings; so that, if the originals be demanded, no man can be deceived. Some of them were copied out and sent to the Rev Mr Pomeroy. So here the century ends with men.[3]

These words come from *The Strange Effects of Faith with Remarkable Prophecies of Things Which are to Come* and are the first published reference to Joanna Southcott's Box of Sealed Writings. Printed in January 1801, the book not only elevated Joanna from local harvest prophet into nationally acclaimed Prophetess, but also propelled her wooden box of sealed writings towards its momentous destiny.

In 1800 Joanna Southcott was aged fifty, unmarried and, having lived for thirty years as a domestic servant in a wide variety of situations, found herself without a home to call her own. Her widowed father, old William Southcott, had been forced to move out of the family farmhouse and into lodgings, so it was fortunate that she had made some good friends in Exeter and it says much for her character that many of these friends were her former employers. There was the Taylor family with their roomy premises fronting on Fore Street. No doubt she could have left goods and chattels with them for safekeeping. Except that Robert Taylor, the head of household, was not altogether sympathetic to Joanna's claims to prophesy. More amenable were William and Mary Symons of Gandy Lane, who not only employed Joanna on and off for seven years and afforded her accommodation while she worked for others, but also allowed her to use the services of their children as scribes and messengers. The fact that William Symons was also a warden at Allhallows, their parish church, and a furniture broker with ample storage space, made him the ideal guardian for Joanna's Box.

Living in Gandy Lane placed Joanna at the hub of the city. By the 1790s, when Joanna came to live at Number 4, the streets all round were being modified to accommodate the increased number of carts carrying fish, grains, oats and potatoes from the newly opened market whose entrance was from Gandy Lane. Opposite the Symons's house was an imposing medieval residence, the former home of Thomas Bodley, founder of the Bodleian Library at Oxford. In 1778 the house was occupied by William Nation who acquired an ancient carved stone, known as Toisa's cross, from the recently demolished Exe Bridge and sank it into the ground at the corner of Gandy Lane and High Street to stop the carts buffeting his property. The stone stood there for about 130 years before being removed to St Nicholas Priory.

In 1794 when Joanna first entered their lives, the Symons family included William, Mary and their children John Tremlett, Mary Anne, Gracey and the new baby – christened George Bolt. The family was having a difficult time. Mary was already forty-seven when she gave birth in September and at some point during the year all the family lay very ill.[4] In these circumstances Joanna would have been welcomed as an extra pair of hands and quickly formed close bonds with the parents, even if her relationship with their children was at times less than cordial. While on 29 May, 1800, Joanna was delighted to receive a gift of gilded oak apples from Mrs Symons's children,[5] in an undated Communication she was told that: 'Simonds is thy friend, but her children are against thee but William is not'.[6]

An advertisement in the *Exeter Flying Post*, 2 August, 1792, affords a glimpse of Number 4, Gandy Lane, home of William Symons, and first location for Joanna Southcott's Box of Sealed Prophecies.

> To be Sold, the fee simple and inheritance of the estates of Thomas Sweetland, Baker, a bankrupt, situate in Gandy's Lane, and adjoining to the Way leading from thence into the New-Market, in the Parish of Allhallows, Goldsmith Street, in the City of Exeter, at a Public Survey, to be held at the Globe Tavern, in Exeter, on Tuesday the 21st day of this instant August, 1792, at 5 o'clock in the afternoon, when the same will be put up in the following [6] Lots . . .
>
> Lot 4. Another SHOP fronting the same Way, with a Room over it, a Kitchen with two rooms over it, and a Court and Cellar in the occupation of William Symons, Broker.

By the time John Tremlett Symons was old enough to join his father in business, trade had evidently expanded. The acumen of the younger man is seen in the following advertisement in the *Exeter Flying Post* of 10 April, 1806:

> J.T. Symons, General Appraiser, Auctioneer & Undertaker, 4 Gandy Street, begs to return his most grateful acknowledgements to his friends, for the favours he has already received, and wishes to inform them and the public in general, that in future he intends to sell at auction all household furniture, plate, linen, china, books, etc. committed to his care (either at his house, or in his sale rooms) at 2½% instead of the usual price of 5%. J.T.S. having been in the habit of purchasing and selling household furniture of every description, to a very great amount, for many years past, consequently knows the exact value of almost every article in the business; and those ladies or gentlemen who will be pleased to honour him with the care of their furniture etc. may have (if required) security to the amount of £1000. N.B. The king's duty is charged to the purchaser. Dated 4, Gandy's street, Exeter, April 7th, 1806.

It is not recorded whether Joanna had to pay Symons for taking care of her Box. William Symons could well have acted altruistically, but it would have been out of character for his son, John, whose mercenary nature caused her much embarrassment when, in June, 1801, the Reverend Stanhope Bruce sent her a gift of money to help finance the printing of her books, and was promptly presented with a request for more – not from Joanna, but from John Symons. Joanna dissociated herself from Symons's action, declaring to Bruce, 'You are right about the money. I am sorry it should be mentioned: I did not desire any thing of you; but only to make plain the paths of the Lord'. Moreover, to ensure that such a thing could never happen again she wrote to Bruce on 1 August, 1801, asking him in future to check that all letters purporting to come from her bore her signature.

That John Symons's attempt to exploit Joanna's wealthy new friends did not cause a permanent rift between her and the Symons family was due to the close bonds already forged. While Mary Symons held Joanna in great respect and a degree of awe after she had successfully predicted the quality of harvests in 1799 and 1800, John Symons proved most helpful in copying out Joanna's otherwise illegible writings. When, at Christmas, 1800, the Reverend Pomeroy suddenly called for some of Joanna's writings to be copied out, the Symons family were central to the proceedings. At their home in Gandy Lane, they hosted a gathering of at least twelve local people including four members of the Taylor family, John Jones, William Ratcliffe Coomb, Elizabeth Boucher, and Sarah Ware to act as witnesses when the sealed papers were produced from Joanna's Box and cut open. Mary Symons later attested to the fact that as soon as any papers were unsealed, witnesses signed their names upon them for future identification. At the end of seven days the papers were sealed up again in the presence of witnesses, and replaced in the Box which was left in Mary Symons's care.

Describing the episode later in a letter to the Reverend Thomas Webster,[7] Joanna wrote:

> There is a mystery in my writings you will be at a loss to explain, concerning the seals they cut open at Christmas, by the order of the Rev Mr Pomeroy, and some of them were copied out; but not the tenth part of the things that are near at hand. I had a limited time fixed to have copied out what was to be put in print, for the present, to try the judgment of men, before they were proved, and then to have my writings sealed up by men; and every man was to put his seal to them, and write his name on the outside, which was done by 5 different men; and after that put all together in a box, and nailed up by one of the 5, never to be broken open till they are brought into the presence of the 12, who will meet as judges of them.

Life was not altogether happy in the Symons's household in the next twelve months. In the summer of 1801 Joanna grieved with the family when their youngest son, seven year old George Bolt Symons, died, and she was heard to lament the fact that this was not the only calamity that would happen in their house in the course of twelve months – a remark that was remembered the following year when the Symonses' two daughters died within the space of one week. 1801 was also marred by the tragedy that befell Parnell, a friend of the Symons family who sought refuge at their house after killing a fellow farm worker in a fight. Amidst such dark shadows Joanna's announcement that seven eminent gentlemen with whom she had been in correspondence were about to visit Exeter to inspect her writings and judge whether she was a genuine prophetess, must have been received with delight. William and Mary Symons agreed to act as character witnesses when the Seven Stars (as they were dubbed) asked to meet people who had known Joanna Southcott for years and, together with the Taylor family and the Joneses, they testified that Joanna was honest, industrious, virtuous and sane, adding that she had prophesied accurately about the war, the harvests, the weather and other events. The enquiry reached a dramatic climax when Joanna was told by the Spirit to commit all her writings to the care of the Seven Stars:

> So let thy writings made in 1792 be sealed again with seven seals, as at first, by thy own seal, and another paper put round them. And let Mr Taylor write on the paper he was present at the breaking of them, and wrote on every leaf, and sealed them again in seven days; and they will find his name within and without. Then deliver them to the Rev Mr Bruce. The sealed book that is in print, give to the care of the Rev Mr Foley, and seal that up with seven seals. And seal the seven books together, and give to the care of the Rev Mr Webster. The box to the care of Mr Sharpe. And the copies of all thy letters and thy other writings seal up in the different parcels and commit to the other three sealed up with the seven seals. The book that is sealed which concerns Mr B. Bruce must be sealed up with seven seals, and sent to Mrs Bruce. So let all the work be done in six days, and give all into their hands the seventh.[8]

On Monday 4 January, 1802, Joanna went with Mrs Boucher to fetch her sealed Box from Gandy Lane where it was being stored, and brought it round to the Guildhall. The precious papers were then distributed among the Seven who left for London, each carrying a sealed parcel which he had sworn to guard, unopened, until summoned

*Exeter Guildhall, the medieval building that stands in Fore Street. It was here that the contents of Joanna's Box were examined by the Seven Stars on Monday, 4 January, 1802, before being taken to London.*

by Joanna to produce it before twelve judges. So it was that in the first week of January, 1802, Joanna bade farewell to her seven new friends and, while herself remaining in Exeter, allowed them to take away her precious Box holding the greater part of her writings. Bound by cords, fastened with seven seals, the Box was entrusted to the eminent engraver, William Sharp. 'Instead of setting in judgement on My Writings they are carrying them out of the town . . . and what was not sealed before was sealed this night and taken away, the Old Christmas Eve 1802.' (Communication to Joanna, transcribed by Benjamin Howe.)[9]

The departure of the Seven Stars from Exeter marked the end of the first phase of Joanna Southcott's Box. For three years it had been stored in Gandy Lane, exciting little attention, safe in the care of William and Mary Symons, who remained her loyal friends. It was Mary Symons who accompanied Joanna to Exeter's Guildhall in the last week of January, 1802, to answer a charge of blasphemy, a case that was subsequently dismissed. The name of Mary Symons also featured prominently in the list of those invited to be present at the public examination of the writings that was held at High House, London, in January, 1803.

Although the Symons family no longer looked after Joanna Southcott's Box their store room continued to receive tangible reminders of her mission in the form of consignments of books. By the end of 1802 Joanna had published over a dozen books, and William Symons played a major part in their distribution in Exeter. Prices varied, but the normal arrangement was for him to buy copies from Joanna at something like 1/9d and resell them for 2/3d each. On 30 July, 1802, Joanna had written to him, wanting to know if he had received the 140 books sent but not yet acknowledged.[10] When her eleventh book was published in August, its list of distributors included the name of W.

*LONDON:*
Printed by Marchant and Galabin, Ingram-Court; and sold by W. Tozer, Chapel-Place, Duke-Street, Westminster-Road, Southwark; also by W. Symonds, Gandy-Lane, and the Miss Eveleighs, St. Sidwell's, Exeter; S. Hirst, Leeds; W. Wadman, York; James Light, Coventry-Street, Stourbridge; Edmund Baker, Ilminster; C. Bradley, Digbeth, Birmingham; R. Goldsmith, Gravesend; and T. Turpin, Greenwich.

1813.
*(Price One Shilling.)*

*An advertisement for the Third Edition of A Word to the Wise, which was Book 17 in Joanna Southcott's canon of 65 books. The name and address of W. Symonds figures in the list of distributors.*

Simmonds [sic] at Gandy's Lane, Exeter, and his name, variously spelt, continued to appear in following years despite frequent wrangling over the exact number of books that he should have had in stock and payment for those sold. On 4 December, 1803, Joanna wrote to Mary Symons from Leeds explaining that if she had not written before it was through 'lack of time not lack of love'. She appreciated the fact that her friend had sent for hundreds of seals to distribute in Exeter. In view of such loyalty it was natural that, when a third trial of Joanna's writings took place at Neckinger House, Bermondsey, that December, the name of Mary Symons was again foremost on the list of those invited, even if her son's name was omitted. John Tremlett Symons, whose cavalier attitude to accounts and general mischief-making had been troubling Joanna all summer, was understandably furious, especially when he discovered that those invited were being provided with new clothes and expenses. He wrote Joanna an insolent letter which she answered with a sharp reprimand. Recognising that there was no trifling with Joanna, Symons climbed down and humbly asked if he could appear in London to testify on her behalf. This she condescendingly allowed, but unlike other guests from Exeter, John Symons had to travel at his own expense.

He appeared before the assembly on Wednesday, 5 December, 1804, to say that he had known Joanna Southcott for ten years. He had been employed by her to copy all the letters which she read to him from her own writings and later published as the first four books of *Strange Effects of Faith.* He admitted that he had been sceptical at first, not believing that Joanna's writings were the works of the Lord. He had also written to the Reverend Nutcombe Nutcombe, Chancellor of the diocese of Exeter, on Joanna's behalf, asking him to study Joanna Southcott's writings in order to judge whether they were really from the Spirit of God. Asked what he thought of Joanna, he declared that her character was in general 'unblamable'. As for the Reverend Joseph Pomeroy, he had often come into their shop in Gandy Lane and in the course of conversation always spoke well of Joanna, believing her works to be very good and certainly from the Lord. However, Pomeroy later changed his tune and told him to have nothing more to do with Joanna. 'He said, we had troubles enough in our family already, without believing in such nonsense, meaning the accidental deaths of my two sisters in one week.'[11] When Symons challenged Pomeroy about the change in his attitude to Joanna, the clergyman became very angry and told him that it would be better to confine his beliefs to those of the Church of England.

The following day Mary Symons was examined. She told the assembly that she had known Joanna for at least ten years and found her to be a faithful, honest, Christian woman. She had also had conversations with the Reverend Joseph Pomeroy about Joanna's writings, explaining that she would not want her son to be copying anything that might have come from the devil, but Pomeroy had laughed at her, and said, 'there was nothing of it that came from the devil, for it was good'.[12]

The Trial at Neckinger House was probably the last occasion on which Joanna and Mary Symons met, although the friends continued to keep in touch by letter. On the last day of 1807 Joanna wrote to Mary with the joyful news that her sister, Susanna Carter (formerly Southcott), had at last come into the fold and actually sent for a seal. Moreover, after a second sealing of the faithful had been launched, John Symons reported that people in Exeter had been streaming in to sign again and there were many new enquirers. A year later Joanna would no doubt have heard of his marriage to Sarah Melluish at St Paul's Church, Exeter. Sadly, the birth of their first child the following October was followed by the deaths of both mother and baby within a fortnight. John Symons, still under thirty, might have been expected to remarry and start again. Instead, having enrolled in the military, he was sent abroad as Clerk of Stores in the Field Train Department and died in Sicily in October, 1814. His mother, Mary Symons, had died at home in Exeter the year before. His father, William, died a few weeks after John.

It is a sad fact that none of the Symonses' children who had presented her with gilded oak apples in May, 1800, survived Joanna. The last record of Mary Symons in her correspondence is a letter she sent to Charles Taylor on 23 February, 1812. Joanna had just had her portrait engraved by William Sharp and it seemed that all her friends in Exeter wanted a copy. Young Charles Taylor must have mentioned this to Joanna, for she writes, 'if you wish, you can have one of Mrs Symons['s] as I have sent more than was bespoke'.[13] In other words, loyal Mary Symons could be depended upon to allocate Joanna's portraits, just as her husband had taken charge of the distribution of Joanna's books and looked after her precious Box of Sealed Prophecies.

# 2

# Trials and Stipulations, 1802-1820

The man who took charge of Joanna Southcott's Box of Sealed Prophecies in January, 1802, viewed his new responsibility very seriously and was in no doubt that he had in his care an object of the utmost importance. In *An Answer to the World for Putting in Print a Book in 1804* William Sharp justified this attitude by repeating the history of Joanna's writings:

> From the year 1792 to the end of the year 1794, her writings were sealed up, and after being witnessed, were put out of her possession; and the same caution was observed at the end of each succeeding year, and were at each time placed in the hands of persons of credit, until the arrival of myself and friends in Exeter when at our departure, which was at the beginning of January, 1802, the whole of her sealed writings were put in our possession, properly sealed and witnessed. The Box, containing the greater part, was given to my care, and a parcel, also sealed and witnessed, was given to the Rev. Stanhope Bruce; and one to each of the other friends. And I think it necessary to add, that whilst I was at Bath, on my return from Exeter to London, I had a large case made, which enclosed the whole box, for the cords round the box were sealed with seven seals, and I had a quantity of tow put between the box and the case to preserve the seals from being broken.[1]

When he reached London, Sharp took the Box to his home at 50 Titchfield Street. William Sharp was born on 17 January, 1750, and baptised at Holy Trinity in the Minories on 13 February. He was the second son of William and Sarah, whose address in Haydon Yard, Minories, gave a clue to the father's profession, for the area was famous for its gunsmiths, and the elder William Sharp started life as a gun-maker before becoming an engraver. His was a masculine household, because his wife died young and of his three sons (Richard, William and John) and three daughters, only the boys survived into adulthood. Whilst Richard Sharp set up business for himself in Leadenhall Street as a carver, gilder, and picture frame maker, his younger brothers followed in their father's footsteps and became engravers. Having shown an early talent for drawing, the younger William Sharp was apprenticed to Barak Longmate, an engraver famous for his

*Trade Card engraved by William Sharp for his brother, Richard, who had set up in business as a carver, gilder, and picture frame maker.*

knowledge of heraldry. Then, upon his marriage to a Frenchwoman, William set up shop as a writing engraver at 9 Bartholomew Lane, Royal Exchange, producing mostly trade cards. However, in 1775 he made a drawing of Hector, the old lion at the Tower, and after engraving it on a quarto plate he exposed the prints for sale in his window. The experiment proved a commercial success and marked the start of his transition from jobbing craftsman to most celebrated engraver of the age.

From all accounts the young William Sharp was a handsome man, middling in height, finely proportioned, with a broad forehead and commanding features. He was also ambitious, and within a few years had sold his shop and moved to a private house at Vauxhall, where he began to engrave from paintings and to develop a sophisticated technique that combined dot-work with all the refinements of preliminary etching and fine stroke-work. He was quickly recruited by Benjamin West, and in 1782 produced a major plate from his *Alfred the Great Dividing his Cloak with the Pilgrim.* By dint of hard work and perseverance William Sharp had achieved professional success, even if financial pressures meant that he had little leisure in which to enjoy it. With the deaths of both his father and brother John early in 1786 he inherited wealth enough to move up the social scale and live in comparative luxury. Almost immediately he moved from Vauxhall to a larger house – 8 Charles Street, Middlesex Hospital – and from here published many of the prints that made him famous, including portraits of Garrick, Mrs Siddons, Dr John Hunter, St Cecilia and the Prince of Wales.

In April, 1793, William Sharp published a portrait of Thomas Paine, a subject that reflected political sympathies that would plunge him into deep trouble. As a republican and member of the Society for Constitutional Information, he became involved in proceedings for high treason taken against Horne Tooke in November, 1794. At one point

*William Sharp (1749-1824), the celebrated engraver. As First Custodian of Joanna Southcott's Sealed Prophecies, Sharp took care of the Box from 1802 until his move to Chiswick in 1820 prompted him to deliver it into the safe-keeping of Jane Townley.*

William Sharp found himself arrested and examined before the Privy Council to see if he too should be charged with high treason, but fortunately the ready tongue that had exposed him to danger proved his salvation. After being plagued with interminable and what he considered to be irrelevant questions, Sharp decided to enliven proceedings by fishing in his pocket for a prospectus of a portrait of the Polish patriot, General Kosciusko, that he was then engraving. Handing it to William Pitt and then to Henry Dundas, he asked them if they would care to subscribe to the portrait and pass his prospectus on to other members of the Privy Council. The bold innocence of the man set the assembly laughing. They decided that he looked too jocular to be a revolutionary; the case against him was dropped.

With time, Sharp's radical enthusiasm waned. Not so his religious fervour. He was a staunch believer in the Scriptures and was convinced by those prophets who were proclaiming that God's chosen people were about to be restored to the Holy Land. In January, 1794, Richard Brothers published '*A Revealed Knowledge of the Prophecies and Times, wrote under the Direction of God by the Man that will be Revealed to the Hebrews as their Prince*'. The following year Sharp published a portrait of Brothers with the inscription: 'Fully believing this to be the Man whom GOD has appointed – I engrave his likeness'. Nor was Sharp alone in declaring his allegiance to Brothers. He had joined a distinguished group of believers who included Nathaniel Brassey Halhed, Orientalist and M.P.; the Reverend Thomas Philip Foley; the Reverend Thomas Webster; the Reverend Stanhope Bruce; and a group of businessmen in the north where Brothers's writings were distributed by provincial booksellers. So influential was the movement that the Government took fright and ordered the arrest of Brothers under an old statute for 'maliciously publishing fantastical prophecies with intent to cause disturbances'. The Privy Council then called for a report on his mental condition with the result that two doctors certified him as insane and he was confined in an asylum for eleven years. Although this long detention shook the faith of Brothers's disciples, many remained convinced that the Second Coming was imminent, and cast around for another prophet to guide them through future trials. It was in this climate that William Sharp and his circle of friends came across the books of Joanna Southcott, published in 1801, and set out to judge for themselves whether their author was divinely inspired.

The man who arrived in Exeter in December that year must have been striking in appearance. He loved food and drink and had grown quite stout but he had fine features 'of the Roman cast' and his forehead was broad and capacious with 'signs of great intellect'. Although almost bald by middle age he had a few grey whispery hairs hanging down over his shoulders and the crown of his head was described as 'remarkably silvery and beautiful'. Moreover, he was an energetic man, fond of outdoor exercise. He never wore a wig and to prevent catching cold washed the whole of his head in cold water every morning. He was also an expert swimmer who, when in London, took a daily dip in the Thames. At the height of his career, he had recently moved house from Charles Street to 50 Titchfield Street, and it was here that Joanna Southcott's Box of Sealed Prophecies was deposited in January, 1802, for safe-keeping.

It might have been expected that Joanna, when she arrived in London on 22 May, 1802, would have rushed to be reunited with her Box, but this would have been to misunderstand her attitude. The validity of her claims rested on the fact that her Box had always been deposited with reliable friends, people of integrity, who could vouch for the fact that no one had interfered with her writings once they had been sealed. She therefore took up residence in the home of Mrs Maria Bruce in Jermyn Street, whilst the Box remained at 50 Titchfield Street in the care of William Sharp. And there it remained until taken to High House, Paddington, the scene of what is called the Second Trial, when a further attempt was made to have Joanna Southcott's Writings brought before the world to be judged in a proper forum.[2]

The Reverend Thomas Foley and his wife had taken up residence in the prestigious High House on the last day of November, 1802, and much of the following month was occupied with practical preparations for the 'Trial'. William Sharp was a frequent visitor, taking his turn with Foley in copying letters and Communications for Joanna. On Sunday, 12 December, the day of Richard Foley's christening, Sharp shared with Joanna the honour of being a godparent to the child, even though he could not be present at the ceremony, and arrived so late that the company feared he had met with an accident.

By 9 January, 1803, Thomas Foley's forty-fifth birthday, all was ready for Joanna's formal entrance into High House. Sharp joined more than a dozen other guests to welcome her. At six o'clock in the evening, after a religious service that included the taking of the sacrament as preparation for the 'Awful Trial of proving Joanna's writings on the Twelfth; whether they came from the Lord God, or whether they are a delusion the Box of Sealed Writings was deposited in a vault below stairs where they were to remain until eleven o'clock on 12 January when they would be taken up to the Great Room.' [3]

Foley's Diary contains an entry for 12 January: 'By Divine Command this day Joanna Southcott's Writings commenced being proved after a general invitation to the whole Country, Clergy, Nobles and Laity. Twelve Judges and Twelve Jurymen are to be appointed', he wrote. There follows a list of the Sealed Writings that were in the Great Box:[4]

1. John Jones – Seal – February 28, 1801
   The Seal – Figure of Hope leaning on an Anchor.
   Seals – 4 – Good Friday – 1798
2. William Coombe – July 8, 1801
   Cut Seals – Seven – Figure of Hope
   This was cut at the end of 1800
   & four of the Old Seals N:C: [Not Cut]
3. John Jones – February 8

Seals Seven – Figure of Hope
Seals of Joanna's Two
Writings sealed of 1794

4. John Jones – February 28, 1801
This sealed up with Four Seals
Writings of October 1796
Figure of Hope
5. Writings in 1795
Figure Hope – Figure of a Sp[h]inx –
Dove & Olive Branch
Sealed with four seals – 4 loose
William Symonds – February 8, 1801
6. William Coombe – February 8, 1801
Seals eight – and seven Fasteners
Figure of Hope – N:C:
7. John Symons – Seals 4 – February 8, 1801
Writings in 1795 Witnessed S.Minafay, M.Woollan
Joanna's seal – Dove & Olive Branch, 1794
8. Writings 1795 – signed S.Minafy, M.Wolland
February 8, 1801.
Witness'd Will. Symons – 1794
Figure – Head – Joanna's seal.
9. J: Jones – Feby. 8, 1801 – sign'd John Symons
nine Seals – writings 1796-97
Figures – Dove & Olive Branch
One seal with a Thimble
Charity & the Child
10. John Jones – Nine Seals Feby. 8, written
Figure Dove & Olive Branch – N:C:
Eight seals Fasteners – Loose papers – 1795
11. William Coombe – 8 seals wrote Feby. 8, 1801
Figure of Hope & Joanna's Seal
In a paper within side wrote Nov. 1793
12. Miss Wolland – 1794 – Signed by Joanna
sealed with Three seals of Joanna's –
single Rapper

Foley's list was followed by a day to day description of the Trial in which William Sharp's name appeared among the list of twelve judges. There is no record of Sharp's wife, who had possibly died by this time, but his housekeeper, Mrs Ann Eikenhead (referred to elsewhere as Hannah Eikenhead), headed the list of 'Ladies at the Trial'. After the Box was opened the sealed writings were examined for seven days by the twelve judges and twelve carefully selected jurymen and then, whilst some were set aside for publication, the rest were sealed up again in the Box.

Among the sealed papers opened on 12 January, 1803, to be copied was the Communication dated 12 May, 1798, containing the early reference to Joanna placing her writings in her Box and in the copy made at this time Joanna added that 'this to be Put with the Seals First shewn and Copied off from 1797 if Kept Two years. This appeared, and they were Put into the Great Box which Mr Sharp Kept one year. Finis. Signed Joanna Southcott.[5]

In other words the precision in Joanna's actions meant that there was little room for doubt about the provenance of her writings – that they dated from the times she said. As William Sharp was later to write:

> I must observe, that all these precautions of Joanna, about her writings, in sealing, etc. could not prove her an impostor; neither, from these circumstance, could the Spirit that so directed her, be a false Spirit; neither was it possible for us to be deceived respecting the *identity* of the *writings* delivered to us: and which remained secure with us until they were conveyed by me to High-house, Paddington, where the Box and parcels were opened, and the seals broken, in the presence of above forty persons, who were assembled together by public notice, and which was at the beginning of January, 1803. And after the writings were taken out, each paper was signed by three persons, before they were delivered to Joanna, for them afterwards to be copied off.[6]

In a manuscript written by one of her followers, probably Elias Carpenter, in 1803, there are details of how precisely the Seals were placed in the Great Box before he nailed it up on 2 May, 1803 [New Style].

> On Sunday, April 24, When Joanna came down Stairs in the Morning, She said to Bruce, Foley, etc. 'Gentlemen, I am desired to inform you that you must take notice of the Thunder, Lightning, Hail & Rain for this Day. For I have had a Communication this Day that My writings must be sealed upon the 2nd of May, new Stile; and likewise you are Commanded to take notice of the High winds Last week.'
>
> Mrs Wilmot and our Brother Abbot was at Foleys and heard the above; and to the Surprise of many that heard it by Dinner Time there came on a Storm of thunder, Lightning, Hail & Rain and the Hail in particular was so large that we seldom see such.

On the 2nd day of May Joanna's Box of writings was sealed up for the 3d. and Last time in the following manner – they were Divided in 7 Equal parts and then 7 Seals put on Each parcel as follows: Joanna in the Middle – then Foleys on one side and Bruce on the other to Represent the three One God. Then Sharps on one Side at one end, and Wilsons opposite, then Webster Close to Sharp, & Carpenter opposite by Wilson. Every particular about the Sealing was given by the spirit and I was there as Carpenter to Nail & Cord up the Box which I did with Twelve Nails, and Corded the Box with a new Cord and 7 seals put on the Nots of the Cord and then conveyed to where the Lord order'd, till her Last and Awful Trial Comes on

Now as near as I can give it from Memory, the 3 Sealings and 3 Cuttings of her Cords are thus Explained, to answer to the 3 great Events of Scripture History. Namely, the First time the world was Cutt was by the Fall of Man – then it was Sealed up to go on again in the Promise given to the Woman etc. The 2d. Time the World was cutt was by the dreadful Efects of the Deluge. When the Lord said he would destroy Man, yet preserved him in the Ark to go again a 2d. time. The 3 time the world was cutt was by the Crucifixtion of our Lord and the Destruction of Jerusalem. So when her Cords are Cutt a 3d. time, the powers of darkness will be Cutt in like Manner, for God will so seal her mission after the next Cutting her Cords so that he will disperse the Powers of Darkness as our Poor Brethren the Jews were dispersed.

I am Desired to inform you that Joanna Left London on munday morning, June the 6th, 1803, from here she & Mrs Foley went to Mr J Southcotts Bristol, where she stays about a week – from thence she Goes to Exeter, and Stays about a month where you may Direct your Letters, or to Mr Foley where we Expect she will go to from Exeter, and will Stay at Foleys several weeks – and from there She will come to Yorkshire to Perform the work the Lord has for her to do, and She desires me to say She shall Seal the People while She is with you – therefore Brother Jowett must Rest Satisfied, and you also, as you cannot have no more Seals Till She comes amongst you; where she will Stay (I believe) till the time her awful Trial comes on.[7]

Many of these same details appear in a letter from E.J. Field to Mr Ingall, 9 May, 1803, with the added information that Joanna's 'awful Trial' was to come on the following year and 'after that, the Lord will visibly display his power and he has informed Mrs Southcott that the Destruction of the human race will be so Great, that there will be only *one* Man in Ten Left. But there are some Men *now alive*, that Shall Live the whole of the Milenium upon this Earth'.[8]

In the meantime, while Joanna spent the next ten months on her travels, her Box of Sealed Prophecies was taken back to 50 Titchfield Street, where it remained in the custody of William Sharp and Ann Eikenhead. Writing to Sharp from Oldswinford on 7 August, 1803, Joanna ended her letter with her best wishes 'to you and Mrs Ann'.[9] When she returned to London in April, 1804, she took up temporary residence with William Sharp and his housekeeper in Titchfield Street, and was thus reunited with her Box, if only briefly, for Sharp soon introduced her to his friend and neighbour, Jane Townley, a wealthy spinster, with whom Joanna was to live for the rest of her life. To begin with, Joanna and Townley occupied lodgings above a grocery shop, just six doors down from Sharp in Titchfield Stree, and it was from here that they proceeded to Neckinger House, Bermondsey, in December, 1804, for the third 'Trial' of Joanna's writings.

The 'Trial' opened on 5 December, 1804, before twenty-five 'Witnesses of the Truth' and amongst those called forward on that first day to testify to Joanna's good character was William Sharp who, when examined, named all the books he had published for Joanna since 1802 and described their method of working together: 'She read them to me from her own manuscripts, and I wrote from her reading.' The Box did not make an appearance until twelve o'clock on the second day 'at which time the box of sealed writings was put on the table, and the different parcels of sealed papers taken out of it'.[10]

Sharp continues:

> It is necessary here to introduce a general account of the beginning of these writings, as delivered to the assembly. From the time of Joanna's visitation by the Spirit, in 1792, different papers were sealed up, year after year, and deposited with her friends; and the whole of these were put into a box together, at the end of 1794, after having been first sealed up by her friends. The communications given in the subsequent years were added to the former, at the end of each year, and put into the box, and thus remained in the possession of her friends, until the year 1800. The writings were first cut open, by the desire of the Rev. Mr Pomeroy, at the end of the year 1800, in the house of Mr Symons, at Exeter, and in the presence of twelve witnesses, five of whom were present this day, some of whose names were signed on every sheet of the writings; and some of

> the writings, thus signed, were delivered into the hands of Joanna, in order to be copied and deposited with the Rev. Mr Pomeroy. They were again sealed up in the presence of six witnesses, about two months after the opening of them, or in the spring of 1801, and were left in the care of Mr Symons of Exeter. Having been after that committed to the possession of Mr Sharp, of Titchfield Street, London, they were cut open a second time at Paddington, on January 12, 1803, in the presence of forty-nine persons in all, twenty-three of whom acted under the denomination of judges and jury. The writings were again verified there, leaf by leaf, generally by the signature of three of those denominated judges and jury. Some parts were read to the audience, and others were given to be copied, from which the book called *The Sealed Prophecies* was printed. At six o'clock in the evening of May 2, 1803, the writings were sealed up again, in the presence of six of the judges, Joanna, and four or five others. Each of these judges affixed their seals and signed their names on each parcel, and Joanna put her seal thereon. The bundles thus signed and sealed, being six in number, were exhibited this day, December 6, 1804, and the signatures and seals on them were acknowledged, by the Rev Stanhope Bruce, Rev Thomas Philip Foley, Rev Thomas Webster, John Wilson, Elias Carpenter, and William Sharp, as their own respective signatures and seals. At the conclusion of thus identifying the bundles of writings, taken out of the box, agreeably to the directions of Joanna, that is about one o'clock, she became very faint, and was helped out of the room, after signifying that the writings were not to be cut open till she had strength to be present.[11]

On the third day a Communication received by Joanna that same morning was read to the assembly:

> Now, if they are all satisfied without thy trance, let thy seals be broken this day. And I have told thee what must be put aside and sealed up, and never broken while thou art alive: but all the others must remain never to be sealed any more: but what is to be sealed, must now be sealed in the presence of the whole. And I shall teach some one to read thy written hand, when thou art no more: but thine is a hand no man can forge: all that will happen till my Kingdom is established, is in thy writings; but not to be known at the present: but nothing shall be concealed from thee, that I will do upon the earth.

After the reading of this communication, the Assembly instantly stood up and, with uplifted hands, one and all cried out: 'The will of the Lord be done!' Then, at half past eleven, Joanna cut open the sealed bundles of her writings and explained the nature of the 'Trial' before retiring at four o'clock to receive another Communication, which she presented an hour later. 'Having concluded this discourse, Joanna began to look over her writings which were cut open, for the purpose of selecting such as were to be sealed up till after her death; and to identify their being opened, by putting signatures thereon.'[12]

The fourth day was largely given over to singing and prayers and an account by Joanna of her mission.

The fifth day the assembly did not meet until three o'clock in the afteroon to give Joanna more time to select those writings which would be sealed up till after her death. Then Joanna read a communication that she had just received:

> Now, Joanna, I shall direct thee; for the way thou art going on to look through thy writings thou canst not accomplish it by the days that are fixed; for know, I told thee what is sealed not to be revealed, must be sealed by the seventh day. So let the parcel be cut that Sharp brought thee; and when it is cut, I shall tell thee what shall be sealed up for good, in that and in the others: and thy work must be done in haste; for I have other communications to give unto thee, before thou meetest the public; therefore thou hast but little time to spend with friends. Let them have the communications, weigh them together, and pass their judgments thereon. So when the whole are assembled together, let the seals be cut; then bring up the whole, and search them through; place them as I command thee, to be sealed.[13]

Little happened on the sixth day until Joanna appeared in the afternoon to deliver a further Communication followed by an account of her prophecies and Scriptural proofs of her mission.

On the seventh and last morning the assembly met in a field to receive a stirring address from Joanna until proceedings were interrupted by a jeering mob. They retreated to Neckinger House, where in the presence of an attorney, John Scott, several Resolutions were passed by the forty-eight named members of the assembly – twelve designated as judges, twelve as jurymen, and twenty-four elders. In the evening wine and cakes were handed round and, as they drank, everyone repeated the words: 'May I drink deep into the Spirit of Christ, and may his Blood cleanse me from all sin.' After everyone had supped, Joanna declared, 'As we all have drank in one cup, may we drink into one faith, and may that faith be in Christ!'

> At nine o'clock Joanna sealed up the writings, which are to be kept till after her death, and the signatures and seals of several present were also added; and the packet was then delivered into the possession of one of the judges.[14]

This unnamed judge was almost certainly William Sharp who was once more entrusted with the Box. In his *'An Answer to the World'*, published in 1806[15] is the message: 'for I now tell thee, as thy writings have been hid, and *twice cut open, and proved by man,* and yet as the promise that was made is not fulfilled, they must wait till the THIRD TIME, that thy trial cometh by *Friends* and *Foes'*. The Box remained in Sharp's custody for the rest of Joanna's life, and there is no record of it being opened again during this time. Meanwhile, his professional star continued to rise. Engravers were excluded from full membership of the Royal Academy and Sharp had already rejected an offer of associate membership as degrading of his art. He was, however, proud to accept his election in 1814 as honorary member of the Imperial Academy of Vienna and of the Royal Academy of Munich. By this time he had moved house again, and Joanna's Box would probably have gone with him when he moved from Titchfield Street to London Street, Fitzroy Square. By September, 1813, he was also using an address 'near the church, Acton.[16]

In the shocked aftermath of Joanna's death and all the controversy as to whether Shiloh had been born or not, for many the one certainty was that the Box still existed and had not been opened. No matter what else was in doubt, this fact was not. For the believers it was their rock – just as its custodian, William Sharp, was always referred to as their 'Rock', steady and unshakeable in his faith.

The confusion among the believers is reflected in letters that the Reverend Thomas Philip Foley, Oldswinford, wrote to Charles Taylor in early summer, 1815:

> Mrs Townley tells me that Tozer has opened his chapel to read Mr Turner's Communications and there are many private Houses opened once a week to read them. Our dear Joanna's Writings are quite neglected – and the lyes they invent about Underwood, me, and those that do not rely on them would much surprise you. . . . Tozer says he has Visitations, so it is fine confusion. Mrs Townley desires her opinion of Mr Turner's Communications to be made as public as possible. . . . Miss Townley tells me Mrs Wetherall is desperately ill but she and her husband still steadfast in the faith. Sharp is as firm as a Rock, but Colonel Harwood very shaken and possibly faith

> quite gone. . . . Faith of all the Roberts quite gone, but I have persuaded them to keep their seals whole though John Roberts tells me he puts no value on them.[17]

Slowly amidst the confusion, different groupings emerged. There were those who found comfort in the belief that Joanna had taken on the appearance of death but would one day return to complete her mission. Townley was one of these and pictured how it would be. They would find the form of Joanna lying on her bed: 'She will appear much like a ghost, and will remain in that state, till the Spirit of the Lord enter into her'.[18] Townley also believed that a spiritual birth had taken place, writing on the morning after the postmortem examination of Joanna:

> It was made clear to my mind, that it was a spiritual, and not a temporal birth we were to look for; and particularly from the following words: 'The woman's fears of thee are over; the wilderness receives her child.' This was a proof to me that someone was spiritually born, as that character, which corresponded with what is said in Revelation XII of the dragon's being ready to devour the child. But at that time it was concealed from me to whom the character particularly alluded; though, in my own thoughts, a certain individual appeared to be the one; and I wrote his name down.[19]

She meant Pomeroy, for in December, 1815, Turner wrote, 'Townley and Underwood have found that Pomeroy must be the man'; and later Owen Pughe, her secretary, confirmed this: 'Pomeroy was chosen as the man-child, but, having acted in disobedience like Saul, his kingdom was rent from him'.[20]

Sharp was equally convinced that Joanna would return. Writing to Foley on Christmas day, 1815, he recalled the conversation he had with Joanna eight days before she died. They had talked for about two hours, during which time 'the Infant was there struggling within her to be born'. He believed that Joanna would return any time, that Pomeroy would depart and return with her and their son, now one year old. Sharp finished his letter with, 'These are my opinions but as I am not redeem'd I am liable to error'.[21]

Had everyone shown such humility there would have been less falling out among friends. Instead, there was a sudden rush of claimants vying for the leadership, and there was little that the faithful could do about them because one of Joanna's last commands had been 'No more meetings or publications till Shiloh comes'. Illiterate Mary Boon from Staverton in Devon claimed that Joanna now spoke through her and began to issue voluminous 'communications'. Joseph Allman, calling himself Zebulon, claimed Joanna's mantle and launched on the world his doctrine of the Woman-God. In London Samuel Sibley headed the Household of Faith whose chapel in Smithfield was soon attracting a congregation of more than five hundred. Alexander Lindsay rented a chapel in Southwark and with William Tozer's help gathered two hundred members of the old Duke Street congregation to accept his leadership. But the man who secured the widest allegiance was George Turner, the merchant from Leeds and one of the Seven Stars who had visited Exeter in 1801. For years he had been directed by a 'voice' and had published three volumes of Communications, one of which had been approved by Joanna. Within weeks of her death he announced that his 'voice' had appointed him as Joanna's successor and he sent orders to every Southcottian group in the country to acknowledge his leadership.[22]

Many accepted him as Joanna's successor and when Tozer re-opened his chapel, it was to read George Turner's Communications to the congregation. Reporting this development to Charles Taylor on 26 April, 1815, Foley stressed the fact that Miss Townley had completely rejected Turner's pretensions. William Sharp's attitude was also unequivocal. He would have no truck with Turner's claims. In an attempt to bring Sharp round, some believers told him that he was like the Unbelieving world who condemned Turner's Communications without hearing them, so Sharp consented at least to listen. But when they came to 'Those who do not believe in Turner, their Eye is not to the Honour and Glory of God', Sharp's patience snapped. 'That is a lie and I will hear no more,' he declared, 'for though I don't believe in Turner I am sure my Eye is for the Honour and Glory of God'.[23]

The attitude of those loyal believers in the provinces who were desperate to understand events and to continue to work for the Great Cause was exemplified by Edmund Baker of Ilminster, Somerset, in a letter to Townley and Underwood on 31 January, 1815:

> At a meeting of the friends of the late Mrs Joanna Southcott at Ilminster on Sunday, the 15th of January 1815 the following resolutions were entered into and agreed upon:
> We the Believers assembled do acknowledge before God & the Church that by our own foolish judgment we have foiled ourselves by thinking the Child promised would be a Temporal one; but that we now see and acknowledge our weakness and rely upon the Mercy and goodness of God to direct us in future. We now believe the Child promised was the Holy Spirit of God, and that to fulfil the Holy Scriptures, that Spirit was in

> our Beloved Mother Mrs Joanna Southcott and at her death was caught up to God and we hope and trust that God will return the same Spirit to every faithful individual to make the Church the Bride according to the Promise of God through the death and merits of our Saviour Jesus Christ that we may now become the children of the Freewoman. . . . And now leaving all mysteries to be made clear to us by the wisdom of God we will endeavour to follow up our former faith till it shall please the Almighty to manifest himself more clear to his People; and till then, we humbly beseech him to Bless, and Prosper our undertakings, and crown them with success.

On a personal note, Baker went on to explain how he had drawn up certain Articles of Faith which he was persuading believers to sign in an attempt to 'keep them together' and he was happy to say that

> this seems to have spirited many of them up who were drooping. One man who I was much afraid of when he heard it read said 'No one could refuse to sign that.' So I hope I shall not lose so many as I at first feared. . . . And all former Directions I will endeavour through the Grace of God strictly to adhere to till the Lord shall appoint some way of direction to us. 'You say as to Mr Tr. opening the Chapel you have nothing to do with it, or with him.' By this he is off the Cause.

With regard to his own reaction to Joanna's death, Baker admitted,

> I suffered much for 3 Days and Nights; but I think I have a more sure Faith, and more true Sight than ever; but yet I sometimes find a strange Dart from Satan I think. But now the writings and Scriptures open ten fold more than ever. And I am fully persuaded that our Dr Joanna was as much Christ as ever he was, who was crucified; for the 'Flesh profiteth nothing'. 'In disguise before your Eyes, I am in the Woman's Form'.[24]

But if Baker supported Townley in judging that Turner was 'off the Cause', Ann Underwood's attitude was less categorical. Writing to Samuel Hirst, Leeds, 15 April, 1815, she declared:

> believe me dear Friend there is no shyness on my part towards you, Mr Turner or Mr Senior, though I cannot rely upon the Communications given to Mr Turner as you do, without having some proof they are from the Spirit of Truth. I was very thankful when the sign was set of our dear Mother's appearing, and earnestly prayed I might be permitted to see her, but since that time I have not even had a dream about her, neither have I

> heard that she have appeared to any one, which make me fearful, knowing Satan will come as an Angel of Light to deceive, and that he could not do it so effectually through any person as Mr Turner, whose character and faithfulness in the cause of the Lord is so established. . . . I most earnestly and sincerely hope that the Lord will keep, guide, and guard us on all sides, that we may do his will, and that only.

Before she had chance to finish writing, Ann Underwood's equanimity was shattered:

> Thus far I had written when your letter came on Saturday Noon from which I am so much hurt I cannot at present say any further . . . but will enclose you a letter in answer to some things you have repeated which is not exactly correct, but I will assist your memory as fare as I can – in the meantime remember us as faithful servants of the Great Jehovah and as faithful servants to do the Will of the Lord as far as we know it. Mrs Townley write with me in kind Christian love to yourself, Mr Turner, Mr Senior and all Friends.[25]

If Joanna's death had caused no lasting damage to Townley's faith, it had certainly shattered her nerves. One sign of this was the fact that from this time on, she rarely left home. 'From the time of the death of Joanna I have made it a point of duty to confine myself invariably to my house, so as to be at all times ready in case any inquiries concerning the mission should be made', she wrote in her *Letter to the Editor of the Council of Ten* published in 1823. Her anxiety is apparent in her complaints about a mysterious gentleman who called repeatedly on her from November, 1815, till May, 1816, and then visited her twice in January, 1817, with a view to leaving some writings in her care; as he was about to leave England for Paris. She refused and saw him no more, but thought he might have been employed by the government. Small wonder then that, when she wrote to Fanny Luscombe, 5 November, 1816, she confessed to being 'very nervous at the moment and have been very ill this last fortnight with spasms in my stomach'. Mrs Underwood too was 'very indifferent and so nervous' and her daughter, Mrs Barnard, had been dangerously ill but was now recovered: 'she has two lovely children and both sweet tempers which is a great blessing', she wrote. There continued to be 'great divisions among the believers who did not go to Turner', and there is a tinge of envy in the way Townley reported that 'Mr Sharp now resides entirely in the country. . . . He and Mr Owen keep out of all contentions'.[26]

By 1817 George Turner was making increasingly wild claims and predictions. His announcement that the earthquake foretold in Revelation VI, v.12 would take place on 28 January, 1817, had disastrous effects. Many stopped work, sold their possessions, and prepared to go to London for the coronation of Shiloh. When the day came and went without the expected catastrophe, Turner admitted his mistake, explaining that his 'voice' had allowed him to err to keep him from growing conceited. The authorities, however, were unimpressed and had him, like Brothers, arrested for high treason and then confined as a lunatic.

Writing to the Reverend Samuel Eyre on 27 August, 1817, Foley reported:

> Turner still goes on with his visitation and will not own that he is led by a wrong Spirit, although he has been so often and completely deceived by the Spirit that visits him and which ought to shew him that it comes from the Father of lies, the Devil; I sincerely pity him and earnestly hope his eyes may be opened before it be too late. . . . Scott our Solicitor at the *Neckinger trial* has (I understand) joined himself to the new Prophet *Blake* who is filled with witchcraft and goes on very abominably. . . . I hear *Hows* is going to publish a book; he has separated himself from us and Field has joined him. I had the happiness to hear by Miss Taylor from Exeter that their whole family continues true and steadfast in their faith. It grieves me much to inform you that our dear friends the Roberts of Painswick are gone totally from their Faith. . . . Poor Coll. Harwood's faith went immediately on the Death of our Beloved friend and the fatal consequence has been that he was thrown into Norwich jail for Debt and I hear is there at present. From all the accounts I hear of Tozer, he must be a very bad and abominable character indeed. He has treated Turner shockingly and with the greatest cruelty. He knocked his head against the Wall, he broke his shins by kicking them, and broke his own chairs by shaking of him, and now by Mrs Townley I find that Turner & Tozer are forever separated, and on the 7th September Tozer's Chapel was shut up because there was not a Congregation, and Mr Smith informs me that 4 fifths of the believers in Turner are come back again to the *True* standard, *the Woman*, and are willing to wait Joanna's *Return from the Wilderness*, when all mysteries and difficulties will be assuredly and fully cleared up.[27]

Sharp was not mentioned, but his name was prominent among those Foley listed in June, 1818, as true to the cause: 'Bruce, Eyre, Sharp,

Smith, Wetherall, Malkin, The Troups, Owen, and a little band besides.'[28] Sharp had in fact moved to Acton, still in possession of the Box of Sealed Prophecies. Edmund Baker, a reliable witness, saw the Box opened at Sharp's home in 1818, and has left a record of this in an undated note:

> All is given to Joanna and sealed up in Bundles and locked in a Chest and Mr Wm Sharp have them at his house. I saw the chest opened in July 1818 and the writing of Joanna safe and in them the rest of her Mission is contained and will be copied by Woman and printed for the Public when ordered by the Same Spirit who gave them see 91 Pa Trial Bk.[29]

With Sharp now at Acton, residing 'entirely in the country', and busy as ever with his professional work, believers visiting London made for Weston Place to catch up with news of what was happening in the movement. When Joseph Jowett, son of one of the judges at Joanna's 'Trials', accompanied his partner on a business trip to Brighton in May, 1818, he reported to his brother-in-law:

> We called upon Miss Townley as we came through London. She seemed very glad to see us. . . . She very kindly asked us to stop tea, and indeed pressed us, which we accepted. Mr Lowe was very sleepy in consequence of travelling all night which she perceived and told him to lay down on the sophy and get a nap and she and Mr Jowett would have a dish of chat, and this we did. She wished us to go again when we could stop longer. . . . Mrs Underwood is got so fat that I really did not know her at first sight. I asked Mrs Townley if there were any Believers at Brighton, she said she did not think that there was but I rather think there are, for the Preachers of different denominations here both Church and Dissenter are exclaiming against them, and I saw a paragraph in the paper much in the same strain. . . . I think it advisable to be very quiet upon the subject as it is impossible for any good to be done by revealing what we are.[30]

Joseph Jowett's letters betray a general anxiety among believers. They wanted their position with regard to the Great Cause to be clear, but in the absence of public meetings it was difficult to keep abreast of what was happening in the movement and whose loyalty might be suspect. Foley wrote to Charles Taylor, 23 July, 1818, to tell him that he had received a letter from Townley who was well, though the Cause was quite quiet, and there was news that the Reverend Thomas Webster, who had deserted the standard, had been attacked, robbed and had his throat cut, but was now recovering.[31] Later that year, Foley wrote again to Charles Taylor, telling him that Turner was still in York Asylum and that Tozer, 'that most strange and unaccountable of all men', had recently demanded that the stone be lifted from Joanna's grave because he had received a Communication that she would rise again as soon as the stone was removed. Foley had replied with 'a decisive negative'.[32]

Amidst the gloom which had descended after Joanna's death it was people like Sharp, Townley and Foley who kept the flame of her mission alight by stressing that there was no point in trying to understand what had happened, for that would be to rely on man's wisdom rather than God. The friends should 'judge nothing before the time that the Lord comes who will bring to light the hidden things of Darkness', Foley wrote in a letter which was much copied and distributed among the faithful. He also suggested that people should watch to see whether Joanna's Visitation would fade away like that of false prophets. If it did, then it was not true. If it did not, then it was true, and the rest was up to God.

The fact that the movement did not fade away was largely due to Foley himself, to his stability and steadfast faith. If William Sharp was a rock, never wavering in his personal faith, then Foley was a beacon, who never ceased to radiate the light of his encouragement to the friends. As Rector of Oldswinford since 1797, he was not only regarded as a pillar of society but was strategically placed to keep in touch with believers in the West Country, London and the North of England.

'I was at Mr Foleys last week, when he was very well and was enquiring about Father', wrote Joseph Jowett, Birmingham, to his brother-in-law, James Kidd of Halifax in November 1818.[33] A week later Foley was sending him an order for dress material which Jowett passed on to Kidd, with an assurance that Foley thought very much as they did about the Visitation.

> [Foley] said that he believed we should yet have a Child for if even the writings upon the subject could be dispensed with how, he asked, was it possible that the scripture could be fulfilled without the Child, and he was equally strong concerning the return of Joanna, in fact he and I have always agreed so far.[34]

It was important to have someone like Foley, stable and capable of inspiring confidence, when the paths others were pursuing threatened to wreck the movement. John Hows, for instance, had accused Townley of deception declaring that he would never rest until he brought the works of Joanna Southcott and her supporters into a Court of Justice.[35] The effect on poor Townley's nerves may be imagined, so William Owen Pughe and Ann Underwood agreed to meet Hows and his party to discuss the matter.

> Last Monday Mr Owen accompd. me to Mr Hows own house where the meeting was appointed to be. Present: Mrs Field; Parker; Haggar; Soarsby; Mrs Hows & her sister; Mrs Spurgin. The battle begun at 2 o'clock & lasted till half past ten. It was opened with Symonds business & the statements made by Mrs Field were in writing. Mrs Field said she would prove Joanna was the Jezebel and then she will bring her out the Bride. Mrs Field said she is to be the first to cast a stone at Satan.[36]

The meeting possibly cleared the air, because when Jane Townley wrote to Charles Taylor later in the year she was able to report that her health was very much better (even if her fingers were so cold that they could scarce hold her pen) and Mr Hows had gone back to his old shop in Shadwell 'and he and all his party are silenced'. She also said that Sharp had recently walked all the way from Acton to see her and that he was well and looking younger than she had ever seen him.[37] Perhaps Sharp had walked over to see Foley who was in London that same week.[38] Whatever his motive, Sharp would have wanted to consult both Townley and Foley about his latest plans which involved moving house again, this time to Chiswick, on the bank of the Thames, about six miles from London. His new house would give him every opportunity to indulge his passion for swimming and it afforded him much better light for his work. However, his move further into the country prompted Sharp to make new arrangements for Joanna's Box of Sealed Writings and he delivered it into the care of Jane Townley who became its next official custodian.

Sharp's move to Chiswick did nothing to dim his devotion to the Cause. He never lost faith in Joanna Southcott's divine mission nor expectation of her reappearance. He was still accompanied by his loyal housekeeper, Hannah Eikenhead. Although he suffered from gout, he enjoyed good food and drink, swam every day and was an avid reader, being particularly fond of Cobbett 'of whose writings he was to the day of his death a great admirer, and of which writings he used to say that for the greater part of his life on Saturdays, after dinner in his easy Chair he had experienced great pleasure, in the reading of his register, in which work he said there was always something new, something out of the common way, something to smile at, or downright laugh at, something to open the chest, so as to admit large gulps of fresh air into the lungs, so conducive in his opinion to longevity'. The only thing he found to criticise in Cobbett was the way the man kept changing his opinions – in marked contrast to Sharp's own steadfast beliefs.

There are occasional glimpses of him in the correspondence of friends who invariably reported him happy in his new home. 'Mr Sharp is very well, he removed to Chiswick and is very pleased with his new residence,' wrote Townley to Charles Taylor on 29 November, 1820.[39] And Foley found Charles Barnard and Owen Pughe at Sharp's house when he spent a happy day with him at Chiswick the following May.[40] The only thing to mar this period of his life was the dispute that erupted after Townley announced that she had experienced a Visitation of her own that was a continuation of Joanna's mission. For Sharp there was no one like Joanna; no one who could take her place; so, gentle and tolerant though he was, he could not endorse Townley's claims.

Sharp had inherited substantial wealth and had worked hard all his life, so his contemporaries assumed that he would die a wealthy man. Because of the number of good causes he espoused, this proved far from the case. Nevertheless, his Will made in May, 1823, shows his determination both to secure the interests of those he loved and to safeguard the objects he held dear:

> To Hannah Eikenhead, my housekeeper, the lease of my dwelling house in Chiswick Mall and all my household furniture plate linen and effects together with my Proofs and Impressions of my Copper Plates and the reasonable and proper use of my Copper Plates in having such Impressions taken therefrom as she may think proper during the time of her natural life and after her decease I give and bequeath the said Copper Plates to the children of Mr Charles Barnard of the Post Office Lombard Street, London, who shall be living at the time of the decease of the said Hannah Eikenhead.

He also appointed Hannah Eikenhead and Charles [Vincent] Barnard as executors.[41]

William Sharp died at 3.45 in the morning of 25 July, 1824,[42] from a second attack of dropsy on the chest. Shortly before he died he received a present and a Communication from Townley, sent as a token of reconciliation.[43] It was said that he had moved to Chiswick so that he could be buried in the same churchyard as Hogarth 'whom he esteemed as the most extraordinary painter that ever existed'.[44] The burial records of St Nicholas Church, Chiswick, contain the following entries:

> 1824 July 29 – Sharp, William, Chiswick, the Eminent Engraver, age 74.
> 1838 March 5 – Hannah Eikenhead, Hammersmith, age 67.

In his '*Memoirs of English Engravers*', Thomas Dodd included a printed brochure of the works of the late William Sharp describing him as 'one of the first engravers the world has produced, and whose engravings rank in the very highest class of art'.[45] Today the truth of this assessment may be judged by examining the fine examples of his work in the National Portrait Gallery and in the Department of Prints and Drawings of the British Museum.

# 3

# The Women at Weston Place, 1820-1825

Jane Townley, custodian of the Box for the next five years, was a woman of considerable wealth and social standing. She was born near Rochdale, at Belfield Hall, a stately mansion approached by a long avenue of cherry trees, and was the fourth child of Colonel Richard Townley, High Sheriff of Lancashire, and his first wife Ann (née Western). Her mother died in 1761 – possibly in childbirth, as Jane was christened at St Chad's parish church on 19 August that same year. Little is known about Jane's early years, but it is clear that she grew up in a cultured and privileged household, under the influence of a highly principled father.

Colonel Townley was known as a man 'of literary tastes and philanthropic zeal'.[1] In 1791 he published *A Journal Kept in the Isle of Man* and he was a friend and patron of the Lancashire poet John Collier, alias Tim Bobbin, of whom he wrote the short biographical sketch published in Aikin's *Manchester* in 1795. Townley, a pioneer of popular education and Sunday schools, also helped Robert Raikes in his work. An active, outdoors kind of man, whose favourite exercise was walking, he spent his last years in the Lake District where we catch a brief glimpse of him in Dorothy Wordsworth's Journal, 12 December, 1801: 'A fine frosty morning. Snow upon the ground. . . . We walked with Mrs Luff to Rydale and came home the other side of the Lake, met Townley with his dogs'. He died at Ambleside in 1802. Perhaps his death left a painful gap in his daughter's life that she needed to fill, for the following year saw Jane writing from London to offer Joanna Southcott a home.

In 1803 Jane Townley was a spinster aged forty who for years had been treated as an invalid. Writing to the Editor of *The Council of Ten* some twenty years later she set out to give an account of herself in connection with Joanna's mission:

> From early life I had a strong impression upon my mind that I should be restored to perfect health, and live to see the Millennium, notwithstanding the hopelessness of my case, in the opinion of all my medical attendants, until I put myself under the care of Doctor Moseley, in 1798, who said, from my having a good constitution, I might, in time and by perseverance,

> be perfectly restored; and I have been since answered, that his skill and penetration were gifts from the Lord: and by pursuing his plan I am now restored to health. It was this impression that often cheered me in sickness and adversity; but I could form no idea how, or by what means the happy period which I looked for was to be brought about, until the month of May 1803, when I heard of the books of Joanna Southcott, which I thought it my duty to read, and then to judge for myself. And that others might do the same I sent some of those books to my relatives and friends; but not even the receipt of the books was acknowledged by any of them, which caused me much sorrow of heart; being then totally ignorant of the powerful influence that Satan had over the human mind, to work blindness and unbelief. However I was comforted by being answered through Joanna, that by sending the books I had done all that was then required of me; and that I must set my heart at rest, and leave both relatives and friends to the Lord; for it was not in my power at *that time* to awaken them.

Her older sisters, fearing that she was gullible and easily exploited, had tried without success to wean Jane away from Joanna. Although Jane remained steadfast in her loyalty to Joanna, she was always conscious of her family's honour and the danger of bringing the Townley name into disrepute. For Joanna to be allied to someone of such assured social standing and unimpeachable integrity was invaluable to her, and the fact that they lived together for upwards of ten years meant that when Jane Townley vouched for Joanna's honest conduct over matters like the alleged sale of seals, her word carried weight.

While Joanna was alive, Jane Townley had looked to her for guidance in everything, obeying her 'as anyone must have obeyed the Duke of Wellington, who was an officer in his army'. Joanna's death had left Townley in a state of nervous collapse. Quite apart from natural shock other matters added to her grief. Exactly one week after the death, she fell out with William Tozer, the rough-hewn lath-cutter from Exeter who had become one of Joanna's preachers. In the course of their quarrel he declared that he saw the devil in Jane Townley and had long seen it. Her response was to banish him from her sight and she never saw him again.[2] Later that year she started to receive visits from the mysterious gentleman whom she suspected had been sent by the government to spy on her and these continued until the end of May, 1816.[3] And, as if this was not enough to tear her nerves to shreds, she was at the same time being bombarded with abusive letters from Richard Law. Purporting to be madly in love with her, this notoriously unbalanced man extorted money from her, growing increasingly malicious as he did so. He mercilessly played on the susceptibilities of an ageing spinster, alternately flattered and cajoled, then bullied and threatened her. On 13 May, 1816, he wrote from Doncaster to tell her that she had been to him 'the blooming Maid of Paradise, till you was deceived by the serpent, and persuaded to change your angelic form. . . . You have drove me mad[;] you have made me run distracted, and you have bewitched me out of my wits, as all my letters to you will most clearly testify'. His letter carried a postscript: 'Townley, you and I are married by ANAGRAM. e.g. Jane Townley = Yet one in Law.' Dubbing her 'Inexorable Jane,' he added, 'Come, come, don't puff yourself up about Virginity, it is through such proud, insolent, conceited Nuns as you that many a brave and proper man goes Wifeless and childless to the Grave . . .[so] boast no more of your Vile Virginity and since you have sent word by your tractable servant in iniquity that you are determined never to see me any more I shall now tell you the amount of your debt for which I demand instant payment viz: £100 six children and 25 years of conjugal love – all this you owe to me I swear it by the Devil's capstone which is your own heart.' Making it clear that he was prepared to settle for £100 sent immediately under cover to Canterbury Post Office, he threatened to send the letter to several London papers and, unless he had satisfaction, he would do much worse.[4]

On 14 June, 1816, he wrote again, this time to vilify Joanna:

> O Impious Wretch thou hast destroyed the Happiness of so many innocent individuals, come stand forth and answer for thyself – Townley, it would be impossible to paint the miseries my mind [h]as experienced from that Wretch Joanna. No longer believe she was sent of God for if you do you will be blasted from the Earth with bitter Destruction.

He concluded by repeating his demand for money:

> Townley Mark I leave Town this day the 100 pound I have demanded payment for is what Joanna Southcott justly owes me for the unnecessary trouble she gave me in journies and in letters and in pain of mind, you have succeeded to her property [therefore] pay the £100 and I will let you rest if not I will write to you from all parts in Sheets of Fire.[5]

The abusive letters continued. On 23 June, 1816, Law wrote:

> It matters not to me how good you are; or how wicked; how great your faith; or how blind your superstition, pay me my demand is all I want of you . . . though the Witch is dead, her

> spells yet continue, and are set with the most infernal art; you were easily caught by the fascinating delusion; because you was unskilled in the way of Religion.[6]

From a letter written six days later it is clear that Law called at 17 Weston Place but was refused entrance by a servant who threatened him with legal action.[7] On 7 July, 1816, Law repeated his demand for one hundred pounds, at the same time threatening, 'Have you forgot there was once a Townley's head on Temple Bar and I swear by the sun and moon and all the stars in motion that if I have much more aggravation it will soon be ornamented again'.[8]

The effect of this on a fifty-five year old spinster of nervous disposition may well be imagined. And the letters continued, growing ever more abusive, especially in Law's remarks about Joanna.

> She was the most ungrateful woman that ever was befriended by man; Many a rich present she got through the instrumentality of such men as myself, but she forgot us in her will nor even left us a single trinket to keep for her sake . . . she lived like a Hog and died the same; leaving behind her a litter of pigs who grunt and act like the sow that brought them forth. . . . I seriously and religiously believe this Mother is gone to Hell and there her gentlemen and ladies will soon follow her . . . before you knew her you had humanity towards your fellow creatures, but she soon froze up the springs of tenderness in you, and made your heart as hard and as cold as the floating mountains of ice in the southern Ocean. Self confidence and presumption swelled your mind you conceived you was sure you was in the right road to Heaven, and as to your fellow beings they might get there how they would for what you cared.

And always the letters concluded with a demand for money.[9] After all, he wrote to Townley on 17 July, 1816, 'you have £700 a year or more – what is £100 to you? . . . as for me I have often been chopped up and made into mince pies to please your Ladyship'.[10]

In the face of this onslaught, coupled with the quarrels among even those believers who had not joined Turner, it was no wonder that when Jane wrote to her young Exeter friend, Fanny Luscombe, on 5 November, she complained that she was feeling very ill. Failing the support of Mr Sharp and Mr Owen who 'keep out of all contentions', Townley was finding solace in the company of Ann Underwood's two grandchildren. 'I have the Boy here very often for he is quite an amusement to me.'[11]

Law's harassment continued all through 1817 even though there is no evidence that Jane actually read his letters. 'Why do you tempt me by your wicked and malicious silence?' he wrote from Doncaster in May, before renewing his demand for one hundred pounds.[12] Two days later, in the midst of some extravagant religious fantasy which prompted him to identify himself as Richard, 'Bishop and Patriarch', he drew on the parable of the fig tree to imply that she was barren and should be cut down.[13] The letters may have been the product of a diseased mind, but their malice was carefully contrived to undermine Jane Townley's belief in herself and her mission. On 23 July, 1817, he summoned her to meet him on the solemn morn of 29 December to shake hands with him over 'the awful Sepulchre of the Prophetess'.[14] The following month he told her,

> I am determined to have love or money . . . if you deny me love I will sell you for Gold . . . to the Manager of Covent Garden Theatre for £1000 . . . as Laumanza's Witch . . . burnt every night before thousands of spectators . . . and I in some unknown corner enjoy the spectacle . . . so I entreat that you will remember what you are – that you are a lovely woman, and all your actions ought to be lovely – then write me a lovely letter. . . . let us become like two turtle doves.[15]

In the continued absence of any reply, Law turned to Ann Underwood for help. 'It is a good thing to have a Friend at Court,' he wrote, before pouring out his hard luck story about walking the streets of London to look for work.[16] His attempt to reach the mistress through her maid proving ineffective, he continued to importune Townley for money and subject her to malevolent threats for the next four years. But perhaps Townley never saw the letters, as it would have been natural for Underwood to protect her mistress from such unnerving communications. It was, however, impossible to shield her from missiles fired from nearer home, such as the charges made by Hows in 1819 that Townley had been guilty of deception. Such an allegation injured Jane deeply: it impugned her honour and her good name. For this reason, Ann Underwood and Townley's good friend, William Owen Pughe, went into battle on her behalf. Their triumph did much to strengthen her position among the loyal believers at a time when Sharp, having moved to the country, was retiring from the fray.

Writing to her protégé Charles Taylor on 7 December, 1819, Townley reported the depressing news that 'All the followers of different Visitations had joined Turner except Sibley. Mr Turner is still in the Asylum and his followers say he is quite restored and are angry the Governor will not release him.' She added, however, 'Benjamin Wyatt the architect has bought all the books we could procure for him and his butler says his Master reads with great attention'.[17] 17 Weston Place was still seen as the headquarters of the movement, and new enquirers went there for information about Joanna's mission and to purchase her books. 'A clergyman has been with Miss Townley 2 or 3 times and purchases the Books very freely and appears to be well convinced of the truth of the Visitation, but will not declare his name for the present,' Joseph Jowett wrote to James Kidd on 12 December, 1819. This anonymous clergyman had evidently arrived at Townley's house one day when the Reverend Thomas Philip Foley was visiting and, seeing the latter's hat in the hall, turned away rather than meet a fellow clergyman in such delicate circumstances. Others were affected by personal rather than professional considerations and, according to Foley, rejected the cause simply because they did not like Miss Townley.[18] She was also being victimised by a new landlord who was trying to force her to leave 17 Weston Place, so life was far from easy.[19] Nevertheless, when Sharp relinquished the Box of Sealed Prophecies in 1820 no one questioned the fact that Jane Townley should be their next custodian.

Even if there was no official announcement, a tremor of excitement seemed to run through the believers that year. 'I think that things will come on fast now that the King is dead', Joseph Jowett confided to James Kidd in February.[20] And Jane Townley's correspondence shows her new preoccupation with Joanna's Box. 'I have been so extremely nervous, but thank God I am now much better', Townley admitted in a letter to Charles Taylor that November.

> I hope the time is not far distant when we shall all meet, as the Prophecies are now so rapidly fulfilling . . . as Bonaparte was a Scourge to the Nations abroad so I consider a certain great lady [Queen Caroline] is the scourge to this nation and like him I expect she will go on till the Writings are demanded or a heavy stroke comes from the Lord . . . the believers in London have provoked me by comparing her to Joanna. . . . Mr & Mrs Wyatt are both strong believers in Mr Turner's Visitation . . . and expect Shiloh to appear next January. I expect the delusion will go on till Joanna's Writings are demanded.[21]

Followers of George Turner also had cause for excitement in 1820, when in July their prophet was set free from York Asylum after being declared sane. He promptly announced that all who wished to be Brides of Christ must be married in a service designed by himself and set off on a tour during which he travelled three thousand miles and performed this bizarre ceremony over fifteen hundred times. A measure of his success in attracting followers was seen at Westminster on 30 August when seven hundred believers arrived, as instructed, all dressed in blue, to attend a 'Marriage Supper' presided over by him. Their joy knew no bounds when he announced that Shiloh would appear in London on 14 October that year. The day came and went with no such appearance, but still Turner's followers kept faith, saying, 'God has disappointed us to test our love for Him'.[22] Soon Turner's 'voice' came up with another date and it was announced that Shiloh would arrive on 10 April, 1821. Again the day came and went without Shiloh making any appearance, and this time Turner was devastated. He took to his bed, tended lovingly by Simon Gompertz, his chief disciple and Lord High Treasurer of his cause.

Writing to Charles Taylor on 17 July, 1821, Foley mentioned that he had visited London in May and spent ten days with Townley at Weston Place. Since then he had received a letter containing ominous news from John Smith, the man who had gone through a marriage ceremony with Joanna shortly before she died. It seemed that the Turnerites were now saying that there was no point in reading Joanna's writings any more or even mentioning her name, because she had done her work and by bringing Christ in the Spirit into the world her mission was finished. Foley's comment was that, if there had been some excuse for Turner when he was insane, there was none now.[23]

When George Turner relapsed into a coma and died in September, 1821, many of his followers cast around for someone who could explain what they themselves found inexplicable. At the same time Townley, now custodian of the Box, seemed to be wrestling with the need to reach a decision.

> On the 16th of December, 1821, I became exceedingly nervous, trembling and restless, and on the following morning it was explained to me, that if my feelings should be changed at the end of seven days, the time of my departure from Weston Place drew near; and when the morning of the 23rd of December had arrived, it was perceived by all in the house, that I was become perfectly composed and comfortable. On the morning of the 24th I was powerfully commanded to inform Mrs Underwood of my having had a spiritual communion at various times ever since the death of Joanna, a circumstance that I had not before revealed to any one. I was also ordered to tell my medical attendant, that I was to lie in a trance, as a sign to the Bishops; also to inquire of him whether he would be my attendant at the time when it should take place.[24]

A new certainty creeps into her tone as she picks up on Joanna's 'Voice':

> January 6th, 1822, being old Christmas-day, Mrs Underwood and myself were ordered to wear white clothing; and to drink a glass of wine; and on our taking the wine, I was to pronounce these words: 'May Christ's glorious and peaceable kingdom be speedily established, and Satan's power destroyed; may love, peace, unity, and harmony prevail over the whole earth.'

A few days later Jane was ordered to send for Underwood's two little grandsons, Charles William and George, of whom she was fond. Both seemed equally pleased to see her as she sat them down, one on either side of her, and gave them some wine and cake. However, when she started to speak the words: 'May Christ's glorious and peaceable kingdom be speedily established, and Satan's power destroyed . . .', George, the younger child, turned his back on Jane and clung to his grandmother. His father, Charles Barnard, told him to say amen, but little George said he would not and could not. His father then told him to look at Jane and thank her for the wine and cake. The child replied, 'Me won't, but I love the wine and cake – give me more'. When Townley asked him to kiss her; he pointedly refused. The older boy, Charles, on the other hand, showed her more than usual affection.

Townley might have taken mortal offence at the younger boy's behaviour had not the Spirit explained:

> The two boys stood as a type of the Jews and the Gentiles; the eldest standing for the Jews, and the younger for the Gentiles; therefore that many faithful believers, who had formerly shown me great kindness and attention, like the youngest child, would reject my visitation, until the manifestation of the Lord's power; when all things would be made clear; and that some would say, had the visitation been to Mrs Underwood, they would have received it. This I have seen perfectly fulfilled; so that the type was set for my comfort, and to prevent my imputing to them anything unkind: for as they expect Joanna to accomplish the whole mission, they cannot receive anything as coming through me as an instrument.[25]

And there was the rub. Jane Townley was convinced that she was the instrument of a divine visitation and therefore Joanna's natural successor, but others failed to see her this way. Even in her own household Ann Underwood, devoted servant that she was, could not bring herself to acknowledge that Jane's visitation was real. And, as the news spread, there were others whose opinion she had always respected – people like Sharp – who refused to accept that she had been divinely appointed to continue Joanna's mission. And why were they so blind? Not for petty personal reasons, but because, like the two little boys, they too stood as types of the Jews and the Gentiles.

All in all, it must have been a very tense time at 17 Weston Place. Not only did its occupants have to contend with the agitation and stress involved in their mistress's Visitation, but tragedy was unfolding in Ann Underwood's family. Coming to work for Townley as a young widow, Underwood had been accompanied by her only child, Ann, who had grown up in the household and become a great favourite with everyone. There had been great rejoicing in 1813 when she married Charles Vincent Barnard, a fervent believer in Joanna's Mission, but her health had never been robust and on the first day of February, 1822, she succumbed to the combined effects of consumption and childbirth. A fortnight later her poor mother was said to be 'bearing up with great fortitude'.[26] Townley made no mention of Ann's death, but perhaps her feverish activity at this time was partly in response to the chill wind of mortality that she felt blowing. On 7 February she was given a list of ten names, which included Foley, Bruce, Eyre, Charles and Robert Taylor, and commanded to send them each the following circular letter:

> Dear Friend,
> I am ordered to inform you that the writings will be demanded, before the expiration of this year; but at what time is not made known to me; but you must prepare yourself to be ready to come forward when called upon, as you are chosen to be one of my disciples; for it is my cause that the Bishops are to take in hand, according to the 42d page of *Prayers on the Fast*. None of the believers can be admitted, except those who are chosen to go with me. Probably you may wish to know by what authority I write the above. I answer: by the same authority by which I have rejected Turner's and all other visitations, and have been guided and directed by, ever since Joanna's death, according to the 87th page of *Second Book of Sealed Prophecies*. I remain yours, faithfully, in the work of the Lord.
> Jane Townley.[27]

Foley's response was enthusiastic. 'I told her that I had received her most welcome & heart cheering letter and I felt myself highly honoured in being chosen one of her Disciples – and that I should be glad and most happy to come forward at an hour's warning to attend her in London whenever my presence was deemed necessary', he wrote to Charles Taylor on 13 February, 1822, before cautioning him 'to keep these things as much secret, as you possibly can for the present because it will prevent misrepresentation, and many falsehoods'.[28]

Such caution proved unnecessary, for that same day Townley wrote another circular letter, this time to the Friends in general, explaining by what authority she acted and exactly what she had done.[29] But if Townley's Visitation was no longer a secret, its detailed implementation was still a source of misunderstanding. For instance, were women to be included amongst her disciples? Lucy Taylor clearly thought so, and concluded that the letter addressed to her husband had really been intended for her. Outraged at the notion, Townley quickly wrote to Charles Taylor so that he could set his mother straight:

> Surely, my dear friend, you must be convinced a Female could not be a Disciple therefore I lose no time in rectifying the mistake, as it is your Father who is chosen to be one of my Disciples. I shall be truly happy to see both your Mother and Sister afterwards, but how soon I may be permitted to do so I cannot venture to say till I have further directions, no Female is to go with me but Underwood.[30]

Although within days of Joanna's death Townley had become convinced that a spiritual birth had taken place on 25 December, 1814, she was not sure about the identity of the Man Child. But she later admitted that 'in my own thoughts, a certain individual appeared to be the one; and I wrote his name down, which I sealed up, and requested some friends to put their signatures thereon'. The name was evidently that of Pomeroy, for Owen Pughe later wrote, 'Pomeroy was chosen as the man-child, but, having acted in disobedience like Saul, his kingdom was rent from him.'[31] By 1822 Townley, now aware of her mistake, was preparing to acknowledge the real name as it had been revealed to her.

> On the 9th of March, I was ordered to write a letter, with a duplicate, announcing the name of the Man Child; and my medical attendant coming in just as I had finished, he saw me in the act of sealing them without having the contents imparted to him. One of the letters was put into the custody of Mrs Underwood on that day; and the other was delivered the next day to that professional gentleman.[32]

Meanwhile Townley's chosen disciples were writing to each other with mounting excitement. Foley wrote to Charles Taylor on 18 May, 1822:

> I rejoice exceedingly that your Father and yourself have accepted the offer sent you by our Dear Friend Mrs Townley of being her supporters at Hers, and our Trial – and before this year has finished its revolving Round we shall certainly be summoned to the Metropolis, but how soon that may be, we know not, for the day & hour is unknown – & it must come sudden & unexpected upon us. I see clearly by the Writings (and Townley says so too) that Pomeroy must be called forth and must appear at the Trial. Indeed we cannot do without him. . . . Miss Townley has written to tell me not to make any judgments of my own – I gladly obey the Deborah placed in our late dear and beloved friend's place.[33]

When William Oldfield wrote from Stockport on 7 July to a friend in Huddersfield to tell him about Townley's circular, he was clearly delighted about her Visitation, but mentioned that Sharp was 'the doubting Thomas'.[34] Then came news of the death of William Shaw, a prophet who had gathered a group of Southcottians around him from 1819 onwards.[35] This could be taken as another sign that Townley's time had come.

In April she had appointed Dr Owen Pughe to act as her secretary and in August he sent out a letter on her behalf, explaining to all believers that a communication about the late king, sent out by Joanna and then ordered to be destroyed, had been intended as a test of their obedience. He also tried to make it clear that when, after the coronation, Townley had been told that it was 'the last king who should ever reign', that communication should not have been construed as ominous for the monarchy. What had *really* been meant was that George IV was 'the last king who should ever reign *under the Satanic power'*.

The following month, Pughe wrote to Charles Taylor, explaining that 'Mrs Townley and Mrs Underwood being so nervous they seldom can write much themselves,' but, he said, it was their opinion that Joanna herself would return when Townley came out of the Trance, and that all the believers assembled in London would then see her.[36] It appears from later correspondence that Charles Taylor, always very sensitive, was profoundly disturbed by this notion. On 10 October, 1822, Pughe wrote to Lucy Taylor to confirm that Townley was looking forward to seeing her and her daughter, Fanny Luscombe, soon after her trance and he described how Joanna would return and be laid on a bed, appearing much like a ghost. As for Townley and Underwood, Pughe was glad to say that their health was better though they remained very nervous and expected to stay that way until called forward by the bishops because this would show that they could do nothing of

*William Owen Pughe (1759-1835), the celebrated Welsh antiquary and lexicographer, was a friend of William Blake and loyal adherent of Joanna Southcott. As legal adviser and secretary to Jane Townley, he was responsible for the despatch of the Box of Sealed Prophecies to the Reverend Thomas Foley in 1825.*

themselves. So, he added, 'don't be uneasy if Charles Taylor remains in a similar state'. Less encouraging was his news that Mr Sharp continued to be the doubting Thomas and seldom visited Weston Place and that Peter Morrison, one of the Seven Stars, had 'broke out again in rebellion'.[37]

That Townley, now over sixty and used to being treated with respect, was able to retain any semblance of composure that October speaks much for her inner strength, for those who rejected her visitation did not mince their words. One believer in Joanna's mission called on the morning of the 18th and implied that by exalting herself Townley had given Satan power to lead her into delusion through spiritual pride. 'These words wounded me most severely', she said, writing to him the following day to say that, if she was not called forward by 13 January, 1823, then he would never see her again in this world. Ten days later, still very agitated, she wrote, 'In my distress of mind, before I was up this morning, I formed a plan, that were it possible for me to be deceived, I would then retire to a distant part, and pass the remainder of my days in retirement, among strangers. To this I was answered, that, in such a circumstance, it was the only resolution left for me to pursue.'

Townley was also receiving censure from further afield. '[O]ur spirits are very much depressed', wrote James Kidd of Halifax, on 31 October, 1822, after reading a letter that had been sent to the friends at Manchester which debarred them from meeting together in future.

> We are not aware, that the manner in which we have acted have been contrary to any command given thro' Joanna. We have neither singing, prayer or preaching (which constituted a meeting for religious worship) but have as far as I can learn, done precisely as you do at Weston Place, viz. reading & conversation. And this is agreeable both to the Scriptures & the writings. . . . And now I shall notice the letter sent to friend Crossley, dated Oct 1st, wherein a good deal is said of the manchild, but not a word about the Prince of Peace, of which so very much is said in the Scriptures, & the writings & it is this character my eyes are directed to, without which I see no necessity whatever for the other.

But Kidd's most wounding criticism was that believers were finding it difficult to distinguish the words of the Spirit from Townley's own ideas.

> Now I shall notice another thing which appears to be necessary to prevent wrong notions from being received, which I have several times heard mentioned by the friends, that they find it difficult to distinguish what you have had given to you from your own judgment. If therefore the Communications were given, as was Joanna's practice, it would obviate this difficulty. I should be glad to know in what manner you receive your directions, if it is by a Voice. Hoping soon to have the pleasure of hearing from you, to the clearing up of all these difficulties, I remain with kind Christian love to yourself, Mrs Underwood, & the friends, Yours etc.[38]

In her circular letter to her ten chosen disciples the previous February Townley had declared that the writings would be demanded before the expiration of that year. As 12 January, 1823 (New Year's Eve, Old Style) approached she was clearly feeling the strain. On Saturday, 4 January, a visit from several of the friends left her so exhausted that next day she was directed not to receive them in future, but that same day twelve others called at 17 Weston Place, some for the first time in years. Expectation was in the air. Townley wrote,

> The time limited in my circular of the 8th of February being to end on Sunday, the 12th of January, I and all in the house were consequently looking forward with much anxiety and depression of spirits, on that day, as being the last, for the fulfilment of the letter, by the demand of the writings; but at two o'clock while at dinner I said that I felt my spirits rising; I then burst into tears of joy, and not of sorrow. . . . When the hour of eleven at night had passed over, without the looked for

> fulfilment, several writings were sealed up; and indorsed thus – 'Enclosed are papers which Mrs Townley was commanded to deliver or send to His Majesty George the Fourth, if he announced himself the Paul, before twelve o'clock at night of January 12th, 1823'.

And this was witnessed by two signatures. The next day a circular was sent to the believers:

> The 12th of January is past, without our hearing any thing; therefore Mrs Townley has nothing more to say. She sends her love, and hopes you will not take the ways of the Lord in question, as she is resigned to his will. I am yours, etc. Wm Owen Pughe.

Concluding that her work was finished, Townley then wrote a public letter to the Bishop of London, reminding him that in 1814 she had requested his opinion on Joanna's visitation and had taken his silence as an acknowledgement that she was right. She added that since Joanna's death she had found herself guided and directed, and everything had been perfectly fulfilled except a circular letter sent out to the friends last February, announcing that she (Townley) would be called forward, and that Joanna's writings would be demanded, before the end of the year, by a Paul. Now it had been revealed to her that His Majesty was the Paul who would summon the bishops to take the cause in hand, but as 12 January was past, and the prophecy had not been fulfilled, she had nothing more to say. She finished by saying, 'But it is my intention to publish to the world what has been revealed to me, to prove that I have acted upon the strictest principles, for the honour and glory of God, and for the good of mankind; and that I have neither disgraced myself nor my family'.

In view of her previous medical history Townley's closest friends must have felt anxious for her in the aftermath of her 'visitation', but she bore up surprisingly well. 'Notwithstanding the late disappointment Mrs Townley is perfectly happy and composed in mind, and what with that and her improved state of health, she is to us quite a wonder', Underwood wrote to Miss Eveleigh in Exeter, adding, 'The friends in general have borne the disappointment uncommonly well, nor do they meet with any mockery.'[39] Pughe also reported that Townley was in good spirits when he wrote to a friend on 28 January, 1823, but he hinted that such equanimity had been achieved at a cost. 'She cried almost incessantly for days and at night cried herself to sleep . . . but now her Spirits are quite restored and her mind is all peace and happiness, for she feels in herself having obeyed every command given to her, through Joanna and herself.'[40]

Such hard-won serenity was dealt another blow a week later with the death of her brother, Richard Greaves Townley, a man of property whose son would become Member of Parliament for Cambridgeshire. In contrast to their sisters, Richard had proved very supportive of Jane in recent years. He had been residing at the Cork Street Hotel in London and, although not a believer, had offered to wait upon the bishops on her behalf or do anything else that she wanted. In her tribute to him, Townley wrote, 'though it was not the will of the Lord that he should stand forth in my defence, his offer was well-pleasing; and it rested a blessing upon him, as was evidently shown before he departed this life for a world of glory'.

Jane Townley could ill afford to lose such support when even close friends such as Ann Underwood and William Sharp had refused to acknowledge her visitation. Their attitude was something she might have found impossible to forgive had she not realised that she was not to take it personally. 'Had not a little Type explained Mr Sharp's conduct towards me it would almost have broke my heart,' she wrote to Fanny Luscombe on 6 May, 1823. Then, after describing how, when she had offered the Barnard boys wine and cake, the elder had looked at her with delight whilst the younger turned his back and clung to his grandmother, she explained that this was because Ann Underwood 'stands like Joanna to the Gentiles . . . and he stood a Type of Sharp and the Gentiles who thought Joanna was all in all and therefore they cannot receive anything through me'. And the reason Townley had appointed Dr Pughe rather than Underwood to write for her was to show that 'we stand distinct though both handmaids to Joanna, and I was to obey her in all things, both Spiritual and Temporal – as the Type of the Jews being subject to the Gentiles until the fulness when all will join in Christian unity'. She described her sufferings after 12 January – 'I wept almost incessantly for many days which relieved me greatly and finding the Friends were not cast down as I feared, my Spirits gradually recovered and I became very happy and comfortable,' and finished by saying that she had had no Visitation since, though she frequently felt the influence of the Spirit, and she did not expect any more directions 'until the Paul awakens which I ardently hope will be soon though it may not till the end of the year'.[41]

In fact she received new directions within days, for the following order was put in writing and witnessed by four of her friends:

> Saturday, May 10th, 1823 – It is powerfully worked upon me, that I must not consent to go forth to meet the bishops, without having a solemn pledge given me for all commands given through me, respecting the trial, to be complied with. Jane Townley.[42]

Her new sense of authority was further evidenced by a command she received on 20 May to answer certain points brought forward by James Shergold Boone, Editor of *The Council of Ten*, a short-lived periodical that first appeared in June 1822. She accordingly published *A Letter from Mrs Jane Townley to the Editor of the Council of Ten, in Answer to His Remarks and Misrepresentations Respecting the Mission of Joanna Southcott*. It began:

> Sir, Having read in the twelfth number of your publication, the animadversions made by you upon the visitation to Joanna Southcott, it is incumbent upon me, in justice to her character, for my own honour and credit, and in justification of her faithful followers, to correct the various misrepresentations made by you which otherwise must lead the public to conclude, from her having lived with me for upwards of ten years, that I must have wilfully countenanced deception, notwithstanding the solemn promise made by me to my friends, of my determination of exposing whatever might appear incorrect, with regard to all matters concerning Joanna and her mission. . . . The writings of Joanna declare that the work therein announced should, after her departure, be carried on by myself and Mrs Underwood; and, as a testimony of the verity of that declaration, I have, under the guidance of the same spirit as visited her, been led on through all the various difficulties that were raised against me, ever since her death, without the aid of human counsel, and often contrary to my own feelings, and the calculations of human wisdom.

After a brief account of her own actions in connection with the Visitation, she thanked the Editor

> for announcing the names of those clergymen who at various times examined into the writings of Joanna; and I hope others will soon follow so good an example, by examining such of her writings as are still sealed up, and deposited, not in an iron-chest, as you have so safely placed them, but in a box of common wood.

Townley's efforts left her very agitated but her thirty-eight page publication met with general approval. Foley was full of praise of it, and Sharp said, 'It is an Honest Book.'[43] Twelve-months later, hearing that he was unwell, Townley sent Sharp a conciliatory gift, and news of his death on 25 July, 1824, left her devastated until the Spirit reassured her:

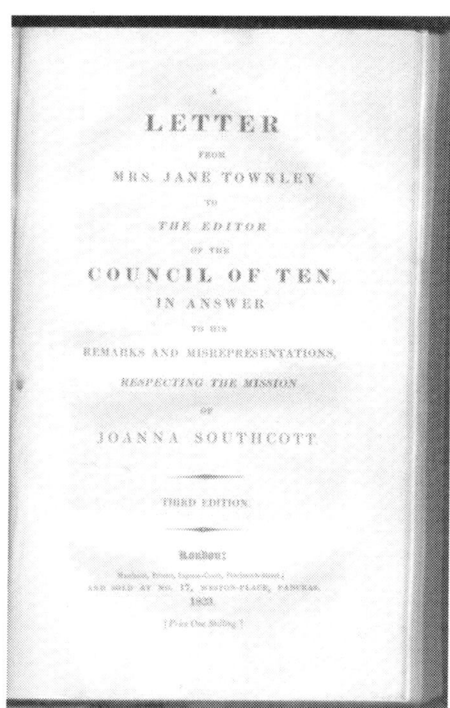

A

LETTER

FROM

MRS. JANE TOWNLEY

TO

*THE EDITOR*

OF THE

COUNCIL OF TEN,

IN ANSWER

TO HIS

REMARKS AND MISREPRESENTATIONS,

*RESPECTING THE MISSION*

OF

JOANNA SOUTHCOTT.

THIRD EDITION.

London:

AND SOLD AT NO. 17, WESTON-PLACE, PANCRAS.

1823.

[Price One Shilling.]

*Frontispiece of A Letter to the Editor of the Council of Ten, written by Jane Townley in 1823. The Council of Ten was a monthly magazine, first published in June 1822 by James Shergold Boone (1799-1859), its editor and almost sole contributor. The magazine expired after twelve issues, but Boone went on to take holy orders and held the incumbency of St John's Church, Paddington, until his death.*

> I know it is a great blow to thee. . . . I never told thee that Sharp would not die, but I left thee to draw thy own judgment – I tell thee thou wilt see him in Glory, though not in the manner thou didst expect, for, he is gone before thee, as no one will welcome thee more than Sharp; – I restored Sharp according to thy expectations; and I healed his leg according to thy expectation and I worked upon thee to feel great love and compassion for Sharp, and to send him a present, and a communication was also sent him, saying that Satan had been permitted to prejudice his mind against thee, the time was now come that he ought to do thee justice, which thou knowest he has not done; which I tell thee stands a type of thousands, who have good hearts like Sharps but their pride will keep them from acknowledging their errors, therefore I shall take them as I have taken Sharp. I do not require either believers or unbelievers to bow to thee, as thou art only the instrument but they must bow to the command given by one through thee.[44]

For Townley this was the heart of the matter. People must accept that she was the instrument of the Spirit, the person divinely entrusted to continue with Joanna's mission. She believed that Sharp, despite his virtues, had been led astray by Satan and that was why he had been blinded to her own Visitation. Underwood had been similarly deluded. 'Now I shall answer thee of Underwood,' Townley's Spirit announced on 6 August, 1824.

> She acted wisely in acknowledging to Waring how Satan had worked upon her, for since the death of Joanna she had not been happy, but she could not recollect how she had aggravated thee, that though she loved Joanna much more, still she loved thee, and this I know to be true; for Satan has worked as powerfully upon her, to prejudice and blind her mind against thee, as he did upon Sharp. And I know Satan spoke many things through her which wounded thy feelings, and that she no more recollects, than Peter [Morrison] remembers the random things, which Satan speaked through him. Therefore she will act wisely in future, to pity Peter in stead of blaming him. At my appointed time I shall take her to Glory, and as Joanna and her were kindred spirits on Earth, so they will be in my Kingdom above – And thou hast promised to take the grandchildren under thy protection. Whatever I shall have for her to do on Earth, I shall enable her to do it until she has finished; Therefore let her set her heart at rest, and grieve not, that she cannot see clearly into My visitation. For she and Sharp have stood like the Jews of old, who believed God was all in all, therefore they could not receive me. In like manner Sharp and Underwood thought Joanna was all in all, therefore they could not receive thy visitation; but no blame is attached to either.[45]

In a letter to her friend, Lucy Taylor, written on the same day, Townley described with some feeling how she had been at odds with Underwood who had been unable to accept her Visitation because 'for her Joanna had been all in all'. In fact, Underwood and Joanna were 'kindred spirits', she concluded.[46] What she did not say was that her own health was deteriorating and she was beginning to suffer again from the nervous anxiety that had bedevilled so much of her life. On 7 August, in what reads like paranoia, Townley raved about Lord Sidmouth and others, who were accusing her of fomenting rebellion, and how she would agree to give up every paper in the house if demanded. Her deranged mental state may have been due to the medical draughts, possibly laudanum, that Townley was taking, for she quotes the Spirit as saying:

> I restored thee to health to leave off the draughts, to have a good appetite and to sleep, and, for a time, thou didst feel no agitation, but had I freed thee from every infirmity of nature I could not have worked in thee as a type of the King; for when thou art freed from every infirmity of nature, thou wilt feel no confusion

> in thy mind about anything. . . . I told thee that the King and Sharp stood in one likeness, for Satan has worked as powerfully upon the King against thee, since Joanna's death, as he worked upon Sharp. And as Sharp upheld Tozer against thee, the King has upheld the Ministry in a similar manner, and the Habeas Corpus Act was suspended to seize thee, and had Frazer left his Papers in thy house, thou couldest not have cleared thy self, but I permitted thee to consent to have them brought here; which, I tell thee, confounded them![47]

For years Townley and Underwood had been at odds. The health of both women was now suffering, and illness seems to have prompted Underwood to make the first conciliatory move. On Sunday morning, 12 September, Townley received the following Communication:

> The unity and harmony that has been since last Monday morning between thee and Underwood stand a deep type of the end, how Jews and Gentiles will be united in Christian unity and harmony. . . . I have frequently told thee, that I could not take Satan's power from Underwood, until she acknowledged how Satan had blinded her respecting thee, which, thou knowest, she did on Monday morning, which turned the blow on his head, and I took his power from her.[48]

Having acknowledged her failings, Underwood sealed their rapprochement by leaving Jane Townley her diamond hoop ring when she made her Will three days later.

Now that the friends and fellow handmaids of the Lord were reunited it seemed that the mission would go quickly forward. It was announced that Townley would have a Visitation on the night of Sunday, 19 September, 1824, but she was disappointed. She was told the following morning,

> Thou hadst no visitation whatever last night, and now I shall answer thee. . . . I have told thee, that thou wilt be called forward before the expiration of this Month, Old Style, but I have not told thee when thy trial will take place, for reason must tell every one, that after thou art called forward, there must be a time for arrangements to be made, as I am a God of order and not of Confusion.[49]

So, they settled down to wait until the end of the month, Old Style, but still to no avail. On 13 October, 1824, Pughe wrote to Mrs Pye, 11 Red Lion Court, Fleet Street, as follows:

> Dear Friend, Mrs Townley directs me to inform you of the following particulars. Yesterday terminated the time for the fulfilment of the words given to her and of which you have been made acquainted. She and her inmates waited until midnight, without having their expectations realised. Mrs Townley exerts her fortitude and resignation as far as could be expected. She and Mrs Underwood unite in Christian love to you and all the friends.[50]

Fortunately Townley had the support of good friends during this difficult time – friends whose faith in her had never wavered. One such was George Troup, for years a loyal follower of Joanna and now 'a friend at court', having served as 'Pagesman' to George IV for over 35 years. Troup retired in September, 1824, but continued to live at St James's Palace, and to support Townley despite the fact that they sometimes fell out.

> I have left thee for a while to confound Satan, for great have been his accusations against thee and Troup – that thou wouldst murmur and complain; and that if Troup were foiled, he would upbraid thee and curse the Lord,

the Spirit told Townley in October, 1824. Yet,

> thou knowest that Troup instead of upbraiding thee, has felt more for thee than for himself and is resigned to my will. I ask thee how I could mock thy temporal enemies if I had not set a time to foil thee – to let them rejoice for a little season, thinking that all was over, crying peace and safety, before sudden destruction come upon them.[51]

But Townley did not live to see any 'sudden destruction'. Her spirits never recovered after the second disappointment. She had made her Will within days of Sharp's death, and in early March, 1825, she anticipated her own by giving detailed directions for her funeral. After this she became very lethargic, falling into almost a continual sleep, waking only to wet her mouth with a little tea.[52] On 26 March, 1825, William Owen Pughe wrote to the Reverend Foley:

> Dear Friend,
>
> I am concerned to communicate to you the Melancholy Tidings that Mrs Townley is no more. She was seized with violent convulsions yesterday morning at Eleven which so continued till about ½ past One – and then they gradually abated so that at about ¼ past 2 she seemed to get into a Doze and in another Quarter of an hour she ceased breathing. . . . Mrs U. continues very unwell.[53]

Her funeral was private, with only Owen Pughe and Mr Bancroft following the hearse to St Martin's churchyard, Camden Town, where she was laid to rest at the head of Ann Barnard. Her Will included bequests of five guineas each to her two sisters, and a hundred pounds to Owen Pughe. She left all her personal property, goods and chattels to Ann Underwood, but she had probably not died a wealthy woman because, as Charles Barnard explained to Edmund Baker, 'there cannot be much left as she has lately supported so many'. Now that Townley was dead, Barnard also volunteered an opinion that he had not dared express before: 'My mind has for some time back been undetermined about the visitation to Mrs Townley but I thought it most prudent to say nothing.' As for Ann Underwood, his mother-in-law, Barnard made it clear that nursing Townley had left her completely worn out: 'her weakness is extreme; that I cannot at present trouble her with much conversation as her strength enables her to sit up only a few hours in the course of the day'.[54]

Underwood never recovered after Townley's death, so it would have come as no surprise when, six weeks later on 5 May, 1825, friends received another message from Pughe:

> I have to acquaint you with the sad tidings, Our Dear Friend Underwood is no more, she departed at 20 minutes before 4 this morning after a long time of sufferings & agonies till nearly the end, when she became quite collected & perfectly happy.[55]

There are several accounts of Ann Underwood's last days. Charles Barnard said that about a week before she died she dreamt that Mrs Townley came to her and called her.[56] Another witness said that, during her last days, when she was sitting pondering over her troubles, Underwood was heard to mutter repeatedly: 'Ye fearful saints, fresh courage take, The clouds ye so much dread, Are big with mercies, and shall break, With blessing on your head.' Once, suddenly roused from sleep, she said that she had awoken with the words, 'Christ is the rock' and later murmured, 'I want no temporal comfort; I have spiritual comfort.' On her last night she kept repeating, 'Lord have mercy on me.' At about twelve o'clock she asked for some cherry wine, and whispered, 'It was so good', when she drank it. Her last words were, 'God bless you all. I must leave you. I have done all I can.'[57]

Ann Underwood was buried on 11 May, her coffin being set upon Jane Townley's at the head of Ann Barnard, her daughter. Edmund Baker, attending the funeral as one of the mourners, reported that he was present when Joanna's Box of Sealed Writings was opened before being sent on to its next custodian. He left the following note to this effect:

I also saw the Chest opened at Mr Barnards with Bundles of the same writings in them in May 1825 Mr Sharp being dead, after this Mr B sent them to the Revd Mr Foley. Signed Edmd Baker.[58]

# 4

# Riveted to My Soul, 1825-1835

The Reverend Thomas Philip Foley was a natural choice to succeed Jane Townley as custodian of the Box of Sealed Prophecies, for no one had been more loyal. One of the Seven Stars who had visited Joanna Southcott in Exeter in December, 1801, Foley had immediately embraced her cause and his faith in her mission had never wavered. He had arranged for the Trial of her writings at High House, Paddington in 1803, and poured money and energy into the printing and distribution of her books. This is shown in his Diary, where an entry for 25 September, 1804, reads: 'Reced. 5748 of Joanna Southcott's [books] of Mr Heming and brought them to my House at Oldswinford'.

A son of the Reverend Philip Foley, Rector of Shelsley in Worcestershire, and kinsman of Thomas, Baron Foley, in 1797 Thomas Philip Foley accepted the family living of Oldswinford, a Worcestershire parish which covered almost all of what is now the borough of Stourbridge. He also held the living of Wombourne in the Lichfield diocese. Known at Cambridge as 'the handsome Foley', as a young man he had gained a reputation for fashionable dress and fast living. His account book shows that he was addicted to card playing and gambled away considerable sums of money. A typical entry reads:

> Tuesday, April 21st 1801: To a Baronett's Brother
> at 2 Handed Whist Lost at Cards £9-0-0
> Never to play it again. TPF.
> Thursday, April 23rd 1801:Lost at Cards £0-1-6

He enjoyed the theatre, recording expenses of £0-14-6d to see Mrs Siddons at Birmingham in August, 1800. He subscribed to the local bowling club, the library and the hunt, causing dismay in his parish by appearing at some funerals with his surplice thrown over his hunting pink. Parishioners also rumoured that he kept a white horse saddled in Oldswinford rectory stables in readiness for the time when he would be summoned to witness the birth of Shiloh.

Among the day-to-day minutiae of Foley's life recorded in his Account Book is an entry for 30 June, 1800: 'Elizth. Beach came for a month on trial at Four shillings a week.' Exactly one month later Foley notes: 'Agreed with Betty for Seven pounds a year from this time. A months wages or a months warning. Thos. P. Foley.' From this it may be deduced that Elizabeth (or Betty) Beach had made a good impression and been offered a more permanent position in the household. Then, on 16 September, 1801, Foley records: 'A white and auspicious day to me, as Charity & Justice were performed. On this Day I offered myself & was kindly accepted. TPF.' What Foley's Account Book had not shown was the birth of his son, Richard, on 18 July, 1801. Nor did it record his marriage to the child's mother, Elizabeth Beach (or, more correctly, Bache) on 6 October, 1801, at the church of Saint Pancras, Middlesex. There is, however, a brief Memorandum for 24 July, 1803: 'My wife first appeared in Oldswinford Church accompanied by Mrs Joanna Southcott & Miss Taylor from Exeter.'

Foley was a kind-hearted, impulsive, man whose enthusiasms must have sorely tried the patience of his more pragmatic wife. He and Elizabeth had not always seen eye to eye about Joanna, and in the aftermath of her death, Foley found any criticism of their 'Spiritual Mother' hard to bear. His diary gives evidence of the tension he was labouring under at that time.

> Sunday, Jany. 15, 1815: There was a very large congregation, it being the first time that I made my appearance at Church since the death of Joanna Southcott, my much lamented Friend.
>
> Monday, Jany. 16, 1815: A very hard frost in the night and also in the morning and so continued. . . . I am truly grieved to say that my wife and self are now quite opposite in our opinions respecting Joanna's works & most uncomfortable is our present state; for one of us must be going deeply into sin, Oh, may the LORD be pleased to shew us which is right! And what is HIS Blessed Will in this matter! . . . I read dear Joanna's works till suppertime.
>
> Wednesday, Jany. 18, 1815: I had a violent breeze with my wife after dinner abt. Joanna's works, and she asserted a most gross lie, and for which & other exasperating language I was obliged to put her out of the room. Oh, may it please the LORD to judge between us & shew us who is right! And what is HIS good will & pleasure concerning us! May the devil be soon chained into HELL that he disturb mankind no more during Xt's Millennial Reign upon Earth. Amen, & Amen.
>
> Tuesday, Jany. 24, 1815: I can assure the Doctor [Reece] that Truth, Honor, & Uprightness has ever swayed the proceedings of the tried & proved Friends of our dear & lamented Spiritual Mother, Joanna Southcott, and so *the End*

*The Reverend Thomas Philip Foley (1758-1835), Vicar of Oldswinford, Worcestershire, and Custodian of Joanna's Box of Sealed Prophecies from 1825 until his death in 1835.*

> will shew to the whole world. Matters cannot long rest as they are. We humbly and confidently leave them now with the LORD to manifest forth whether the work is HIS or whether it be only a Delusion. In the latter case we are willing to make every reparation in our power for what we have done in this cause, wh. however I still think must proceed from the GOD of Truth* (*from the many truths wh. have been already fulfilled. TPF.)

Despite the occasional 'violent breeze', domestic harmony gradually returned to the Foley household, and whilst Foley continued to be an encouraging beacon for believers, his letters being copied and widely circulated, his correspondence shows that he was also the model father. His concern for his last born, four year old Alfred, is apparent in a letter he wrote to the Taylor family in January, 1822. 'Dear Alfred in the autumn had the scarlet fever which has been very prevalent abt. us, but he is now thro' the divine favor perfectly recovered.' Although disturbed by the prevalent crime – 'We have had in this neighbourhood within the last six months near 20 horses stolen out of grounds & stables' – Foley found cause for celebration in the fact that 'Our Great & Glorious Cause seems to be advancing with rapid steps – and I think the Time is near at Hand when the Great & Learned will demand Joanna Southcott's Divine Writings to be placed before them – Then they will be disputed upon & then proved by 24 agt. 24 for 7 days and then it is promised by the Spirit of Truth that their Work will be clearly shewn to proceed from the Mighty God of Jacob.'[1]

He found further cause for celebration when, the following month, Townley announced her Visitation and informed him that he had been chosen as one of her disciples. Unlike Underwood and Sharp, Foley did not doubt that her Visitation was real and immediately communicated the 'Glorious News' to his wife and eldest son, who agreed to take his reply.

> This very day, I believe that dear Richard (who is returning to Emmanuel College after the Xmas vacation) will deliver my answer to my beloved Friend in Weston Place. I told her that I had received her most welcome & heart cheering letter and I felt myself highly honoured in being chosen one of her Disciples – and that I should be glad and most happy to come forward at an hour's warning to attend her in London whenever my presence was deemed necessary.[2]

Foley's high expectations were reflected in the depth of his disappointment when the events promised by Townley failed to take place, but he was still not disillusioned. 'Our strength now is to stand still, & to wait till it pleases the Lord to manifest His Power amongst us,' he wrote to Charles Taylor, 7 March, 1823. And, on a personal front, he must have found some consolation in the achievements of his eldest son.

> I have the happiness to inform you that dear Richard has very greatly distinguished himself in taking his A.B. degree in the Senate house Cambridge in January last. It has exceeded all our most sanguine expectations, & what pleased me more than all the rest, was that He gave the whole praise & Honor to the Lord – for, he said, on 1st days Examination he felt a Spirit enter him that gave him skill & wisdom more than he ever had before in his life. He was the 6th Wrangler of one of the greatest years of the last 50. . . . the College was so pleased with what he had done that they intend to present him with a cup.[3]

Despite paternal pride and family feeling, Foley was never one to compromise where principle was concerned, even if it jeopardised his standing in the community. While Joanna was still alive his attachment to her cause had attracted much ridicule from his parishioners, as a result of which he had largely withdrawn from local society. However, the fact that he was a kinsman of Lord Foley of Witley Court, one of the most influential men in the neighbourhood, saved him from ostracism. When his relationship with that gentleman was threatened by a rash vow taken years earlier, Foley still refused to sacrifice principle on the altar of expediency. He wrote to Lord Foley on 22 July, 1824,

> My Lord, When I returned Home after a very pleasant visit to Witley, I then learnt that Oliver and Harwood had fixed on Tuesday next to have a Public Dinner for Your Lordship at the Talbot Hotel, and it grieves me exceedingly that I cannot make

> One of the Party: because abt. 14 years ago from the Persecution and great unkindness of many of my Flock I made a Hasty and Foolish Vow To the LORD that I would not Dine out at any Public Meeting, or accept of any Private Invitation of Pleasure at Stourbridge – or Just Around it till after a certain event had taken place, and which has not yet been Fulfilled. Still, I am certain it will Come to pass, as sure as I am now in Existence, although I cannot fix the Precise Time – that being only known unto the ALMIGHTY. I would sooner (under the Divine Aid and Strength) suffer Death than break my Vow; because I should then be most miserable and wretched during the remainder of my Life But . . . if Your Lordship will do me the favor of Taking a Bed at my House on Tuesday Night, and will spend the next day with me, I . . . will make Every Exertion to make your Lordship comfortable. . . . I still have a little Quantity of De La Maine's Port in my Cellar of 25 years old, and, I hope, it is as High Flavoured, as when I had last the Happiness of seeing your Lordship at the Rectory. . . .

Lord Foley replied the same day, courteously declining the invitation to stay at the Rectory and adding, 'I am sorry that you will not Dine with us as I have always great Pleasure in meeting you. But had you not given yourself the Trouble of making the Explanation you have, I should not have Believed, or Attended to any reports or reasons that either Malice, or Ignorance might have assigned as the reasons for your Absence. . . '.[4]

Foley was one of the first to be informed by Pughe when Jane Townley died on 26 March, 1825. Six weeks later he received another letter from Pughe, this time telling him of the death of Ann Underwood which, Pughe said, 'completes the type in 1804 when Joanna & Mrs Townley set off for Bristol leaving Underwood to follow the next morning'.[5] Underwood was buried on 11 May, 1825, and Edmund Baker, a mourner at her funeral, was present at Charles Barnard's house where he saw Joanna's Box being opened around this time. He did not say whether anything was added to its contents, but it is possible that some of Jane Townley's Communications were placed in the Box before it was locked and shipped off to its next custodian.[6] The decision to ask Foley to accept this responsibility seems to have been taken by William Owen Pughe, in consultation with Charles Barnard and possibly others such as Edmund Baker, the Reverend Samuel Eyre and John Crossley. Pughe's letter to Foley on 16 May, 1825, implies that he had been in touch with believers in all parts of the country:

> Dear Friend,
>
> Your letter dated the 13th instant afforded me great satisfaction, under existing circumstances; as I consider the general view taken by you of the Progress of the Visitations to the Women (Joanna Southcott, Jane Townley, Ann Underwood) to be equally correct as Conscientiously Faithful. Letters have come from the Revd S. Eyre and from Mr J. Crossley which agree with ye sentiments expressed by you; and their Resolution now is to wait Resignedly and Patiently for the Manifestation of the Will of the LORD towards the fulfillment of our Expectations for Establishing HIS Kingdom on the Earth. . . . Everything will be cleared off from Weston Place without delay. But Mrs Waring has taken rooms at No 16 (Weston Place) next door to 17, and she will store some of the Books there as we are at a loss for room for all of them. Any future Letters will be taken in by Her, or at Mr Barnard's, No 3 Prospect Cottages, Barnsbury Park, Islington. Peter Morison still remains at Mr W. Oldfield's, Carrs, Stockport, I had a letter from them a little before the death of Mrs Underwood but no Answer to my Announcement of her Death. If I were to fill a Few Cases with Books, could you give them Room? For we shall find it difficult to keep them here. I am also proposing to send the Box of sealed and other writings to be put under your care in *TRUST* for the Executors, if you consent.[7]

Foley wrote back to express his consent in no uncertain terms: 'With lively joy and gratitude to the Lord for this distinguished blessing, I will gladly receive the Writings and take the strictest care of them, and may I be found a true, grateful and courageous steward of these invaluable treasures, even unto death.'[8]

And how were these 'invaluable treasures' to be moved from St Pancras to Oldswinford? Fortunately, Oldswinford was very near Stourbridge, whose iron and glass products had for years enjoyed the advantages of canal transport, so Pughe despatched Joanna's Box by water. He wrote to Foley on 3 June, 1825:

> This Day 4 cases of Books, with the Box of Sealed Writings, have been sent off for Whitehouse's Boat, I forgot to send the Key of the Box of Sealed Writings. Therefore, it shall be left at Mr Smith's, No. Princes Street, (Cavendish Square) for Mr Richard Foley – or Any other Friend to call there for it, on coming through London. The account for the cases and carriage to the Boat of your own books is £1/11/6d, that is £1/7/0 the

> cases and carriage 4/6. After you shall have paid the carriage of the cases *now sent*, you will please to inform me of the balance for a future settlement. Your future letters to me had been better addressed to Mr Barnard, General Post Office, and then he will open them that you may be answered in case I shd. be in Wales; for when in London I am at his house. Should anyone want the Portraits of Brothers, with the name blotted out, you might sell them *for the present* at 1/6d each. You will see below what books are sent in the cases. Hoping that yourself, Mrs Foley, and the young family enjoy health and presenting my respects to all, I remain, Dear Friend, Yours truly, Wm Owen Pughe.

Pughe then carefully listed the numbers and titles of all the books contained in each case.[9]

It must have been an anxious time for Foley, waiting for the boxes to arrive. His relief is palpable in a letter written to Owen Pughe on 29 August, 1825, acknowledging that he was overjoyed to have received that day five large boxes, including the 'New Ark of God'. He and his wife had been very ill, he said, before asking Pughe to pass on news of the whereabouts of the boxes to 'my dear and beloved friend Troop' and to all other true believers in their glorious cause. Sensing that where the 'Ark' rested might become a place of pilgrimage, Foley extended a welcome to the rectory at all times and concluded, 'We all unite in Christian love and kind wishes to yourself and all true ones around you from the Giver of all Good.'[10]

There were, however, pernicious rumours circulating about Foley. One in particular suggested that, after the death of Joanna, he had not only renounced his faith in her Divine Mission, but had publicly recanted from the pulpit. When John Crossley wrote to ask if this was true, Foley immediately defended himself. He wrote on 22 September, 1825,

> There never was a greater lie sent forth by Satan than that of my reading the Recantation of my faith in Joanna Southcott's Divine Mission and Writings from my pulpit. My faith in those heavenly Works, blessed be God for it, was never stronger or more riveted to my soul, than at the present moment. I shall therefore kindly thank you, to do away that abominable wicked lie, propagated by the agents of Satan, wherever you possibly can. . . . I have been shut for a long time from giving any written opinion, or of drawing any judgment upon Joanna's Divine Works till after the great & awful Trial takes place: and therefore you must excuse my silence on that head. In respect

to the Sealed Writings, I shall feel happy in giving you a copy of my Circular Letter lately sent out, and which will explain many things unto you: and if yourself or others should derive the least comfort or light from what I shall spread before you; I shall be most amply gratified.

Foley finished by saying that he had been very ill for the last six weeks with a gouty complaint in his stomach and dreadful cough, but that he considered this little affliction as a blessing from the Lord, because it had kept him humble and resigned to the Lord's will and not 'lifted up too much with joy'.

*Circular addressed to the Friends of the Rev.Foley on receiving the Trust of the Sealed Writings*

Oldswinford Rectory,

September 1825
To the Friends

It is with much pleasure I take up my pen on the following very interesting subject;

Some short time ago, there was a Discussion in London (upon the br[e]aking up of the housekeeping in Weston Place) where the Sealed Writings and others should be deposited; and they unanimously agreed they should be placed under my care; if it should be convenient for me to receive them. With lively joy and gratitude to the Lord, for this high and distinguished Blessing I instantly returned an answer to say, that I should most joyfully receive them, and I would take the strictest care of them. Accordingly they were sent to my house, & arrived safe. I assure you, I consider *the keeping of this New Ark of God* – of *the Covenant of Joy, Love, and Peace for a thousand years for all the human race* (who will accept it) *to be the greatest blessing which could possibly be conferred upon an individual*, and as such, with the deepest love and gratitude to the Almighty do I humbly receive it. And may I be found a true, grateful and courageous Steward of these invaluable treasures, till they are *properly demanded by the Great and Learned, as set forth in Joanna Southcott's Divine Writings*. My soul's desire is to do the will of the Lord according to the power with which he hath blessed me. The enemies to our glorious cause have from a singular circumstance been made acquainted where the Sealed Writings are deposited; and a short time ago I have been permitted by Dr Pughe to make it fully known to all the True Believers in our glorious cause; and

> therefore with great joy do I now give them the intelligence.
>
> You know from the Scriptures of Truth that there was '*An Ark*' given to the Jews at first, before they entered into the promised land; and *that Ark* went before them, and *Victory* was their sure and constant attendant. So now both Jews and Gentiles (being united) form the *True Israel of God, and the Ark a Second Time* will go before them under the Direction of the Lord God, and will be the sure token of victory during their journey to the promised Land, to enjoy that Sabbath of Rest for a thousand years, of Love, Joy, & Peace before the General Judgment. Blessed, blessed be God for it; this happy and exalting period is fast approaching. These are High and Mighty Blessings, and may we be worthy (as far as sinners can be) to receive them. And may we be ever grateful, true, and obedient soldiers, servants, and friends to the Captain of our Salvation & Redemption, the Lord Jesus Christ.[11]

Soon after explaining his position to the Friends and putting their minds at rest, Foley received a disturbing letter from William Tozer who, having alienated Jane Townley after Joanna's death, had espoused first the cause of George Turner, then of Alexander Lindsay [or Lyndsey] who had announced himself as 'Laban, who is Paul according to the Spirit'. Hearing that Foley was the new Custodian of the Box of Sealed Writings, Tozer wrote,

> Reverend Sir,
>
> I have had a wish to write to you for many years – but seeing you so united in party difference it kept me from writing; but now the time being fast approaching for the fulfilment of the prophecies, I think it is time to join in that great cause we first engaged in: which I have always very strictly followed, to the best of my knowledge: relying wholly on the Lord Jesus Christ, to be my whole Guide. . . , what the world, or my brethren, have said concerning me, I care not, it cannot hurt my faith, for that is a gift of God – and man cannot overthrow it: and I am very happy to see you so gladly received the Ark of the Covenant – and I hope to God you will make the use of it according to the Will of God, viz: not to keep us in party discord – but to unite us all in one body of people – and to learn the New Song of 'Moses and the Lamb' – as the true Israel of God; and in the name of God, let us have the Ark of the Covenant to go before us. And I apply to you – as I always looked on you as one of the head, now to come forward and

> meet the Heads and Rulers of the great and high calling in Christ Jesus – that is to say, the Judges and Jury that are living of the First and Second Trial of that highly favored character Joanna Southcott. . . .
> Dear Sir, I hope you will excuse the liberty I have taken, and what I have written, as I have done it with my best wishes, to unite our brethren together, as I think the day is fast approaching; and I should wish, if agreeable to you, to be on the 12th of January 1826, as that is the first month in the twelfth year, after her death. . . .
> [Please to direct your response to William Tozer, 9 Duke St, Westminster Rd, London]

What sounded to be a reasonable approach was belied when this letter, having failed to elicit from Foley the desired response, was incorporated by Tozer into a printed circular sent to believers such as Charles Taylor. In an effort to increase the pressure on Foley to summon all those judges and jury who were still alive and had been present at the Trials at High House and the Neckinger, Tozer resorted to sinister threats. He described how, for instance, fifty to sixty people had met on Sunday, 6 February, 1825, to curse Townley – 'the sign was that Townley, Townley, Townley should go the road of all flesh in 3 months; and within 3 months her death took place'. Then, on 3 April, 1825, twelve people (W. Tozer, J.K. Williams, Mrs Wood, Mr Bacon, Mrs Barnes, Mr Pye, Mr Dynes, Mrs Sharlock, Mr Marshall, Mrs Jones, Mr Vaughan, and Mrs Archer) had been sent to warn Mrs Underwood to 'come and see' or send her answer. When no answer was received, double the number was sent. When there was still no answer, these twenty-four people returned to the chapel at White Horse Court, Southwark, and carried out certain malevolent actions. They opened a trap door in the floor, shut it again, then trampled on it 'as a sign to Underwood and her death followed'.[12]

The effect of such an unpleasant letter on the sensitive mind of Foley, who was already physically ill, may be imagined. 'I received a circular letter from Tozer some months ago but I returned no answer to it, as I clearly saw it proceeded from the evil source – and I am glad you did the same,' he wrote to his young friend, Charles Taylor on 4 March, 1826. 'My friend Smith returned to Lieut Lyndsey (their Paul, who it seems is the leader of the Party) a strong letter from Joanna's works proving clearly they were wrong & were led on by the Satanic power. Smith received no answer.' Foley mentioned that he had been an invalid for the last seven months, and that his wife and daughter had been ill, but he was still most grateful for 'the high & distinguished honour which the Lord has been pleased to confer upon me, viz: The Keeping of the Ark of the Covenant of God, of Love, Joy and peace for a 1000m. years before the General Judgment . . . and I daily thank Him for it and pray to Him every morning that He may keep me a Firm, Faithful, Grateful, Noble & Glorious Champion of these Inestimable Treasures till they are properly demanded from me by the Great & Learned as set forth in Joanna's Divine Writings – and then having the Lord's Sanction, may I deliver them up to such a Call, Freely, Safely, & Cheerfully'.[13]

A trip to a seaside resort near Liverpool that summer enabled Foley to regain his strength in time to meet the next onslaught from those believers who were convinced that it was time for the rank and file followers of Joanna to advance the movement by bringing her writings to Trial. On 20 September, 1826, he received a very long letter from John Ley of 35 Wellington Place, Southwark, explaining that since the previous May a group of people had been meeting at his house once or twice a week to read the printed and manuscript writings of Joanna Southcott. They had sent a copy of *A Dispute between the Woman and the Powers of Darkness* [Book 11], together with a petition, to the Society for the Suppression of Vice, urging them to bring forward the Trial so that Satan's Blasphemy could be judged, and that Society had met three or four times on the subject without coming to a conclusion. Meanwhile, the group meeting at Ley's house had chosen twenty-four people plus one shepherd to guide them and had all taken the following Oath:

> *I . . . . . . swear by Him that liveth I will obey in all Things Thy strict commands given through thy Handmaid, Joanna Southcott, And it is not all The Powers of Earth and Hell shall make me turn To the Right or the Left, but Thy Command the Living Lord of Heaven & Earth I will obey.*[14]

Citing *The Parable of the Flock of Sheep* (Book 22, page 8) as their authority to act, John Ley was now writing to urge Foley to join their group.

Foley seemed at first excited by the prospect that something of great moment was about to happen, but the fact that Ley had not given him the names of any of the twenty-four other than his own made him suspicious. He sent a brief reply asking for names and details of the twenty-four. On 4 October he received another very long letter with the names of the twenty-four: John Hagar, John Ley, Ann Ley, John Pye jnr, Elizabeth Pye, Thos Malby jnr, Elizabeth Malby, Thos Malby snr, Sarah Malby, Wm Stevens, Chas Waites, Wm Baker, Ann

Baker, Chas Sherlock, Ann Were, Benjamin Conguer, Wm Sugden, James Sinnack, Jonathan Parkis, Susanna White, Eleanor Mac Malkin, Richard Bouffs, John Pye snr, & Elizabeth Tozer. The letter also contained the name of the shepherd they had chosen to lead them. It was William Tozer. 'When I saw the names of the 24 and the one Shepherd to lead them and the plan they were pursuing, then I knew how to proceed with them, and I sent the following Letter to John Ley,' Foley wrote.

> Sir, Last week I receiv'd your long letter and I have pondered it over and over in my mind and I must say that I am not at all satisfied you are now acting under a right influence of the Holy Spirit of God and therefore I shall beg leave not to have anything [to do] with your party or with your schemes. In respect to myself and W.Tozer it is clear we can never agree together in our opinions because we are as much at variance in our belief of the Glorious work before us as the East is from the West and therefore I shall decline having anything more to do with him whatever. When he sent out his Circular last year I would not answer it because it was so completely hostile to my beliefs. I have sworn by order of the Spirit of Truth to stand by the 3 Women viz Joanna Southcott, Jane Townley, and Ann Underwood and the Lord giving me strength and power I shall stand by them even to the end, be the consequences what they may because the Spirit of Truth has declared they stand as one in His sight. . . . Mr Tozer for some years deserted two of the Women viz. Jane Townley and Ann Underwood, and he was forbidden to come to Townley's house and therefore it is impossible for us to draw together in the Heavenly work before us. Time will show who is right and who is wrong and to time I shall leave it. I remain, Sir, as I fully hope and trust to be found, a true and faithful soldier and servant, even unto Death, of the Mighty God of Jacob. TPF.[15]

Foley had no doubt that his response was the right one, but his expectations had been roused. 'We cannot possibly tell when the Writings will be demanded but I fully believe that things of high moment are at hand,' he wrote to Charles Bradley on 24 October, 1826. 'We must watch this November because much is said of that Month that things of high importance will take place.'[16]

November, however, when it came, was accompanied by the realisation that the Movement still had many opponents.

> Our enemies no doubt are waxing strong against us, therefore we must wax strong in faith and Prayer to the Lord Jesus to be with us, and in the End to make us Victorious over all our Enemies, for He alone can do it. . . . We cannot tell when the Writings will be demanded by the great and learned, because it will come on us unexpected, but I fully believe that things of high moment are nigh at hand. We must watch the month of November because it is said by the Spirit of Truth,[17] that month some time or other will bring forward events of high consequence to this Nation, and Oh may we be prepared to meet them. Remember the Lords November begins the 13th. He goes to the Old Style. . . . Any news about Tozer and his party and what they are doing, or any news about our Glorious cause will be gratefully received.[18]

Most of the news in succeeding months was concerned with efforts being made by members of the London group, especially Mrs Lavinia Jones, to collect any hitherto unpublished manuscripts connected with Joanna Southcott's Mission. The most important of these manuscripts were, of course, those that had remained sealed and were being kept safe under lock and key in the Great Box – and that to be opened only in the right circumstances. The London group refused to accept this situation and began to agitate for all Joanna Southcott's Communications to be opened and made public. It was not long, however, before they were deprived of the guidance of their 'shepherd', for William Tozer died on 4 May, 1828. In accordance with his wishes, he was buried in St John's Wood cemetery in the same grave as Joanna, and in what may have been a conciliatory gesture before he died he sent all his private Communications to Foley.[19]

A few weeks later Foley, on a visit to London, called on a few of the old, staunch friends but was sad to see how their numbers had dwindled. He was also shocked when he went to pay his respects at Joanna's grave.

> One morning in July I went with my wife to St John's burial ground near the Regent's Park to see the gravestone of our late dear Spiritual mother Joanna Southcott and you may guess how my feelings were deeply hurt when I saw the stone placed a little out of the way and most carelessly put down upon the earth. It then pleased the Almighty to work upon my mind to remedy the above evil by securing the stone from being removed in future. First I pressured a few friends to assist me in this highly praiseworthy business. We first intended to place an

iron railing round the stone to secure it but as the churchyard is divided into two parts, one for the Rich and one for the Poor, and dear Joanna was buried in the poor's ground, when we applied to the trust for an iron railing round the stone and grave they would not hear of it or allow it upon any conditions. After much difficulty we procured permission [to] put up a stone on the wall . . . about 22 feet from the grave. . . . J. Malkin then gave orders to the mason to prepare a handsome black marble tablet; the letters after being engraved were to be handsomely gilt with gold with a star at each corner of the Tablet. The size of the Tablet to be five feet long by two feet 6 inches wide and 3 inches thick, to be let into the wall 3 or 4 inches in order to secure it. J. Malkin will have all the words copied from the first stone and put on the second stone as T.P.F. desired, but another stone being now put up after such a length of time had elapsed we judge it necessary to add something more . . . [so that] the people who read it will see that we have still strong grounds for retaining our faith even after the very great disappointment which befell us in the year 1814 when our dear spiritual mother died and winged her flight to the Realms of Bliss.

We have selected three verses from the scripture of truth . . . to be put under Mr George's words on this new stone. . . .

2 Esdras, ch. 7, v.26: *Behold the time shall come that these tokens which I have told thee shall come to pass and the Bride shall appear and she coming forth shall be seen that is now withdrawn from the Earth.*

Habakuk, ch. 2, v.3: *For the vision is yet for an appointed time but at the end it shall speak and not lie though it tarry wait for it because it will surely come it will not tarry.*

2 Esdras, ch. 7, v.27: *And whosoever is delivered from the aforesaid evils shall see my wonders.*

The expense of putting up this stone may be about £40 and though a few of us would gladly have paid the expense we thought best to let all the true believers (who sincerely wished it) to cast in their mites. . . . J. Malkin, No 30 Princes Street, Soho, London . . . will joyfully give a true account of every penny that will be expended on this very praiseworthy business.

Foley ended this letter, written to John Crossley on 2 October, 1828, with a reference to the fact that both the Reverend Samuel Eyre of Bristol and Charles Taylor of Exeter were supporting the project.[20]

Something that Foley did not mention was the fact that, while they were in London, he had taken his wife back to the church where they were married. Elizabeth Foley had been seriously ill for two months and it is possible that there was something playing on her mind that she wanted to put right. When she had been asked to sign the marriage register at St Pancras church on 6 October, 1801, her name had been entered as Elizabeth Beach and she had made her mark with a cross, as if unable to write her own name. On 4 July, 1828, the curate supplied an extract of the entry to which was added two formal statements:

> I do hereby most solemnly Declare I was in the habit of writing my name before and after the 6th October 1801 – Elizabeth Foley.
>
> The above is Truth, And the Day when we were Married She was so much Agitated that she could not Sign her Name, and, which She has ever since much regretted: and It is by her particular desire that This Statement is made. Thomas Philip Foley.

That little matter settled, they returned home to Oldswinford and Foley settled down to wait with as much patience as he could command, refusing even to accompany the family on pleasure trips if this meant turning his back on the Box.

> I am preserving the Spiritual Ark of God – and the Divine Writings are now as safe and untouched as when deposited under my care. We must wait with patience and prepare ourselves for the time when the Lord assembles His soldiers to meet the storms of the Great Trial. I would gladly have gone with my wife and friends to Plymouth, but, having the Ark of the New Covenant in my house I dare not leave it; I daily pray to be kept a firm and faithful champion of these great treasures till they are properly demanded from me by the Bishops, as set forth in Joanna's Divine Writings,

he wrote to a friend in March 1829.[21]

Others, however, were growing increasingly concerned about his health. For years Foley had been suffering from a recurring chesty cough and gout for which he took a variety of medicines, and his letters and diary show that he had a keen interest in home cures. There are payments for 'chymists drugs', analeptic pills, and an entry for December, 1801, reads: 'For the Itch: 4 oz.of quicksilver boiled in Two Quarts of water down to one. Wash yourself well with it & drink it at your Meals instead of Beer.' Whether it was the toxic effects of drinking solutions of mercury, or simply old age, by 1829 Foley was beginning to show signs of that affliction that eventually caused him to

*Oldswinford Rectory, a gracious house dating from 1700, built in the style of Wren but probably designed by his pupil, Nicholas Hawksmoor. The Rectory was the home of the Rev. T.P. Foley, and Joanna's Box was stored here, 1825-35.*

retreat entirely from the world.'I understand that Mr Foley has been very poorly some time and that he thinks he shall not live long but this I have only from hearsay,' Joseph Jowett reported to his brother-in-law, James Kidd, on 14 March, 1829.[22]

Although Foley's grip on the world was beginning to weaken, he was still the beacon, sending out encouragement to friends and believers in an effort to stop them straying from the true path. He wrote to Mr T. Pierce in July, 1829,

> My Dear Christian Friend,
>
> On July 12th I received a kind letter from my friend Mills, who has seen you at Nottingham, and who has given you a copy of my circular letter; and I rejoice that you approve of it. . . . My friend Mills asks me my opinion concerning Turner's books. . . . we had better for the present moment to leave them alone; because some only have been approved of by the Spirit that visited our dear and beloved mother, Joanna Southcott. . . . In respect to the meetings of the believers in Joanna's visitation, they were decidedly forbidden by the Spirit,

> in August, 1814, until Shiloh came among us. . . .
>
> You ask me my opinion of Charles William Twort's Book, entitled . . . *Vision of Judgment, or the Return of Joanna from her Trance*? I do not believe one tittle of it. . . . Through the mercy, kindness, and goodness of the Almighty Jehovah, I have been most highly honoured and blessed in having 'the Spiritual ARK of God' in my house more than four years, safe and untouched; then, do you think, when the time is arrived for the writings to be demanded by the great and learned, that I should have no notice whatever about them? Or about our dear and beloved Friend's return from the realms of bliss? Especially when that glorious time is arrived, they will be placed under different names, and in a secret place provided for them by the Lord; and DEATH is set forth in Joanna's writings, that will fall upon the believers or unbelievers who will DARE to find out the spot where they are, except those few friends who will be permitted to carry on the work of the Lord, through their communications given from the Almighty to them by Joanna Southcott, Jane Townley, and Ann Underwood. From some communications of Joanna's, I think the above most happy Trio will come again to us at the Lord's appointed time. T.P.F.

This letter was printed the following year in *The Living Oracle; or the Star of Bethlehem: written in answer to a letter of the Rev T.P.Foley, addressed to Mr T.Pierce of Nottingham.*

Meanwhile, Foley was still being troubled by people who wrote claiming to be Joanna's true successors.

> I have received eight extraordinary letters from a 'Mary Joanna' who lives at Staverton, desiring that I should invite her to Old Swinford. She says she is to fulfil Joanna's writings. I have had a letter too from a 'Zebulon' in London, who says Joanna is returned and Shiloh; and in another an 'Issachar' from somewhere in Devon tells me the same thing.

In a letter to Charles Taylor, 4 August, 1829, he mentioned that he had decided to ignore Issachar, Zebulon and John Field, whom he considered to be false prophets but who kept writing to him.

> Satan is working to deceive the True Friends in our Glorious Cause, because it is not likely for Joanna to be in various places, and with various People at the same time – and not to give any Information to those who are preserving 'The Spiritual Ark of GOD' (which is Joanna Southcott's Divine Writings) and they are *now* as safe and untouched, as they were when deposited under my care. . . . We must wait with patience, and prepare

> ourselves to the utmost of our Power to meet the Bridegroom* whenever He comes forth to assemble his soldiers and servants to meet the Storm that will come upon the Sealed People.

That Foley identified the Bridegroom with the Reverend Joseph Pomeroy is shown by an asterisked query in the margin: 'Pray is Pomeroy alive?'[23]

As his mind became increasingly befuddled and anxious the one thing that remained clear was his duty as Custodian of the Box. After his second son, Noah Philip, married his cousin Rosa Foley in August, the couple set off for their new home in Devon accompanied by the groom's mother and sister. Foley said,

> They very ardently wished me to be of the Party, and which I should have most gladly accepted, had I been perfectly free and independent; but, having the high and distinguished favour from the Almighty JEHOVAH of keeping 'ye Spiritual ARK of God' in my House, and which has been there for more than 4 years, I dare not leave it upon any account; because it is said in dear Joanna's Divine Writings that 'the Ark' Will be demanded from me sudden & unexpected by the Great and Learned & therefore I must be ready & prepared on my Watch Tower to meet them whenever It should come to pass.[24]

Furious at being ignored, John Field decided to link up with Charles William Twort and Charles Bradley, and go with them to confront Foley in person, but when they arrived at Oldswinford Rectory on 11 March, 1830, and Foley refused them admission, they went away in a dreadful rage after waving their fists in his wife's face. Bradley, a tobacconist from Birmingham, later sought revenge by writing a letter to the Archbishop of Canterbury, accusing Foley of idolatry and blasphemy, citing as evidence the stone erected in St Johns Wood and Foley's belief that Joanna, Jane Townley and Ann Underwood – 'this happy Trio' – would come again. Moreover, Bradley threatened to put his letter into print if the Archbishop did not call Foley to account. He then sent a copy of the letter to Foley, expecting him to buckle at the thought of receiving such admonition, but the Rector saw how even this might be turned to good account.

> Perhaps that very letter may be the means of bringing forward the Great & Grand Trial of 24 agt. 24 for 7 days. The Lord chusing one 24, agt. the Great of the Earth chusing the other 24, but they must be True Protestants, and not false Sectarians,

he wrote to Charles Taylor.[25]

This noble restraint did nothing to deter his tormentors who now resorted to shouting his name through the streets coupled with dark threats on his life. In August 1830 an old acquaintance, Robert Rockett, sent Foley the following description of a scene he had recently witnessed:

> Your name on a printed paper was cried in the streets at Bristol, this paper was relating to whom the writer called two prophets at Birmingham whose predictions, it stated, had been verified by the removal by death of Townley and Underwood for refusing to give up the writings of Joanna, and now the fatal treasures were in your hands (name and residence at length) who was to follow the above for a like refusal.[26]

Small wonder that Charles Taylor had recently written to deplore 'what a most woful state the Evil Power has brought the human race to'. But there was good news too. In Exeter Mr Pascoe was enthusiastically studying Joanna Southcott and had all her books except five, which he was anxious to acquire.[27] When Foley wrote back on 25 August, 1830, it was to say that he had sent Charles Taylor four of the required books, but could not at the moment lay hands on *The Long Wished for Revolution* because it 'is shut up in one of dear Joanna's Closed Boxes, which cannot be opened at present, but as soon as I possibly can, having the power, I will keep one for you'. He continued,

> Things at present relating to our dear and Beloved Mother's Divine Works are at a stand still; but, I fully believe before the end of this year finishes its revolving round, something of high moment will take place. . . . I have heard not a syllable from the London Friends for several months, and therefore I am quite in the dark of what is going on in that Quarter of the World, as now I have very few friends there at this moment – and of course I hear very little concerning our blessed and Glorious Cause. We all unite here in our kindest and affectionate wishes to Mrs Taylor, to your brother and Sister, and to All your Relations – To the Miss Eveleighs – and to All the dear Friends around you and may health, peace and happiness flow down upon you All from the Giver of all good![28]

Penned in his usual firm, strong hand, his words have a valedictory air and, although he lived on for another five years, this letter was possibly one of the last Foley wrote. Certainly, from this date we see him, if at all, through the eyes of others.

One such observer of Foley was Joseph Jowett, son of William Jowett, a steadfast supporter of Joanna and a judge at her London

'Trials'. In 1830 Joseph was living near Birmingham, within walking distance of Oldswinford, and so he kept his family and friends informed about Foley. 'I have not seen Mr Foley since I came home as I have not been able to walk there and back on one day', he wrote to his brother-in-law, James Kidd of Halifax, on 24 February, 1831.[29] By the following year there was no point in Jowett making such an effort, for he wrote: 'I understand that Mr Foley has almost entirely lost his memory, that they will not suffer him to preach, and that the doctors do not like anyone to see him more than is absolutely necessary.'

It must have been hard for believers to accept that Foley, one of the brightest of the Seven Stars, was no longer in a position to guide them. Of the three Anglican divines whose support had been crucial from the earliest days of Joanna's Mission, the Reverend Stanhope Bruce had died in 1823 and the Reverend Thomas Webster in 1831. As the Old Guard were falling, the younger generation of believers – men like Matthias Crossley, school-teacher son of John Crossley – showed themselves desperate to gain all the wisdom they could from those who remained. 'You live in the neighbourhood of Mr Foley, and when you have anything to communicate respecting our glorious cause, you cannot send it a more direct road into Yorkshire than through Derby', he wrote to his uncle, Joseph Jowett, soon after moving to that city.[30]

The truth was that Foley had by now lapsed into senility and wandered about the Rectory hardly aware of what he was doing. Although his last years were spent in this sad twilight zone, the end, when it came, was sudden. In the early hours of 4 September, 1835, he was seized with sickness which lasted for about five hours and ended with his death at ten minutes to seven. He was buried in Oldswinford Churchyard on the following Thursday. When the news reached Joseph Jowett in Birmingham, he found it so hard to believe that he summoned his daughter, Martha Ann, to accompany him to Oldswinford. It was already after nine o'clock when they set out, so, having missed the coach, they walked there and back, a distance of twenty-five miles – and when they arrived, the church was so full they could not even sit down. They did not get home again till evening, but neither of them went to bed until they had written letters giving accounts of the day to their relatives. Joseph wrote first to his brother, Samuel, in Leeds.

Birmingham. Sept 13, 1835

My Dear Brother
I lose not a moment in giving you the following information. I this morning heard that Mr Foley was dead, not being satisfied as to the truth I determined to go there and Martha Ann went

> with me. . . . We arrived there at the church about 10 minutes before one o'clock, when the clergyman was just finishing the funeral sermon. When Mr Richd. was coming out of the Church he see me and imeadeately returned and came to me and asked me to please to walk into the house. His Father has been childish for years and died so. He died at about 5 hours sickness, which was very sudden. Mr Richd said he should like us to stop and dine with them, but under the present circumstances he begged that I would excuse it, and wished us to take wine or anything else.
> I think the first twelve must all go and When the Lord has gone his round like a clock then he will chose 12, as he had 12 in the Days of his flesh. Mr Foley died on the 4th inst about 10 minits before 7 o'clock. He was interred on Thursday last. Hope you will excuse this hasty scrawl as it is now a late hour. We all unite in very kind respects to yourself, Sister and Family and all Friends. Yours affectionately, J. Jowett.[31]

Joseph Jowett then wrote a similar account to his brother-in-law, James Kidd at Halifax, but giving more detail about Richard Foley who had 'seemed much cut up but treated us in the most gentlemanly manner'.[32]

The death of Foley, preceded as it was by that of William Owen Pughe who died on 4 June that year, left the believers uncertain of the future of the Box. There had been no question about the Reverend Thomas Philip Foley's fitness to be its custodian after Townley's death, but there was no clear successor now. An obvious candidate was the Reverend Samuel Eyre of Bristol, but in October he wrote a circular letter to believers, explaining why he was reluctant to take on such a responsibility.

> With regard to any interference in respect to the Security of the Sealed Writings, however prudent it might appear to human wisdom, from the danger in which they are apparently placed by the late solemn event, I cannot find my mind guaranteed on such a principle to advance one step towards altering their situation, when I recollect the awful fate that befel Uzzar of old, who was struck dead for merely putting out his hand to keep up the Ark of God, which seemed to be falling. This surely was intended as an awful example to all the succeeding ages, not to intermix *our wisdom* with the *Divine proceedings*. I fear I may hear of many attempts of the same nature among the various bodies of believers as noticed by our friend in your letter now received, but I would have them take great care, that their presumption does not cost them dear. I feel this to be a matter of too great importance to move at all in, without

> *special direction* & in the next place, to pray earnestly to God, that in such a *critical affair*, (in His Great Mercy) He may not suffer me or any other believer to be led astray *herein* by the teaching of a false infernal visitation – Such are my present decided sentiments. . . . I think it is singular that the life of Mr Pomeroy is so wondrously preserved . . . perhaps the time may be drawing nigher than we expect when the interview between *him* & *Joanna alone*, alluded to in the books of Wonders, may take place, by her being commissioned to him with a *message from God*, commanding him to lay before the ruling Authorities the whole subject of the visitation . . . & intimate to them the present situation of the *Sealed Writings* to be brought before them.[33]

There were other, more personal, reasons why Eyre would have been reluctant to become next custodian of the Box. There were the feelings of the Foley family to consider. Eyre had recently been sent the following extract from a letter which Miss Esther Foley had written to a friend three weeks after her father's death:

> Ours dear madam has been no common loss, for he was indeed the kindest, the best, the most affectionate of husbands and fathers, & as long as he was able (for 4 years his memory & faculties were lost) his greatest, his chief delight was to do the will of the Almighty & to do to others as he would that others should do to him. His health had been for many years but very indifferent, & the greatest care was necessary. We sincerely hope he was not a great sufferer, no, not even at his death which was to us sudden at last. It was not till the morning of his decease that we had reason to apprehend that there was any danger. His was indeed the death of the righteous, as the sting of death was mercifully taken away, not a groan, struggle, no, not even a sigh. It was just like a Babe sinking into the sweetest slumber, so calm & peaceful was his end.
>
> With respect to the Sealed Writings of Joanna Southcott, I am desired both by Richard & my mother, that they do not intend to part with them. Signed Esther Foley.
>
> PS. Perhaps you will kindly let the believers know that we do not intend to allow the Sealed Writings to go out of our possession. (26/9/1835)[34]

Eyre immediately complied with the Foley family's wishes. 'As things at present appear I think the believers have no reason to be dissatisfied with Mrs Foley's decision,' he wrote to Joseph Jowett, '& I think myself that there is rather a singular coincidence in it, with the principles of my circular letter'.[35] It therefore fell to Jowett and William Bown Harrison, from Manchester, to visit the Foleys on behalf of the friends in order to form some judgement of the situation. They went to Oldswinford on 9 October. Two days later, Jowett wrote to James Kidd:

> I doubt not but that both yourself and the friends around you will be anxious to hear the determination of Mrs Foley and Mr Ricd. respecting the writings now left in their possession, particularly the Sealed ones. Ever since the death of Mr Foley I have had a desire to go over as soon as I thought it prudent so to do, But as we were in daily expectation of Mr Harrison I thought it best to wait till he came that he might accompany me there, and that being two of us it might have a better effect and more satisfactory to the Believers in general, consequently as soon as I had ascertained when Mr H would be here . . . I wrote to Mr Richd to say that we, Mr H and myself, should be there (if agreeable and convenient to them) on the Friday following. He wrote by return of post to say that they should be happy to see us on the day named.
>
> Accordingly we went to the appointment, but unfortunately Mr Richd had been suddenly called out to see after a Living, as they will be oblidged [sic] to leave Swinford Rectory next Saturday week, the living being sold. Mrs Foley expressed great sorrow at the disappointment, but said that Richd desired her to give his respects to us and say that he was much disappointed at not being able to be at home according to appointment and that they were determined that wherever they went, there the Sealed Writings should go also – But as it was very likely they would be oblidged to go into a small house, or into lodgings they would be oblidged to part with all the printed Books which they had for sale, and I assure you there is a good cart load . . . they had agreed that Mrs Waring should hold them and she had agreed to do so. We told Mrs F and Daughters that we thought it would be best for them to be in the hands of some who might make them useful by disposing of such of them as might be wanted, and handing over the money to her. She say'd she should have been glad for me to have had them, and wished that she had known when I was there before, and asked why I did not ask to see her, as she was determined they should not go into the hands of any but those who had been long and steady Believers. We therefore proposed that they should be divided between Mr H

and myself, But she said she could not do that without consulting Richd which she would do. We made the same request respecting the private Comns (which Richd is now examining) and I think is not inclined to part with, But we have promised to return to him any that he may favour us with the sight of, so that we do not despair of yet having some part of some of what they hold. I was very glad to find that Mrs Foley is not, even now, without faith, as she very soon told us that the aspect of affairs are now such as Joanna prophesied of, and that the Sealed writings would yet be demanded, and also that it was in the time of danger they would be demanded.[36]

# 5

# Enter Mr and Mrs Jones, 1835-1842

During his last sad years, with his memory gone and no longer allowed to preach, the Reverend Thomas Philip Foley presented a lonely, confused figure wandering about Oldswinford Rectory, hiding money in odd places. When, after his death, the family were given notice to quit their home and faced the prospect of having no roof over their head, the whereabouts of any valuables became crucial. Richard Foley, as eldest son, took the decision to open Joanna's Box to see if his father had hidden any money inside. In the circumstances it was a natural thing to do. He could not have known that in opening the Box he would be letting out all the mischief associated with Pandora – in the shape of Lavinia Elizabeth Chapman Jones.

Lavinia was the wife of Daniel Jones, a prosperous architect and builder of Bradford-on-Avon in Wiltshire. She had been twenty years old when she married him in 1821[1] and she is probably the 'Mrs Jones' who appeared in the list of twelve people sent to warn Ann Underwood in April 1825 and one of the perpetrators of malevolent acts designed to bring about her death.[2] There is an undated letter, apparently postmarked 22 April, 1827, from Lavinia Jones, 12 Harrow St, Lant St, Southwark, to Mr Jowett, Printer, Mill Hill, Leeds, in which she explained that, despite frequent bouts of ill-health, she was determined to advance the cause by collecting together as many of Joanna's unpublished manuscripts as she could find. She further explained that she had arranged a gathering of believers in London to hear them read and wondered why some of the invitees had failed to reply. Penned in a scratchy hand, looking as if their author is pressed for time, her words convey Lavinia's distinctive tone. She is fervent and determined.

> Dear Friends and fellow labour[er]s
> It is most painful to me even to imagine any mistake, yet how is it that I have had no acknowledgement, either of my parcels or of my last two letters? I will withhold no effort that shall appear consistent to keep the union among us wh. I have struggled so hard to obtain. Now I must request you to write by return and let me know the result of your consultation respecting the plan of our all meeting in London for the express

purpose of hearing the pure word without note or comment. I arrived on Monday and have today come to an arrangement to sojourn for the present with Mr and Mrs Dickinson (late Miss Boyle). . . . But should it be that I should require more accommodation I have the offer of a spacious room in the city. This will be regulated according to circumstances.

I left the Bath friends amidst the tenderest sympathies – for I was indeed very ill, and reached Exeter – being met by our most worthy and excellent friend Mr Pascoe. He submitted to my care first all our dear lamented friend Mr Rocketts collection out of wh. I gathered a few [manuscripts] – they were principally made up of Miss Eveleigh's collection – but not at all so weighty as I should have expected. I then went over Mr Pascoe's books – Mr Tapp's and Mr John was so good as to meet us upon the subject – So that I saw all the friends at Exeter. . . . I was again thrown upon a sickbed so that I could scarcely handle the papers – however I felt impressed to strive to reach London – but it looked like madness – yet after we had held several consultations I was placed on board a steamer and passed two nights on the water – the first we were for 2 hours in decided danger and our ships company were all in the utmost consternation – I was considered as past all hopes for the Captn. And all said if I had the ague I should not survive 3 days on shore: but what is man that we should trust in him. . . . Here I am – perfectly recovered – I can walk! Take my food with companions – and have actually recovered my appearance. Now what remains but that I should show my gratitude by a double effort of activity and that I should turn round and tell you all these astonishing things that we may indeed encourage each other to bear up under the least appearances of hope.

Let us strive for the unity of the spirit and above all things keep out contentions, whisperings, 'imaginations' from among us – This I say because I find from Mrs Dickinson's visit to Mr Harrison that he questions her as to the Believers I associate among in London. Could he gain the knowledge of them all – what is that to do with my public walk among you all? He must judge me from my words and what he has seen if he wants to scrutinize – but as to 'associating' you know from our frequent meetings my mind – I go in search of truth – and I find it only in the written word – I have not yet entered one House where I can fully 'associate' neither do I expect it – until the kindling coal from off the altar kindles us like fire among us all. Therefore mine is an universal love to all the signed people – and were I to forsake one house to meet the fastidiousness of one party – or another house to meet another, my work would never have been done – for who am I to judge among you? Or to raise a standard in any house. Mr Harrison's expression was that 'All the friends would support me if I had no connexions with certain people.' How can this be? God is the supporter of us all and now I send out my invitation it is *to all* – to hear what he has spoken I intend writing to Manchester directly I have heard from you and shall go over this same subject again – as you know how careful I am respecting preferences.

Mr Eyre and Mr Baker refused me their Comns. Mr Eyre writes to me that I might do a great harm by 'spurious Comns.' Now I send him the challenge to come and correct my MSS [manuscripts] before I circulate them among the believers, and I tell him I intend throwing them before the whole body of believers if they will assemble. Farewell. Offer up a prayer of thanksgiving to the throne of goodness for thus strengthening me. Silver and gold I have none but my table will be spread with an abundance dainty enough for even a marriage feast, the fruits of the spirit.

Kind love to all. Mrs D. sends hers – farewell – Lavinia.[3]

Lavinia Jones continued to collect as many Southcottian manuscripts as she could lay hands on in the next few years, despite continued problems with her health. On 14 March, 1829, Joseph Jowett of Birmingham reports that she had been very poorly, and two years later, writing to James Kidd, he mentions that 'Mrs Jones has been very ill indeed and no hopes of her life, but is now got about again.'[4] Her brush with death did nothing to diminish her zeal and as soon as she was back on her feet Lavinia renewed her efforts to unite the believers.

On 19 March, 1832, an advertisement appeared in the *Morning Advertiser*:

JOANNA SOUTHCOTT

*The persons who assisted at the Inquiry instituted in the year 1804 at the Neckinger, Bermondsey, into certain particulars respecting the above mentioned Joanna Southcott (commonly called the Prophetess of Exeter) and who acted as Judges or Jurymen at that Inquiry are requested to send their address post paid directed to A.B. to be left at the Bar of the Albany Arms Tavern, Albany Road, Old Kent Road.*

As John Haggar happened to be in town that morning he decided to call on Thomas Stephens, who had been a Juryman at both the High House and Neckinger Trials, and he told him about the advertisement. As a result, Stephens went along to meet 'A.B.' who explained that he was merely an agent in the affair and could not divulge the names of his employers, but that their motives were good. Stephens was sufficiently impressed to write to William Jowett, the Reverend Thomas Philip Foley, the Reverend Samuel Eyre, and Thomas Senior. The fact that someone outside the movement was taking Joanna Southcott's message seriously enough to consult those who had been officially appointed by her was encouraging, especially to the London group who had been trying to unite the believers.

John Haggar wrote from George Street, Richmond, to Joseph Jowett,

> We in London think Pomeroy is at the bottom of this, as things wear a most awful appearance & we do most earnestly expect & believe this Spring will bring a revival of the grand work of the Lord. I shall thank you to make known the purport of this among the friends around you & shall be happy to hear from you what your thoughts are & that of the friends on the present aspect of affairs. The cholera or with me the forerunner of the Plag[u]e, is making great havoc in London. I have just recd a letter from a friend of the name of Wm Baker, who I think you know, stating that his daughter, aged about 21 & her infant fell a sacrifice to this dreadful malady last week. This is the first instance I have yet heard of a Believer, or any of their children being attacked, but as it is so, the will of the Lord be done.
>
> I must conclude, trusting the time is now arrived when the Lord will begin to display his mighty-power to the confusion of his enemies & to the comfort & justifycations of His friends & may He protect us in the coming storms & shelter us under His almighty wings.[5]

Wherever they looked there were catastrophic signs of economic distress and political unrest. The letters of Joseph Jowett in Hockley were full of woe. He wrote to James Kidd.

> The trade here is in a most dreadful state, a great many have nothing at all to do, and those who have a little receive so little for it that they can scarce exist, and many declare that they should be glad to see a Revolution tho' they should be the first to die by the sword. We have heard that John Crossley has gone over to old Jacky [John Wroe], but I suppose it is another of their lies.[6]

In Manchester their friend, William Bown Harrison, was having trouble after his wife was injured in a coach accident. She received £50 from the coach company but he was now searching for a 'stout' servant girl to do the housework. He explained to Samuel Jowett,

> I would rather have a believer than an unbeliever, provided she is eligible in other respects. . . . With regard to wages we shall not quarrel provided she is not extravagant in her ideas. . . . we think of removing the next week, & as my wife continues very unwell we are anxious to have some person about us. With regard to my faith I am happy to say that I do not recollect that I ever felt anything like doubt on the subject of the visitation, since the death of Joanna in 1814, and then it did not last for many hours. The subject was one of daily conversation when I lived with my grandfather 28 years ago, it is bred in me, it has grown with my growth, & strengthened with my strength, and is likely to form a part of my nature so long as I live.[7]

Harrison was an accountant and a firm believer. Another of his heart-felt testaments of faith was expressed in *A Letter Addressed to a Friend, explanatory of the object and manner of Christ's Second Coming, and Proving that Isaiah 7 v.14, and Micah 5 v.3 were not fulfilled by the Birth of Jesus Christ*, printed by Samuel Jowett, Top of Mill-Hill, Leeds, on 12 January, 1834 [New Year, Old Style].

As a close friend of the Jowetts, he was constantly passing between various members of their family carrying messages and parcels. 'I take this opportunity of sending a few things for sister by Mr Harrison he arrived here this morning,' Martha Ann wrote to her uncle, James Kidd, in October, 1835, before explaining that her father, Joseph Jowett, and Mr Harrison had just gone to Oldswinford to see the Foley family. She ended with a plea for her uncle to acknowledge her letter and send all the news as soon as possible 'as I think Sister's promises are like pie crusts made to be broke'.[8]

While the old guard in the persons of Joseph and Samuel Jowett, W.B. Harrison, James Kidd, and Samuel Eyre marshalled themselves behind the Foleys to ensure that the Box of Sealed Prophecies would not be opened until the exact conditions were met, others saw the death of the Reverend T.P. Foley as the moment when the movement must surge ahead. They believed that this would happen if all the Sealed Writings were now to be published to the world. Daniel Jones set out their reasons in a letter to the Reverend Joseph Pomeroy, 21 December, 1835.

Revd Sir,
From the confused state of all churches at the present time we are apprehensive that the principal cause is the total suppression of the divine truths contained in the writings of Joanna Southcott which from the year 1796 to 1800 were according to evidence committed to your care as an appointed minister of our established Church. . . . We extract from the Book of Wonders page 27:
*Copy of the Deed of Trust committed to the care of the Revd Mr Pomeroy to prove the truth of Joanna Southcotts mission from the Seven Seals:*

| | | |
|---|---|---|
| 1st Seal | The death of Bishop Buller of Exeter in | 1796 |
| 2nd Seal | The events which took place in Italy | 1797 |
| 3rd Seal | England seeking for peace but in vain | 1797 |
| 4th Seal | The Harvest of the year | 1797 |
| 5th Seal | The large sums of money demanded | 1797 |
| 6th Seal | The Harvest of the year | 1799 |
| 7th Seal | The Harvest of the year | 1800 |

Our object in addressing you is to ask if these things were made known to you at the time and times above named for if so the substance might certainly follow on the shadow and it will be fatal for yourself and the nations if these secrets are any longer concealed. The writings of Joanna affirm that these events were fulfilled and the history of the Nations appears to us to corroborate her testimony. . . . Therefore Revd Sir to conceal such events connected as they are with the present and future well being of millions of professed and professing Christians is a crime which the Almighty will repay with heavy afflictions on all such as are wilfully guilty.

We find in many parts of Joanna's writings the very events that are daily occurring in different Nations testified by the public newspapers, particularly those concerning Spain, the dreadful distresses that are upon our own Nation, also the distress and disgrace upon the Clergy. . . . Now we call upon you before we proceed further to come forward and put in the hands of those who are appointed those prophetic writings placed in your hands. Lay them before the Arch Bishops & Bishops of this land, now that the evils are come upon them. . . .We the undernamed Committee have thought fit to make this short appeal to you considering the time is arrived that the word of the Lord must be obeyed to which appeal we most respectfully entreat a reply from you within seven days of the post date hereof – Daniel Jones.[9]

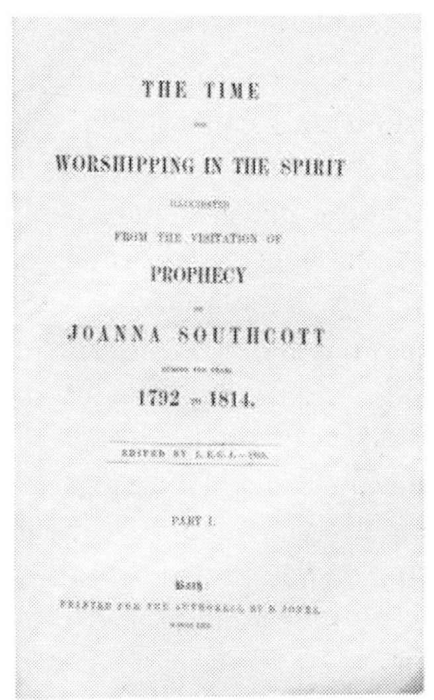

THE TIME

WORSHIPPING IN THE SPIRIT

PROPHECY

JOANNA SOUTHCOTT

1792 – 1814.

PART I.

*Title page of an unfinished book published in 1853 by Lavinia Elizabeth Chapman Jones and printed by her husband's private press at Bath. The couple produced many compilations of Joanna Southcott's published and unpublished writings.*

Meanwhile, the Box of Sealed Prophecies was again in transit after the Foley family had been served notice to quit their gracious home at Oldswinford where they had lived for thirty years or more. Foley's personal papers were also inaccessible because of the move. Joseph Jowett wrote to James Kidd on 31 December, 1835,

> When I last wrote to you I was in hopes that before this time I should have recd the Private Comns. belonging to the late T.P. Foley, but to the present have been disappointed . . . as the Family were oblidged to leave the Rectory and be in lodgings where they could, among their friends, till Mr Richd could meet with a living which I believe he now has done, and is to go to it as soon as the house is ready, which was to be about this time. The living is at Kingswinford about ten or eleven miles from here. If I do not hear from him in about 2 or 3 weeks I intend to go over to see him. I understand there is a Comn. where a circle is drawn in which are three stars which are said to represent Bruce, Foley, and Webster, that there is a single star outside the circle which represents Eyre, and that he sees the work clearer than all the others. I give you these particulars that you may make all the enquiry you can for the Comn, as I have reason to believe it has been taken, by what I call unfare means, from Mr Foleys. The way it was taken was as follows: A lady from London visited Mr Foley some 2 or 3 years ago, professing herself a strong Believer, therefore had free access to the Private Comns which he possessed, and that she also visited during her stay at Oldswinford two ladys of the names of Brown and Boucher, that this Lady took a Book or Books to those ladys and left them there and that they have not yet been returned, and that this Comn is in one of these Books but I have not been able to lay hold of it yet.[10]

Although the 'lady from London' was not named, it was possibly

Mrs Lavinia Jones, up to the kind of tricks for which she was soon to become infamous. For the moment, though, the believers were intent on obtaining all of the unpublished Communications that T.P. Foley had kept. His eldest son and heir, the Reverend Richard Foley, expressed himself happy to oblige as soon as he could make suitable arrangements for this particular Box of Writings (not the Great Box) to be delivered to Joseph Jowett. 'I must apologize for not having sent you the Box of Writings before but I have been waiting till a neighbour of mine, who occasionally attends Birmingham Market, goes – he has promised to let me know, & as soon as he gives me information I will write to you stating the Inn where he puts up,' he wrote from Bromley Lodge, Dudley, on 26 February, 1836.[11] Six weeks later Richard Foley wrote again: 'Dear Sir, My brother will be coming to Birmingham either on Saturday or Monday, when he will bring the Box, which he will leave for you at the Albion Coach Office. I am sorry no opportunity has occurred before.'[12]

While the Jowetts studied and distributed among their friends the Communications they received from Foley, Lavinia Jones was still intent on extending her own collection. In November that year Thomas Stephens presented her with an original manuscript,[13] and on 22 October, 1837, Samuel Jowett gave her a copy of a letter from Ann Underwood to Samuel Hirst, dated 15 April, 1815.[14]

By this time she had already sent Richard Foley a letter asking him directly for the Sealed Writings. He refused her request. She suggested visiting him in person. He replied that he would rather she did not come. She went anyway, only for him to repeat his refusal. But if he thought that would be enough to deter her, he was mistaken. What he had seen was but the opening of her campaign, and her armoury contained some formidable weapons.

> It seems she is connected with Mrs Essam and Mrs Haggar. . . . I have been informed that Mrs Essam has been collecting a great number of private communications from different parts of the Kingdom and intends to keep Open House in London over Whitsun for all who want to examine them,

the Reverend Samuel Eyre told Mr Symes of Bath in September, 1838.

With regard to Mrs Jones, Eyre described how he had invited her to Bristol from Bath, but she had written to say that she did not think it right to come until she had completed her plan to read aloud all the Communications to public meetings in London, starting on Whit Tuesday. The readings would take seven days, and she hoped that he would come to them. Eyre curtly refused, protesting that she did not have the authority to hold such meetings.[15]

Confronted by this new impulse in the movement, the old guard began to close ranks. Samuel Jowett, regretting his generosity in giving Lavinia some manuscripts when she called on him the year before, inveighed against 'the so-called believers' who were reprinting Joanna's writings, and he quoted passages to prove that this had been strictly forbidden.

> I think I can tell you who is the Instigator of the whole – it is Mrs Jones, who once began to print the Writings before, but finding, if she persevered with it, she would not be able to accomplish the object she had in view of getting all the MSS Comns. so she dissisted from it, till she had accomplished her purpose. The first day she spent in Leeds, I was not at home, but she told more of her plans that day than she did all the time afterwards, & one part of her plan was to print & she requested my son to do it for her.[16]

The trouble was, whether people agreed with her or not, Lavinia Jones was bringing energy into a cause which for some was beginning to pall. 'Disappointment after disappointment during a period of 24 years, more than half of my life, has cooled me down,' W.B. Harrison confessed to Samuel Jowett, 'so that though I am as anxious as ever to hear the opinions of our friends, I have no confidence either in my own or those of other people'.[17]

Richard Foley, meanwhile, was faced by another onslaught from Lavinia Jones. At Christmas, 1839, he received two letters from Collings Robinson M.D., of Clarence Place, Exeter, claiming the Box of Sealed Writings on behalf of Mrs William Southcott, widow of Joanna's brother. He had been given to understand, Robinson said, that the Box contained not only manuscripts but silver plate. His informant, it seems, was Mrs Jones. Richard Foley replied that he had no plate in his possession belonging to anyone but himself, and would never give up the Sealed Writings until they were demanded by the 'great and learned', which he understood to be Joanna's command.[18]

This firm response stiffened Lavinia's resolve, and a desperate disease called forth a desperate remedy. At about six o'clock one evening in the following February, when it was after dark, an old woman in a large cloak, accompanied by a young man, called on Kingswinford Rectory, where the Foleys now lived. They asked Mr Foley's manservant if they could speak to Sarah, one of the other servants. Having explained that she was upstairs, he shouted for her and was about to turn away when he heard a rustling noise among the coats hanging in the servants' hall. At this moment Sarah appeared, carrying a lamp, and he saw what he took to be a man, carrying under his arm a wooden box about eighteen inches square. 'What have you got there?' he challenged. 'That does not belong to you. You must leave that behind you.'

Foley, who was at dinner, overheard the noise and came out. As soon as he saw the intruder, he exclaimed, 'Why, it's Lavinia Jones!'

In the altercation that ensued Foley pointed out to Lavinia the enormity of her offence and the consequences if he decided to prosecute. His words must have had some effect, because next morning he received a note asking him to call upon her at her lodgings, so that she could give him an explanation of her conduct the previous evening. He promptly replied that he would do no such thing, nor would he have anything whatever to do with her.[19]

Unabashed, Lavinia immediately set about the next stage of her project. She entered into an arrangement with Mr Walters, a bookseller of Dudley, whose shop she used as a postal address, and in March, 1840, he printed the following circular:

> Mrs Lavinia E.C. Jones, announces with sincere pleasure to her friends and all lovers of Scriptures of Divine Inspiration, that her Work of the Commentary of the books of the Old and New Testaments . . . is in a forward state towards publication. Being a Work of some considerable extent – probably of about 42 Numbers, at 6d each, it will not be begun until the proposed number of Subscribers are obtained. . . . An exact estimate of the extent of the Numbers cannot be given, since a part of the manuscript *belonging to the Work* are withholden – the circumstances of which will be *fully* explained in the Introduction. Should these manuscripts be conceded they will add a great additional value and extent to the work. . . .
>
> Mrs Jones has toiled under most untoward circumstances in obtaining the *extensive* collection of curious and interesting MS documents she holds, they have been collected from many obscure places in various parts of England; and, with the exception of those before mentioned, she is informed by persons who have been long acquainted with the Work, that she may rest satisfied in believing she has accomplished the arduous undertaking of rescuing nearly the whole. . . .
>
> Mrs Jones does therefore expect the Work will interest almost every class of CANDID – THINKING minds; and her object being anything but gain of money, she intends yet to continue with every perseverance the pursuit of tracing for these singular documents for further perfecting the Work, should any opportunity offer. Address, post paid, Mrs Lavinia Jones, Mr Walters, Bookseller, Dudley, Worcestershire.[20]

When Lavinia said, 'with every perseverance', she meant it. On the morning of Monday, 25 May, 1840, four gentlemen (one of whom may have been Lavinia, again in male attire) appeared on the Reverend Richard Foley's doorstep. Their spokesperson was Samuel Cook, a notorious Radical mercer of Dudley, and they had come armed with several petitions demanding that Foley hand over the Sealed Writings to them. This he refused, on three grounds, viz: that he would render himself liable to prosecution; that they were not the proper persons; that he had received letters from other believers requesting him not to do so. Apparently satisfied with this reply, they left. However, in the course of conversation, Foley had inadvertently let slip that he had opened the Box containing the Sealed Writings soon after his father died – and it was on this fact that Lavinia Jones pounced. Immediately she sat down to express her sense of shock (perhaps tinged with triumph) at the revelation.

She wrote to James Kidd,

> My work has come to a crisis. . . . A deputation of four gentlemen have waited upon Mr Foley this morning with several petitions signed by parties all round about here. The event is that 'The wise and learned' may call upon the honourable and trustworthy and conscientious clergymen of England's disgraceful church – but they will 'call' in vain. The box has been opened and the contents – we can tell nothing about more than there are some sealed papers just left in it – Now what can we say to this dark deed of secret treachery – Will the people be any longer priest-ridden and hold in reverence such ungentlemanly conduct as this and suffer themselves to be robbed without any reckoning? If *they* do, *I* will not. I have sacrificed my property – my health and all the talent I possessed, and could obtain, to seek to the bottom of every truth – and I will now wait your sentiments whether we can act in any way harmoniously about it. I tell you candidly I do not intend to stop – but had rather that a friendly feeling should subsist in the church – and that we should act together – But – I have my measures waiting, and I hope you will call a meeting and not be long in writing to me – I am willing to bear the heat of the day and care nothing about 'what people think'. What I am aiming at in this matter is Universal Good – and intend to pursue this or any other cause which I consider may benefit society at large. Yours in Christian respect and hope, Lavinia Jones.[21]

When word spread that the Reverend Richard Foley had opened the Box, his fitness to be Custodian of the Sealed Writings was brought into question, especially as he was not a believer. Samuel Jowett of Leeds was particularly exercised by the problem despite having little time for Mrs Jones, whose letters he ignored after she declared that she would leave no stone unturned to accomplish her ends. On 28 May he asked W.B. Harrison to visit Foley and find out the truth of what had happened.[22] Before he could do so, Harrison received a letter from Foley containing a full explanation.

> The true account is simply this. At my father's death, on looking through his papers, a considerable sum of money was missing and, as he had for the last years of his life been in the habit of hiding money, it was thought proper to search every likely & possible place. Amongst others I certainly did unlock the Box in which the Sealed Writings are, but I positively declare that no seal was broke and that all the Papers were safely restored.
>
> My mother and one of my brothers were present at the time, that any suspicion of fraud might be obviated. Since then to the best of my knowledge and belief they have been seen by no person; certainly not with my consent. The papers are kept in a Box, which itself is enclosed in another Box; both have keys of a large size. Had the inner Box been sealed, my object in searching would have been satisfied, I am not certain whether I ever mentioned my having opened the Box to you, but it is what I never made a secret of, as under the circumstances I conceive I was quite justified.
>
> Mr Mellor of Birmingham has enclosed a letter, from Mr Eyre, of Bristol, and I have written to him as above, adding that I shall be happy to give any two or three or more of the believers ocular demonstration that the Sealed Writings themselves are in the same state of security, as when committed to my Father's care. I have also said that if there is any dissatisfaction among the believers I shall be happy to hand them over to the care of Mr Eyre, who from his station in Society and long standing among the Believers appears the best qualified for the Trust. Signed R.Foley.[23]

The Believers were satisfied with Richard Foley's explanation, but they were left with a problem. It was not so much their confidence in Foley, as Foley's confidence in himself as Custodian, that had been shaken. He was a godson of Joanna, and as a small child had played a significant part in the Trials of her writings, but he had not received the trust from Joanna Southcott, Jane Townley, Ann Underwood, or any of their Executors, and so he was vulnerable to any impertinent intruder who pretended to be voicing general dissatisfaction among the believers. This situation had to be remedied somehow. Harrison suggested to Joseph Jowett,

> I think a circular letter explaining the conduct of Mrs Jones and the duty of believers would do good if printed with the names of some of the old and tried friends. One good would result from it to ourselves – we should be able to refer to it hereafter to show that we had entered our protest against the proceedings of this vile woman and done all in our power to prevent her from leading the weal astray. If you approve of this let me have a sketch of what you think ought to be written. I have written to J. Crossley and your brother Samuel for their views. After we have all written we may leave James Kidd to point out what part or parts of each letter were the best for the object intended.[24]

But the 'vile woman' had not finished with her tricks. On 31 May her husband, Daniel Jones, wrote a disarming letter to Richard Foley, saying that he understood that Mr Foley had been applied to 'by a lady' to give up the Sealed Writings, and he for one hoped he would not do so. Nonetheless, he expressed a wish that Foley would let the writings be printed.

After studying the letter, Foley concluded that it had been written by Mrs Jones in a disguised hand. He also noticed that, although it carried a penny stamp, there was no post mark, so it had either been put into the Office at Kingswinford or been delivered by hand.

While various versions of their Address to Foley were being circulated among the 'old and tried friends', W. B. Harrison and Joseph Jowett dined with the Foleys and explained what was being planned. Richard Foley, however, made it clear that he did not wish to be involved in any public demonstration or to receive any delegation.

> I am neither ambitious, nor desirous of being brought into public notice, preferring to pass thro' life in an humble & quiet manner. I feel equally obliged to the gentlemen who have signified their intention of calling upon me, but beg leave respectfully to decline the honor. Any written communication on the subject shall be attended to & an answer sent by return of post.[25]

He could not have made his attitude more clear: He was not a believer, but as a man of the cloth and a conscientious son, he would carry out his duty. After some discussion the believers agreed that this was what was most required in a Custodian of the Box – someone whose integrity was beyond question. 'I feel quite satisfied that the writings are perfectly safe where they are, & that the Devil with all the assistance of Mrs Jones & the Chartists will not be able to get hold of them,' James Kidd wrote to Joseph Jowett.[26] With renewed vigour the friends then turned to settling the details of the Address. There are several drafts in existence, evidence of the immense care they took.

> To the Revd Richard Foley
> Revd Sir
> We, the undersigned being believers in the Divine Mission of the late Joanna Southcott, beg to express in the strongest terms, our unqualified approbation & approval of your conduct with regard to the Sealed Writings of the said Mrs Southcott, which were intrusted to the care of your late honored & worthy Father, &, which Trust has descended to you as his Heir –
>
> We are fully aware of the great annoyance to which you have been subjected by Mrs Lavinia E.C. Jones & others under her direction, who have applied to you to give up the said Sealed Writings to her or them, & we are highly gratified by the firm but dignified & gentlemanly manner in which you met those applications.
>
> We consider the circumstances under which you were placed at the time you opened the Box of Sealed Writings were of that nature that fully justified your doing so, and we beg to say in the most unequivocal terms that we are perfectly satisfied with your conduct on that occasion.
>
> We beg further to state that it is the seals on the parcels that we wish to be held sacred and untouched, having no particular feeling about the Box itself being unlocked or opened, and we feel firmly convinced that no circumstances will induce you to violate the trust reposed in you as a gentleman, a christian, and a Minister of the Gospel of Christ, we therefore beg to express our wish and desire that the Sealed Writings should continue in your hands feeling assured that they could not be removed to a place of greater safety. . . .[27]

Samuel Jowett's suggestions included:

> We seek not to inquire what may be your own particular views with regard to those writings, having a firm conviction that no private views or feelings of your own would ever induce you to violate the Trust reposed in you as a gentleman, a Christian,

> & a Minister of the Gospel of Christ; we therefore beg to express our wish & desire that the Sealed Writings should continue in your hands, feeling assured that they could not be removed to a place of greater safety.[28]

Another variation added:

> Revd Sir – We are not afraid for the safety of the Box of Writings under your care – He who has given them will protect them, and it is in him alone that we confide for that protection, but he works by human agency and the peculiarity of your circumstances as regards them, appears to us to render it necessary to address you in this manner, being all the support we can at present give.
>
> Had you yourself received this trust from Mrs Southcott, Mrs Townley, Mrs Underwood, or any of their Executors you would have been prepared with your authority when assailed by any impertinent intruder; but this not being the case, exposes you to the tampering of the ignorant, or designing, and you are left to question within yourself whether these impertinent annoyances do not proceed from general dissatisfaction among the believers; to obviate this, we present you with our assurances of the unqualified approval of your conduct, and our firm belief that an unerring providence has directed the sacred treasure to the place where it now rests.[29]

As much care was taken over the form of the Address as the content. Samuel Jowett described to a friend how they set about compiling it.

> We agreed for the Address to be wrote on a large sheet of paper & then all the names to be wrote on the same sheet by one person, which fell to the lot of Mr Harrison. The names were given under the separate county's they came from, & the towns were aranged in alphabetical order under each county. Yorkshire first, then Lancashire, Cheshire & Warwickshire, etc. The number of names signed to the Address were 435, besides what was sent from London.[30]

The reward for all their trouble was a brief but gracious response from Richard Foley.

> Kingswinford House,
>
> 21st July, 1840
> Gentlemen,
>
> Absence from home has prevented me from writing sooner to thank you for the kind manner in which you have expressed

your satisfaction at my conduct on a late occasion.

I consider the papers in question as a sacred deposit from my late father, and as such shall, with the Divine blessing, endeavour in the disposal of them *to act as he would have done*.

I beg again to thank you all and those who signed the Address for this mark of confidence, and shall conclude with wishing, in nearly your own words, that the Lord may so bless both you and me that we may in all our words and works endeavour to increase His Glory and promote our own eternal salvation.

I have the honour to be, Gentlemen, Your obliged humble servant, Richard Foley.[31]

Foley's reply was promptly acknowledged by Samuel Jowett:

Reverend Sir,
In the name of my Friends & Brothers that signed the Address, I desire to return you our most cordial thanks for the kind acknowledgement I have received; & we beg to assure you that on *any* or *every* future occasion when you may require information, or assistance respecting our Sacred & Godlike Cause, that it will most readily & cheerfully be given, according to the best of our information & abilities, with thanks for what you have hitherto done for us.[32]

The crisis was over, at least for the time being. What it had revealed, however, was the need for some intermediary to be appointed. Should any future emergency arise – in the shape of Lavinia Jones or an approach from the Bishops – the Reverend Richard Foley must know whom to contact for assistance or advice. In 1840 the obvious candidate was William Bown Harrison and it was he who took it upon himself to maintain regular contact with Foley on behalf of the 'old and tried' believers. Not that Harrison did not have troubles of his own in the next few years.

In November, 1840, his letters to Samuel Jowett were full of complaints about the shortage of money and other signs of imminent financial collapse in Manchester. By Christmas his financial woes were compounded by horrendous boils on his leg and thigh that prevented his visiting Leeds and joining the Jowetts in their festivities. He bemoaned:

I know of no place that I would have so soon visited, I know of no company I would so soon have joined. If any man on earth has reason to hate the devil I have . . . in 15 years I have

> had no peace or comfort. A few months ago I was . . . robbed and plundered – since then my Assurance Agency has been taken from me . . . and I am now left pennyless & without the means of support. What I shall do I do not know.[33]

As far as Lavinia Jones and the London Friends were concerned, all these signs of economic distress merely highlighted their belief that the Great Cause was being held up for want of the opening of the Sealed Writings and they redoubled their efforts to secure unity in the movement. In response to a circular that he received from them in 1841, Samuel Jowett wrote:

> I wish to ask two or 3 plain questions. . . . Ist. Is not one object you have in view to get possession of the Sealed Writings? 2nd. Is not another object you have in view to cause the great & learned to inquire into the truth of J.S.'s writings by your preaching etc.? Do you believe that the manifestation of the Cause can take place & the writings be fulfilled without the Return of Joanna Southcott? It is very necessary that we should have an understanding on these points before we can unite with you. . . .
>
> Again, we are informed that Mrs Essam has been to Mr Foley applying for the Sealed Writings. We cannot express too strongly our disapprobation of such conduct. Were you privy to it, or had you anything to do with her on this occasion? It appears that your request for an union of the friends in prayer, on a certain day, is only the *first* of a *number* of things which you have in view to accomplish. If by *these means* you intend to compel the Lord to make manifest his Cause, you will find that you are mistaken. . . .Was it to be done by man, the Lord would be *robbed* of his honor, & it would be given to man. But this cannot be!!![34]

From this it may be gathered that the 'old guard' did not welcome approaches from the London group. On the other hand, they were prompted to re-examine their own reluctance to take any initiative to bring about the opening of the Sealed Writings. According to Matthias Crossley the Spirit had announced through Joanna that there should be no more meetings until the birth of the Child, and the Child had not been born because in 1814 the bishops had refused to grant a marriage and so there was no father.[35] The Jowetts agreed that there should be no public meetings and in October, 1841, Samuel Jowett, Leeds, printed *A Copy of a Letter Addressed to the London Friends*, refuting their justifications for holding a public meeting.

> You will no more have the power of the Lord made manifest, *as at the day of Pentecost*, than Mrs Jones had at her meeting in 1838 (which she anticipated would take place *then;*) because it would be contrary to His word; and the object which she held forth to draw the friends together, (viz. *Union*) was the *same as yours now is*; but as hers vanished like the baseless fabric of a vision, not leaving a wreck behind, *so will every effort that is made by the believers* to raise the Cause; because the work *is* the *Lord's, and* HE must execute it. . . . it appears from your circular that you anticipate an *union* being made of the different views entertained by the believers in our mother's visitation . . . is it likely that by a number of discordant believers assembling together from different parts of the country, that they will become united, form one harmonious body, and ALL be brought into one way of thinking in a few days?[36]

To judge by their correspondence it would be difficult to imagine any being brought into one way of thinking. As Joseph Jowett pointed out,

> No doubt but every section of believers consider that they have the best and most correct views of the work, with this consideration I have, ever since Joanna's death when I have found others take different views to my own, begun to re-examine mine . . . as we could not be all right. I have hitherto always come to the same conclusion that mine are better than those that have opposed me [ie to stand still and not stir until the Lord directs]. . . . Mr Lowe has sent me one of the London pamphlets, but I shall take no notice of it. . . . The state of the Nation and the State of the Believers or rather pretended believers give me great hopes that we shall not be left much longer without our helpmeet, and I heartily and sincerely pray God hasten the time of her return, for we know by woeful experience we are not good alone.[37]

The Reverend Samuel Eyre, while against the London group's efforts to accelerate the Trial, agreed with their view that there had been a spiritual birth in 1814. For this reason he refused to distribute a circular expressing other views sent to him by Joseph Jowett, much to that gentleman's annoyance. When W.B. Harrison published a printed version of a long letter written to the Reverend Joseph Wolff in response to his request for information about Joanna Southcott, the indignation of Joseph Jowett knew no bounds. He had been snubbed by Eyre for publishing his views and now here was his friend, Harrison, printing a pamphlet for sale to unbelievers when it was agreed that nothing should be done to convert them. 'Know that the Lord has told us that the Communications which are in print are for the unbelieving in common with the believers, but those that are not printed are for Believers only,' he stormed. 'I know not of any thing that has given me such a shaking since that of the death of Joanna.'[38] Harrison was mortified, and the situation was made worse by the fact that the pamphlet had been printed by Joseph's brother, Samuel Jowett, who was thus drawn into the row.

Writing to Samuel Jowett on 23 March, 1842, Harrison wondered how neither of them had realised that printing extracts from Joanna's writings was to be disobedient. He had now withdrawn all of his pamphlets, he said, even though it meant losing as much as twenty pounds, and in future he would avoid doing wrong by doing nothing at all. In fact, with the exception of Samuel Jowett, he was going to drop contact with believers. 'Your brother no doubt means well, but he does not act judiciously,' he concluded. It was left to Harrison's wife, Jemima, to explain that his book had never been intended for any unbelievers beyond Dr Wolff and to convey how hurt her husband had been by the incident.[39] Joseph Jowett, in mellower mood, wrote to suggest that perhaps Harrison's book could be altered so that it was addressed to believers in and around Manchester, and thus avoid setting a precedent to those who were all too eager to publish to the world.[40]

For the rest of 1842 a pamphlet war was waged between the London believers, led by Hagger, Copas, Pye and Malby, who wanted to meet in assemblies and campaign for the Box to be opened, and the 'old and tried' believers, led by the Jowetts, who insisted they must wait on the word of the Lord before doing anything. Samuel Jowett was also involved in a correspondance with Samuel Sibley of the House of Faith, Hoxton, in which each wrote long letters minutely refuting doctrinal points made by the other.[41] And, while all these struggles for influence were going on, the Box had quietly resumed its travels. In 1842 the Reverend Richard Foley had been appointed Rector of North Cadbury in Somerset, a living in the gift of his old college, Emmanuel. Here he set up home with his mother and sister, the latter causing some commotion when, soon after arrival, she reported that a letter containing a five pound note had gone missing. Official enquiries resulted in the local postmaster being found guilty of theft and transported for life.[42]

# 6

# Embattled Custodian, 1842-1861

When the Box of Sealed Prophecies arrived in Somerset it entered the orbit of another group of loyal believers, some of whom had known and loved Joanna in her life time. Edmund Baker, for instance, had led a group of believers in Dowlish Wake, near Ilminster. The Somerset Southcottians had their own traditions. Their special festival was 14 October, the date on which Joanna had experienced her Visitation in 1813, and on this day in 1842 Edmund Baker was host to twenty friends who included Sealy Stuckey and his wife, Anna.[1] Their assembly certainly would not have included Richard Foley, who continued to lead a private life aloof from Southcottians.

On 25 May, 1843, the London group, in another attempt to bring about a degree of unity among believers, sent *An Invitation to the Southcottian Churches in London, Birmingham, Manchester, Stockport, Warrington, Ashton, Worcester, and all other parts of England,* calling on them to set apart Sunday, 4 June, as a day of united prayer.[2] At the same time Thomas Parton Hudson in Birmingham had taken it upon himself to publish a pamphlet entitled: *Copies of deep and important Letters, addressed to the Queen, Prince Albert, the Archbishop of Canterbury and others, on the Cause of England's Distress, and the Remedy*. In one of these letters, written to the Bishop of Worcester on 5 August, 1842, Hudson attributed the nation's economic and political ills to the bishops' failure to call for

> the SEALED WRITINGS given to the late Joanna Southcott concerning the distressed state of the nation (also what will befall it). I now acquaint you that the same are in the hands of the Rev. Richard Foley, late of Kingswinford, in your diocese; and to prevent the awful stroke from the Almighty God coming on this nation, I do hope you will cause the same to be demanded, to save this kingdom and give it the promised peace and happiness.

Hudson's initiative met with the usual resistance. Richard Hill Norris, for instance, wrote from Birmingham with reasons why he, for one, could not support the new 'movement party': he abhorred Lavinia Jones's antics and he needed proof that the Child had been born spiritually. Failing this, he was in favour of 'standing still'.[3] But members of the 'movement party' received a boost when they heard about the Will of Ann Essam, a wealthy member of the Hampton Court Group, who died in 1844 and left all her property to be dedicated to printing, publishing and distributing the writings of Joanna Southcott. Ann Essam's niece, Eliza Thornton, contested the Will on the grounds that Joanna's writings were 'indecent and immoral' and the case dragged on for years before being settled by the Master of the Rolls in May, 1862. Both sides had cause to celebrate when he declared that Joanna Southcott was shown by her writings to have been a very sincere Christian, and her works, though confused and incoherent, were written with a view of extending the influence of Christianity, but he decided that the Will fell within the limits forbidden by the Statute of Mortmain and was therefore invalid.

> Had this bequest been made out of pure personalty this Court would, in my opinion, have supported it and regulated its application as well as it could; but as it is given out of land, in my opinion, it is void by reason of the prohibitions contained in the Statute of Mortmain.[4]

In April, 1844, the Southcottian friends in London published another pamphlet: *An Address to the Protestants of England especially the Queen, the Archbishops, Bishops and Clergy, to every sect of professing Christians and every one who believes the Bible to be the True Word of God*. In this they declared that they possessed part of the law by which Satan was to be judged, but that the remainder was still sealed up and in the possession of the Reverend Richard Foley, North Cadbury, Somersetshire.[5] Five months later Samuel Jowett replied in a pamphlet designed only for believers in the Visitation. Immediately after Joanna Southcott's death, he wrote, 'because things had not taken place as expected, plans were begun to be devised by some of the believers, to bring in the promised Shiloh, and complete the redemption of man in a way of their own, contrary to the prophecy given; declaring also that Joanna Southcott had done her work, and that it was now left to be completed by *them*. Thus . . . one impostor after another has risen up, to lead away the believers from their faith in the woman's mission'.[6]

Ignoring Jowett's jibes, the London group organised a seven-day conference from 19 to 25 November, 1844, with James Sinnock acting as treasurer, and Mr and Mrs Spencer providing accommodation for delegates.[7] At 9 p.m. on the last day the meeting culminated with the drawing up of the following *Indictment against Satan*:

> The free subjects of our Lady the Queen, do present upon their oaths, and say, that a certain Being, known by the designation (viz.) – Dragon, Old Serpent, Devil, and Satan, did – to wit, in England, from January 12th, 1804, to November 25th, 1844, wilfully, wickedly, and with malice aforethought – tempt and persecute the Sealed People, contrary to the Law made in the year 1804; and did blaspheme to Most High God: - and also did murder the late Joanna Southcott, against the Peace of our said Sovereign Lady the Queen, her crown, and dignity, and contrary to the Statute in that case made and provided.[8]

In a lengthy pamphlet published the following January, the Chairman, John Hagger, set out the aims and achievements of the Conference. He said that they met in love and joy and with the desire to find out the real duty of the believers, and how they were to perform it. 'This Conference not being a self-created body, but chosen and elected by the free unbiased votes of the different churches they represent, are now a compact body, to whom applications can be made for information, and to whom the same can be sent by any believer who wishes to assist the Conference in its work, to obtain justice for God and man.' He mentioned the names of fourteen men who signed their approval: John Hagger, John Spencer, Joshua Lowe, T. Parton Hudson, J. Potter Wardle, John Vincent, Joseph Graystock, Thomas Malby, John Pye, Benjamin Howe, James Sinnock, William Parker, George Hinds, Wm Shingleton. He then appended the names and addresses of thirty-three professed believers who had objected to the Conference.[9]

One person who objected to the Conference was Samuel Jowett, but he was too overwhelmed by private grief to pay it much attention. 'Since I last wrote we have had a domestic affliction in the death of a son, nearly 21 years of age, he had been afflicted a long time and confined to his bed many months, not being able to turn himself without help,' he wrote to Edmund Baker on 20 January, 1845. He then explained why he and the friends in Leeds preferred to celebrate 12 January every year. The question of coming together for 14 October had been conditional on 'if I bring thee into prosperity', and that condition had not yet been fulfilled, but 12 January, 1804, was the evening when the List of names signed for Satan's destruction was sealed up by Joanna in Leeds and so that day was sacred.[10]

In early summer, 1845, W.B. Harrison visited London, from where he was able to report 'I am now pretty well acquainted with the Believers in this great city and I am sorry to say there is not amongst a population of 2 millions of human beings *one* intelligent, well informed, consistent

Believer'. He had been to see Mrs Waring, who was still living in Joanna's old home in Weston Place, but found that she believed in Townley's visitation and had a head full of notions about fallen angels returning to earth for redemption. 'I should feel ashamed of the world knowing that such extraordinary opinions existed amongst us', Harrison wrote to James Kidd. 'Not *one* expects the return of Joanna, there is not one who wishes for it.' He had also met up with Hudson's party, who had got hold of about four hundred seals signed by Joanna and were preparing to use them to seal members of their group.[11]

Meanwhile in Somerset the believers clung to their own traditions, meeting on 14 October for special celebrations. The twenty friends who gathered at the home of Edmund Baker in Langport Street, Ilminster, in 1847 included James Hayward, a baker from Bridgwater, and Sealy Stucky, a confectioner who was about to move from Odcombe to Burnham-on-Sea. Writing to describe the event to a friend, Edmund Baker's hand was clearly shaky, sad evidence of a recent seizure.[12] Life for him had been a struggle since the death of his wife in 1839. Now aged eighty-one, he was determined not only to minister to his flock for as long as he was physically able, but to make proper arrangements for their spiritual welfare thereafter. On 4 May, 1849, he wrote to the friends,

> As in all probability my Time cannot be long with you I think it my Duty to draw out some form or plan for the church in and round Ilminster to stand upon when I am gone. First I think it right to put down the Names of all the Male Friends that have been in our Great Cause from my first coming to Dowlish which I shall term Elders. Then I shall choose one of the whole Seven men of sound judgment in Joanna's Divine Writings *only* or such as are sanctioned by the Spirit through Her to conduct the affairs of the Church so that no unsound Doctrine creep in and to hold fast to what the Lord has given to us until a further Revelation be given.

The Seven he chose were: James Pearce, Joel Vile, William Vaux, George Churchill, Sealy Stuckey, James Hayward and Samuel Galpin. George Churchill from Curry Rivel was to hold the Register of Names and take care of the two silver gilt cups and the Bass Viol.[13]

Edmund Baker lived on until 1857, but with his departure from Ilminster the Southcottian movement in Somerset shifted focus. At North Cadbury, thirty miles away, the Box of Sealed Prophecies slumbered in Foley's dressing room at the Rectory while the Rector himself was busy making changes in his life. In 1850, his fiftieth year,

*North Cadbury Rectory, Somerset, where the Reverend Richard Foley stored the Box of Sealed Prophecies in his dressing-room from 1841 until his death in 1861.*

the Reverend Richard Foley entered marriage for the first time, taking to the altar Frances Essex Talbot, a wealthy widow who had been born in 1802 at Ilminster, where her father, Vincent Langworthy, was an attorney. She was the mother of two daughters, one aged seventeen, the other, ten. The marriage was not a success, for Richard did not know that Frances suffered from mental illness and had recently been confined in an institution for seven months. The strain of her new marriage proved too much and within three months she suffered a total breakdown.[14] While Richard Foley was struggling to come to terms with this tragedy, his life was further complicated by a fresh assault on the Sealed Prophecies by Mr and Mrs Jones.

The first he heard about it was in a letter from Leeds, dated 7 April, 1852, containing a second Address from Samuel Jowett and his friends, assuring him of their entire satisfaction with his custodianship of the Box, but warning him that Lavinia Jones might be about to make another attempt to get the Sealed Writings from him. The reason for their concern was that Daniel Jones had recently managed to gain possession of all the books and manuscripts that had been left at 17 Weston Place. Mrs Waring, who had lived there since the death of Townley and Underwood, had been taken away after falling dangerously ill. In her absence, Charles Barnard, Ann Underwood's grandson and one of her heirs, was left to clear out the house. Acting on the instructions of the Reverend Samuel Eyre, Daniel Jones visited Barnard and arranged to buy all the printed books, the twelve Visions of Joseph Prescott which Joanna had taken round the country in 1803, and a collection of manuscripts and letters. Jones paid him fifty pounds for a load that weighed almost five tons and needed four large vans to take away.[15]

It was not, however, the monetary considerations that vexed the believers, but rather the fact that the manuscripts included certain important letters that had been sealed by Joanna in 1813 with strict instructions as to when and in what order they should be opened.

Their seals were still unbroken and many believed it was vital that they remained so.

Daniel Jones disagreed and was determined to go ahead and read them, even when opposed by Samuel Eyre, his friend and mentor. He set out his justifications in a letter to T.P. Hudson, 28 April, 1852:

> In many cases, my friend, the Revd S. Eyre has great sway over me, and perhaps I may say no one more so, yet on the question of my right to open the letters which came into my hands, I think his judgment quite childish, and such (through right and duty to those under bondage) would have been to me (a child of freedom) an act of decided disobedience. My first intention was, when I had the letters, to assemble at least a few friends to consult on the propriety of opening them, but I soon found that this decision was not good, and that it would lead to an immediate division. I therefore took all responsibility on myself to prevent if possible so unpleasant a first step.

With regard to his right to open the sacred letters, Daniel Jones explained:

> The letters on the outside are written on and witnessed with these words, 'First letter to be opened,' 'Second letter to be opened,' 'Third letter to be opened'; but no command is therein given not to be opened, therefore I opened them with the same intention I should do one of your letters to me, namely to know the will of the writer; and when I did so I found that it is the publishing of these letters that will bring on 'The Trial'. This is the purpose I have in view, on which I entreat all friends to suspend their judgement until they have an opportunity of reading the letters and meditating thereon, for it is not until then that a right judgement can be found, and even then some may see the case clear while many will doubt until they have seen the seventh book.

To queries about the published book and whether the seals had been broken when he received the letters, Daniel Jones replied,

> The seals of the box were broken, but the seals of the letters were perfect when they came to my hand. The title is taken from the letters, except the words *Sixth Book of Wonders*, which are mine and will be inserted as such. I believe there are more manuscripts which ought to be forth coming, but not likely to be brought to light unless we could prevail on the Revd R. Foley to bring out what he has.[16]

Apprising the Reverend Richard Foley of these events, the believers declared that her husband's triumph

> has so elated Mrs J. that we thought she might be making another attempt, either direct or indirect, to get the Sealed Writings from you. Not that we feel the least alarmed at what she might do, having unbounded confidence in your integrity, not to give them up to any person or persons, till you are perfectly satisfied they are the proper parties to receive them; & we hereby tender you our cordial thanks for your kindness hitherto, in protecting the Sacred Treasure, believing that our Almighty Father, who caused them to be placed in your hands will enable you to keep them from every person desirous of obtaining them, till they are demanded by the Great & Learned, as stated by the Lord to Joanna Southcott. We are wishful for you to do by the Writings in your possession as Joseph of Arimathea (as recorded in the Gospel) did by the Body of our Lord & Saviour Jesus Christ. . . . Signed: Samuel Jowett (Leeds), James Kidd (Halifax) W.B. Harrison (Manchester), Wm. Bonehill (Warwick), Lee (Wolverhampton), Wm. Oldfield (Denton).[17]

The friends had taken trouble to warn, whilst at the same time reassuring, Foley. They had no idea of the strain under which he had been living since his marriage to Frances Talbot, no idea that his health had deteriorated and that he had left North Cadbury for the time being to live in Montaubon, France. As a result, their letter failed to reach Foley before one arrived from Daniel Jones informing him that he and the Reverend Samuel Eyre were keen to collect all Joanna Southcott's works, were in a position to meet any demands that might be made on them and wanted to know if Foley would resign to their keeping the Sealed Writings in his possession, whilst reserving to himself any interest that might later arise from them. Richard Foley was outraged.

> I beg to say in answer that my objections to handing over to you the papers in my possession are as strong as ever they were, and that consequently I respectfully decline complying with your request. I have no pecuniary interest in retaining the papers in question, nor do I expect ever to obtain anything by doing so.[18]

When the Believers heard that Jones had already approached Richard Foley it seemed that their worst fears were being realised. W.B. Harrison wrote immediately to Eyre:

> Having just heard within the last few hours that yourself and Mr Jones of Bath have made a demand upon Mr Foley to give up the sealed writings of Joanna Southcott now in his possession, we thought it better to address a few lines to you to ask whether such be really the fact and if it be so, perhaps you will be kind enough to favour us with a few lines stating what circumstances have occurred to induce you to take this step.[19]

He wrote a similar letter to Foley, addressed now to Montaubon.

> Within the last few hours we have been informed that an application has been made to you by the Revd. S. Eyre of Bristol & Mr Jones of Bath to give up the Sealed Writings of Joanna Southcott. Anticipating some such proceedings, an address, signed by five friends was forwarded to North Cadbury on the 12th April last to hope & request you would continue to hold those writings as you had hitherto done. From a brief acknowledgement from some person at your residence we learned that you were in France, we therefore now send these few lines hastily written to beg you will not on any account whatever, be induced to give up those Writings until you are fully satisfied that the parties making the demand are fully authorized by Church & State to do so.[20]

Foley wrote back immediately to say that he had no knowledge of the earlier letter, but on receipt of Daniel Jones's letter he had written to his curate at North Cadbury telling him not to give up any boxes in the house to anyone. He had also warned him against being imposed upon by anyone, even if carrying a letter professing to come from him.

> I do not of course mention the particulars of my directions as it is better that they should remain a secret between me and him, but I expect that they will prove sufficient to prevent Mr Jones or any other person obtaining improper possession of the Sealed Writings.

Foley then explained his presence in France.

> I have been unwell since the Thursday after midlent Sunday, & though somewhat better, am not yet quite recovered. I am in hopes however that with the summer & change of air & scene I shall, by the blessing of God, recover my usual health. I propose to leave this place at the end of the month, & have not as yet made up my mind where I shall go, but if you wish to write to me, & will forward a letter with a foreign stamp

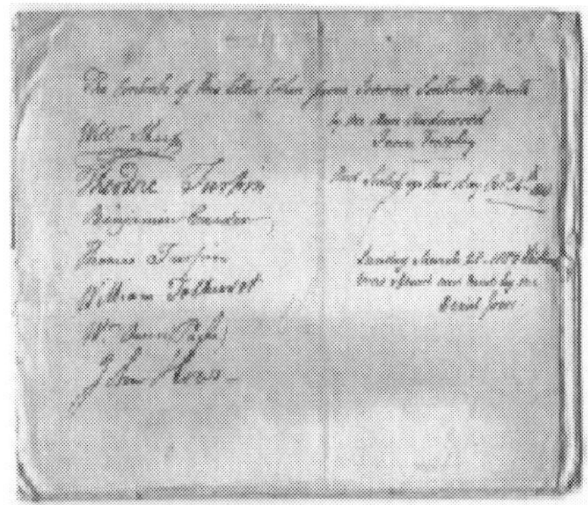

*One of the six sealed letters opened by Daniel Jones on 28 March, 1852, and published later that year in The Sixth Book of Wonders. The book caused a furore among the followers of Joanna Southcott, many of whom refused to accept that the letters were genuine.*

upon it (for the English one is thrown away) to my curate at North Cadbury, he will always know where I am to be found.

He ended on a curmudgeonly note:

> I have forwarded this letter unpaid as I cannot be expected to pay postage both ways.[21]

Richard Foley's letter might have set the minds of the 'old and tried' believers at rest, had not Daniel Jones not committed further outrage by announcing that he had already broken the seals and read the six letters that Joanna sealed on 13 September 1813, despite her words: 'I cannot enter into particulars of what was revealed to me; as it was ordered to be sealed up, in the presence of seven friends, and put into a box, that is not to be opened till my TRIAL.'[22] Moreover, Jones had declared his intention to publish the letters under the title 'The Sixth Book of Wonders.'

The friends moved to limit the damage straight away. Harrison offered to visit Lavinia Jones who was judged to be the puppet-master pulling her husband's strings.

> If this be contrary to the Lord's plan He will defeat it, but as I have no intention of doing wrong in any way I feel no fear about meeting Mrs Jones, on the contrary I feel I shall be able to manage her and I think I can gain as much information from her as can be gained by any man,

he confidently assured Samuel Jowett.[23] However, on the day, he reported:

> I got here [Leamington] this morning about eleven o'clock and have spent some hours with Mrs Jones, but it will be impossible for me to do more than give you a sketch. Five sealed packets have fallen into the hands of Mr Jones by whom they have been opened. Three of them were letters sealed with Joanna's seal & signed by the seven & marked first, second, third letters, a fourth was like a written pamphlet & a fifth a letter written

> by the seven expressing their opinion of the proceedings of that period (1813) – the first four were all written by Mrs Underwood and related to Joanna's Marriage. These letters & papers Mr Jones has resolved to print and he thinks of entitling it, 'This day – the Revd Joseph Pomeroy married to Joanna Southcott, the great prophetess & the wonder of the World', or the Sixth book of Wonders. The first part of this title as a quotation is from one of the letters mentioned above. He thinks it will form a pamphlet of 90 or 100 pages. . . . The above sealed packets were found in a sealed Box opened by Mr Barnard.[24]

The following day Harrison wrote a temperate letter to Daniel Jones:

> I address you with the knowledge and approbation of your wife. . . . I have been a believer in Joanna's mission about 47 years and during the whole of that period I have never lost sight of it. . . . I do not feel I have any authority to blame you for what you have already done or to dictate to you with regard to the future.

In the same tone of moderation he then pointed out that, as a believer, Daniel Jones should not print the sealed packets, because there were so many passages in Joanna's writings against it.[25]

Daniel Jones was not open to this kind of reasoning. He justified his actions in a letter to Messrs Miller and Norris. He had not demanded the Sealed Writings from Foley, he told them. He had merely explained what had transpired at Weston Place and that he had removed the books to Bath where he intended to establish a depot for the sale of the printed books and a place of deposit for the Sealed Writings if Foley would give them up to the care of himself, Mr Eyre and a few others, who would be answerable for their safety. Foley had refused this request. Jones's letter then took on a threatening tone:

> [I] urge upon every member of the church to endeavour to bring in Richd Foley by faith, as an imperative duty, & should he refuse beyond God's appointed time, some calamity of a very serious nature will fall upon him to give the box into the hands of those who will faithfully make known its contents for the general welfare of all believers, or into the care of another Man-child.

With regard to the box of sealed letters that he had purchased, Jones explained that he had opened them and intended to print a few copies just for those believers who wanted them. He wrote:

> The Books of the sealed writings are most particularly the properties or the legacies of the Mother to her children to gain the long lost inheritance which by the fall was lost. Every man therefore who believes the writings of Joanna Southcott to be the unalterable will of God is justified in claiming a share in this *will* . . . as there is nothing but the writings that can give the kingdom, as long as they are secreted from the believers, so long shall we be deprived of our inheritance. I therefore hope that every believer will make his house a Booksellers shop for the sale of the printed books.[26]

When Harrison realised that his eminently reasonable approach to Daniel Jones had not worked, his anger exploded. He wrote to a friend:

> D. Jones is ignorantly a prime servant of the devil, & I am persuaded that nothing but death will stop his proceedings (I have no doubt but he will threaten Mr Foley with God's judgments, therefore I think we ought to do something to support him. I think he [Foley] ought to know that the majority are with him on our side.

Fuel was added to his fury when he heard that Mr Graystock, a believer from Birmingham, had called on Mrs Jones and found her already setting up the type for printing the sealed letters opened by her husband.[27] Warning Richard Foley to be on his guard, Harrison wrote,

> We feel assured there is nothing which D. Jones is not prepared to do to accomplish his purpose. We think it probable that you will again hear from him, & we are prepared to expect he will attempt to influence you, first by persuasion, & next by threats, & you must not be surprised if you should receive from him a letter threatening you with all the vengeance of heaven, if you do not give up the Sealed Writings to him. . . . I think it only right to inform you that Mr T.P. Hudson of Birmingham has no discretion. All the information he obtains from your mother or sisters relative to your views & intentions he communicates to some person in London, by whom it is conveyed to D. Jones. A copy of your letter to that gentleman dated May 1st was read to him in London before he got the original. I have no wish to advise you, at the same time I think it proper that you should be put in possession of facts, & so long as you have to deal with parties like Mr & Mrs Jones I think it would be better to keep them in ignorance of your plans.[28]

At the same time Messrs Norris and Miller from Birmingham sent a strong protest to Daniel Jones.

> You direct the believers as an imperative duty to urge the Revd Richd Foley to bring forward the sealed writings, or you say some serious calamity will fall upon him. We think before you had given utterance to a sentence of this nature, it was your duty to have shown some authority beyond mere human opinions. That gentleman is acting in accordance with those who have preceded him in taking care of the Sealed writings till demanded by those in power. The same judgement you think will come upon him for not opening the sealed writings was equally liable to fall upon his father, Townley, Sharp & even Joanna herself, when each had the care of the sealed writings. . . . You charge Richd Foley with frustrating the will of God & keeping the believers out of their possession. If this be true, by what right did Joanna keep them sealed from 1804 till her death?

Norris and Miller pointed out that only impostors had tried to force custodians to bring forward the writings, citing Mr Bradley who came to a sad end after offering a lawyer £500 to force the sealed writings into the King's Court and bring on the Trial. The safest course, therefore, was 'to wait the Lord's time and not to force the Almighty'. It was wrong to suggest that humanity was being deprived of its inheritance by the detention of the writings because 'There are to occur events in the order of Providence, to make those sealed writings fruit in its season; & that we may see the beauty of the flower, we should not nip the carnations in the bud, or make bold assertions without direct authority.'[29]

As the expected date for publication drew nearer, Harrison went to Birmingham in an effort to curb Hudson's involvement with Jones. After talking to Foley's unmarried sister, Anne Elizabeth, and other friends, he concluded that both Hudson and Daniel Jones believed that whoever had the Sealed Writings when the Work began again, would be the Man-child, and so each was manoeuvring to get the writings from Foley, and they were deceiving each other.[30]

When, despite the protests, Daniel Jones persisted in his plans to publish, believers were left with a dilemma. Samuel Jowett asked James Kidd.

> Should we have anything to do with the book at all if offered to us? We believe Satan has influenced Mr Jones to disobey in breaking open those sealed letters. . . . Is not Mr Jones's object in presenting his book to the believers to draw them into disobedience, like himself, & then having done so, may he not

> turn upon them with these words: You condemned me for opening the sealed letters to gain a knowledge of what they contained; but I have no sooner offered to you the *forbidden* contents, than you have received them with eagerness? . . . I intend to answer all the questions for myself, but I do not wish others to be biased by me.[31]

At a meeting held in Manchester in July to discuss Jones's book Samuel Jowett was dismayed to hear that Daniel Jones had recently applied to Mrs Waring's niece for another box of sealed letters, but this had been refused him.[32] The meeting agreed to disseminate a printed paper outlining their objections to Jones's proceedings. When Jones received his copy, he was furious to find that they had discussed him without giving him the opportunity of being present. In his printed response, he declared,

> It is my opinion . . . that all the printed books should be put again into free circulation throughout the world. . . . His Word given to Joanna Southcott is the 'Will of God', given for the purpose of gaining the Kingdom, and of dividing the kingdom among the twelve sealed tribes. I deny that any command has been given to withdraw the Word from circulation. But it is clear that the errors and conceits of Believers have had this effect, that thereby the Church has been slain, and most of the Believers numbered with the dead. . . . However, it is my intention to publish the Word, and I expect that it will bring on the trial.[33]

In a personal letter Jones expressed his dismay at finding Harrison's name amongst those who were trying to persuade believers to shun his book. He had assumed that Harrison understood the stand he was making and he was at pains to point out how far advanced the project was.

> Forty pages are printed off and the others (which may be about 40 more) are in progress, but as I am doing it on my own premises and have only one compositor the progress is slow, so slow, that I fear many of the lukewarm Believers hopes will die away before it is completed although I expect to see it completed in one month from this time. . . . I can hardly believe that out of a body of 700 believers 500 will be so indifferent as to content themselves with not seeing the book.[34]

If there is a twinge of self-doubt in his letter, it may have been due to difficulties in Daniel Jones's family. For years he had worked in partnership with his brother, Charles, a fellow land surveyor and builder. Together they had built up the business inherited from their father until between them they owned more than a score of properties and employed dozens of labourers. Then, in the autumn of 1852, Charles died, leaving a widow and young son. For a moment this tragedy diverted Daniel from his dispute with the Believers. 'I intended to have written you a long letter last Sunday but family circumstance prevents me', he wrote to Harrison on 26 October, after informing him that the *Sixth Book of Wonders* was now ready for circulation.[35]

Harrison, meanwhile, had thought the matter over and decided that he had a duty to read the book, if only to be in a better position to advise others.[36] On 7 November he wrote to James Kidd, 'I last evening got a copy of the Book published by Daniel Jones, which I have read through and will now give you my opinion thereon. . . . I do not expect any perceptible change to be effected by its publication, either amongst the believers as a body, or in the nation at large. In my own mind I feel a moral conviction that its publication has been under Divine direction, and that it is now sent in mercy to the Believers and I think it ought to be read by all.'[37] And, in answer to those who feared that Jones might have tampered with the text, Harrison argued that Jones did not have sufficient knowledge to understand it or make any significant alterations.[38]

Such arguments failed to convince Samuel Jowett, whose main fear was that believers would be led to assume that Joanna's marriage was only spiritual and miss the fact that the temporal marriage was the beginning of the fulfilment of her writings. He continued to insist that believers should shun the published letters: 'As Mr Jones' book is now out, it appears that now the believers will be put to the trial of their obedience, that will show really who is on the Lord's side.'[39] Samuel Jowett's friends were exasperated by this kind of tone. 'If I mistake not, Mr Jowett's habit of laying down the law amongst all those believers where he is accustomed to visit, has unfitted him to judge correctly of his own feelings & motives. . . . Before we can reasonably expect the Lord to direct us, our desire to be directed by Him must be pure & sincere & free from any lurking wish of our own', wrote Harrison to James Kidd in December, as the argument rumbled on.[40]

On 12 December, 1853, the Rev. Samuel Eyre, aged seventy-seven, died at Bristol. In his last years his reputation had suffered from his association with Daniel Jones, even though he made it clear that he had never sanctioned Jones's opening of the sealed letters or publishing their contents. Against a background of trouble in the Balkans that presaged the Crimean War, Daniel Jones approached the Reverend

Richard Foley again, urging him to allow the Sealed Writings to be published.

> Most reluctantly do I address you on a subject which I fear may be unpleasant, particularly when I reflect that in April 1852 I wrote you on the same subject & recd a reply refusing to comply with my wishes; yet I cannot refrain from calling your attention to the papers you hold relating to the Mission of the late Joanna Southcott, to entreat you to take some decided means to have them made public. I do not wish to dictate the most proper course to be taken, nor do I solicit that you should give them into the hands of those in whom you have no confidence; but I do most earnestly entreat you to examine them & make the contents known amongst believers, for most certainly as the Revd Mr Pomeroy was afflicted for so many years for keeping back the writings intrusted to his care, others have nothing less to expect.
>
> The writings which were at No 17 Weston Place, London in the care of Mrs Waring, & which were the property of C.Barnard & Brother, were purchased by me, & are now in my possession. Amongst them I found some unpublished MSS [manuscripts] which I have since printed & published as the 6th book of Wonders, a copy of which I shall be happy to send you if I can do so without giving offence.
>
> In conclusion I once more entreat you to bring forward those papers you have, to see whether they contain the seventh & last book of Wonders, which the believers expect, for nationally we have entered on the long expected 'Famine' – the sword of War – Pestilence, earthquakes etc, etc. precisely as predicted, and therefore the people should know the cause.[41]

The reply was brief and to the point: 'Mr Foley presents his compliments to Mr Jones and begs to say that his opinion remains now exactly the same as it was when he wrote Mr Jones in 1852.'[42] Foley sent both letters to Harrison together with news of his mother, Elizabeth Foley, now very infirm. Her death that summer raised the spectre of Richard's own mortality. Writing to express his condolences, T.P. Hudson launched on the subject of the Box of Sealed Writings in Foley's possession, beseeching him to commit to paper what he wanted to happen to them. Foley, whose health was poor and his marriage childless, saw the sense in what Hudson was saying. 'Life to each & every one is most uncertain, & I think the idea a very proper one,' he told Harrison; 'and I have therefore written to you to inquire to whom you & the body of believers with whom you are connected would wish me, in case of my death, to leave the Box of Sealed Writings. Without such an appointment the papers would necessarily pass with my other papers to the custody of the Executors of my Will'.[43]

Harrison immediately sent copies of Foley's letter to Samuel Jowett, James Kidd, Matthias Crossley and William Bonehill. 'I have no idea that Mr Foley will die before the Writings are called forward, but not withstanding this we ought to make a proper selection,' he said, after pointing out that they were all the same age or older than Foley, and that he could think of no one in Exeter, London, or Birmingham who was a suitable candidate for the trust.[44] Throughout October and November, letters flew to and fro as the friends tried to decide who would be the next custodian or, if they failed to agree, how to avoid Foley's willing it to some other ambitious individual such as Hudson. While Matthias Crossley took the view that the Lord would take care of matters, Samuel Jowett was more pro-active. After canvassing the friends at Leeds, he found that they all agreed that he himself should look after the Writings in the event of Richard Foley's death.

> They said – as my father being one of the 12 judges, it seemed to be by right to descend to me, there not being anything objectionable in my character, as a steadfast believer from the beginning of the Visitation being made known in Yorkshire, they thought I was the most eligible person for the trust to be reposed in. As to my age, it was said, that I had a son that was a steadfast believer, & was I to be suddenly taken away by death, after the Writings were committed to my care, he would legally step into my shoes, as Mr Foley did into his Father's & take as good care of them as I should.[45]

These arguments failed to convince the friends, so it was decided that matters should remain as they were, and that when Richard Foley died, the custody of the Writings would devolve on his Executors.[46]

For Believers 1854 was a crucial year, because it marked forty years from the death of Joanna. When it passed without anything happening to advance the movement they were deeply disappointed. Harrison confessed to James Kidd:

> I do not recollect any cycle in the Scriptures of a longer period than forty years, and as those are now fulfilled we are without data to calculate from, & I must confess so far as regards forming an opinion when the fulfilment of the Lord's promises will take place I am quite at sea.[47]

This loss of bearings laid some believers open to the new enthusiasm for spirit-rapping that was sweeping in from America. It was a phenomenon eagerly embraced by Lavinia Jones who, in 1855, launched a new periodical called *The Comforter,* uniting Joanna's visitation with spiritualism. Horrified by the notion, Samuel Jowett demanded, 'What can be more opposed to the ways of the Lord than spirit rapping?' [48]

Her new enthusiasm increased Lavinia's determination to get possession of the Box of Sealed Prophecies. Moderating her tone, she wrote an unctuous letter to Richard Foley.

> Rev & Respected Sir,
> It is indeed truly melancholy to stand still & witness the departure of so many of the suffering people who have supported so devout an attachment to the Cause of Joanna Southcott go away from this life without any realization of the promises they have so tenaciously held to. Rev. Sir, would you write me on the subject of those papers you have in your possession. I have a residence in Bath, 17 Argyle Street, where I shall be from next Saturday, 5 p.m. to Wednesday 5 p.m. A call from you would be much valued, when I would in every way as far as I could enter into your views. Accept my thanks for many past favors, & believe me, Rev. Sir, sincerely in the hope to promote peace & good will, Lavinia Jones.[49]

Foley politely declined the interview and forwarded Lavinia's letter to Harrison with the comment: 'she is unusually civil, & I consequently suspect some mischief to be brewing'.[50] Samuel Jowett, on the other hand, drew comfort from Lavinia's move, seeing in it an admission that the Joneses publication of the *Sixth Book of Wonders* and *The Comforter* had not achieved the desired effect forcing them to make another effort to get possession of the Box.[51] The friends were also gratified by Foley's no-nonsense reply and Harrison quickly wrote to tell him so.

> I have consulted those old & steady friends with whom I have long been intimate & the whole body, without one exception, highly approve of your reply to Mrs Jones. . . . Should you at any time require our advice & assistance in any way, a word from you will command it at once. . . . Many years ago Mrs Jones stated to Mr Jowett of Leeds that she would leave no stone unturned to accomplish her object, consequently he has the worst opinion of her, as I have myself . . . and we both agree that she will make some other attempt. I feel pretty sure

> she is capable of robbing your house if the means of doing so were possible without detection. Excuse me therefore suggesting that if you leave home you give clear directions to your household for the protection of what we deem a sacred trust. We have no doubt about God's power to protect His own word, but notwithstanding this we have no wish that any person should feel self condemned for any want of thought, of which however we have not the slightest reason to suspect you.[52]

Matthias Crossley of Derby entertained no higher opinion of Lavinia Jones:

> Mrs Jones has said that she would leave no stone unturned to obtain possession of the sealed Writings, and I believe her; her own natural perseverance & energy, combined with the designs of hell in a shape sufficiently veiled to deceive her as to their object, are a sufficient guarantee that she will make good her promise; but her disguised master as well as her, are subject to the control of Him who can say,
>
> 'Hitherto shall thou go & no further, and here shall thy proud waves be stayed'; if she got possession, she might be paralysed in action, and unable from a hundred different causes to reap what she considered to be the benefit of her labours; it is more than probable that she would not be able to decypher them.[53]

Whenever Richard Foley had anything of importance to convey, he contacted the believers through William Bown Harrison. In September, 1857, he wrote a long, lugubrious letter with sad news that his brother, Noah Philip, had just died in Bombay, leaving two crippled sons and another whose education he would have to pay for. As far as his own health was concerned, he had been suffering from pains in the head since an attack in France the year before, and to make matters worse he had nearly been killed when forced to leap from his carriage after his horse bolted recently. As a result, he wrote, 'I feel myself far from well, and I begin to be apprehensive that without some alteration for the better, my days upon earth may soon be shortened; God grant that I may be prepared for the hour of my departure.' He added a note: 'The sealed writings are all safe in my dressing room'.[54]

With Foley in a debilitated state and his wife prone to mental instability, it may be imagined how they felt when, on 27 December, 1858, Daniel Jones landed unannounced on their doorstep to demand the Sealed Writings, which he claimed were national property. The reaction of Frances Foley must have been dramatic to call forth the apology she received from Jones the following day.

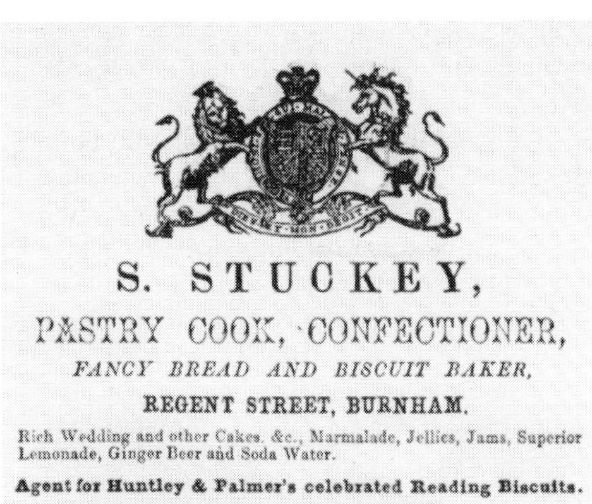


*Advertisement for Sealy Stuckey's Confectionery business at Burnham-on-Sea, Somerset, published in 1859 in J. Salisbury's A Guide or Handbook to Burnham & its Neighbourhood.*

Madam,

I regret exceedingly that I had not more calm time allowed me to subside the disturbance caused in your mind by my visit yesterday. In my application to the Rev R. Foley for an answer to my intended questions there was no ill will or cause for excitation intended, nor was I aware that the subject was so distasteful to you. . . . Seeing you desire to understand fully the nature of the business we came upon. . . . I feel it my duty to explain to you something more of this troublesome business which has occupied my attention for at least twenty five years. . . .

In 1814 the dissolution of Joanna Southcott occurred & the disappointment of the birth broke up the cause for the time, there were certain sealed Papers which ought to have been examined & published to the world immediately, then the nature of the Birth would have been publicly known & with some appreciated, instead of which these papers have been kept secret by the late Revd T P Foley & the present Revd Richard Foley for forty four years which expired yesterday. My object in visiting the Revd R. Foley yesterday was to explain that keeping secret these papers from the world brought a deep affliction upon the late Revd T.P. Foley & that I was under the greatest apprehension that the present Revd R. Foley would bring a similar calamity on himself if he still persisted in keeping them unpublished.

Think not, Madam, that I am thus explicit with any intention of creating any ill will between you & Mr Foley for you may believe me when I say that there are no two names on record

> of my most intimate friends or relations for whom I have a greater veneration than those of the late Revd T.P. Foley & the present Revd Richard Foley, therefore it is not from sinister motives but purely to prevent if possible a National disgrace which is being incurred through a mistaken zeal in the keeping secret that which should be published openly. I consider the Papers National property & shall most certainly make the matter known more publicly to the Bishops & Ministers of Church & State that the cause may be further tried & proved.
>
> In conclusion allow me to speak personally & to reassure you that it is far from my wishes to act hastily & if you will favour me with a letter I will use every effort to promote your wishes as far as possible if we can any way meet on the subject.[55]

Richard Foley was so disgusted that he could not bring himself to answer the letter on his wife's behalf. He forwarded it to Harrison and asked him to return it to sender.[56]

As the decade came to an end, a cloud of melancholy settled over the Believers. Their numbers were dwindling. Joseph Jowett had died in 1848. Early in 1860 William Bonehill died and W.B. Harrison was suffering from the kind of depression and ill health caused by 'hope deferred which maketh the heart sick'. [Proverbs 13,v.12.][57] His death in March 1860 raised the question of who would be the new channel of communication between the believers and Richard Foley, and it was considered urgent that someone should undertake the role quickly in case the Joneses took advantage. Matthias Crossley proposed Samuel Jowett for the task, if his advanced age and difficulty with writing allowed it.[58]

Samuel Jowett, approaching eighty and about to dispose of his printing business, was happy to accept the responsibility and immediately planned a visit to the West Country.[59] By June he had arrived at Burnham-on-Sea to stay with the Stuckeys, who invited friends each evening to meet him and discuss the Visitation. There ensued long, lively debates, especially with James Hayward, who had lost his leadership of the Bridgwater group when his views came to reflect those of Mr and Mrs Jones.[60]

Daniel and Lavinia Jones, meanwhile, were having troubles of their own. Daniel, after more than thirty-five years, had lost faith in Lavinia and, after declaring her work useless, refused to pour any more money into printing her books. The blow fell in January, 1861, when her next publication was already in the press and within three or four sheets of being done. She wrote to David Wells, a friend in London, begging him to send her ten shillings and describing the conditions under which she laboured.

> The weather is getting in my favour – the printing press is up in a very high place and ink – paper wetted – and type freezes before we can work it. But I hope we shall get no mishaps and then all will be well done.[61]

Samuel Jowett's visit to the West Country seems to have injected new energy into the group of local believers led by Sealy Stuckey. In the census of 1861 Stuckey is recorded as living over his shop in Regent Street, Burnham-on-Sea, with his wife, Anna, and their children, Sarah Ann, aged twenty, and Robert, aged eighteen. A recent guide to Burnham had included an advertisement showing that Stuckey had been awarded the royal warrant as pastry cook, confectioner, fancy bread and biscuit maker. His business had thrived since he came to the town, and he found that he did not have enough time to copy as many of Joanna Southcott's Communications as he would have liked. Hearing that Joseph Graystock was now living in London, but out of work, he wrote to ask if he would like to take on the task.[62] Before there was time for him to receive a reply he was shocked by an obituary in *The Times*. Thomas Crocker, a believer who lived in Glastonbury, saw a similar announcement in his local newspaper, and hastened to convey the news to John Marshall Jowett, son of Samuel. He wrote on 2 June, 1861,

> I did not intend writing to you before Monday, but I have been startled this morning by seeing the death of Revd Richd Foley announced in the paper & as you hinted you was going to have a meeting of the Friends Sunday I felt I shd like you all to know it. . . . he died 16th May. My dear friend this is what we did not expect. All the Judges in the shadows are now dead. I wonder what may be the next surprise.[63]

# 7
# The Finger of God, 1861-1876

The Believers were caught out by the news of Richard Foley's death and had no clear idea what should happen next to the Box of Sealed Prophecies. Some years previously, after failing to settle on the identity of the next custodian, they had left the matter to be decided by his executors. Now, there was a sense of panic, as they realised that this was just the kind of circumstance that Daniel and Lavinia Jones might exploit. As soon as he heard, Samuel Jowett, who was staying with his son at 58 Elmwood Street, Leeds, despatched a letter to Richard's widow.

> Respected Madam,
> We were sorry to hear through the newspapers of the death of your dear and worthy husband, and with most sincere regard we offer to you the expression of our sympathy in your bereavement. It is about a twelvemonth ago since I had the pleasure and gratification to be the recipient of your kind and generous hospitality, and had a first interview with your husband on a subject of surpassing interest in our estimation – viz – the safe custody of the box of Sealed Writings of the late Mrs Joanna Southcott, the *sacred trust* of his late father the Rev Thomas Philip Foley.
>
> We are now very anxious to learn what provision has been made for their care, and if I might not be considered presuming, it would greatly oblige us, believers in her Mission, if you would favour me with a line of information as to how they have been or are to be disposed of, or allow myself and a friend the pleasure to wait upon you for an hour or two at your convenience to learn the particulars adequately. I fear you will not fully estimate our solicitude, but I beg to assure you that the deposit we regard as sacred and that we believe the Lord God of Heaven will order them to be called forward in furtherance of his own great work, of man's redemption as was effected by your late husband's father.[1]

Samuel Jowett's letter to Foley's widow must have crossed in the post an official communication from Foley's married sister, Esther Pickthorn, who was staying at North Cadbury, while she sorted out his estate.

> Sir, It is with sincere grief I inform you of the death of my dear Brother, the Rev. Richard Foley, which sad event took place the 16th May, leaving Mr Bache (my brother-in-law) and myself executors; and we are of opinion that the Box of Sealed Writings should be placed in the care of one or more of the oldest Believers, as may be agreed on by the generality. Having understood that Mr W.B. Harrison, of Manchester, is dead, I have written to his son, requesting him to acquaint the Believers and ascertain with whom they wish the Box to be placed; but not having heard from him, I fear my letter may have miscarried. Will you kindly have a meeting as soon as you can, and let me know the result, as the sale will (D.V.) take place here in about three weeks, and it would be desirable to have it removed before then. Not having a house of my own, I and my sisters must decidedly decline having the permanent charge of it.[2]

Esther Pickthorn's letter must have set Jowett's mind at rest, at least for the present. The Box would be handed over to 'one or more of the oldest Believers', so now it remained to sort out how this person – or persons – would be chosen, bearing in mind that there was not much time to make a decision. The sale of Richard Foley's goods would take place before the end of the month, and any delay might still lay them open to the Joneses' machinations. Fortunately, John Marshall Jowett was a printer and it was a simple matter for him to produce and distribute a voting form. On 4 June, 1861, a letter was sent out to all supporters of the cause.

> Apple Hall, Leeds Old Road, Bradford, Yorks
>
> Dear Friend,
>
> The following letter has been received from the Executors of the late Rev Richard Foley, who died on the 16th day of May last. To his death he had charge of the Box of Sealed Writings, in trust from his late father the Rev Thomas Philip Foley.
>
> As a believer in the mission of the late Joanna Southcott, you will please fill up the following form, as to whom you wish to be empowered to receive them, and post the same to me not later than Sunday Evening next, that I may receive it on the following day.
>
> Should you know other believers in your neighbourhood, be kind enough to make known the purport of this note, and forward their wishes with your own. I am, dear Friend, Yours

> sincerely, in the work of the Lord, John Marshall Jowett.
> I wish Friend ———
> To have the Box of Sealed Writings delivered to his care in trust, as held by the late Rev. R. Foley
> (Signed), ———————[3]

In London Joseph Graystock read his letter to the group of believers who met every Wednesday to study Joanna Southcott's writings and found that everyone there agreed that John Marshall Jowett would be the proper person to take charge of 'the Ark of the New Covenant'.[4] In Somerset Samuel Galpin visited Sealy Stuckey to find out what the friends thought about the Box being moved from North Cadbury, and found that they were also in favour of John Marshall Jowett being custodian, although they declined to sign the form because they wished 'to leave it in the hands of the Lord'.[5] Thomas Crocker of Glastonbury nominated Samuel Jowett and John Sandell of Wells in Somerset as the proper persons to have charge of the Trust, as they were the two oldest Sealed believers, but he found that the Stuckeys felt that they themselves should take priority over Sandell, as their whole family were believers and they had a house of their own. Poor Mr Sandell was deeply hurt when he heard this. After much discussion it was then agreed to nominate Samuel Jowett for the trust despite a lingering desire for the Sealed Writings to stay in Somerset, and some notion of inviting him to make his future home there.[6]

In the event, although three places, York, Dukinfield, and Stanningley, failed to return their votes, nearly two hundred people voted for Samuel Jowett, who was accordingly appointed Trustee of the Sealed Writings, with the task of collecting them from North Cadbury. As soon as the result was announced John Marshall Jowett received a flood of letters from believers expressing their approval. Samuel Galpin wrote from Beaminster, Dorset, on his return from Somerset.

> To see such a number of names standing for your worthy Father quite overcomes me with joy, and when I trace his journey last year in the West, the very great respect the deceased Mr Foley paid him & Mr Stuckey by shewing the Box of S.W. and the travelling case, combined with the great light he opened to his Friends in the West, I cannot but conclude *It is the finger of God.* Why then Dear Friend Should we tempt the Lord, (as I fear our Friends did on Sunday) by wishing to cast Lots, to find where the Ark should rest. And mar the pleasure of all the Friends by holding a contention on the subject the whole of the afternoon, which our Friends Crocker, & C. Hill did. . . . Although Dear Friend this Pearl of Great Price is going so far

> distant from us, I shall not require a Bond of £2,000 for its safety (as Mr Caleb Hill offered on Sunday, if it was placed in Mr Sandals possession) Because I can discern the hand of God in it, and am perfectly satisfied to let it rest with Him whose suretyship is Sure.[7]

Thomas Crocker also wrote to explain why some of the Somerset friends had proposed John Sandell of Cheddar as a worthy custodian of the Box. They had understood by the circular that one or more of the Oldest Believers would be appointed, so they thought it would be a good idea for Samuel Jowett, as the Sealed representative of Yorkshire, and John Sandell, as the Sealed representative of Somerset, to act jointly. On the other hand, they were perfectly satisfied with the choice of Samuel Jowett.[8]

Several letters warned about the machinations of Lavinia Jones, who had been publishing circulars and canvassing so-called believers in an attempt to gain possession of the Box of Sealed Prophecies. Joseph Graystock wrote from London with rumours that she was resorting to tricks 'worse than in 1840' and had gathered signatures, not only by false pretences but also by vilifying the characters of honest men.[9] The urgency of the situation became clear when it was reported that Daniel Jones had called on Foley's sister, Esther Pickthorn, at North Cadbury Rectory on 10 June and asked her to hand over the Box of Sealed Writings. She refused. Then, on 14 June, Lavinia also paid her a visit, only to find herself very coldly received, and her request denied. On this same day Samuel Jowett, who had travelled south via Bristol to stay with the Stuckeys, arrived in Burnham-on-Sea, and sat down immediately to write to Esther Pickthorn to ask when it would be convenient to call on her to collect the Box. Her reply came on Sunday morning.

> North Cadbury Rectory, June 15, 1861
>
> Sir, I shall be happy to see you on Monday morning, but hope you will be able to come in the early part of the day, as I expect after one o'clock to be engaged.
>
> I am, Sir, yours truly, Esther Pickthorn.

Accompanied by Sealy Stuckey, Samuel Jowett left Burnham on the Monday morning at seven o'clock, and arrived at North Cadbury before midday. Pleased with their reception, they took the opportunity to ask questions, such as, had Foley left any instructions in his Will about the Box? She answered, No. They then asked about Foley's last illness and death, and learnt that he had been in poor health for some time, had suffered an apoplectic fit whilst at dinner on 11 May, and

*Samuel Jowett (1784-1876), fifth Custodian of the Box. An ardent follower of Joanna Southcott, he produced many pamphlets and as a preacher and prolific correspondent was regarded as the leader of the movement in the north.*

had died five days later. Esther and her sister had been telegraphed for, but by the time they arrived on 14 June, Richard was in a coma.

Jowett asked if there were any other writings in Richard's possession besides the Box. Esther went to look and returned with an armful of sealed packets, books, and beautiful gifts that had been made for Shiloh. After that the conversation was frequently interrupted by her leaving the room to fetch something else that she remembered. Eventually she presented Jowett with a key and drew his attention to a slip of parchment tied to it, on each side of which was written: 'JOANNA'S BOX'. The Box itself was delivered to Jowett and Stuckey on leaving. Although it was already nailed down and apparently locked, they had taken a new cord with them to put round it for security. Having transported it to Castle Carey railway station, the station master decided that it looked much too heavy for the normal weight allowance and had it put on the scales. It weighed 156 pounds, which was forty pounds over, so they had to pay the excess.

They were back in Burnham by about eight o'clock that evening and took the Box to the Stuckeys' home in Regent Street. 'Had you seen the faces of all the family on its arrival here, you would have thought some unexpected good news of importance had arrived that caused them all to be nearly frantic with joy. The Box will remain here till I leave for Yorkshire,' Samuel reported to his son, John Marshall Jowett, before asking him to address a few lines to Mrs Pickthorn, thanking her on behalf of the friends for keeping the Box safely till his arrival. He also enclosed a copy of the receipt that he had given to Esther Pickthorn earlier that day:

> This is to certify that I have this day June 17, 1861, received at North Cadbury Rectory, from Mr Bache and Mrs Esther Pickthorn, executors of the late Rev Richd Foley Rector of North Cadbury Somerset, the Box of Sealed Writings belonging to the late Mrs Joanna Southcott, committed to my care by the believers in her Divine Mission, as a deed of trust on their behalf.
>
> Samuel Jowett, 58 Elmwood St, Leeds.
>
> Witness to the above, Sealy Stuckey, Burnham, Somerset

In a postscript he added, 'You may print what you think proper of this letter and send 20 copies to me.'[10]

John Marshall Jowett quickly circulated the good news so that believers, especially in the North, could rejoice at the prospect of the Box of Sealed Prophecies coming into their midst. Thomas Molineaux, a school master in Warrington, had recently taken advantage of a general holiday to visit believers in Manchester, Salford and Stockport. He

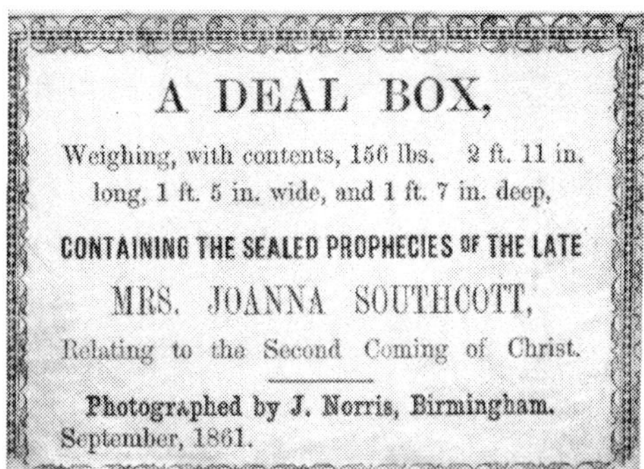

A DEAL BOX,

Weighing, with contents, 156 lbs. 2 ft. 11 in. long, 1 ft. 5 in. wide, and 1 ft. 7 in. deep,

CONTAINING THE SEALED PROPHECIES OF THE LATE

MRS. JOANNA SOUTHCOTT,

Relating to the Second Coming of Christ.

Photographed by J. Norris, Birmingham.
September, 1861.

*The Box of Sealed Prophecies as photographed in 1861 by John Norris after the death of the Reverend Richard Foley, its fourth Custodian. What we see is the travelling case referred to by Samuel Galpin in 1861, and Joanna's original Box should be inside. The dimensions of the outer case are given on the reverse side of this faded* carte-de-visite.

saw profound significance in the sudden emergence of objects connected with the Cause. 'It seems to betoken that the believers long hidden from the view of the world are soon to come out of obscurity, and the truth darkened through unbelief be made to shine forth again,' he wrote to J.M. Jowett. Apart from the Box, there was the magnificent crib prepared for Shiloh which had the previous year been donated by W.A. Howes to Salford Museum, where it was publicly exhibited

> bringing strikingly before our minds the strong love and faith of the believers who provided such a costly offering, and this year along with the 'Ark of the New Covenant' moving before us, as the Ark did before the Children of Israel to find out a resting place for them.[11]

There were one or two discordant voices. The heirs of W.B. Harrison criticised the way that the Jowetts, father and son, had manipulated the situation. When they also objected to Samuel Jowett's becoming custodian of the Box on grounds that he spent too much time away from home, Matthias Crossley suggested that 'if this is the case he is bound . . . either to remain at home to protect its contents by his presence, or to place it in such a situation that there is every reasonable probability of its safety from burglars & from fire; his responsibility is great, and he cannot evade it; it is great in the sight of God & man'.[12] Nevertheless, Crossley raised the question with his cousin, John Marshall Jowett, who said that his father proposed that in the event of his leaving home, Samuel would transfer the care of the box to him. This did not please Matthias Crossley, who declared that those who had voted for Samuel Jowett had not voted for his son, and Samuel Jowett had no right to delegate his trust.[13]

In general, however, the believers expressed their approval. 'We feel great pleasure at the turn which these events have taken,' wrote R.H. Norris from Birmingham. 'We do not think Mr Jones did himself much credit in the way he & his wife acted in the matter but on the contrary it seemed to us a piece of great folly.'[14]

The perpetrators of this folly had not given up their campaign to gain possession of the Box, but now they turned to subtler means. On 28 June, Lavinia Jones wrote from Bradford-on-Avon to ask Samuel Jowett, who was still at Burnham on Sea, if he would care to go to her house to peruse some Communications which were not to be seen elsewhere.

> It occurs to me that here I am with all these boxes of MSS [manuscripts], visions, and books, etc etc – all open for believers to visit, and many MSS original with Joanna's own signature which were among Mr Ingall's books, and which have never yet been circulated. . . . It seems such a pity that now Mr Jowett is so far from Leeds, that he should not take advantage of all he can, in visiting this hill. Miss Stuckey could lead the way having once been here. I write this from the sincerity of my wishes to do what I can to offer Mr Jowett and all friends (as I did when I first saw him in the year 1838 or 9) all I had brought for the benefit of all. And now I know that I can add much information to this great and glorious work, and I repeat my invitation for a quiet, domestic friendly visit, as is the duty of all – seeing how the last strokes are approaching.[15]

Believers who knew Lavinia were immediately apprehensive. 'I hope neither your worthy father nor any other friends will enter her door,' Miss Mallinson warned J.M. Jowett. 'She failed to gain her ends over the late Rev R.Foley. She is now trying a new dodge which I trust they will all see thro' & not one of them set foot in her house. I have wrote a few lines to your father to this effect. Hope you will do the same (if you have not) I could not rest till I did so, but at the same time I trust they *all* will be aware of her *arts*.'[16] Matthias Crossley was also worried that his uncle might fall into Lavinia's trap.

> I cannot pretend to say what is her ultimate object in giving this invitation, but I think he ought not to accept it; I think he is not a match for her wiles; if he avoid contact with her, he will so far do wisely; I shall feel some relief when I know he has left the neighbourhood in which she resides.

Perhaps they would have been less worried if they had realised what personal problems Lavinia was facing at that time. She had not only been unwell but matters between her and Daniel had reached such a sorry state that she was spending less and less time at Bradford-on-Avon. As usual, she confided in her friend, David Wells.

> I have had so much anxiety lately – I cannot always bear up – I am now waiting to receive letters – about finding me a room in London and if that is done I may send up some furniture and keep a place in London. You must try to take a run down here while the cheap trips are going. I will let you know when I am in London. Mr J[ones] is still firmly persuaded in G Turner completing what was begun by our one and one only Spiritual Comforter.[17]

David Wells decided to act on Lavinia's suggestion and take a cheap excursion to Bradford-on-Avon. Writing to him in August, after Lavinia had left for London, Daniel sounded pessimistic.

> Your note is before me in which you seem to fancy a run to the West in hopes of finding Shiloh's Throne, were I inclined to travel for that purpose I should go to the North in hopes of glad tidings. . . . [Y]ou may find what I cannot; I once had an expectation of finding Jerusalem, the gate that led to Paradise or some other Holy spot, but now the cup is dashed from my lips and neither North, West, South or East furnishes any clue to the inner temple. . . . If you should wend your way to the West and spend a day or two with us and could bring a few of Sibley's writings in your packet I should like to see them as there may be some corn amongst the chaff and I like to be gathering if I can also avoid being scratched by the thorns.[18]

Meanwhile, Matthias Crossley was scandalised by the fact that his uncle, Samuel Jowett, had not yet returned to Yorkshire with the Box of Sealed Prophecies and did not seem to be taking his responsibilities as custodian seriously enough.[19] When he did eventually arrive at 58 Elmwood Street, Leeds, Samuel announced the fact to the friends:

> It is with pleasure that I inform you I arrived safe at home on the 30th September, with our *treasure*, the Box containing the ARK of the NEW COVENANT, without any mishap taking place to it or me; thanks and praise be for ever ascribed unto our Heavenly Father for his care and preservation while on the journey, and for preserving my home when absent.[20]

In 1862 the Great Cause became once more the subject of national debate as the case of Thornton versus Howe, which had been dragging on since Ann Essam's death in 1844, came before the Master of the Rolls for final judgment. Caleb Hill felt so strongly that he wrote to Sir

John Romilly urging him not to give a decision until he was in possession of sufficient evidence about Joanna Southcott to guide his opinion in the case.[21] Renewed interest in Joanna Southcott was reflected in the gathering which took place that July in Little James Street, Gray's Inn Lane, London, where followers came to meet Samuel Jowett and his son, John Marshall Jowett.[22] The organiser of the meeting was George Bennett, who lived in North Finsbury. He was a friend of Lavinia Jones, who often delivered pots of cream to him from his West Country friends, whilst he supplied people like John Vincent and Thomas Molineaux in Warrington with Southcott manuscripts to copy. The Bennetts' home acted as a focus for believers, and when Richard Hill Norris came on a visit from Birmingham in October, 1862, he found several London friends came to North Finsbury to meet him.[23] Later that month Mr Taylor brought his daughter and granddaughter to stay with the Bennetts so that they could visit the Exhibitions in London, and Taylor described an angry exchange he had recently had with Sealy Stuckey about the birth of Shiloh.[24]

By December Lavinia had gone home to Bradford-on-Avon whence she wrote to James Hayward junior the following April in a spidery hand, apologising for not writing before but admitting that she had nothing firm to say.

> Family affairs are keeping me in abeyance and [I] have no money-power wherewith to move. If I were at work upon Engines & wood & stone for Temporal things I should brisk about and do as merchants do – but – the building of the Spiritual Church is another affair altogether. . . . I am longing to be at active work – but at present have no powers. . . . But my young friend let us be clearly satisfied in our own minds – when we lift up our wings & sail forward – or when we drop these energies and keep still – I will tell you as soon as I know myself. I should very much enjoy a longer party here at Whitsuntide – but none of us seem ready! It looks as if I shall hence to go to London but it is impossible to tell.[25]

While Lavinia lamented that her work was in the doldrums, others were being dragged unwillingly into arguments. John Marshall Jowett, for instance, had fallen out with James Kidd over the Box of Sealed Prophecies which, he insisted, should come to him, as of right, after his father's death. Thomas Molineaux agreed with Kidd that Jowett's son had no more right to the Box than anyone else and was acting reprehensibly. 'It appears the devil is trying to make head against us, by working contentions about the box,' Molineaux wrote to George Bennett, 'when we need not trouble ourselves about it as the Lord is sure to see that it shall be in safety until the time comes, that they will be enquired after and demanded'.[26]

In the midst of this dispute with his uncle, John Marshall Jowett was possibly gratified to receive a respectful letter from Daniel Jones, explaining that he was about to publish some tracts on Shiloh compiled from Joanna Southcott's Books and wanted to know if J.M. Jowett still published the *Bradford Advertiser* and, if so, what were his advertising rates and would he encourage correspondence on prophetical subjects. Jones also asked after Samuel Jowett and what hopes he had of Joanna's return to carry on her mission.[27] The fact that Samuel Jowett believed that Joanna would return in the body had become another bone of contention among her followers; Sealy Stuckey tended to agree with him, but David Wells maintained that Joanna would return as the Man/Woman or Second Adam.[28] As the debate raged on among believers, Daniel Jones was preparing to enter the fray for one last time with a direct challenge to those who claimed the right to withhold the Sealed Writings from the world. He issued the following circular and voting forms:

> TO THE BELIEVERS IN
> JOANNA SOUTHCOTT'S WRITINGS
>
> THE REVELATIONS given through JOANNA SOUTHCOTT, and published to the world, from AD 1801 to 1814, present to the reader one of the greatest Wonders of the World, ancient or modern; but, through some error, in not opening a BOX of Sealed Writings at the death of JOANNA SOUTHCOTT in 1814 to know the WILL of the Lord, there has been, since that time, a death to the circulation of the Word; which death cannot be succeeded by a resurrection of the Word until the Box of Sealed Writings are openly published to the world: I therefore send forth this opinion, and most earnestly submit the proposal to all believers to sign one of the two Voting Papers I herewith present, to know how many votes there may be for keeping the writings sealed as they now are, and which have been given to the care of Mr SAMUEL JOWETT by the Executors of the late Rev R. Foley, and also how many will vote with me to have them openly published under the care of an appointed Committee of Believers.
>
> I remain, Yours truly, DANIEL JONES, Bradford-on-Avon, Wilts. February 1865.[29]

Jowett's response was to draw up a counter statement addressed 'To all whom it may concern:'

> This is to certify, That I, Samuel Jowett, Leeds, in the County of York Have had committed to my care (By the executors of the Late Revd Richard Foley, Rector, Castle Carey, Somerset) A Box Containing *Sealed Writings*, Belonging to the Late Mrs Joanna Southcott, To be preserved *Unopened* till Demanded By Ministers, mentioned in A Communication taken from the Sealed Writings in 1802, beginning with the Following Words: 'When they see the Truth in Public Print, etc.' and also in *many other Parts of Her Writings*. This is to Testify Should my death take place before the Box and Writings are Demanded (as specified in the Passages alluded to) By the Bishops and Clergy That I Hereby Leave them to the Care of My Son, John Marshall Jowett, Printer, Bradford in the County of York. *To Preserve Unopened* Till Demanded By the Authorities above Alluded to, as Witness My Hand and Seal.[30]

The following year he signed a formal 'Disposition of the Box of Sealed Writings':

> I hereby bequeath to the custody of John Marshall Jowett, my son, the Box of Sealed Writings of the late Joanna Southcott . . . to be by him held in trust unopened until demanded by the Great and Learned. Signed by the Testator, as his last will and testament in our presence, this 23rd Day of September 1866. Signed: Samuel Jowett. Witness[ed]: Joseph Hebblethwaite; Sarah Taylor; Edwin A. Jowett; Mary Jowett.[31]

It is not clear how much time Lavinia Jones spent with her husband in this last year of his life. She was in London in the late spring of 1866, meeting David Wells, Thomas Molineaux and Frederick Greed. She took the latter to a lecture on the Theory of Spiritualism, an 'entertainment' then highly fashionable. Mr Greed wrote to a friend on 24 May, 1866:

> [N]ever was a more aristocratic audience – churchmen, doctors and private gentry. . . .You have no doubt heard of this Spiritualism but it prevails very much here amongst the higher class of people. It is a lady lecturer. I think she comes from America – she is supposed to be under the influence of the Spirit to answer any questions put to her. . . . Mrs Jones, I believe, is in favour of Spiritualism under this system. . . . I have seen some very strange things since I came to London – there is a woman Mrs Jones took me to see by the name of Mrs Marshall, a believer in J. Southcott, but she informs me that she is visited by the spirit as Joanna was. I spoke to her for some time and advised her to be very careful by what Spirit she was visited.

Although impressed by the answers he received to questions about his parents' health, Mr Greed dismissed the medium as a 'vulgar working woman – not at all spiritual in appearance and her expenses are met by her profession'.[32]

On 27 November, 1866, Daniel Jones died at his home in Bradford-on-Avon. He was seventy years old and shortly before he died he had been painting a series of Joanna's visions, some the size of a table and very beautiful.[33] If those who had found Daniel Jones a thorn in the flesh registered a sense of relief at his passing, this feeling was soon overtaken by events. On 5 March, 1867, Samuel Jowett's son-in-law, William Bowes, suffered severe injuries in a train that crashed in the Bowling tunnel between Bradford and Low Moor.[34] In July his nephew, Matthias Crossley died, aged fifty-nine. Samuel's sister, who was over eighty, was very unwell, as was Miss Mallinson and James Kidd. 'From the foregoing you will see that the small number of believers in Yorkshire are getting fewer so that indeed we are a little Flock,' Samuel Jowett wrote to George Churchill in Somerset, 'but the Promise still stands on record – Fear not little Flock'.[35] A memorial card sent out the following year recorded that James Kidd of Binns Cottage, Southowram, died on Thursday, 30 January, 1868, in his 77th year, and he was interred in the Borough Cemetery, Halifax.[36]

Lavinia, meanwhile, left to face the chill winds of widowhood, found them colder than she had imagined. Daniel, a wealthy man, had taken care of her interests in his last Will and Testament made six weeks before he died. It came as a dreadful shock to find that he had added a Codicil to this Will one month later, substituting the name of his solicitor for that of Lavinia as trustee and executor, which meant that she was left with no control of his assets. It seems that Daniel, aware of his wife's passion for the Cause, had decided to safeguard the inheritance of his young nephew, Charles John Jones. Lavinia would have a life interest in his properties but would not be able to invest the capital in printing manuscripts or sponsoring public meetings. Lavinia, naturally, contested the validity of the codicil, and it took eighteen months before the matter was resolved. When the court pronounced for the force and validity of the Codicil, the effect on Lavinia was traumatic.

'I will give you a real truthful statement – as to the precise position I am in,' she wrote despairingly to a friend.

> It is a curious state to be in after 45 years of intensest hard work – economy – and much deprivation and then [in] 1866 possessing £2,700 funded property 17 freeholds in houses of my own, purchased with my own private monies. Now I am dispossessed of all and this given to the family of a common

> prostitute – and I am allowed to keep one room as it is which contains my night couch. . . . Now all this is a glaring fact – brought about by simply causing the dying man to put his signature to what was trumped up – and done too while the words were in his mouth "No, no, I do not wish that – no, certainly not." Truth has ever been my motto – and from an infant too much plain truth has many hundred times cut me off from would-be friends. . . . Accept my best wishes and I herewith sign my deep felt belief that a Spirit for life and right mindedness towards God and each other will be aroused – and then the enemy will not be able to tear us all to pieces as he does now.[37]

Lavinia had never been strong and now her health collapsed under the strain. Miss Selina Worthy, a retired schoolteacher, whose family had benefited from Lavinia's generosity in the past, went to stay, but found her patron's ill temper more than she could bear. 'She said I was a burthen upon her because I was afflicted and not able to work about the house. . . . I thought to find a dear gentle kind lady but I met with the reverse,' Selina wrote to James Hayward, 'I hope you won't mention this to anyone because she is so violent at the smallest thing'. But as a believer, Selina Worthy had additional worries. Whilst staying with Lavinia she realised what written treasures she possessed. 'I think Mrs Jones ought to make a will, for who will inherit all these books and papers if she does not. We know life is uncertain till the Kingdom comes, and I think she must be near 70 years old. She was married in 1821 and she must have been grown up then!'[38]

With probate settled, much of Daniel Jones's property came under the hammer and believers feared for the fate of the manuscripts and paintings. Fortunately Lavinia was able to keep the painted visions, the six sealed letters and other items out of the auction. She was also able to buy in what she liked cheaply, because two-thirds of the proceeds came back to her.[39] Nevertheless, her grief was palpable in the black-edged letter she had written on 9 October, 1868:

> Dear Friend,
> I feel it best to write again just to picture to you how things look here. I am sitting in a chair lotted 26 – and yesterday all the things were lotted. Next Tuesday these men come again to arrange for the Sale on Wednesday. As yet I have not had any prospect of deliverance but my health is returned – and those exhausting pains are gone – It occurs to me to propose that I wd give my life interest in some houses – or land for the use of £100 before this calamity culminates – but as to any original

> paper or book I would not for £1000 – and the devil shall feel some years that a woman can and will hold fast what the Lord himself has strengthened her to profess. I have travelled on foot – the length and breadth of this land – England. I have not made myself an easy campaign and I feel there is much more yet to be done. . . . I never will barter the treasures now under my care.[40]

In December, 1868, Selina Worthy visited Bradford-on-Avon again and found Lavinia in much better spirits. She was given Daniel's old room to sleep in and wrote to James Hayward: 'Mrs Jones is very kind to me and does all she can to make me comfortable.'[41] Early the following year Selina took up more permanent residence in one of Lavinia's houses and for a while had nothing but sympathy for her patron. 'Mrs Jones has been most cruelly treated. They made her pay £90 for the papers etc. and £60 for part of the furniture and they have carried off everything else – yet the place appears to thrive.' Selina also mentioned that there was a large room at the top of Lavinia's house being made ready to receive all the writings.[42] By August, however, the women's friendship had again worn thin. 'Mrs Jones has no idea how to treat those with ill health,' Selina complained to James Hayward, before mentioning that Lavinia had booked her into Bath a fortnight before to take the cure.[43] They were joined in Bath by Lavinia's sister, Abigail, who lived in Brighton and had been left a wealthy widow by her late husband, the Reverend William Edelman. Abigail spent a month with Lavinia but, possibly sharing Daniel's fears about her prodigal ways, gave her sister many gifts but did not offer to pay her debts.[44]

Although Lavinia suffered from swollen legs and feet that summer,[45] her ailments did nothing to diminish her zeal for the Cause; nor did her chagrin over Daniel's Will do anything to lessen her respect for her late husband. She was convinced that his publication of the *Sixth Book of Wonders* had been vital and that it was now up to believers to have the six sealed letters 'proved' in the same way that the rest of Joanna's Communications had been proved by her Trials. For the moment, though, she put all her efforts into studying them. 'I wish to read them for I have agreed altogether with our great friend Daniel Jones that there is a link wanting to lead us up to the great judgment day and maybe it is to be found there amongst those letters,' she had written in June.[46] She was disappointed at not hearing from her London friends. Then, when David Wells at length contacted her, it was to say that he was a ruined man and could she spare him some money. She sent him five pounds. He then employed someone to write on his behalf demanding twenty-three pounds in rent from her, which left her feeling outraged.[47] For the rest, she still poured money into good causes and was rumoured the following year to be creating a spacious chapel.[48]

Lavinia spent the cold early months of 1872 painting watercolours of Joanna's Visions.[49] A year later she was in correspondence with Eliza Thornton, Mrs Essam's niece, arranging for her to send down some articles from Hampton, Middlesex, that had been kept in store for her. '[Y]our Boxes are here & they will not be any more expence to you except the railway carriage. The door of the room you occupied was locked & the boxes exactly in the same corner you left them the room was clean & in order ready as though you were expected to return, which I believe was the case. Now about sending them to Bradford if I can get them to Twickenham they would come via Reading to you without so many changes & the carriage ought to be paid from here to insure their safety I could not get the Boxes till this evening too late for luggage train from here.'[50]

Two years earlier Lavinia had hired William Godward, a stonemason, to repair the marble tablet erected to the memory of Joanna Southcott in St John's Wood burial ground.[51] In October, 1874, Godward wrote to inform her that he had made a thorough examination of the tablet and found it in such a sorry state that nothing could be done except replace the facing with a new marble slab 'as the old one is in so many pieces it will never stand long if repared again and will be loose again in a short time through the shaking of the Trains under it, the slate at the back is quite sound it is only the face that is gon – awaiting any further commands from you I beg to remain – Wm.Godward'.[52] After a further consultation in which it was decided to preserve the original marble, the work was put in hand.[53] As a result, on 12 June, 1875, a gathering took place of Lavinia Jones, Eliza Thornton, Mr S.J.B. Pawley, George Bennett, Thomas Copas, Thomas Belsey, and Frederick Greed for the rededication of the tablet, and at the same time instructions were given for the stone on the grave of Richard Brothers and John Finlayson to be repaired.[54] Lavinia paid for the repairs to both monuments.[55]

Little had been heard about the Box of Sealed Prophecies since it had travelled north in 1861 in the safekeeping of Samuel Jowett of Leeds. Samuel, once a prolific correspondent, was now over ninety and finding it difficult to hold even a pencil. A dismal letter from his son, John Marshall Jowett, in October, 1875, mentioned that he had not heard from many people lately, and that 'In the cause the friends seem all to be dying out – Very few are left and none, so far as I know here, coming in. It is, however, the Lord's own work, and He will bring it about in His own good time. May he speedily hasten his work. The double 7 has been noted by several; we cling to straws as drowning men.'[56] But if Samuel Jowett had been expecting great things from the double seven, he did not live to see them. He died, aged 92, in the early weeks of 1876.

# 8

# Resting in Paradise, 1876-1918

News of Samuel Jowett's death rang alarm bells for believers who immediately wanted to know what would happen to the Box of Sealed Prophecies. When Richard Foley had died, a voting form had been sent out asking them to vote for a particular name. Afterwards a *List Of The Names Of The Friends Who Voted In Appointing A Trustee Of The Sealed Writings* was published. It showed that there had been an overwhelming majority for Samuel Jowett, who received over two hundred votes. James Kidd of Halifax scored thirty-one; Samuel's son, J.M. Jowett, four; Samuel's nephew, Matthias Crossley, just one. Of these candidates, only John Marshall Jowett was still alive in 1876, and this gave him some claim to be custodian. What counted for more was that the custodianship of the Box had been bequeathed to him by his father in a document signed in 1865. In any event, there seems to have been no dispute about the fact that the Box of Sealed Prophecies was now taken to Bradford, for safekeeping.

When Thomas Belsey of Great Suffolk Street, Borough, wrote to James Hayward to tell him that he had heard that the Box of Sealed Prophecies was still in the care of Mr Jowett's family, he seemed more concerned with the fate of all the books and manuscripts collected by Lavinia Jones, who had recently been hurt in an accident.[1] Believers had cause to feel concern because Lavinia had made no Will and, when she died on 8 April, 1879, at 8 Montpelier Gardens, Brighton, the home of her sister, it was left to Abigail Edelman, as her only next of kin, to settle her estate. It amounted to less than £200, and Abigail arranged for Lavinia to be buried, not in Bradford-on-Avon with Daniel, but near the Reverend William Edelman in Merton, Surrey.

Meanwhile, the Box of Sealed Prophecies was stored in an upper room at Apple Hall, 207 Barkerend Road, Bradford, a substantial semi-detached house that became the heart of John Marshall Jowett's property empire – he would die owning more than two dozen houses in the surrounding area. In his portrait, bearded and strong featured, John Jowett gives the impression of being a typical Victorian patriarch. His wife, Mary, had been born in Cork, Ireland, and was six years his senior. They had seven children, all of whom married except their daughter, Sarah. Of the four sons William Henry became a newspaper

*John Marshall Jowett (1816-1898), sixth Custodian of Joanna's Box. Born in Leeds, son of Samuel Jowett, he settled in Bradford, where he made his fortune as a publisher and builder. A typical Victorian patriarch, he brought up his sons and daughters to reverence the Box of Sealed Prophecies that was stored in his home. He specified in his Will that Sealy Stuckey should become its next Custodian.*

editor; John Samuel, a printer; Joshua Jowett, the proprietor of the Royalty Theatre, Wakefield; and Edwin Armstrong Jowett, printer and bookseller. Two daughters, including Sarah, became music teachers. According to Edwin, their youngest son, all the children were taught to hold both the Box and the subject – Joanna's Visitation and work – in veneration. Others reported that Mrs Jowett was happy to show the Box to interested callers. When Mary Brownell, for instance, visited Bradford from Stockport in 1881, she was disappointed to find John Marshall Jowett away from home on the day she called at Apple Hall. However, his wife made Mary and her friends welcome, and invited them all to go upstairs to see the Box.[2]

To some people John Marshall Jowett appeared dour and 'dogmatical',[3] but an incident related by his youngest son suggests that he had a wry sense of humour. Apparently, one day an American gentleman called at Apple Hall and announced that he had been instructed by the Lord to request the custodian to hand over the Box of Sealed Writings, which he was to take away with him. John Jowett smiled and said that, as the Lord had not informed him of this fact, he could not oblige. The stranger departed, crestfallen.[4]

After his wife died, John Marshall Jowett buried his grief in work and, with all his professional responsibilities as printer, publisher, and developer, he was a busy man whose patience was stretched when he was drawn into other people's disputes. One such dispute occurred in 1887 when the New & Latter House of Israel, or 'Jezreelites' became the subject of controversial reports in the national press. The Jezreelites were a group founded in the mid-1870s by James White, who had renamed himself James Jershom Jezreel and set himself up as a prophet after being expelled from the Chatham group of Southcottians. In 1879 he married Clarissa Rogers, who promptly renamed herself Esther, and the couple toured the United States collecting funds to set up a centre for the elect. On their return they purchased twenty acres of land outside Gillingham (Kent) and started to build a temple large enough to hold twenty thousand people and designed as a vast cube, a hundred feet high, a hundred feet wide and a hundred feet long. Jezreel also began to publish his revelations in a book called *Extracts from The Flying Roll*. The enterprise flourished even after Jezreel's death in March, 1885, when his twenty-five year old wife took over the leadership of the Community and opened new chapels in London, Liverpool, Manchester, Leeds, Lincoln, Ashton, Maidstone, Brighton, Belfast and Glasgow.

In October, 1887, John Marshall Jowett wrote to Mrs Jezreel, pointing out certain errors in an article recently published by the *Daily News*.

Stewart Legg replied on Mrs Jezreel's behalf, saying that she had already written to the editor pointing out the same errors, but he had printed only those corrections which he deemed relevant to the article. Possibly sensing a potential convert, Stewart Legg added:

> Mrs Jezreel is indeed glad to hear that you are a firm believer in the mission of Johanna Southcott as we all are. She feels how much you are losing by not partaking of the feast which the members of the House of Israel are so privileged to partake of. She would be glad to hear from you again & to answer any questions upon the work that you may feel moved to ask.[5]

Jowett's reply on 10 November was couched in terms that left no room for doubt as to where his own loyalties lay, and it offended Legg who demanded to know why, if Joanna was to seal the 144,000 and yet not have a successor, did she not do so? And if Joanna was to bruise the serpent's head and yet not have a successor, how is it that death was still rampant? To Jowett's criticism of the Jezreelites' use of 'thee' and 'thou' in the writings, Legg declared that these terms meant anyone upon whom the Spirit rests and who is used as an instrument to fulfil scripture. As for Joanna's real mission, Legg suggested that it was possible that Joanna herself, like other inspired writers, did not understand her own writings, and, he added, 'Pardon me for saying so, this same want of knowledge has dictated your own letters to us'.[6]

Their exchange had left little room for conciliation. It had also rattled Jowett enough for him to report the affair to his friend, Sealy Stuckey, and even ask for advice. Stuckey replied:

> You wish to know what I would say to such a letter. I should not enter into a long controversy with her, as it appears she wants you to do. . . . How could we be led away to follow a host of prophets, that she mention. . . . if we did we must be very simple. . . . I was sorry to hear you say that you had but such few friends true to Joanna's Cause. Are they led away by this woman? I hope there are more than you mention, that have not bowed the knee to Baal. . . . She attributes your want of knowledge in your letter – but I should not write her a long letter any more for that. A relative called here yesterday – she said that a lady lent her brother-in-law living near Sherborne *The Flying Roll*, but he did not approve of it. I told her it was a false alarm. We have had contentions about our cause several times.[7]

Mrs Jezreel's sudden death the following year, at the age of twenty-eight, left her followers devastated. Her father became Overseer for a time, but failed to hold the community together. The main body moved into London and opened a chapel in Camden Road.

A splinter group, known as the House of Israel and Judah, set up their headquarters at Harrow. A number of North Country groups, calling themselves Outcasts from Israel, became centred on Dewsbury. The great temple, Jezreel Tower in Gillingham, was left unfinished and years later, after its upper walls had been dismantled, found use as a cinema, dancing school, billiard saloon and a Seventh Day Adventist chapel.

In December, 1887, John Marshall Jowett received a letter from Walter Begley, East Hyde, near Luton. Neither signature nor address provided clue that his correspondent was an Anglican clergyman, and Begley did not mention that he was the great grandson of the Reverend Thomas Webster, one the Seven Stars who visited Exeter in 1801. He wrote,

> Sir, I hope you will excuse me, a perfect stranger, for writing to you, but the reason is I have a very large collection of books, manuscripts & pamphlets relating to Joanna Southcott and as I find from them that your father was one of the most prominent 'old believers' I am in hopes that you may be in possession of some books or pamphlets that are new to me, & would be useful to me in preparing for the press an account of the Woman's Church. . . . I am told that you have the sealed writings of Joanna, once in the possession of Mr Foley – I know their history, at least their earlier history, and of course they will remain in your possession till they are demanded in the proper way & by the rightful persons & of this I see no signs at present. I do not refer to the sealed writings when I speak of books & pamphlets that might be useful to me, nor do I refer to Joanna's printed works, or Turner's printed works for I have complete sets of both – but small out-of-the-way pamphlets for or against Joanna, Wroe, etc.[8]

Jowett replied within six days, but still apologised for the delay caused by the fact that he had to work till the early hours most week days. He explained that he would not provide manuscripts, pamphlets, or letters for publication because he believed that there should be no publicity or interference with the Lord's work. The task of believers was 'to wait with patience'. Possibly still smarting from his recent exchange with Stewart Legg, he added,

> The duty enjoined on Believers as amongst themselves, or with those who avow being believers, but take the liberty to act at discretion, whether as Turnerites, Wroeites, or under other names – is *obedience*. This I must observe, or I may lose my 'Crown'. I do not feel at liberty to identify myself as furnishing materials, with any enterprise – literary or religious, which should even have the *appearance of being a departure from the ground of the Visitation; or causing anyone to think I looked in any measure for the resuscitation of the Lord's work by human effort.*

He did, however, give Begley the address of George Bennett in Walthamstow and suggest that the latter might supply him with letters published by the London friends.[9]

Walter Begley, disappointed, wrote again to explain that he was in no way trying to proselytise and so could not understand Jowett's reluctance to supply him with information:

> My own opinion is, until the Bishops of the Church of England come forth to claim the sealed writings the work must be at a standstill, but I am not a believer myself . . . & I have no wish to propagate any doctrines whatever in my history, which will simply endeavour to be a fair & impartial account of the Woman's Church & its various branches, without note or comment from me except perhaps the expression in the preface of my own opinion that Joanna has had but scant justice in the literary world, & that the brand or title of Impostor so universally accepted by the world of letters is altogether wrong & misleading.[10]

On 12 January, 1888, John Marshall Jowett hosted a gathering at Apple Hall to celebrate New Year, Old Style. Sadly, the friends from Stockport could not attend. Mary Brownell wrote to say that she was unwell and in any case always kept the twelfth at the home of George and Mary Taylor, who lived locally. She did not find the situation easy in Stockport where the unbelievers mocked her as 'an old Joanna', but she was firm in her faith and grateful for the day she had gone to see Mr and Mrs Scott [MacLaughlin] who had introduced her to the mission of Joanna Southcott.[11]

William and Mary Scott MacLaughlin lived in the Boat House at Powderham, Devon, where William had plied his trade as waterman. In 1892 William was approaching seventy. He was a friend of Sealy Stuckey, an exuberant correspondent, and someone who took a warm interest in the welfare of John Marshall Jowett, who was nearly ten

*Apple Hall, 207 Barkerend Road, Bradford. This large semi-detached house became the heart of John Marshall Jowett's property empire. Here, in an upper room, Joanna Southcott's Box stood for over twenty years. The house has since been demolished to make way for high-rise flats.*

years his senior. 'I feel vexed at the last part of your letter, for I see that you are alone, and that should not be so at your age', he wrote on 5 May, 1892, before suggesting that he would book into the nearest hotel to Jowett, who should spruce himself up like a smart young man and the two of them would 'go a little into the Town; and have a Bath etc'. This was a reference to the Turkish baths which John Marshall Jowett had established next to the Junction Hotel, Leeds Road, Bradford, but, Scott stressed, it was not bathing but talking with his friend that most interested him.[12]

By 1893 John Marshall Jowett was seventy-seven and feeling his age. In March he made his last Will and Testament, appointing his four sons as executors and leaving his substantial estate to be shared equally by his seven children. A separate clause read: 'I also will to confide in trust to Mr Sealey Stuckey of Paradise, Burnham on the Sands, Somersetshire, the box of sealed writings of the late Joanna Southcott Prophetess of Exeter bequeathed to me by my father Mr Samuel Jowett. That he, the said Sealey Stuckey, shall keep the same unopened until called for by the Archbishops and Bishops of the Church of England And in case of his demise or refusal of the trust then to Mr Wm. Scott MacLoughlin of Powderham Kenton Exeter.'

In one way Sealy Stuckey was a strange choice as custodian of the Box of Sealed Prophecies, because he was aged seventy-nine, which

*Paradise Cottage, the home of Sealy Stuckey and his family near Burnham-on-Sea. The Box was kept in Sarah Anne Stuckey's bedroom until her death in 1918, and it was sent to Edwin Jowett in Morecambe in 1925, shortly before Robert Stuckey sold the house. Renamed Athol, and then Greenways, the building was subsequently used as a nursing home and recently converted into flats.*

was two years older than Jowett. In other ways Stuckey was the natural candidate. He had been a believer all his adult life and his faith was unshakeable. After he had accompanied Samuel Jowett to fetch the Box in 1861, it had rested under his roof in Regent Street, Burnham-on-Sea, for many weeks before Samuel was ready to take it back to Leeds. During this time, whenever there was any debate about the future of the Box, it was deemed important that it go to someone who lived in their
own house and whose whole family were believers. Sealy Stuckey was such a person. When they retired from the baker's shop in Regent Street, he and his wife, Anna, moved into Paradise Cottage, a delightful residence on the outskirts of Burnham. It was situated in the hamlet of Paradise, whose name derives from a local legend that Joseph of Arimathea landed near here on his journey from the Holy Land to Glastonbury, carrying the Holy Grail. Both of Sealy Stuckey's children, Sarah Anne and Robert, became firm believers in Joanna Southcott's mission despite the fact that their faith must at times have been sorely tested.

1883 had been a particularly tragic year for the family. In April, Robert's wife, Albenia, died suddenly of heart disease. Less than a fortnight later, his mother, Anna, also died. The following month Robert's only child, Alice May Stuckey, died of diphtheria. It was a series of shocks that Sealy surmounted, but Sarah Anne was left with nerves so severely shaken that she never fully recovered. 'Miss Stuckey is rather nervous', her father wrote to Mr Hayward in 1889.[13] And again, writing with his condolences on the death of Mrs Elizabeth Hayward the following year, 'I thank you for your kind invitation to attend the funeral but as my Daughter is still very nervous I could not possibly leave home'. It was a sad letter, but his reflection on his friend's death revealed the strong fabric of Stuckey's faith:

> I assure you I felt it much, having known her so many years. I think about fifty years. We can feel assured that she is gone to a world of happiness. She came to see my dear wife a few days before she died and now she is gone to meet her again and other dear friends. We are told in 7B 37p [*Strange Effects of Faith*, Part 7, page 37] that they arrive to the first Heaven on the third day and the saints meet them there.[14]

James Hayward, confectioner of Bridgwater, and another of Sealy Stuckey's lifelong friends, died in April, 1887.[15]

But life for the Stuckeys was not all gloom. In the spring of 1886 Robert had married again. His bride was a former employee, Lily Kirby Herbert, and two years later, after the couple had moved to Bristol to open a restaurant in Wine Street, she gave birth to a son, Ralph Herbert Stuckey. By 1893, when John Marshall Jowett made his Will, the Stuckey family comprised Sealy, his daughter, Sarah Anne, and his son Robert, who had a wife and young son. They were prosperous, well-respected and regular attendees at church.

When, in March, 1894, John Marshall Jowett wrote to ask W.B. Harrison's son for some addresses, he must have been surprised to receive an eighteen page reply from John Harrison, saying that he would have written sooner had he not been so very busy. Harrison lived in Cork and was clearly delighted to hear from a fellow believer, especially one so estimable as Mr Jowett. He asked, '[A]re you the Mr Jowett that has the Box of Sealed Writings in your possession; that were formerly in the care of the late Rev. R. Foley?'[16]

Although by 1895 memories of the Box were fading, one lady visited John Marshall Jowett at Apple Hall that year and later recalled:

> I remember, as we were looking at the Box, the custodian said to us, 'Now at one time we (ie several Believers of the district) found that a mouse was gnawing its way through one corner, so we put it, for further safety, into a larger box.'

By 1895 membership of the little groups of Southcottians was also growing thin. In London the death of John Pye in 1895 caused George Bennett to write to the widow,

> We have forgot how to sing the Hymns without the music. . . . Can you lend us John Pye's music book, then we shall be alright.[17]

On 23 March, 1898, John Marshall Jowett died at 53 Hillside Villas, Bradford, the home of his unmarried daughter, Sarah Procter Jowett. He had nominated his four sons as executors of his Will, but as Edwin

Armstrong Jowett, the youngest, lived at Brighouse, only seven miles from Bradford, his brothers appointed him to settle the estate. Following his father's instructions, Edwin forwarded the Box of Sealed Writings to Sealy Stuckey, who replied on 8 April, 1898:

> Dear Friend,
> I received the Box of Sealed Writings quite safe but not the Key. I thank you to forward the Key. It is called Joanna's Key.
> I hope these Writings will be very soon called for by Divine authority to prepare for the coming of Christ to bring in His Glorious and Peac[e]able Kingdom for a Thousand years. With kind regards I remain yours sincerely, Sealy Stuckey.[18]

Edwin had also found among his father's effects a parcel containing robes, caps, shoes, shirts, tippet, receiving blanket, long flannel, and other garments. Many were accompanied by letters saying that these were gifts made by the faithful 'for our blessed Lord of Lords'. Edwin consulted his brothers and they suggested that he send the items to Salford Museum, where the cradle made for Shiloh was kept on show. He wrote to the curator, but found that they lacked space to display the articles, but would be pleased to have them. Edwin then got permission from his brothers to keep the articles himself, together with some seals, signed and unsigned, a Communication by Joanna in her own handwriting, a large portrait of Joanna by William Sharp, and a declaration sent by the Seven Stars to members of the Government on 29 May, 1802. 'These things I have religiously preserved', he later wrote.[19]

Clearing up his father's estate was a doleful task, for Edwin had not only to deal with things, but with people. John Marshall Jowett had been a conscientious correspondent and it took time for news of his death to reach some believers. Poor John Harrison in Cork was still writing in mid-May with no idea that his intended recipient had died over six weeks previously.[20] In fact, it took two months for John Marshall Jowett's Will to be proved and Administration was not granted to his sons until 23 May, 1898. Five days later his granddaughter, Lilian Oldfield, sent off to Sealy Stuckey a little bag containing the keys to Joanna Southcott's Box that her Aunt Sarah Jowett had just found. She asked Sealy Stuckey to acknowledge that he had received them.[21] But this he never did, because on 25 May, 1898, three days before the keys were sent, Sealy Stuckey had died at his home in Paradise. He was eighty-four and it was said that his dying gaze was fixed on the Box of Sealed Writings that had so recently come into his care.[22]

Until now, every time the Box had changed hands, the name of its

*Burnham Urban District Council, 1908. Robert Stuckey (1843-1931), bearded and bespectacled, is standing fourth from left in the back row. He was the eighth Custodian of the Box.*

new custodian had been made known to the Believers. This time the name of the new custodian had been kept secret and many assumed that the Box had remained in the custody of the Jowetts. For this reason the death of Sealy Stuckey roused no great anxieties among Believers, and the Jowetts readily acquiesced when Sealy's son, Robert, assumed custodianship of the Box in obedience to his father's last wishes. Robert Stuckey was always keen to avoid any publicity that might draw attention to the fact that he had possession of the Box. Not only did he value his own privacy but, because he was living at Clifton in Bristol at the time of his father's death, the role of custodian at first fell on his sister. Sarah Anne Stuckey, who had by now retreated into her inner world and become a complete recluse, lived on in Paradise, cared for by a servant. She insisted on making space in her room for the Great Box of Sealed Writings, which she treated with great reverence.[23]

In 1902 Robert, now sixty, sold his restaurant business in Bristol and brought his wife and son back to live in Paradise Cottage, Burnham, where he could keep an eye on Sarah Anne (and the Box). He entered into years of active retirement. He became a director of Burnham Gas Company and a member of the Burnham Urban District Council, of which he rarely missed a meeting. He had always been a keen sportsman and now turned his energies from cricket to bowls. As a staunch churchman, ardent Conservative and Freemason, his name was familiar to most people in the town, but few, if any, knew about the secret box he guarded in his house.

If, at the turn of the twentieth century, the Great Cause seemed doomed to die out, appearances were deceptive. For, as one by one the old believers departed from the scene, so others arrived to breathe new life into Joanna Southcott's mission. One of these was Alice Seymour. Born at 16 Wyndham Square, Plymouth, on 10 January, 1857, she was the daughter of James Seymour and Lavinia, formerly Day. Her father was a linen draper and from both sides of her family Alice descended from Believers. Her aunt had married John Wroe's eldest son, so her cousins were Wroe's great grandchildren. Moreover, one of Alice's great friends was the Reverend Walter Begley, the Vicar of East Hyde, who had corresponded with John Marshall Jowett. After retiring from the ministry in 1898, Begley had gone to live in Hampstead where he intended, with Alice Seymour's help, to write a biography of Joanna Southcott, but, when he died in 1905, Alice was left to carry out the work on her own. She started the first of two volumes, eventually published as *The Express*, in December, 1907, whilst still headmistress of Headland College, a girls' school which she owned in Plymouth. In 1909, when her book was published, Alice gave up her school and dedicated the rest of her life to publicising Joanna Southcott's teaching.

One of her first tasks was to trace the Box of Sealed Writings. With the help of Samuel Galpin, she made contact with Robert Stuckey who in 1910 invited her to Athol, the house previously known as Paradise Cottage, where she viewed the Box. Years later she was interviewed by the *Daily News* and was reported as saying: 'I have seen the Box. The writings remain intact and sealed as in 1814 with seven red seals. The Box is not sealed externally, but is strongly roped and nailed. It is not in the care of a Church dignitary as has sometimes been stated, but in that of a good Churchman of position and integrity.'[24]

From her cottage at Crapstone, Yelverton, in Devon, Alice Seymour began to edit and issue a monthly magazine called *The Express Leaflets* which included eight to ten pages of Southcott literature, some hitherto unpublished and drawn from original manuscripts in her possession. Annual subscription was three shillings, with sixpence postage, and every edition carried the apology: 'Miss Seymour regrets she is unable to give them away gratis, as she is already bearing a heavy financial burden for the work'. By this she was referring to the reprinting of all Joanna Southcott's sixty-five books, that she had taken in hand. Although success came slowly, Alice Seymour's work paid dividends

*The Reverend Walter Begley (1846-1905), Vicar of East Hyde, Bedfordshire, and a great-grandson of the Reverend Thomas Webster, one of Joanna Southcott's early supporters. Begley inspired and helped Alice Seymour to revive Joanna's cause in the twentieth century.*

and interest in Joanna Southcott gradually revived.

In February 1912 Alice wrote:

> Another unlooked for event has happened this past week. A bishop was visiting at a house, where through the *Expresses* the works of Joanna had been lent. Conversation turned to this subject, and on looking over the books, he declared she was a very good woman, and he would be willing to be present at the opening of the Box of Sealed Writings and that he would try to induce others as well. But on learning from me there must be 24 or their chaplains present, he feels that number is prohibitive. However, this is a great advance and certainly paves the way for a future occasion. . . . We know it must be the 24 elders, who sit *before God on their seats*, that will cast or give up the crowns of their own wisdom before the Throne and the Ark of his Testament when opened (Rev. xi, 19) and they shall reign (or rule) on the earth – this the Bishops certainly do. I do not myself think the Trial can take place for a year or two, but it says that it will be 'hasty and unexpected': also that it will be before the severe judgements as the words 'Hurt not the earth till we have sealed the servants of God in their foreheads' (meaning the name as in baptism) have a great significance: the King and half the nation are yet foretold to sign the Woman's Petition for Satan's overthrow and Christ's Kingdom to come.[25]

Signs of a renewal of interest in Joanna Southcott were seen in the disclosures about boxes, invariably spurious but purporting to be Joanna's, which from this time onwards began to hit the headlines. On

11 February, 1915, the *Daily Mail* carried an article which accurately described Joanna's Box as 'A deal box weighing with contents, 156 lb. Measuring 2'11" long, 1'5" wide, 1'7" deep, containing the sealed prophecies of the late Mrs Joanna Southcott relating to the second coming of Christ. Photographed by J. Norris, Birmingham, September, 1861'. What, however, was far from the truth was the statement that this box came to Mrs Sarah Lea Kenyon from her grandfather, Richard Hill Norris, who was a Believer. To another granddaughter, Mrs Dugard, he had allegedly given a second box, containing several sealed parchments, an inscribed snuff box and silver cup, a scarlet cap and a dark blue robe made for Shiloh, the latter being labelled:

> This robe was made in the year 1814 and put into my hands early in 1815, wich I have faithfully kept, and this day it leaves my hands, October the 9, 1826. Wm Wilson. The people that it belongs to are as follows: William Willson, Timthy Pearce, Joseph Southwick, John Willson, Henry Willson, Mrs Parker.[26]

The Norrises, including Richard Hill Norris, a mathematical instrument maker of Birmingham, were known as a family of Believers and it is probable that they handed down boxes of archives and relics to their descendants. Such boxes were common in Southcottian families who used them to hold the precious copies they made of Joanna's Communications. Some Believers scoured the country for fragments of her writing missing in their own collection, and treasured them as holy relics, in much the same way as medieval pilgrims treasured fragments of 'the True Cross'. In later years these boxes of writings and relics surfaced, perhaps on the death of an old Believer, and were seized upon by gullible people or sharp journalists keen to exploit the column inches warranted by the opening of Joanna Southcott's Mystery Box. Little investigation was made into the provenance of these boxes, some of which contained genuine, others completely spurious, archives. What is clear, is that Joanna Southcott's Box of Sealed Prophecies never featured in any of these public revelations. However, when the attention of Edwin Armstrong Jowett was drawn to the *Daily Mail* article he was shocked and wrote from his home in Morecambe to Alice Seymour, explaining who he was and enclosing photographs of his father and grandfather

> Dear Madam,
> Much has appeared in the newspapers of recent dates respecting the Box containing the Sealed Writings of Joanna Southcott, the prophetess of Exeter. A great deal of what has appeared is untrue, or mere assumption (I think) in order to 'draw'

information from the few believers in her Mission who are living at the present day.

But my object in writing to you is to ascertain if possible if the person to whom *I sent* the Box has been faithful to the trust reposed in him. I am not at liberty to tell you who the gentleman was, but in an article in the *Daily Mail* of Feby 11/15 it is stated that *you* know where the box is and as a picture of the box (or the supposed box) is given, I am at a loss to know by what means this photograph was obtained. . . .

From the article in the *Daily Mail* . . . you would be led to believe that the Box had been in the possession of a Mrs S.L. Kenyon, of Edgware road, London, and that it had been in the possession of her family for many years! Unless there are 2 boxes containing Joanna's sealed writings (and I have not previously heard of any other than the one which came to my father – and which I certainly did not send to Mr Norris of Birmingham) the article which I call your attention to is a tissue of falsehoods. The illustration of the Box in the *Daily Mail* is not a likeness of the one I had in my keeping. Is the box referred to in the *Daily Mail* the one you say you know of but are not allowed to divulge its whereabouts?[27]

Alice Seymour was quick to respond.

Your letter has greatly interested me: I am glad to have the enclosed portraits. I hope I may keep them as their names and personalities have been familiar to me through their letters; so I shall greatly value them. Since I brought out the two *Expresses* . . . I have kept myself surrounded with the portraits of the old prominent believers . . . so that I might take courage from their fidelity. Mr Molineaux I knew personally and greatly admired.

This question of the Box seems to have seized hold of the popular fancy. I have taken no part in this outburst. This latest in the *Daily Mail* on Feb 11th I felt sure was untrue. I expect the woman wanted to see her name appear in print. I promptly contradicted it to the editor. . . .

The gentleman to whom you entrusted the Box still has it as I saw it at his house. He received it from his father as a sacred trust. I always understood his father had received it direct from your father. I am glad that Mr Norris never had it. It may have been a box of writings this Mrs Kenyon received as Mr Norris was a great correspondent. I have been extremely careful to give no clue. I merely said I was quite sure that Mrs Kenyon did not possess the Box. . . .

> I had heard that some of your family lived at Morecambe. Do you know Bishop Troughton of Calton Terrace? He has regularly received all my *Express Leaflets* and has thanked me for them and wished me 'God Speed' in the work.
>
> I am enclosing a portrait of myself just to show you I am no religious crank. My parents and grandparents were all believers; I have loved Joanna's Writings from a child. . . . I have always believed that the Man-child was born on Dec 25th 1814 and caught up to God, thereby perfectly fulfilling Rev XII.[28]

Edwin Armstrong Jowett took time out from his busy schedule as a commercial traveller to reply at length to Alice Seymour.

> Dear Madame
>
> I was pleased to have your long letter, also your photograph and the copy of the *Express*. . . . As a child, and later as a young man I used to sit in Father's 'meeting' room when the believers were assembled, and listen to my grandfather reading from the Bible, and also from Joanna's books, but I could not make any connected sense from what I heard read of Joanna's verses. I have always loved to read the poets, and this was such queer stuff that I rather turned from it than to it. Still I never scorned their faith; and after Mother's (who was also a signed believer) and Father's death, I venerated the relics.

He then described the relics that he had been allowed by his brothers to keep after their father's death and how one of his relations, Fred Lees, a journalist who lived in Paris, had visited him ten years previously and taken photographs of them to illustrate an article on Joanna Southcott that he was writing. 'But I have never heard of the article appearing in any Magazine,' Edwin continued, before going on to remark that,

> Nothing specially important has appeared respecting Joanna's Mission until this year, and some who profess to be believers have been labouring under the impression that this is the occasion when our nation 'is in great jeopardy'. They stated that the box must be opened Jan 12th or that awful judgements would befall our land such as never before had befallen it. In reply to that article. . . . I wrote to the *Yorkshire Evening Post* assuring Believers that the time was not yet, and that the box would not be opened on that date. It seems to me that it is unbelievers, not believers,who want the box opening to gratify their curiosity. My Grandfather and my Father entertained the belief that the time for the opening of the Box will be when our

*Alice Seymour (1857-1947), photographed in November, 1913, at Plymouth, where she was owner and headmistress of Headland College, a private school for girls. After publishing* The Express, *a two volume biography of Joanna Southcott in 1909, she focused her energies on the Cause, moved to Blockley in Gloucestershire ten years later, and founded the Southcott Society.*

> Nation is in peril from an attempt by the Roman Catholic Church to dethrone the Church of England as the State Church. . . .
>
> I know Bishop Troughton very well – am an officer at his Church – the Free Church of England – but was brought up and still love our dear old Church of England. Ritualistic practices compel me to worship *out*side the pale of our Morecambe *Established* Church.[29]

In March, 1915, after forty-two issues of *The Express* leaflets, Alice began to publish the magazine under a new title, *The Two Witnesses* (Christ in the FLESH, and Christ in the SPIRIT). With the country at war she felt her message all the more urgent. She wrote in March, 1916:

> Barak was not successful in the war until he stooped to listen to the Woman, and I see we shall not be so now, until the Shepherds do the Lord's bidding and open the Box of Sealed Writings, when the scenes in England are promised to change; and this is to become the *first* HAPPY LAND to unite all nations under the Gospel. The Lord will not permit the 'nails to be loosed (of the Box) or the Seals broken until the Jews are warned.' We are now sending out the *Third Book of Wonders* to all the leading Rabbis and if any one of them is omitted and will apply to me, I will send it gratis: this is the book that is said will awaken the Jews. Six Jews of repute are to be invited to be present at the opening of the Box, if they express a desire. . . .
>
> Our position as believers in Joanna Southcott's visitation has completely changed during the last two years. Her books are now eagerly read in some of the highest circles in the land. Several of the bishops, too, are now willing to send for the Box, but others are afraid that by so doing they will give the impression that they *believe* in the Writings. This is not the case, as it is only when the enemies are present that the promised WONDERS will be displayed by the lord. These will convince the bishops and convince the Jews who are present of the truth; the latter are the people whose nation will be born in a day – probably that very day. . . .
>
> The bishops, as yet, do not see the necessity to obey the command for twenty-four of their number, or their representatives to be present and thus form a double jury against a double jury, i.e. the twenty-four believers. An attorney is to be present and witnesses called before him and the jury, and carefully interrogated. Thus God has stooped to the laws of man that all may be in order. To the Church of England is

given the privilege of bringing out the truth to the world, because of the fidelity of the three clergymen, who so unflinchingly upheld Joanna's cause: the Rev. Stanhope Bruce, Inglesham, Gloucester; the Rev Thos P. Foley, Rector of Old Swinford, near Stourbridge, Worcester, and the Rev Thos. Webster, Falcon Court, High Street, Borough, London.[30]

Alice mentioned that several of the bishops were now willing to send for the Box, but it was a sensitive situation and she was not yet prepared to name names. In fact, she had been in communication with Bishop William Boyd Carpenter of Westminster Abbey, and was so far convinced that he might be able to persuade his colleagues that she wrote to Robert Stuckey that year urging him to join her in approaching all the bishops. Stuckey declined, convinced that the time was not right. Distrustful of her pro-active campaign, he refused even to correspond with her except through Mr Galpin, a mutual friend.[31] It was also a difficult time for Stuckey whose son, Ralph, joined the colours that April, and was drafted to France the following November. He was a popular figure locally, a keen sportsman like his father and making his way in the banking profession. On 3 May, 1917, he was seen going into battle and later reported missing.[32] It was several weeks before news came through that he had been taken prisoner but had died of his wounds in Wurtt Feldlaz at Fechain. He was twenty-eight.

Robert Stuckey's grief mirrored that of millions who lost loved ones in the First World War. The scale of the tragedy was so vast, the horrors so stark, that many fell to questioning why the war had happened and if there was any kind of sense in it all. It was a climate in which people grasped at anything that promised to shed light on such disasters. As a result, there was an upsurge of interest in Joanna Southcott's Box of Sealed Prophecies and Alice Seymour found herself inundated with enquiries. In October, 1917, she reprinted in *The Two Witnesses*, the following letter which had recently appeared in the Press:

As a great deal of confusion has recently arisen in the public mind respecting the Box of Sealed Writings left by Joanna Southcott at her death, on December 27th, 1814, I should like, as her biographer, to clear up the mystery. Inquiries have daily reached me, and the following reply was sent to a Church dignitary: 'There is only one authentic Box of which we have the names of the successive custodians from the time of the death of the prophetess, when it was placed in the charge of the Rev T P Foley, rector of Old Swinford, Worcestershire. There are other old Boxes , containing copied MSS

> [manuscripts], which are in the possession of descendants of old believers, of which I have one. But these have nothing to do with the GREAT BOX as Mr Foley calls it in his Journal of the Trial of the truth of the Writings, held at High House, Paddington, in 1803. I have seen and examined the outside of this box. It is large, and is strongly nailed and corded; I can vouch for it that it has never been tampered with, but is as left 103 years ago. The past holders, as well as the present, have been men of eminent respectability and of well-known integrity. The present custodian is a staunch churchman, and an active worker in his parish.'
>
> Nothing was placed in this Box but the bundles of Sealed Writings, most of which have remained entirely secret from the moment they were written, as they were commanded to be put into the Box and kept for a future period. It is foretold that it will be sent for by the Bishops 'suddenly and unaware in a time of national danger;' that on its opening all will be convinced of the truth of the Visitation to Joanna Southcott. The scenes in England will then begin to change and this will become the FIRST happy land among the nations. . . .

As Editor of *The Two Witnesses* Alice Seymour added a personal note: 'I do not believe the Box will be opened until *after* the war, as some Communications seem to clearly indicate this.'[33] During the next few months her campaign went from strength to strength as she gained friends for the cause in high places. Chief among these were Rachel Fox, the wife of a Falmouth clergyman and descended from generations of Quakers, and her cousin, Lady Portsmouth. These two engaged the interest of Lady Walburga Paget and Princess Louise, who both took a keen interest in spiritualism.[34] Faced with the submarine menace and a possible threat of famine in February, 1918, twenty-four bishops were persuaded to request that the Box of Sealed Writings be sent to them in London, where Bishop Boyd Carpenter and the Dean of Westminster were willing for the opening to take place in the Jerusalem Chamber at Westminster Abbey. To Alice Seymour and her friends it seemed that, at last, the Church was on the move. The trouble was, the bishops wanted the Box by 6 March and would not wait until May, even though they would be in London at that time for Convocation. Nor would they agree to meet the twenty-four believers for the necessary deliberation before opening the Box. Nevertheless, their request was passed on to Robert Stuckey who, much to Alice Seymour's regret, felt compelled to turn it down. Later she found consolation in the belief that such a turn of events had been predicted:

> as they [the bishops] fulfilled the prophecy that they would come forward suddenly through fear of famine, the next time will be in fury and anger, when they will compel the Box to be brought forward by permitting the simple directions to be carried out.[35]

When Alice Seymour passed on the Custodian's message to her friends, they felt that it was she herself who was standing in the way. Lady Paget wrote to Rachel Fox in April:

> I hope that Bishop Boyd Carpenter will talk Miss Seymour over. She must not at a moment like this insist upon outward forms which can make no difference whatever to the Writings. She ought to facilitate everything as far as her conscience allows.

In the same letter, she explained how Mrs Fox could send a letter to the King via his aunt.

> I would give the letter myself to Pr[inces]s Louise and explain all about it. The thing to guard against most is that if the King is impressed, some silly person should not come & unsettle his mind – Christ when he healed the people said 'Go and tell no man' for He knew the hidden laws of the Cosmos & that is one of them. Believe me yours sincerely – Walburga Paget.[36]

On 20 April, 1918, Lady Paget elaborated on the difficulty of gaining the King's attention:

> I can get your letter to the King but, unless I tie him down in a chair and read the letter to him myself it will be stopped by one of the secretaries or be given to him by the King and they will make fun of it. Joanna Southcott is so little known and the entourage of the King is absolutely ignorant of psychic things and then worst of all they are afraid of being laughed at and compromising themselves. . . . I suggest that you should condense the letter to the King and I have indicated with a pencil what I think will be wise to leave out, but you are the best judge. . . . I have always felt deep down in my heart a terror lest peace should come too soon and England would go back to its old frivolous luxuries, careless, money-grubbing ways.[37]

Lady Paget was clearly giving the matter a lot of thought, for she wrote to Rachel Fox again a week later, to say:

> I think it will be best only to ask the Princess L. to give the letter to the King if Lady Portsmouth would ask to see the Queen and explain matters to her by word of mouth – that would be another matter, and she could hand her the letter for the king. I am going to London on May 15th. If that is not too late I would see Lady Portsmouth about it. One thing you must be quite certain about and that is that Miss Seymour will not at the last moment refuse to have the Box opened for that would wreck the whole thing for ever. . . . There is no doubt but that the present moment is most serious and that any advice we can get we ought to get. It is wrong not to do so. It is quite true that I have no great hopes of finding useful advice in the Box, but at the same time I think it ought to be opened.[38]

Rachel Fox immediately informed Lady Paget that their mutual friend, Helen Shepstone [Helen Exeter] was urging her to see what was being done about the Box. Rachel Fox added that she had decided to try and make her peace with Alice Seymour.

> I therefore wrote what I was proposing to do and asked her co-operation and improvements upon my letter to the Queen, & if she advised such. I am awaiting her reply rather anxiously, I confess. I feel that if she remains an obstruction to the Will of God being done, that she will be removed from the Headship of this movement. If she will not be reconciled after all we have done to solicit it, I think she will surely not be allowed to block the way. That 24 Bishops have gone so far to meet our desires is all to the good for England. I fear we shall have to be driven to greater straits yet – Lloyd George or not – that Church and Nation shall be convinced that the Lord alone shall rule this nation. . . . Mrs Shepstone assures me that I may ask your kind offices to get my letter delivered to Queen Mary if we can get Miss S. to approve.[39]

Rachel Fox also informed Bishop Boyd Carpenter that she had written a letter to the King.

> I feel it right to send it now, as I believe it to be of great importance that His Majesty should know the facts, whether anything comes of it or not. I want you to know what I want to do, and to see the letter in case you should be asked anything about the matter. . . .Your action on behalf of the Bishops has afforded me the greatest comfort through the period of waiting for the time when the Box shall yield its secrets, as I am certain

> it is a great step, and presaging ultimate blessing. As events of dire import to England thicken, the mind of the Lord in the matter will surely be made known to all concerned. He will not let Miss Seymour, or any one, stand in the way of His Will being done when 'the psychological moment' for our country comes. I expect England was not ready in March for the full benefit which there lies for her in the sealed writings, but has to get to her knees in a deeper humility and self purification before her relief can come.[40]

The Bishop's reply was not encouraging.

> My dear Mrs Fox,
> I have no right to dictate to you or to thwart your wish. If therefore you think it well & right to avail yourself of the opportunity you mention, please act as you feel disposed. Naturally I cannot share your view of the importance of the matter. The voice which I hear speaks in other tones; and the attitude of those responsible has shaken my confidence; there seems to be no real wish to know the truth or face it.[41]

On 27 May, 1918, Princess Louise, King George V's aunt, wrote from Kensington Palace, to Bishop Boyd-Carpenter:

> I heard from Lady Paget that you are very willing and ready to speak to the King about the Box. So I have asked his Majesty and he says you may send him the letters – give, perhaps – any way, he is ready to receive it from you. As you have got 24 Bishops to be of the same opinion, why not try? To bring many together in the same belief is a strength and may help many in these anxious times. I am grateful to see strong faith anywhere in what is thought to come from the Almighty, and Faith and Unity is *our one hope* and strength. Yours sincerely, Louise.[42]

Only after Bishop Boyd Carpenter's death in October, 1918, did Rachel Fox discover that her letter had never reached the King.[43]

Meanwhile, on Good Friday, 1918, Robert Stuckey had been dealt a further blow when his sister, Sarah Anne, died at Athol in Paradise, after a long illness. She was seventy-seven and for the last twenty years had religiously watched over Joanna's Box which she kept in her room. Ralph, who had been killed the year before, had been Robert and Lily Stuckey's only child. News of their loss travelled (probably via Samuel Galpin) to the believers in the north.

On 12 September, 1918, Edwin Armstrong Jowett wrote from Morecambe to raise the question of the future custodianship of the Box. In his reply on 1 October, Robert Stuckey gave a brief resumé of the Box's recent history.

> I am glad to note you entertain a lively interest and reverence as to the safety of the Box of Sealed Writings left by Joanna Southcott. As a boy I remember the circumstance of the late Rev Mr Foley of Cadbury, Somerset, handing over the possession of the Box to your grandfather, Mr Samuel Jowett – in the presence of my late father. The Box afterwards came into the possession of your esteemed father Mr John Jowett, whom I well remember. As you know it was afterwards left to the care of my father – who on his deathbed wished me to hold it. . . .
>
> Coming to the object of your letter, which is to know if it is possible for the Box to be placed in your care – this is a question I am not prepared to decide upon immediately. From the correspondence I have had with Mr Galpin I fully understand the London believers are quite satisfied for it to remain in my possession – and I believe Mr Galpin quite understands I will do nothing before consulting or informing him. In a day or two therefore I will write him.
>
> I must inform you I am now childless – my only son, a dear boy, to whom we were most devoted – having given his life for his Country – in France, last year. This has been a tremendous blow to both my wife and self and we are not recovered from the shock. Of late we have been very much away from home and sometimes the idea occurs to us as to w[h]ether we may reside elsewhere – and either sell our house or let it furnished. But this may not take place as we have a very pretty comfortable residence. However, before we make any change – my first care will be the safe custody of the Box. From what I have said, therefore, the matter had better remain in abeyance for the present.[44]

# 9

# End of a new Beginning, 1918-1926

In the spring of 1918 Alice Seymour had left her home in Yelverton and moved to London where she felt better placed to serve the Cause. Then, in October, 1919, she seized on the chance to buy Rock Cottage in Blockley, a house with deep-rooted associations with Joanna Southcott. It had been owned by John Smith, the devoted follower of Joanna, who acted as 'bridegroom' in a marriage ceremony performed six weeks before her death, and it had remained in the possession of Southcottians ever since. Against the evidence, Alice convinced herself that Rock Cottage had been Joanna's home for ten years, and soon the house, seen as a shrine, became a centre for the Southcott Society that she founded.

Meanwhile, in March, 1919, after forty-two issues of *The Two Witnesses*, the title of the magazine was changed again and came out as *The Southcott Despatch*. In the December 1921 issue, after referring to Armistice Day, 11 November, Alice Seymour wrote:

> November, too, is a notable month in the Southcott Writings, and is the last in any year when the Box of Sealed Writings can be opened by the Bishops. . . . The contents – the MSS [manuscripts] placed year by year as ordered, sealed in bundles with seven seals (see Rev.v, i.) still await the faithful zeal of the Bishops to unlock and explore their hidden mystery. . . . Certain it is that the Lord has decreed a time that neither men nor devils can frustrate. It will be an hour of such national danger that the Bishops in their fury at the clamour of the Press and the people will compel the custodian to produce the Box.[1]

If her words were designed to goad Press and people into clamouring, they failed. Two months later she wrote,

> So much apparently must happen to bring the GREAT TRIAL on, to make the Bishops hasten to send for the Box of Sealed Writings the second time. . . . Recently someone printed on a handbill, that the Box must be opened before 1924; there is no warrant for this assertion; I contradicted it *at once,* because a

> similar one was printed in America in a widely circulated handbill, that the Box should have been opened in 1914. It was extensively copied by the Press, and gave me and others a lot of trouble to contradict. We want to consult and work together in our handbill printing, so that they can be freely circulated in this or any other country. It is foolish not to take advantage of those who have read more deeply.[2]

Behind this remark lay a growing conflict between Alice Seymour and other Southcottian groups that had sprung up in recent years.

In November, 1914, Alice had received a visit from Rachel Fox, who had read some of her leaflets and wanted to know more about Joanna. Devastated by the death of her first son in 1894, Rachel had been comforted by the belief that he could communicate with her through automatic writing and had told her that she was being prepared for some great work. She wrote about this to her friend Helen Exeter in Natal, and sent her copies of Joanna's writings. Helen was so impressed that, after writing to the Archbishop of Canterbury urging him to open Joanna Southcott's Box, she set out for England. Upon arrival in 1915, she soon heard about Mabel Barltrop, another friend of Rachel's who shared their belief in Joanna's mission.

Mabel Barltrop, widow of an Anglican curate, had been so affected by one of Alice Seymour's pamphlets that she immediately launched a campaign of her own to persuade the bishops to open Joanna Southcott's Box. However, their lack of interest brought on a nervous collapse that resulted in her lengthy stay in St Andrew's Hospital, Northampton – an experience she later described in her book, *Brushes with the Bishops*. By October, 1916, she was well enough to return to Bedford where she renewed her efforts and in January, 1918, set up an office in her home, appointed a secretary and treasurer, and started to gather in the names of believers. It was the influence of this group that had been largely responsible for securing the co-operation of Bishop William Boyd-Carpenter, who that year announced that he had the names of twenty-four bishops prepared to request the opening of the Box. When this offer was rejected by the custodian via Alice Seymour, who then proclaimed that the time, after all, was not right, a rift opened between the two groups.

After the war the Bedford group flourished. Mabel Barltrop came from a highly-cultured background (her godfather was Coventry Patmore and John Ruskin had been a family friend) and she had a strong intellect. Reading a copy of Jezreel's *Flying Roll* made her realise that Joanna was not the only modern prophet, and she determined to bring together the various teachings. Combining elements from Southcott, Brothers, Turner, Wroe and Jezreel, she published

*Helen Shepstone (1851-1918), photographed in September 1918, just days before she was drowned in a ship torpedoed off Plymouth. Known as Helen Exeter, she was recognised as the 'Seventh Prophet' in the Visitation, and had come to England from Natal in order to persuade the Archbishop of Canterbury to open Joanna Southcott's Box.*

*Keys to the Whole Body of Truth for the Whole Body of Believers*, a booklet that drew many to live in Bedford once they discovered that Mabel herself was a prophet who received Communications. The Community thus established saw itself as the repository of a secret wisdom passed through seven successive prophets – Richard Brothers, Joanna Southcott, George Turner, William Shaw, John Wroe, James Jezreel and Helen Exeter – and once they recognised Mabel Barltrop as the eighth prophet (as in the Book of Revelation), she became known as Octavia. Seeing itself as a society for the gathering of Israel, the Community aimed to live together with as little expense as possible, preparing for the time when the Lord would require all their resources for the establishment of His Kingdom. 'All who subscribe their hands to become members of the Community must live as persons who do not expect to die', was one of their maxims.

In 1919 several members of Octavia's group, including Rachel Fox, experienced a 'revelation' that led them to believe that Shiloh had returned to earth in 1866 when Octavia was born, and that Octavia was in fact Shiloh. The announcement brought pilgrims flocking to Bedford, and as disillusioned Turnerites and Wroeites arrived from America, Australia, and New Zealand, Octavia's dream of drawing together all the strands into one tapestry appeared to be coming true. A new development happened in May, 1923, when Octavia discovered that she had healing powers that could be implemented through the medium of small squares of linen that she had prayed over. As applications poured in for these linen sections that were to be placed in water, which could then be drunk or applied to a wound, the Community adopted a new name: The Panacea Society.

By this time Alice Seymour was ploughing her own furrow and would have little to do with the Bedford group. Ever since she published her two volume biography of Joanna Southcott, *The Express*, in 1910, she had sent an annual letter to Archbishop Randall Davidson. On 18

*Mabel Barltrop, 'Octavia' (1866-1934). This photograph was taken in Bedford and sent to her friends at Christmas, 1919, the year in which it had been revealed to her followers that she was Shiloh.*

July, 1923, the Archbishop's chaplain issued the following note to the Press:

> The Archbishop of Canterbury directs me to acknowledge the receipt of letter respecting the Box alleged to contain certain documents placed in it by Joanna Southcott. The Archbishop has repeatedly urged that the Box be opened forthwith and has done his best to secure that this should be done. Those in charge however, have declined to act save under conditions which would make the whole proceedings farcical. You are doubtless aware that there are rival boxes in different parts of England which claim to be the authentic article. The Archbishop requests that in anything you publish in this matter with regard to himself, this letter be made public.
>
> G. K. A. Bell, Chaplain.[3]

Bell's reference to rival boxes highlighted the problem that faced Southcottians all the time – that the name of the custodian was kept secret. In an effort to dispel the suspicion that there was no particular Box of Sealed Prophecies, or if there was, it had already been opened, Alice Seymour told the *Daily News* in 1923 that she had seen the Box. The *Daily News* canvassed the opinions of the bishops and reported:

> Of the 49 Bishops of the Church of England with whom the *Daily News* has communicated about the opening of the Box, only 21 have thought the matter serious enough to require a statement. Not one of these has offered even to attempt to call a gathering of 24, as required before the Box can be delivered up by the custodian. Six Bishops refuse under any conditions to take part in the opening of the Box; five express no opinion, but plead distance or pressure of business from attending such a ceremony. Two Bishops criticise the conditions attached to the opening, and the remaining eight place themselves unreservedly in the hands of the Archbishop of Canterbury for the settling of the matter.[4]

The article sparked a flurry of letters to the editor, including one from Edwin Armstrong Jowett, writing from 7 Greaves Terrace, Morecambe, on 22 August, 1923.

> Dear Sir,
> The letters which have recently appeared in your columns respecting the Box of Sealed Writings, left by Joanna Southcott, seem to convey an erroneous impression. The Box and its contents are the property of the Believers in the Mission of Joanna Southcott and outsiders are evidently presuming that they can demand the opening of the Box. This is an error: the Box is only to be opened at a time when the nation is in great jeopardy and that time is not yet. Miss Seymour is in error when she declares that she is the only living person (besides the custodian) who has seen the Box, as I was the one who forwarded the Box to the father of the present custodian.[5]

Within days Alice Seymour visited Robert Stuckey and showed him a letter from a lady journalist connected with the *Daily News* which said: 'I have today been informed that Johanna (Joanna) Southcott's box is at Paradise Cottage near Burnham-on-Sea, Somerset. My informant has also given me a history of the box up to its removal there. I am waiting until I hear from you before publishing anything.' The journalist wanted to see the box, and asked Miss Seymour to give her a note of introduction.

Robert Stuckey, antagonised by Alice Seymour's domineering manner, proceeded to reprimand her for writing to the bishops and for publishing private Communications. He reminded her that if the writings were from God, then no earthly power could resist when the time came for them to be revealed. For the present, however, he refused to show the Box as requested, indicating that it was not yet a public matter. Before she left, Alice asked him to keep her informed of any developments. Even this he would not promise, because he wanted to avoid opening any correspondence with her. 'We parted in a friendly way and she complimented me on my firmness and said her visit was in the way of a warning – whatever that may mean', Stuckey wrote to Edwin Jowett, concluding,

> I note your enquiry re the future of the Box – and delighted you have sons who possess the same integrity as ourselves as to its safe keeping. If it passes from me it seems evident it should return to your family. My dear wife knows this. I may refer to this another time. Please excuse more now. . . .
>
> P.S. I do not say to you as to Miss Seymour. But if anything of interest transpires it will be my pleasure to write you. R.S.[6]

*Edwin Armstrong Jowett (1848-1926), and his wife, Emily, at 7 Greaves Terrace, Morecambe. Edwin was Custodian of the Box, 1925-26, and died shortly after moving into the bungalow that he had built and named Southcot. Emily succeeded him as Custodian and took care of the Box until her death in 1934.*

In this way an understanding was gradually established between the two men about what would probably happen to the Box. It would go back to the Jowett family and the future custodian would be Edwin Armstrong Jowett. As if in confirmation of the Jowetts' interest in the Box in September, 1923, the long-awaited article written by their cousin, George Frederick Lees, was published in two parts in *Cassell's Weekly.* It was beautifully illustrated by the photographs of gifts prepared for Shiloh that he had taken at Morecambe twenty years before, which aroused great interest among members of the Panacea Society.[7] As part of their efforts to promote the Cause, the Panacea Society had embarked on a plan to establish a small museum and was actively engaged in bringing together as many books, manuscripts, and relics as they could procure. After they had been approached by Alice Midgley, who lived in Morecambe and was a close friend of the Jowetts, their Treasurer, Hilda Green, sent Edwin Jowett a letter asking whether he would like to sell his collection. His reply was immediate. If they had asked previously, he would have refused. Now, however, his family was under notice to quit the house where they had lived for nearly thirteen years and he wanted to build a bungalow on a piece of land that he owned. He had been thinking of selling the relics to some believers in America, but if the Panacea Society would pay him £250, that would enable him to proceed with the building. He appended a list of articles, books and papers and a note that he had been promised many old letters written by believers which he would forward gratis to the purchaser of the articles listed.[8]

The price was high, especially as the Panacea Society already possessed most of the books and tracts mentioned, but they offered £200, and this was accepted.[9] Alice Midgley took the parcel to Bedford and sent Edwin and his family an enthusiastic account of the Community she found there.

> I had a very pleasant & safe journey, a lovely private motor met me at the station & bowled me along here. Afterwards I went along & had tea with Octavia – motor again. Well? Dear Mr Jowett you would enjoy the business room thoroughly stacked with books & files innumerable & in such an orderly fashion. Everybody seems to be at work & I am feeling something like a drone. A Norwegian gentleman is copying *Fountains of Gardens* & a Frenchman & Madam translating into French. They are all at work in their rooms at the present moment. A meeting is held every evening & very well attended. I cannot say how long I shall be here, the invitation is 'stay where you are'. They were all delighted with the *Layette*, it was opened after the usual evening meeting & the things passed round. It was a good idea to send four photos. There is a photo of Richard Brothers framed and hung up in the Meeting room, so you see I have seen it after all. Also Joanna's Sampler exquisitely done, not in the usual cross stitch, & in lovely silks not wool. Bedford is a nice town & the weather being so mild makes it pleasurable to be out.[10]

Octavia herself wrote to Edwin:

> Dear Mr Jowett
> I enclose a cheque for £200 for the parcel which arrived safely and which we undid when we had got the Believers together so that they all saw the things. I, who am writing to you, am the person who is principally concerned, and I am very thankful

> that you have so faithfully discharged your trust of taking care of these treasures. They are, of course, intensely interesting and very beautiful, & together with Miss Seymour's Collection, which is even more beautiful, they are a valued possession for English Believers. . . . I think you said you would let us have a few more books. It would be very good of you. We are enthusiasts here, and we get all the help we can out of them, for the benefit of the dying world.[11]

The transaction had left a cordial atmosphere. Edwin quickly wrote again to thank Octavia for sending the literature, which he would 'peruse with pleasure'. He also enclosed photographs of his father and grandfather, and invited any Bedford Southcottians to call on him if they ever visited Morecambe.[12]

In March, 1924, the Society's treasurer approached the museum in Salford detailing their own acquisitions and asking if the museum would consider lending the cot prepared for Shiloh.[13] The authorities agreed, and on 15 May the cot arrived on permanent loan from Salford. It seemed as if everything was coming together. The only thing missing was the Box of Sealed Writings. Not that the Panacea Society wanted to possess it, but they needed to know where it was, and that it could be brought forward as soon as the bishops made their request. At the moment their only intermediary was Alice Seymour with whom the Society was barely on speaking terms.

On 25 May, Octavia wrote to Edwin Jowett setting out the problem.

> We are approaching the Bishops once more – this time with a Petition signed by 10,000 people, but my fear is, that *if they write, Miss Seymour will not tell us where the Box is.* As honourable people we have preferred not to know – a secret like that is very sacred. I am sorry that her feelings towards us are so bitter. We have tried all we could to make friends. . . .
>
> Any way we are clear in our conscience, that we have done her no harm and only tried to help her all the time. There is strong public feeling that the Box ought to be opened – but I fear while Miss Seymour is the intermediary, it never will be opened, as she is so bigoted upon the things that have to be done that she will not meet the Bishops an inch of the way, and her answer to the last offer they made, in 1918 to have the Box in the Jerusalem Chamber at Westminster to open it (I have a copy of the letter) has put them all more than ever against it.
>
> I quite agree that conditions must be made and kept to, but the arrangements include the actual return of Joanna, who Miss Seymour says will lie upon a bed (which has to be

*Alice Seymour and assistant, Mary Robertson, photographed in 1933, standing in the Obelisk Corner at Rock Cottage, Blockley.*

> prepared) and will go into a trance. It appears to me that common-sense plays no part in some people's religion.
>
> Our Petition goes in on May 29 – perhaps as Miss Midgley says you know the gentleman who has the Box, you would kindly forward the Petition enclosed, to him, and say that *if the Bishops respond this time, could it be possible that he would act apart from Miss Seymour*?
>
> From what she has told us, it appears to have to go through her. I shall be so very grateful if you will do this for us, as we have spent much labour upon the Petition, and I think 10,000 names ought to tell.[14]

Octavia's letter prompted Edwin Jowett to break the silence that had existed between him and Robert Stuckey for over a year. He wrote, enclosing Octavia's letter, the petition, and his own observations on the split that had opened in Southcottian ranks. He clearly had little respect for Miss Seymour 'the lady . . . to whom you have given the cold shoulder, as she was so persistent you should hand over to her the Box of Sealed Writings'. But the other group, Jowett continued,

> seems to be the more influential and has its Headquarters at Bedford, where they have established quite a hive of industry to spread and speed the fulfilment of Joanna's prophecy. This latter section have obtained from the Trustees of the Salford Museum at Manchester the Cot which was prepared for the use of the child (the Messiah) [of] which Joanna was expected to be the Mother. They have, on two or three occasions, asked me to let them have your address but I have refused as you told me you did not wish to be worried over the matter. . . . The Bedford lot seem more courteous and not so dictatorial as Miss Seymour is, and the remark in Mrs Barltrop's letter that Miss Seymour claims that all applications to you must go through her, shows that Miss Seymour claims to be master of the situation. Personally I don't think the present is a time when the Nation is in jeopardy and certainly not the time for the opening of the Box.
>
> If the Box should leave your care and be forwarded to myself I shall certainly wait until *the Bishops ask* for the Box to be opened and not try *to force* the Bishops to demand its opening as Miss Seymour does. Should you decide to forward to me, may I suggest that you have a strong packing-case made in which to forward it, as undoubtedly there will be people in Burnham on the look out as to where it is sent, to acquaint Miss Seymour.[15]

*Rock Cottage, Blockley, former home of John Smith who went through a form of marriage ceremony with Joanna in London. The house was never lived in by Joanna Southcott but remained in the possession of Southcottians and, after being bought by Alice Seymour in 1917, it became the headquarters of the Southcott Society.*

Robert Stuckey replied to Jowett the following day.

> Yours to hand this morning. I am no less inclined to have anything to do with the Bedford people than with Miss Seymour, in forwarding matters re. the opening of Joanna's Box of S.W. I am very much obliged to you for not divulging my name to Miss Barltrop and others. If my address becomes generally known, there is no knowing to what I may be subject. If the writings contained within the Box are from God, no power of Man can keep them back when the time comes – but it is evident that the time is not now, as I can say No, I decline to surrender them. Really & truly, all must await some divine manifestation. You are at liberty to inform the lady I decline to join her and her party in the steps contemplated, viz to approach the Bishops. You can gather from what I told you about Miss Seymour that I am in no way dictated by her.[16]

Three weeks later, without revealing her source, Octavia reported that she had heard where the Box of Sealed Writings was.[17]

Alice Seymour had meanwhile been joined at Rock Cottage, Blockley, by Mary S. Robertson, a former teacher at her school in Plymouth, who had come to share her home and assist in the work of publicising Joanna Southcott's mission. In 1923 she had written a pamphlet entitled: *The True Story of Joanna Southcott*. In 1924 she embarked on a similar project designed to cover the history of the Box of Sealed Writings, and was put in touch with Edwin Jowett. He wrote to her on 27 November, 1924, and, after giving her a brief summary of its history, made no bones about saying, 'when my father died by his instructions the Box had to be forwarded to a Mr Scott (I forget his address) and in the event of his decease to forward it to Mr Stuckey of Bristol. This I did, & at his death it passed into the care of Mr Stuckey's daughter, and at her death into the care of Mr Stuckey's son – the present holder'.[18]

Mary Robertson wrote back with more questions, but it was nearly a month before Jowett replied.

> As I stated in my last you have all the information I possess – the question of a special cover for the Box I know nothing of. . . . The box when I sent it from home was locked (I presume, though I did not undo the rope with which it was corded to ascertain). . . . Father was one of those who implicitly believed he would never die – that he would live to see Christ's Kingdom come on earth. So did his father. But the Lord willed it otherwise. I quite understand that the opening of the box is to take place at a time when the nation is in great jeopardy – but I don't think that time is the present. As I understand the occasion will be a *religious* war – Roman Catholicism versus Protestantism. Time will decide. . . . The old Joannas were a very devout class of people. Jealousy & self-righteousness will have to be guarded against by the present leaders of the Cause – there are already two Joanna headquarters – or they will wreck the Cause.[19]

Mary Robertson's *Authentic History of the Great Box of Sealed Writings left by Joanna Southcott* was published in 1925. Her timing was good, for that year the country was treated to an abundance of boxes, each purporting to be the Great Box but in fact a sham, or a box of relics left by one of Joanna's followers. First on the scene was the 'Hammersmith Box', which caused nearly every newspaper in early April to sport a headline: 'Joanna Southcott Box Opened', and a description such as: 'Eerie scene in a London Room, where, in the presence of four or five witnesses a small, black, coffin-shaped box, roped, nailed and sealed, was opened.' Its owner, an actor-manager, Mr W.J. Mackay, found inside an old copy of the New Testament, a wisp of silvery hair tucked between its leaves, and a scrap of parchment bearing a prophecy dated 24 December, 1805, supposedly signed by Joanna Southcott. The previous owner of the box, an old lady called Miss Morristown, had suddenly disappeared and, when Alice Seymour sent a facsimile of Joanna's signature for comparison, she found that

*The 'Hammersmith Box.' This picture appeared in the Daily Sketch on 6 April, 1925, and shows the actor-manager, Mr W. J. Mackay, who staged the opening of a spurious 'Joanna Southcott' box at his home in Hammersmith. The box was said to contain a wisp of fine silvery hair and a scrap of parchment bearing a prophecy dated 24 December, 1805.*

the Box and its contents had also vanished.[20]

Later that month the 'Doctor's Box (it belonged to the family of a doctor near Bournemouth) came to public notice. This one contained many original manuscripts and was regarded as a genuine Southcott box, although it had nothing to do with the Great Box of Sealed Prophecies. The fact that it contained a letter dated August, 1839, addressed to Lavinia Jones, led Alice Seymour to conclude that it was one of the boxes acquired by that indefatigable collector.

In May the 'Bradford Box' was launched on a suspecting public. Displayed on the steps of the Town Hall as part of a student Rag, this time it was clearly a hoax. Nevertheless it showed how much Joanna's Box had caught the public's imagination.

Once Mary Robertson's booklet on the Great Box was published, she sent a copy to Edwin Jowett and told him, 'I have reserved some interesting information you were so good as to send me, for a small book later on; but as there has been a steadily increasing demand for some short history of the 'Great Box', we felt something short should be got out now'.[21] That 'steadily increasing demand' for information about the Box was due to the massive press and poster campaign that had been mounted by the Panacea Society every year since 1923. Robert Stuckey, however, was a member of the 'passive' school and did not hold with the methods of this 'Forward Movement'. 'If true, God will work in His own time and method in the fulfilment – but that time may not be just yet', he wrote to Edwin Jowett on 23 July, 1925.

> I note the sensational opening of a Box at Hammersmith and that they are now looking towards Devonshire. Miss Seymour

*Cartoon from the Star, 16 November, 1923, showing Stanley Baldwin, dressed as Joanna Southcott, perched on her box containing details of the trade tariffs that he considered essential to reduce unemployment.*

*Cartoon from the Daily Courier, 20 March, 1925, showing the Chancellor of the Exchequer, Winston Churchill, 'sitting on' details of his Budget which, like Joanna Southcott's Sealed Prophecies, were not yet ready to be revealed.*

> knows of the one I hold in my possession. I think I have already told you how firm I was with her about it and am thankful she does not trouble me now. I am most jealous to keep it from their grasp. I feel, however, that at my age, I may now consider the advisability of putting it into reliable hands. As your family has been so associated with it so much in past years, you are the proper person to hold it. I feel this all the more as you have a son, actuated with the same firm views for its *preservation, until properly demanded by the Nation* – and that he would remain firm in his generation.
>
> Another thing that prompts me is that I may be moving into a smaller house, as only wife and self remain of our family. If, therefore, you are of the same mind as you have before expressed to me, very desirous of holding the Box, I will with much feeling have it forwarded to you. Or if you may be coming down West, you may come for it and superintend its removal. Perhaps I may be hearing from you as to this. I note you have built and removed to a new Bungalow. I hope you may live long and enjoy it.[22]

The Jowetts' new bungalow had been given a significant name – *Southcot*. Edwin Jowett replied immediately to Robert Stuckey's letter.

> I am quite prepared and willing to take charge of the Box of Sealed Writings, whenever you decide to forward them; on the same definite promise and condition that it was forwarded to your dear father, at my father's request – 'to preserve the same *unopened* until such time as demanded by the Bishops of the Protestant Church of England at some time when the nation is in great jeopardy.'
>
> I distinctly disapprove of the action taken by Miss Seymour in trying to force the Bishops to demand the box – in order, as I take it to gratify her curiosity. Her advocacy of the cause as it seems to me, savours too much of a business transaction; as witness her pushing her own and Joanna's works at top prices. She strongly advances and supports the idea that Joanna was really delivered of the child 'Shiloh', but that it was at once caught up (unseen by those present) to the care of the Lord. My grandfather, Samuel Jowett, of Leeds, and my father strongly refuted this idea; and both of them implicitly believed that Joanna would be raised from the dead to give birth to the child; and in support of this strong faith, they argued that with the Lord, any course was possible, to establish the second

*Southcot, the bungalow built in Hawarden Avenue, Morecambe, by Edwin Armstrong and Emily Jowett. After Joanna's Box arrived here in 1925 they kept it hidden under their bed.*

Coming on earth. . . .

Now with regard to your proposal to send the Box of Sealed Writings to my care and my son's after my time, much as I should like it, I cannot afford the expense the journey would incur, as it takes all I can scrape together to provide for my home, and repay the mortgage, and other expenses. So I must fall back upon your other proposition – the *sending* of it by rail.

May I suggest that you get a battened case of inch thick wood in which the box will fit tightly. Then nail it up and despatch it by goods train to: E.A. Jowett, Hawarden Avenue, South Road, Morecambe. Don't mention the name of house, as that might give a clue to inquisitive people.[23]

So there it was, the question of custodianship settled – except that Robert Stuckey was not a man to be rushed. 'Must say it is gratifying to know we are so agreed on points relating to the past and possible future,' he replied, but, 'As the holidays are almost on – and no knowing, as yet, what may happen re. Coal Strike – I think it best to postpone forwarding Box *pro tem*.'[24] In fact he delayed until 17 September before taking it to Highbridge Goods Station and sadly relinquishing it.

I part with the Box with much feeling, remembering its associations and anticipations. One of two things however prompt me, viz. my advanced age and that it is my duty to anticipate the future, as I have no relative to whom I can pass it. It is therefore a comfort to pass it on to you who express yourself so willingly to undertake taking charge of it on the same conditions held by my late father and myself and, long before this, by your esteemed father and before him your grandfather, Mr Samuel Jowett. I personally remember all about this in the sixties of last century. Then again I am prompted by the knowledge of your having a son possessing the family enthusiasm, viz. to keep intact the Box until *properly* demanded by the Bishops, etc.

> I therefore do not know how I could have parted with it except to you and yours. For many years past many things have occurred suggesting great anticipations. But may we not ask, what about the present outlook? Really we must 'wait and see,' we can hardly venture to comment. You know I shall be anxious to hear from you as soon as the Box is delivered.[25]

Stuckey was even more anxious when he heard from Edwin Jowett a week later that the Box had not yet arrived, and he immediately called at the station where an official promised to write off about it.[26] But there was no need. Jowett wrote that same day:

> Dear Mr Stuckey, The box arrived safely this afternoon, and is, apparently, in the same condition, corded across three times, and once lengthway; secured by a lock, and nailed at the top, as it was when I sent it to your father, from Apple Hall, Barkerend, Bradford, in 1898, after the death of my father. My son, Cecil K. Jowett, was at my house when it arrived, and signed for it. Let me assure you that the trust you have placed in me will not be abused – as up to the time of my death it will be preserved carefully and remain unopened – unless, prior to that time it is demanded of me by 24 Bishops of the Protestant Church of England, at some period when the nation is in great jeopardy. Like my father, and his father, I long for the great Advent – the coming of the glorious time of the Millen[n]ium. If your and Mrs Stuckey's health and strength permit, my wife and myself will be so pleased to see you next summer, if you dare travel so far. With every good wish to Mrs Stuckey and yourself, I remain, faithfully your friend, Edwin Armstrong Jowett, aged 77 last 21st June.[27]

Mention of the lock reminded Robert Stuckey of the key, which he had forgotten to send with the Box. He declared that he had never inserted it in the lock and would have considered it sacrilege to even try, and he promised to forward it as soon as Jowett let him know if he would like to receive some of Sealy Stuckey's old books and manuscripts, that were stored in his loft, and a quilt that had been made for Joanna. With regard to other Believers, Stuckey's only correspondent was Samuel Galpin and he had decided, for the time being, not to let him know that the Box had changed hands.[28]

The cold weather set in early that year, preventing Robert Stuckey from sorting out his father's papers, but he sent Jowett the keys on 14 January, 1926, explaining that

> these came to hand in the year 1898 a few days after the death of my father to whom they were addressed. They were sent on to me at my private house in Clifton. These particulars you will see by the accompanying letter signed L. Oldfield, with memo thereon made by me. I shall have letter containing Keys Registered and perhaps when received you may let me know.[29]

Robert Stuckey, now eighty-three, felt the cold dreadfully that winter and was ill over Christmas. No sooner had he recovered than his wife collapsed with heart trouble and was confined to bed for six weeks. Convinced that she would benefit from a change, he decided to let their house to a rich Birmingham family, and move into lodgings on the Esplanade in Burnham for a few weeks, before taking up temporary residence at Clifton. Meanwhile, he packed up the books that he had promised to send Edwin Jowett and sent them to Highbridge Station. When, a few days later, he cycled down to the station to check that they had been despatched, he found that they were still there, because the local carrier thought that Morecambe was in Devon. Describing the incident to Edwin Jowett, he concluded:

> Since parting with the Box of Sealed Writings I have heard nothing from any quarter – even Mr Galpin has not written, making enquiry as at one time. As far as I am concerned no one knows where the Box is now. I often wonder what will be – and when will be – the end thereof – the end of a new beginning. When will the mystery be solved? Who can tell?[30]

The Stuckeys enjoyed the next three weeks they spent breathing in the fresh sea air on the Esplanade and then moved on to Richmond Terrace in Clifton. The change seemed to give them both a new lease of life.[31] Edwin Jowett too was making changes in his life. As a child he had been taught to venerate both the Box and the subject of Joanna's Visitation. Now that he was custodian of that Box, the faith of his forefathers that had been lying dormant for so many years, began to put forth shoots. As a sign of this he applied to the Panacea Society for one of Joanna's seals. On 26 May, 1926, he wrote to Octavia:

> [H]aving the faith I hold, I have attached my name to the seal you forwarded me. I do most earnestly long for and pray that the time is not far distant when we shall realise that His Kingdom has come, and that His Will is being done on earth as it is in Heaven. That Satan's reign – with all its attendant sin, crime, disease, want, pain, and its resultant wages, death – has ceased. . . . If you should ever get to Morecambe – on a visit

> to Miss Midgley – and will give us a call, my daughter, Ursula, shall sing for you, and delight your heart.[32]

The following month Edwin received a cheerful letter from Robert Stuckey in Clifton, where he and his wife were enjoying walks and meeting up with old friends not seen for years. 'Like yourself I am full of interest in; and watching passing events,' Stuckey wrote, after reminiscing about Samuel Jowett and his enthusiastic meetings in Somerset where he expounded his ideas to the friends. 'But all these good people have long passed on and now know the grand secrets unrevealed to us. The past, present and contemplated future causes us hope and serious thoughts and anxiety. Faith is now our great strength – and to watch and pray.'[33]

Amen to that, Edwin might have said, for he was having serious anxieties of his own. He was seventy-eight and his health had been failing for some time. He died on 16 September, 1926, just two months after he had signed a special note:

> In case of a sudden collapse, and that my death should unexpectedly occur before I could make a few last requests I notify a few below altogether apart from my will:–
>
> I should like the Box of Sealed Writings to remain at home up to the time of my wife's death; then if Cecil desires, to be taken charge of by him on the same conditions as it was sent to me; to be kept inviolate (to remain unopened) until demanded by 24 Bishops of the Protestant Church of England – In case Cecil does not care to have the responsibility I desire that the box and 2 keys shall be forwarded to Mrs Barltrop, 12 Albany Road, Bedford, but not to be opened by the Bedford believers – only by the order of the 24 bishops. Edwin A Jowett. 16/7/1926.[34]

# 10

# The Bishops and the Box, 1926-1934

The Jowetts were a musical family. Two of Edwin's sisters had been music teachers and all his five daughters sang or played instruments. In his Will he left his grandfather's clock to his only son, Cecil Kaye Jowett; his harp to his recently-married daughter, Erica Alberta Tunstall; and his piano to another daughter, Ursula Irene Jowett. The gross value of Edwin's estate was less than £400. He had arranged for a trust fund to provide Emily with an income for life, and then the money was to be shared equally by their six children. After these matters had been settled, Emily visited Bedford and later wrote to Octavia, enclosing a copy of Edwin's last note referring to the Box.

> I am enclosing a copy of instructions written by my husband before his death. I saw my son yesterday for a short time. He was very pleased to hear that it was to remain here according to his orders. He did not say anything about going to see you, but I shall be having another chat with him another time. With kind love, Yours sincerely, Emily Jowett.[1]

Octavia wrote back almost by return, thanking Emily for the copy of her husband's last wishes and imploring her to take great care of the documents in her possession.

> It gave me great pleasure that he felt we were worthy to be guardians if your son wished it. I am more than thankful The Box is safe with you all and please assure your son that I much prefer you to have it, for what is in it, no one can say that we had worked along its lines. We all enjoyed having you, one and all were very pleased to make your acquaintance. I will see that somebody writes you a few lines now and again to let you know how we are getting on.[2]

Suddenly in April, 1927, everyone was talking about Joanna Southcott's Box and the general public had little doubt that it was the sealed box that had been handed to Harry Price at the National Laboratory for Psychical Research, with a signed letter stating that it had been entrusted to Mrs Rebecca Morgan (née Pengarth) by Joanna on her death-bed, with the injunction that it was to be opened only in

*Emily Jowett (1856-1934). Born at Rastrick, the daughter of John Aspinall Robinson, a prosperous stone merchant, Emily married Edwin Jowett in 1878 and was Custodian of the Box, 1926-1934.*

time of national need and in the presence of a number of bishops. The writer of the letter explained that for many years his family had employed Ann and John, Rebecca's children, as seamstress and gardener.

Ann Morgan had died in 1914, aged 78. Her brother John had died in 1925, aged 81. On his deathbed he had bequeathed the box to its present owner, asking him to 'do what was right with it'. The owner was now going abroad so he had donated the box to the Laboratory, suggesting that they might send it to the Archbishop of Canterbury.

Needless to say, Harry Price, the publicity-seeking Director of the Laboratory, did not send the box to the Archbishop. Instead he arranged for it to be opened at a public meeting in a large London hall to which he invited the Archbishops and eighty Bishops. In the meantime, he declared himself satisfied that the box had belonged to Joanna Southcott and announced that it would be 'psychometrized' by mediums and also X-rayed.[3]

All this was of course reported in newspapers and, when Robert Stuckey read about it in *The Times,* he immediately wrote to Emily Jowett to ask whether she had parted with the Box of Sealed Writings that he had forwarded to her late husband. He continued:

> I quite understood the Box would remain in your custody during your life, and then to your son, but if this latter declined, to be forwarded to a gentleman at Bradford. My impression therefore is, you would not depart from this decision without communication with some of the old stock of Believers. For more than a hundred years the Box I formerly held in my possession had been sacredly held & guarded with prophetic reverence. I am anxious to hear from you & hope you are quite well & have braved the winter without illness.[4]

THE GRAPHIC, May 14, 1927

JOANNA SOUTHCOTT'S BOX X-RAYED

*Probing the Mystery of Her Sealed Casket*

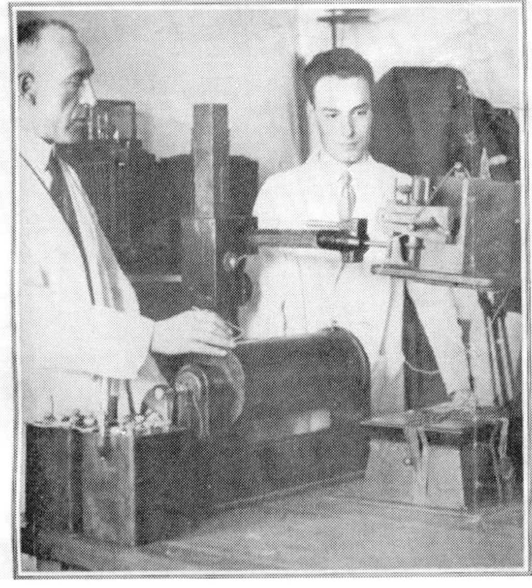

*Harry Price (left) and his assistant at the National Laboratory of Psychical Research look on as his spurious 'Southcott' box is x-rayed.*

*The photograph was published in The Graphic, 14 May, 1927 at a time when the box was creating great excitement.*

Emily also received a letter from the Panacea Society, warning her to be very careful about letting anyone know that she had the real Box in her possession.

> Not that any harm can come to you or the box, but there are always people that are eager to know all they can & it is not always the case that some persons can be trusted.[5]

In fact, Harry Price was never under any illusion that the box he had was the Box of Sealed Prophecies, for on 28 June, 1927, he wrote to Rachel Fox at the Panacea Society, as follows:

> RE. SOUTHCOTT BOXES
> Dear Madam,
> It is the intention of the National Laboratory of Psychical Research to open the Sealed Box in their possession at the Church House, Westminster, on Monday, July 11th, 1927 at 8 p.m. The Council of the National Laboratory are of the opinion that this will be a good opportunity of disposing of all existing Joanna Southcott Boxes and they therefore extend a cordial invitation to your Association to have the so-called 'Great Box' opened at the same time. A similar invitation is, by public advertisement, being extended to all owners of Southcott Sealed Boxes. Trusting that your Association will co-operate with us in this matter, I am, yours faithfully, Harry Price, Honorary Director, and Chairman of Council.[6]

Moreover, the box about which the National Laboratory for Psychical Research was creating so much fuss bore no resemblance to the box that had been measured and photographed in 1861. It was mahogany, ark-shaped, bound with strips of metal, and sealed with black wax imprinted with a head that was believed to be that of George III. Moreover, it was small, measuring little more than 12 inches by 9 inches and weighing only 11 lb. The real Box measured about 3 feet long, 1½ feet wide and 1½ feet deep and it weighed 156 lb. Despite these discrepancies the farce continued. Newspapers had a field day on 5 May when the box was x-rayed. Headlines in the *Western Mail* were typical:

> A JOANNA BOX X-RAYED
> HORSE PISTOL, RINGS & COINS
> BISHOPS TO VIEW THE CONTENTS
>
> The secret of a box which once belonged to Joanna Southcott, the 'prophetess' and which had remained sealed since 1814, was largely revealed on Thursday by an X-ray examination in London. In it were observed: A heavy, old-fashioned horse-pistol; a bead-bag; rings and coins; and what was believed to be either a roll of manuscript, a small tankard, or a dice-box. A little group of scientists, gathered round the X-ray machine at the National Laboratory of Psychical Research in South Kensington, on Thursday, watched the sensitive photographic plate reveal the secret that had been locked up there for over a century. . . .[7]

While scientists and psychical researchers in London were getting excited, Emily Jowett in her bungalow at Morecambe went quietly about her daily business. 'I think that all these newspaper reports are done to find out where the real box is', she wrote to Octavia.

> Some are really so silly. We do not talk or appear to take any interest in the matter for fear someone might come to see us & if anyone did come they would never see it, for it is under the bed that I sleep in and it has a cover on & the valence all round, it only just fits in. My son came in one day & he asked in alarm where it was & when I showed him he thought it was a splendid idea. I have not seen any newspaper cuttings about it or had any sent & I am very glad. The quieter we are about it the better, I think, & you know where it is when called for.[8]

On Monday, 11 July, 1927, the day appointed for the opening of Harry Price's box, London was plunged into darkness and visited by a terrific storm. Under a headline that read: 'Warning Flashes that

*Harry Price in the crowded hall at Church House, Westminster, on 11 July, 1927, cutting the iron bands on his bogus box. Seated on his right is the Bishop of Grantham, and on his left stands Professor A. M. Low. Price's publicity stunt is still cited in reference books as evidence that Joanna Southcott's Great Box has been opened and found to contain trivia.*

Preceded the Great Darkness', the *Evening Standard* reported that, 'the scene in the City was a most remarkable one as darkness developed. "It's just like another eclipse," was a comment that was most frequently heard'. Many on their way to Church House, Westminster, had to negotiate streets that had turned into raging torrents, but the hall was still crowded. The meeting was presided over by Professor A.M. Low and amongst those sitting on the platform was the Bishop of Grantham (Dr J.E. Hine) who had come, he said, 'out of curiosity'. The box was placed on a table in full view of the audience and, after a lecture by Mr Ernest Hunt, the seals were broken and the lid raised. The Professor, the elderly Bishop, and members of the Laboratory then bent over the box and described each object as they found it. 'In an atmosphere of humorous scepticism, amid the titters of an obviously incredulous gathering', the following articles, were revealed: a pistol; printed diary of 1715; Ovid's *Metamorphoses*; two religious discourses (*On God and His Providence* and *On Christ and His Miracles and Doctrines*); a calendar of the French Court, 1793; piece of paper with picture of the Thames, dated 1814; metal puzzle; night-cap; dice-box; lottery ticket, 1796; Jubilee medal, 1791; two ear-rings; bead purse; numerous coins; Brothers's Prophecies, 1795; *The Remarkable Prophecies and Predictions for the year 1796* by Don Johannes Gautier; case containing a medal inscribed 'Augusta, Princess of Wales'; novel entitled *The Surprise of Love, or An Adventure in Greenwich Park.*

*The contents of Harry Price's box, pictured in* The Times, *12 July, 1927, included a pistol, printed diary of 1715, Ovid's* Metamorphoses, *two religious discourses, a calendar of the French Court, an etching of the Thames, a metal puzzle, night-cap, dice-box, lottery ticket, two ear-rings, coins, a bead purse, Brother's Prophecies of 1795; and a novel entitled* The Surprise of Love, or An Adventure in Greenwich Park. *Today the box and its remaining contents are held by the Harry Price Library in London.*

'It is not very illuminating,' commented the Bishop of Grantham when the last object had been taken from the box.

> There was a good deal of laughter in the hall, which was filled with about 400 people. A group of elderly women in evening dress, however, contemplated the whole affair with a sort of reproving gravity. But the general feeling found its most accurate expression in the comment of the woman at the back of the hall, who suddenly exclaimed in a loud, clear voice: 'A lot of fuss about nothing!'[9]

Outside the hall members of the Panacea Society gave away leaflets, with a photograph of the real Box taken in 1861 and proclaiming in large type: 'The Box of Sealed Writings of Joanna Southcott, prophetess, which the 24 bishops will open, remains and will remain in safe custody until circumstances force the bishops to do what they refuse to do'.

Although the affair had been a farce from start to finish, for believers there was a positive side to what had happened. The event had raised the question of Joanna's Box in public consciousness and some said that it had been staged in an attempt to flush out the real box from its hiding place. It also served to focus the minds of those who had the Box of Sealed Writings in their care.

In her recent letter to Octavia, Emily Jowett had implied that the bishops could apply to the Panacea Society for the Box. If this were so, then the Society had to avoid the sort of misunderstandings that had caused problems in the past, by preparing the exact terms on which the bishops could have the Box. On 28 July Octavia wrote to Cecil Goodhall of Messrs. Trotter, Leaf and Pitcairn, the Society's solicitors, with the necessary instructions.

> We must prepare the terms and present them in legal form to the Bishops – a thing that I have always thought ought to have been done before, but until this letter was written to us we had no authority whatever to interfere. Also it seems to me the Custodian should make the offer to us in legal terms, through a lawyer, as we cannot approach the Bishops unless we are confident that the Box would be produced upon our application. . . . Do you not think as a first step I am justified in asking the Custodian to have it all set out in legal terms through their lawyer. It seems to me some statement which would secure that the Box would be produced at any moment, must be in our possession and that the legal statement made by the Custodian should form part of our communication to the Bishops.
>
> We are about to put up Posters in the Tubes again and are printing a quarter of a million handbills, as now is the time to strike, the interest aroused by that ridiculous Meeting in London on Monday, 11th July, being considerable.
>
> I must ask you to undertake to correspond on this matter and to draw up anything yourself as it would never do for even the most reliable of clerks to know about the whereabouts of the Box! America is willing to pay considerable sums of money for the Box, so we must be very careful.
>
> It is quite clear that the Bishops are justified in expecting a very definite and bona fide statement, as they cannot be expected to go about opening old workboxes – still, the Meeting has advertised Joanna's name all over the world as we could never have done it.[10]

Goodhall confirmed that there should be an Agreement between the Society and the Custodian as to the duties each would undertake and suggested that the Custodian should first say what they were prepared to do and, if both sides agreed, the Custodian should then instruct a solicitor to draw up a draft Agreement which could be worked on. He added, 'With regard to the Bishops I think that when the Agreement has been completed a definite statement as to the history of the Box &

proving its Authenticity should be sent them, with the terms as to opening'.[11]

In September Emily Jowett paid another visit to Bedford and took advantage of more leisure to write and reassure Robert Stuckey about the good work that the Panacea Society was doing.

> I am more than satisfied that the opening of the Box will be brought about safely and properly by Octavia, who shows the true spirit of reverence towards this treasure which is in my care. The Panacea Society is spending many hundreds of pounds in acquainting the Bishops and the public with the importance of the Box and I enclose their latest leaflet, a quarter of a million of which are being circulated in London. . . . At the same time, large posters are being put up. . . . It is very wonderful to be here among these devoted people and I am sure those who are dead and gone must rejoice to see the gradual advance they are making, whereby 18 or 19 thousand people are awake to the importance of what is coming on the earth. I am sure that you may have every confidence that the Box is safe in my hands and that Octavia will bring about its opening by the 24 Bishops.[12]

Robert Stuckey, however, was unimpressed. 'I do not believe in the advanced movement now being pursued by the Society you mention,' he replied.

> According to the original belief – as I understand it – the Box of Sealed Writings is to be kept until demanded by *the Bishops, acting on behalf of the Heads of the Nation;* when under some great cause or calamity, we know not what. The Society, of whose hospitality you have been receiving, seem to be acting in a manner *to demand* the Bishops to *demand* the Box to be opened. Is this the right course to pursue? To me it is like trying to force a prophecy to be fulfilled. Is it not the proper way to await the Will of God – and in His Own Good Time? . . . Just contemplate the state of our country at this present time – able to dictate terms in the affairs of the whole world. There is a great lavish of wealth – and pleasure and sport and pastime prevail everywhere. I cannot help thinking but that the people you mention are working in advance of the times – doing no good – but on the contrary provoking mockery and ridicule. . . . There were similar movements sixty years ago – but the old Believers would not be identified with them. I am glad to note in your letter that the Box is still in your care – and sincerely hope it will remain there.[13]

Emily was nonplussed by his reaction when, as far as she was concerned, everything was going so well. Her daughter Ursula had just married Tom Burrow, and the couple had been made very welcome in Bedford when they went on a visit. Emily simply could not understand why Stuckey should be so churlish in his attitude to the Panacea Society. She forwarded his letter to Octavia, asking for advice on how to reply.[14] In her next letter to Stuckey Emily assured him that she would never part with the Box except under conditions that he would find satisfactory and, if the bishops did apply, she promised to let him know.[15] This went some way to appease Stuckey's fears, but still he could not resist lecturing her on the dangers of being 'active'.

> We must not in any way try to force events, which, if of God, will be revealed in His good time. The very word "prophecy" indicates a future fulfilment. So let us be watchful and wait events as our predecessors have done – even as with them who obeyed even unto death. They believed in their reward, if not in this life – in the grand heavenly future. Even so let it be with us – faithful unto death, if it is the Divine Will.[16]

Stuckey was not the only one to air his disquiet. By now Samuel Galpin of Hounslow had heard that Emily Jowett was acting as custodian, and he wrote to explain that when Robert Stuckey was custodian he (Galpin) had acted conjointly with Stuckey to forestall enquiries from those who might want to see the Box out of mere curiosity. Since hearing that the Box was with Emily, Galpin had written twice to Miss Midgley, but received no reply. Anxious only for the Box's safety, he wrote, 'I have told no believer I am acquainted with, where it is & shall continue to keep it a secret, unless you think it may be divulged. My only object is to prevent your being troubled with too many enquiries'.[17] Emily's reply was brief and to the point:

> Dear Mr Galpin,
> I am sorry that you have this anxiety about the Box – I assure you there is no occasion for it – God has guarded it so far & will continue to do so. I have made every possible arrangement for its safety and I have no intention whatever of delivering it up to any person but to the Bishops. If you believe in Divine Providence at all, you must believe that as I am Custodian of the Box I am to be trusted with it. I however thank you for your kind interest and I quite agree with you that the less said about its whereabouts the better. Yours respectfully, Emily Jowett.[18]

*In the summer of 1932 huge posters advertising Joanna Southcott's Box of Sealed Writings appeared all over London.*

*This poster was put up in Piccadilly Circus, London, in June-July, 1932. At the same time 16 sheet posters appeared in Trafalgar Square, Kensington High Street, Finchley Road, West Heath Road, Newington Green Road, Kingsland Road, Stamford Hill, Whitehorse Lane and in Hackney.*

*This poster was placed at Vauxhall Bridge in June-July, 1932, and another appeared in November at Albert Embankment, facing Lambeth Palace.*

*London buses carried the message along routes 9, 25, 29, 59, and 73 in July, 1932, and on routes 14, 18, 27, 88, and 153 in the following month.*

Cecil Goodhall, meanwhile, proceeding according to instruction, was checking dates and details about the Box and asking Octavia to supply all the relevant documents, so that these could form Exhibits to the Declaration when it was delivered to Counsel.[19] On 21 May, 1928, Octavia reported to Emily Jowett:

> I am glad to say the lawyers are taking an interest in this matter of the Box and consider that if we will do exactly as they tell us, we have a very good case. They had no idea that there were any original letters for instance and it is all news to them about the Box travelling from father to son and the serious way in which the members of the different families have treated it, but of course to make a proper case of it they say we must supply as much original writings as possible, they do not care for printed matter at all and *copies* of letters are not very much better from their point of view; what they beg for is original letters. . . . Perhaps you will be able to come and see us again soon, as the summer draws on.[20]

Alice Seymour had been watching the Panacea Society's publicity campaign with grave misgivings. In the September 1928 number of her magazine (now renamed *The Southcott Express,* after *The Southcott Despatch* had run its forty-two issues) she published an article, declaring,

> If I were a bishop . . . I would not be dissuaded from [enquiring into Joanna Southcott's Visitation] by any strange teaching of persons thrusting themselves into prominence by flaring, threatening placards, or interrupting the peaceful Congress of Bishops and other Churchmen by posters, as it is quite contrary to the spirit and teaching given to Joanna Southcott. This sort of thing is apt to come from apparently good, but mistaken people.

Alice, who had no idea that the Box had changed hands, then set out what she believed to be the reason for the failure to secure the opening of the Box in 1918.

> Only one name, the late Bishop Boyd Carpenter was sent, and he was the one who demanded it for the others. Of course, without the twenty-four signatures it was impossible to have it. The Custodian is a gentleman of position and a good Churchman, and unless the Box of Sealed Writings is properly applied for, he would not yield up his trust, so solemnly held from his father. It is not true that the twenty-four Bishops

> must have seats in the House of Lords. Any Bishop of the Church of England is eligible. . . . The Bishops are chosen, because from their position, the Press and the People will believe their testimony. It is also given to the Church of England as a great blessing, because of the fidelity throughout of the three clergymen to the Cause.[21]

By February, 1929, Cecil Goodhall had drawn up a draft Statutory Declaration and sent it to Emily Jowett for her signature, but her son, Cecil Kaye Jowett, objected to a particular clause that suggested that Emily, as custodian of the Box, would deliver it 'to the person or persons authorised in that behalf by the Panacea Society for the purpose of its being opened and dealt with as may be arranged by that Society with authorities of the Church of England, provided that the opening be by or in the presence of Bishops of that Church so far as possible according to the conditions hitherto imposed'. In a prickly note insisting that his mother could not pass the Box on to anyone authorised by the Society, he declared that

> If the Box is not Claimed by the Twenty-four Bishops of the Church of England before her death, it is my Father's bequest that it should come to me. I shall hold it as my father did before me – INVIOLATE and every care shall be taken of it.[22]

Octavia wrote back immediately to apologise for the mistake, explaining that what the Jowetts had been sent was only a proof copy of the Statutory Declaration and could easily be altered. Moreover, it had been drawn up by Counsel from various papers supplied to him and the fact that Cecil's name had been omitted was purely a mistake. She assured him:

> I quite understand that, anything happening to your Mother, the Box would go to you. I have just looked at a copy of the papers I sent to Counsel and I am at a loss to understand why they left your name out. Perhaps when your Mother comes to see us next time, you could travel with her and see for yourself how simple and reasonable an affair this all is.[23]

Cecil Jowett, having made his point, sent an affable reply:

> I must say that I am very pleased that you agree with me that it would have been wrong for my mother to have signed the Statutory Declaration, under its present wording. As you say, lawyers are very difficult people to deal with, and that is why I am most particular that this document be worded correctly, so

> that there can be no going round corners or anything illegal. I thank you very much for your kind invitation to meet you, and I will some day try & arrange to come, as I would very much like to have a talk with you over little matters which interest us both.[24]

Having salvaged the situation with Cecil Jowett, Octavia then had the task of writing to Cecil Goodhall to secure the proper wording in the Statutory Declaration. In his reply on 18 March, Goodhall wrote:

> I received your letter of the 11th inst. and the Enclosures and am sorry that both Counsel and I missed the point which Mr Cecil Jowett [raised.] He is quite right. I think that if the clause is altered as suggested below it will meet the case but of course it should be submitted to Mrs Jowett.
>
> 'I hold it on behalf of the Believers in the said Mission and am to deliver it up for the purpose of it being opened and dealt with as may be arranged by the Panacea Society with the Authorities of the Church of England provided that the opening be by or in the presence of Bishops of that Church so far as possible according to the Conditions hitherto imposed.'
>
> When the time comes Mrs Jowett & her son could together take the Box to the opening could they not?[25]

Octavia found the new clause still unsatisfactory and instructed Cecil's name to be put in the Statutory Declaration. 'Really if anything did happen to Mrs Jowett, we should have to negotiate with the son – there is no way out of that,' she explained to Goodhall.

> It is a very good thing he is mentioned because it lays him under the obligation to guard the Box. Entre nous, his wife has urged that the Box should be sold, but I think he will play the game if he is properly tackled, so will you proceed with getting his name into the Statutory Declaration. I quite understand you are only dealing with Mrs Jowett, but if I may say so, I understand the situation as hardly any other person can understand it, in this degree – that these old Visitation people are very much above the average person by reason of their knowledge – lacking education, they are extraordinarily difficult to deal with.[26]

'Like all spiritual things it is very elusive,' Octavia had told Goodhall the year before,[27] trying to explain that any negotiation with 'old Visitation people' would require delicate handling. Realising that she was the only person with sufficient understanding to steer the situation, she wrote again to Cecil Goodhall:

> I think if you read Mr and Mrs Jowett's letters you will see that they do not intend to let the Panacea Society have the Box so I have put my pencil through what I think is no use, now they have got these ideas in their heads. . . . Mr Cecil Jowett's argument will be now that his Mother must retain the Box there for him to have it at her death – he can make her refuse to let us have it, because the way old Mr Jowett's statement is worded makes it dependent on Cecil Jowett for us to have it . . . it is only Cecil Jowett who could send it to us, as it is 'in case he does not care to have the responsibility' that we are to have it – honestly they would never have found all this out if it had not been for the accidental omission of his name, but as it would have appeared as though we had done it purposely, it is best as it is. Mrs Jowett, in her letter to me says 'I could not sign it for one or two persons to have it' and she is quite right. I have had the proposed substituted clause typed in the only form in which I think they will sign it.[28]

Cecil Goodhall incorporated Octavia's proposed changes in a new draft Declaration which in April was again submitted to Emily Jowett, together with a warm invitation for her and her son to visit Bedford.[29] This time there were no objections, and Octavia must have heaved a big sigh of relief. She wrote to Goodhall on 27 April, 1929:

> At last I am glad to say that Mrs Jowett and her son approve of the Statutory Declaration in its present form. The son is coming with Mrs Jowett to have it signed here probably early in May, any day after the 7th, so it had better be here on Tuesday the 7th. Now the point is, what about the affidavit? When we know the exact date of their coming can this be arranged here? I am sure you will do all possible to expedite the matter of getting the Declaration in form, because it is quite an expensive affair for us getting them here. We naturally have to pay all their expenses and I do want to get it done under Cecil Jowett's eye.[30]

The plan was for Emily and her son to travel down to Bedford for Whitsun, by which time Octavia hoped to have the Statutory Declaration in order and ready to be signed before a Commissioner of Oaths. Until then Octavia and her helpers busied themselves tabulating a sequence of documents charting the history of the Box. These were to be used as Exhibits to the Declaration when it was signed before the Commissioner, and then sent with it to Goodhall so that he could see that everything was in order before he had the Declaration stamped. The Declaration and exhibits were then to be returned to the Panacea Society to hold until required for use.[31]

While all these preparations were taking place, a storm was brewing in the background. Emily Jowett had answered her door one Wednesday evening to find Alice Seymour standing there with Miss Midgley, asking to see the Box. Emily stood her ground and said no, at the same time assuring them that it was quite safe. Alice Seymour, fishing for its whereabouts, said she was most anxious that it should be in a dry place. Emily refused to be drawn. The reason for this sudden incursion was revealed when she was handed the following letter from Samuel Galpin:

> Dear Mrs Jowett,
> Some of the believers feel very anxious about the Box of S[ealed] W[ritings], as they were not consulted when Mr Stuckey decided on placing it in your husband's care, neither after Mr Jowett's death as has been the Custom hitherto. It has been suggested by several believers that it should be placed in your name and mine and two others, in the Chancery Lane Safe Deposit in London, as it may be unsafe to be held in a private House in these times. Miss Seymour will call on you on my behalf to know if this would be agreeable to you, as our only aim is like yours, to preserve it intact until God's appointed time, that it is demanded by the Bishops and heads of the Nation.[32]

Since receiving the Box into her home, the thought of opening her door to find Miss Seymour on her doorstep had been one of Emily's worst fears. Not for a moment did she, or Cecil, consider that there was any virtue in Galpin's proposal. In fact, Alice Seymour's unceremonious visit left both mother and son all the more determined to co-operate with Octavia.

In a letter to Goodhall on 22 May, 1929, Major Carew-Hunt, Secretary of the Panacea Society, wrote,

> Since writing to you we have had a visit from Mrs Jowett (who remains on) and her son & his wife. The son is most favourably disposed towards us, and will gladly facilitate any matter he can. As the result of a talk Mrs Jowett expressed herself as desirous of her son being made co-trustee with herself and both becoming guardians of the Box which would be a wise proceeding and ensure its safety. Already two attempts have been made to induce Mrs Jowett to part with it by some persons inimical to us, and this has made her nervous; hence

> the suggestion above. How can this sharing of guardianship be effected; does it mean a legal document? Or would a simple signed statement by Mrs Jowett suffice?[33]

Goodhall advised that Emily Jowett simply sign a short Memorandum entrusting the Guardianship of the Box to Cecil Jowett in conjunction with herself, and that on no account should they make any alterations to the Declaration now that, after so much trouble, it was about to be signed. The sequence of events was also important. 'The Declaration should be made by Mrs Jowett alone & *before* she signs any such Memorandum as is suggested above,' Goodhall stressed, going on to impress on Octavia the need to make sure that Emily kept in a very safe place the note that her husband had written on his deathbed.[34]

The Jowetts' visit to Bedford was a great success for all concerned. The Statutory Declaration was signed by Mrs Jowett before the Commissioner, who also signed the exhibits. Both Cecil and his wife joined the Panacea Society and afterwards could not speak too highly of the hospitality that they had received from its members.

> Each and everyone of your faithful believers made us so comfortable and at ease in their company that it was impossible not [to] enjoy ourselves. One feature of the visit was that we made clear misunderstandings which evil minded persons had created and now both my wife & I feel greatly relieved at the result of the visit, and in more ways than one. We both loved the little services, which were packed full with most interesting facts. I only wish we lived nearer so that we might have been able to attend more of them. On many instances since those meetings little happenings and incidents have kept flashing through my mind, and pointing out that the world is all wrong and that the time *must* come when *you* will prove to the world that you and your followers can put it right. May this be soon. You will be pleased to learn that we take the water religiously and have also enrolled my wife's mother & father into doing the same. Taking this always keeps you in our minds, besides giving us Divine Healing. I shall be pleased if you will have sent to me each month your little book the *Panacea*. I will remit cost each month. In conclusion will you please convey both Mrs Jowett's and my own best wishes to all the kind friends who made us so welcome. Trusting we may meet again soon. Yrs sincerely, Maud & Cecil Jowett.[35]

In fact, everything had gone so well that Goodhall wondered whether there was any chance of the Jowetts coming to live in Bedford and bringing the Box with them.[36] It seemed an ideal solution, especially in view of the economic crisis that some, such as Major Carew-Hunt, already saw coming: 'The result of the Elections makes one rather think that The Box may now be called for in the near future; there is no doubt that a crisis is looming at not too distant a date'.[37] But, if the Jowetts had no intention of moving south, at least Cecil Jowett's visit had established a good understanding between him and Major Carew-Hunt.

Writing from his home at 38 Cross St, Morecambe, on 2 June, 1929, he wrote:

> Dear Major, Your communication arrived all safe yesterday morning and I was delighted to hear from you, and thank you for your kind wishes. The run home was beautiful and was accomplished in 9 hours steady running. No trouble and no accidents. It will please you to know that I have attached the 'section' (kindly given to me by Octavia) to the car, and certainly feel more secure with it there. Now to business: I have signed the Memorandum, and also the copy which you will find along with this letter. It is quite in order otherwise I would not have done so. I want all done right in connection with this trust, and you can rely on what I told you (when with you) as being the truth. I have no other ulterior motive. Now with reference to the matter of the Statutory Declaration – when Mother returns I shall ask her to let me see the document my father wrote, and do my utmost to get her to let you have it for safe keeping. I cannot do more. Can I?[38]

He enclosed the following Memorandum, duly signed and dated 5 June, 1929:

> My husband Edwin Armstrong Jowett having on his death left in my charge the Box of Sacred Writings by Joanna Southcott to be delivered up to 24 Bishops of the Church of England on the following conditions, namely, that it is to be kept inviolate (to remain unopened) until demanded by 24 Bishops of the Church of England, and having stated his wish in writing that after me our son Cecil Kay Jowett should take charge of the Box, I desire that my said son shall at once join me in the Custodianship of the said Box, and that henceforth we shall be the joint Custodians. And in the event of the death of either of us the survivor shall have sole charge during his or her life time. But in the event of the death of the said survivor we wish the said Box to be sent to Mrs Mabel Barltrop of 12

Albany Road, Bedford, she having given us her undertaking to comply with the conditions handed down from Custodian to Custodian of the Box.

(sd) Emily Jowett
I concur Cecil K. Jowett[39]

When Major Carew-Hunt next wrote to Cecil Jowett he mentioned the possibility first raised by Goodhall that, in view of the present sense of crisis, it might be a good idea for the Box to be brought to Bedford.

> It is not in any way with the idea of influencing you; but in these coming times one must be prepared for all emergencies, and the only safe thing to do is to have ready a plan, so that one can act at once if need be. It might be quite a wise thing to concoct something of a code so that messages could be sent without the outside world knowing their meaning. For instance, we might agree to let the Latin word '*veniat*' (let it come) mean: 'it would be wise to bring the Box here'; 'Bring' because you would, of course, like to accompany it.
>
> Will you think this over and . . . then talk it over with your mother and let me know sometime? You will understand that we have no motives whatever other than doing what we can in facilitating the safe custody of the Box and its due presentation for opening at the right time and place; all is being done to these ends, and to nothing else. We were glad to hear that your mother arrived safely back home from her visit here, and hope that the little change has done her good.[40]

Octavia, for her part, was glad that she was now able to leave the business side of things to the Major, while she communicated with Cecil Jowett on more personal matters. She wrote on 17 June,

> I am thankful that you and the Major can do the correspondence about the business part of the thing, I am sure that you and he will be good friends. Your Mother was saying that she thought if troublous times came and she had any fears for the treasure, we ought to have some little arrangement whereby it could be specially safeguarded . . . but we are taught here not to engineer circumstances, for everything is ordained to a time and will fall out just as the Lord requires, so we will agree to be led entirely by circumstances. It seems to me that much is accomplished in the fact that at last the Lord has secured a little group of

> people (you & us, I mean) who have perfectly upright intentions and can leave the matter to Divine management, but at the same time are willing to act themselves when directed. Please remember that we shall be delighted to see your wife and you up at any time. We thought we sent your Mother home looking very bright and well and we are much indebted to her for teaching us the bread-making and I have just finished my breakfast which I have greatly enjoyed, from the nice loaves she posted to us and please thank her many times.[41]

These letters were not altogether well-received by the Jowetts, who were quick to take exception to any idea that they might wish to deposit the Box at Bedford. On 30 June, Cecil Jowett wrote:

> Now, Octavia, I received the letter from the Major, and am very pleased with it up to a point where he suggests that the 'treasure' should be deposited in the no doubt splendid place selected by the ever faithful Peter [Rasmussen]. When we had the interview about this you may recall that you said you did not want the 'treasure' at all until the appointed time, and you will also recall I gave you my word of honour that as soon as you were ready under the clause in the Statutory Declaration, I would come immediately and bring it. As for the safety of the – I have no fear whatsoever, because the Divine Mother told me that she would protect it and that no harm would come to it; and none shall while I have the care of it, as joint trustee. Mother perhaps no doubt worries on account of her age, but with faith in you all – and the water – no harm shall come to it, and as I have said before as soon as the 'time' arrives we shall come immediately. I don't wish you to misunderstand me in this, and to think that I am selfish, because what I do, I truthfully think is right. My late father made the trust clear and I should do wrong if I did not carry his instructions out according to his request.[42]

The Major was mortified to think that, after such careful building of bridges, such a gap in understanding had opened up. He immediately despatched a telegram to Cecil Jowett: 'A letter follows to correct your slight misunderstanding of my letter – Major.'[43] The letter which followed carried his apologies for having created a wrong impression and an attempt to explain what he had really meant to say.

> Do please put it out of your mind that there was any other reason beyond bringing to your notice that there was this place

of safety, and so that you might feel quite easy in your mind *in case the necessity arose*; there was nothing else. It was all brought about by your mother mentioning that she was nervous on account of her house being a bungalow. . . . We are at one with you entirely in placing implicit trust in the Word of the Divine Mother; but She teaches us also to prepare for any contingencies. So do let us settle, once and for all, that we have no possible interest in the Treasure being brought here, at this stage, nor do we desire it. This does, I hope, explain our attitude.[44]

Meanwhile, the business was not going smoothly with Mr Goodhall. Octavia had assumed that the barrister employed by the Panacea Society would present their petition to the Archbishops and Bishops, and was disconcerted when Goodhall told her that it would be presented by the Society and signed by its principal officers. On 4 July she set out her objections to such a course of action.

You said in your letter, before we saw you, that the Society should send the Petition. Now that is quite useless to us, we should consider the expense and the hours of labour that I have put into gathering the data together as completely wasted because we have done almost as much as before. On one occasion 10,000 signatures were appended to a Petition on Parchment, beautifully engrossed. . . . Therefore my request was – and I repeat it – that you or your firm present this Petition on our behalf with as much legal ceremony as possible.

Next, in regard to the Statutory Declaration, I asked – and I ask you again – would it not be possible to request Counsel to act professionally for you or for us, or for both, by sending the Declaration to the Archbishop, with some sort of covering letter, from his Chambers; or would he do us the great favour (asking him professionally of course) to go in person. . . ?

I feel that, as we are dealing with a National affair, we should combine to do it as legally and *impressively* as possible.[45]

This determination was expressed by the Council of the Panacea Society which met on Saturday, 13 July, 1929, and passed the following Resolution:

'It was resolved by the Council that a Petition be presented to the Archbishop of Canterbury that the Joanna Southcott Box be opened by 24 Bishops of the Church of England and that

*Rachel Fox (1858-1939), first President of the Panacea Society, author of numerous books, and an indefatigable worker on behalf of the Cause.*

> Mrs Fox, as President of The Society, Octavia, as Chairman, and the Secretary to The Society sign such Petition on behalf of The Society.'

To which a rider was added 'that the Council request The Society's Solicitors to deliver this Petition to the Archbishop personally and with as much ceremony as possible'.[46]

On the previous day they had dispatched a long telegram to the Archbishop of Canterbury (Cosmo Gordon Lang), pointing out the dreadful conditions that now obtained in the church and the need for a New Dispensation. They then drew attention to the fact that

> the Panacea Society persistently informs Bishops that they are in possession of knowledge whereby thousands of people are gaining Divine deliverance from torturing sins which the clergy cannot deal with successfully, from diseases which doctors cannot cure, as well as from anxiety & distressing pecuniary and domestic difficulties, and that no Bishop attempts even to enquire into the matter, gives grounds for the allegation that the Episcopate is seriously in fault – for if our work be of God it ought to be supported, if it be not of God it ought to be stopped – a veritable dilemma. This telegram is sent entirely for your Lordships' benefit. As our work is done without money and without price, we have nothing to gain or lose by your action either way. Only a New Revelation at such a crisis will save the Church from disaster and bring benefit to the world.[47]

In this way they prepared the ground for the Petition, which they still hoped would be presented by their Barrister. He, however, having explained that it would not be etiquette for him to do so, suggested that Mr Goodhall's firm first write to the Archbishop for an appointment. Then the Petition should be taken by a small deputation from the Society, and their spokesman should be a man.[48] Octavia ruled out his suggestions immediately.

'Octavia will not for a moment entertain the idea of sending a deputation to the Archbishop,' the Major informed Mr Goodhall on 5 August, before listing her reasons:

> 1. To ask if a deputation can be received is to court a negative reply. Besides we have done this over and over again.
> 2. Even if they agreed to accept a deputation, they might put questions impossible to answer in so short a space of time, & no-one could do the cause justice in so unfavourable an atmosphere. Besides this has already been done.
> 3. The whole object of our applying to you and to Counsel is because we wish to do something in the matter that has never been done before, viz to approach the matter through a legal channel.
> 4. Therefore the only *modus operandi* is either:
> (a) to send, by the medium of registered post, the Petition etc direct from your office with the covering letter enclosed (subject, of course, to any technical alterations that your firm may think necessary)
> (b) to ask you, or a member of your firm, or some trusted confidential clerk, to deliver it by hand to the Archbishop or his Secretary.

He added, 'In Octavia's opinion, the registered post is the better medium'.[49]

Mr Goodhall was quick to accept Octavia's analysis of the situation and, after admitting that he had been uneasy about the 'deputation' method, he agreed that sending the documents by post was the proper way to proceed.[50]

After that there were weeks of letters flying to and fro between the Society and Goodhall as they struggled to get the wording of the Petition exactly right. A typical communication read:

> I received your letter with the draft original proposed letter to the Archbishop, your first draft-proposed letter, & your second, amended proposed draft. Unfortunately you did not send my draft proposals on your first draft, so if I now suggest anything that you have already considered & disposed of please forgive me.[51]

The trouble was, as soon as one difficulty was resolved, another was revealed. On 4 October, Major Carew-Hunt, confirming that the Petition should be despatched on 29 October, wrote to Goodhall,

> We must get over another 'snag' which has just shown up. . . . the Bishops could claim and then deal with the Box according to their own sweet will – which might not be ours! . . . Octavia is writing off to son Jowett explaining this & asking him to add certain conditions, which are essential; it would never do as it is. . . . I have been under the impression that the conditions laid down in Joanna's day obtained today, but Octavia says that it is for the Jowetts, as possessors of the Box, to make the conditions, so there you are. However, I am quite sure there will be no difficulty in getting them to do this. There absolutely must be representatives of our side (as opposed to the Bishops) present, and this must be ensured. . . . [Octavia says] the Bishops would ask for nothing better than to get hold of the Box and then, perhaps, destroy it, or make away with it. . . . You will remember that the original clause 13 had to be scrapped as the Jowetts, as custodians of the Box, were unwilling to allow anyone else to make the arrangements as to the opening and so take it out of their hands, looking upon it, as they do, as a sacred trust.
> *Suggested addition:* 'and in the presence of myself and my son, a lawyer, and not less than 5 other persons appointed by me and my son; a central locality to be arranged to suit the convenience of all parties'.[52]

Goodhall immediately understood the problem and suggested that Emily Jowett be asked to come down to Bedford to make a fresh Declaration.[53] She arrived on 15 October, happy to sign the new Declaration. Major Carew-Hunt wrote to her son explaining again exactly what was happening. 'This time I really think we have provided for everything; it has been the outcome of much anxious thought on our part, and it should ensure that the opening is carried out in the proper way.'[54]

Deletions and changes were still being made right up to the deadline. On 28 October Major Carew-Hunt tried to protect the whereabouts of the Box by ensuring that Emily Jowett's address was omitted from all documents being sent to the Archbishop.

> In case you may have overlooked the fact, the Jowetts' address occurs on the following copies of the exhibition letters: . . . will you block out, cut off, or in any way that seems good to you do away with the address on the above letters – or in any other place that it should occur – if you possibly can. It is important. You won't forget that the documents should be posted on the 29th so as to reach the Archbishop on the 30th. (*vide* pyramid date 29th/30th October).[55]

But it was already too late to make changes and the Major received a telegram from the solicitors that same day: 'Documents being sworn no alteration permissible unless re-sworn therefore despatching unaltered unless we hear before evening post.'[56] 'Bad luck but no delay please', was the message they had back.[57]

After more than two years of incessant effort and enormous expense, the papers were at last despatched. The answer was received within a week. The Archbishop, after acknowledging receipt of the communications drawn up by Counsel, refused to give attention to the 'kind of matter with which the documents deal', and returned the entire 'consignment' to the Society's solicitors. Major Carew-Hunt immediately responded on behalf of the Society:

> If your Grace, as Head of the Church which is built upon the Foundation of the Apostles and Prophets, cannot give attention to 'the kind of matter' with which the documents sent to you deal (which matter is Prophecy), whose duty is it to see if Almighty God may have laid up for this Nation some prophetic word destined to be its guide in some troublous times? . . . On the side of the Believer it is urgently desirable that the Box should be opened, and on the side of the Non-Believer it is equally desirable that the matter should be set at rest. It is therefore good sense that the Box should be opened.[58]

*Cecil Kaye Jowett and his wife, Maud, at Southcot, Morecambe. Cecil acted as joint Custodian of the Box with his mother, 1929-34. After her death he was sole Custodian until 1957.*

When the Archbishop did not reply, the Society waited several months before deciding that it was now their duty to inform the Episcopate of their action, and give its members the chance to investigate the matter for themselves. On 25 March, 1930, they sent letters to the Archbishop of York and to 45 bishops, together with printed copies of all the documents drawn up by Counsel, the letter sent to the Archbishop of Canterbury on 29 October, 1929, and the meaning of his answer. They received fifteen replies, of which twelve were mere acknowledgements and three were brief notes explaining why their authors declined to take the matter further.[59] Major Carew-Hunt then officially informed the Archbishop of Canterbury of the Society's actions and concluded his letter with:

> We should not, of course, disturb your Grace a second time with Documents which you had returned, but it seems proper to let you know that 15 Bishops have replied, in a minimum number of words, and on much the same lines as your Grace, and that 31 Bishops have not replied; all, however, retained the printed Documents. It will, no doubt, be gratifying to your Grace to find that the Episcopate is so united on at least one subject, namely that of its rejection of a possible Divine Prophetic revelation in England, whereby her difficulties would be solved for all time.[60]

There was no reply.

In 1931, out of respect for the illness of the Archbishop of Canterbury, the Panacea Society waited until the third week of May before sending out further letters to the bishops. When their response was negative, it was easy to interpret the earthquake that shook England a fortnight later as 'a Warning of Judgements to come unless the Bishops opened Joanna Southcott's Box of Sealed Writings'.[61] Another exchange of letters took place with the Archbishop of Canterbury,

*3 Mount Grove, Gatley, Cheshire, the home of Cecil and Maud Jowett, where the Box was kept until Cecil's death in 1957.*

who expressed his opinion that the matter of Joanna Southcott's writings had been settled 'some time ago'. Fearing that the Archbishop had been misled by the spurious box opened by Harry Price in 1927, Major Carew-Hunt wrote again – and at length – to clarify the situation. On 15 July, 1931, he received the following reply from Lambeth Palace:

> In answer to your letter of July 11th, the Archbishop of Canterbury directs me to say that he really cannot enter into further correspondence on the subject, nor is he prepared to ask the Bishops to carry out the investigations which you propose. Yours faithfully,
> Alan C.Don, Chaplain.[62]

It must have seemed like a dead-end, but at least the Society had done what it saw as its duty, and on a more domestic front the Panacea was going from strength to strength, as people from all over the world availed themselves of Octavia's 'specific Healing Method by Water and the Spirit'. Among those who flocked to Bedford to experience the Healing at first hand that summer were Cecil Jowett and his mother, who had been unwell. After they returned home Cecil wrote to thank Octavia for her great kindness.[63] It seems that while he was at Bedford he benefited as much from good advice as from their warm hospitality, and as a result he gained promotion at work. 'I am certain that without your guidance and help I could not have accomplished the things that have happened,' he wrote on 1 June, 1932.

> I speak truthfully when I say that ever since I have taken the Divine Water, I have been a different person. Not that I was bad before, but still I am ever so much changed. In conclusion allow me to thank you for your kindness to my mother who is at present at Bedford.[64]

In September, 1932, Octavia embarked on a mission to bring Joanna Southcott's Sealed Writings to the attention of Jewish people living in

Britain, and this gave rise to another exchange of letters with the Archbishop of Canterbury and the bishops. These were met with the same indifference as before and, of the forty-six bishops addressed, only one reply was received. After this, the Panacea Society left it for fifteen months before writing on 27 December when, in the course of a very long letter, Major Carew-Hunt declared:

> Please be assured that we do not for a moment suppose that we can persuade you to do anything about the Sealed Writings; our part is merely to secure that you know about them, and to have all in readiness for the ceremony of the opening. We leave it to the Almighty God to arrange the rest.

There was nothing more to be said – on either side. He received a curt reply:

> Dear Sir,
> The Archbishop of Canterbury directs me to acknowledge the receipt of your letter of December 27th with its enclosures. His Grace bids me say that he has nothing to add to what has been repeatedly said about the Bishops and the Box.
> Yours faithfully,
> A.J. Clements, Secy.[65]

In Bedford Octavia celebrated her sixty-eighth birthday on 11 January, 1934. On this same day Emily Jowett died at her bungalow, 'Southcot', in Morecambe. She was seventy-eight. Her death meant that Cecil K. Jowett was now sole custodian of the Box, and within a week he was writing from his home at 3 Mount Grove, Gatley, Cheshire, to 'The Divine Mother'.

> In this letter I have great pleasure in assuring you that the 'Treasure' is now quite safe at my new address as above, and is well protected by Your Divine power. The conditions that have governed so long, will be the same and you can rest assured that my father's wish will be adhered to. My dear mother's passing is a great loss to all of the family, but I do say that, as she suffered so, it is much the best way. We have all the happy knowledge that she was an ideal parent and mother. We shall miss her happy smile and cheery manner. I take this opportunity to thank all of your good people at Bedford for the kindness and patience shown to her during her visits south. These visits, I may say, were very dear to her.[66]

# 11

# PLACE OF MY GLORY, 1934-1957

News of Emily Jowett's death took longer to reach Blockley where Alice Seymour was still busying herself trying to ensure that the right procedures were followed in any contact with the bishops. On 16 January, 1934, she wrote to Octavia that it was vital for the bishops to come forward of their own volition and not in response to any invitation. With regard to their status, it was not necessary for the request to come only from bishops who were members of the House of Lords.

> I consider any English bishop eligible to be one of the twenty-four for the Trial, or representatives sent by them. Somehow I feel the Great Trial is not far off. You and your people have been most valiant in this matter.[1]

It was a friendly letter, a sign of their improving relationship after Octavia had taken the initiative by sending Alice the Panacea Magazine each month and inviting her to visit Bedford. 'We could easily send a car to fetch you, and could put you and Miss Robinson [sic] up. But of course it will be wiser to wait for the better weather,' Octavia replied, unaware that Alice had not left her house to visit anyone for years.

> We never forget what we owe you as the Pioneer in this wonderful work, and one can only hope, though we have travelled along divergent paths, that we shall both arrive safely at the journey's end and find that all things have worked together for good. I am glad you feel that we have been valiant in the Cause, and I note what you say about not 'inviting' the Bishops, and also about the House of Lords.[2]

In this new spirit of co-operation Alice Seymour wrote to Octavia on 26 January with what she imagined would be startling news.

> As you probably know Mrs Jowett had the custody of the Box of Sealed Writings after her husband's death. . . . She died just after Xmas, and was buried on Jan.12th of this year. It will be best for you not to say you have heard from me as for some reason or another the son is rather opposed to me (his father disliked my bringing out the *Expresses*) and does not wish me to know his address in Manchester where he has the Box. I think you know Mrs Jowett and the son. . . . It seems to me, it is rather a serious

> matter for us, as formerly when the Box was removed a few of the old believers were consulted. If the son were a believer, I should not mind, but I believe he and his sister Ursula, Mrs Burrows, are rather worldly people. I heard about the death from Miss Midgley, 4 Brunswick Road, Morecambe; she was left executor; there is very little money left for them – under £100 each, I think. You have done so much towards getting the Box opened, I would rather it was in your charge than theirs. I think if you suggest his bringing it to Bedford, and you would then *present* him with a sum of money, it would not be buying it, as no one has the right really to sell it, as it belongs to the believers. But you could then hold it until demanded by the Bishops. This is only a suggestion, but it is rather a serious matter for us. Perhaps he will let you know his address. I am not at all anxious for any prominence when the Box is opened, but we want to know where to send for it, if demanded. The son went to live at Manchester and as Mrs Jowett felt she should not get better she let him take the Box there. That is the address he does not wish me to know. But he may not mind your knowing. . . .
> P.S. If you get the Box, I should keep it absolutely private that you have got it, or in these days of wicked bandits and others, your peace would be gone.[3]

Octavia was cautious in her reply.

> I hasten to answer your letter, in order to allay your anxiety about the Box, as far as I can. I cannot put into writing what I *know*, but I am confident that you can rely upon the fact that the Divine Power which has so far guarded the Box is continuing to do so. . . . Now, I should like to say one thing, and it is this – that it would be impossible for you not to take a prominent part at the Opening of the Box, as it is your right. . . . Anyone here would tell you that I constantly refer to you and your work as being the foundation, humanly speaking, of the whole affair. . . . I am glad to say that Mrs Burrows has written to me about her mother's death. I assure you that I will not mention you or anything in your letter in connection with the Box, and I rely upon your not mentioning me, either! . . .
> P.S. I do feel that you ought to know everything there is to be known about the Box and that we ought to work together about it, without any intermediary. Also I quite appreciate your remarks about the need of great caution.[4]

Alice was clearly relieved when she read this letter. She wrote; 'I have every confidence in your honour and as you say it is in safe keeping, I feel I can rest assured it is so'. She also enjoyed the conspiratorial atmosphere, assuring Octavia that she would keep all her future letters under lock and key.

> I think it will be best not to let anyone know of our correspondence on this matter, and if you post to me either on a Saturday or a Sunday I will take in the post myself on that morning, as Miss Robertson sees the postmarks but does not open my letters. She is quite a good help to me and is not at all narrow-minded about religion, but I think it is wise to keep this matter private. I shall tell her [that] the address where they are to apply for the Box, if anything happened to me, is in my locked bag of sealed papers.

Alice then proceeded to outline what she thought should happen when the bishops requested the Box.

> You could wire to me, or I would wire to you and come over at once if they sent to me for it. It is said, it has to be taken wherever the Bishops direct for the Trial to be held. Last time it was to have been in the Jerusalem Chamber. The first day no women are to be present but a few can remain in an upper room, so if called as Witnesses can appear. The Second Day they can all be seated together. Is this what you consider should be done? I am glad you know of the six Jews to be present. What a wonderful thing it all is, and how unexpected it will be to the World! I expect the rooms you have prepared will all be found useful. I have the Banner, and shall hope to bring it, if I am spared, but I only desire God's Will to be done in and through me. . . . I have never lost my love for any of you.[5]

If Alice hoped her excitement would meet an answering echo she was disappointed. Octavia had suffered an accident to her eye that made it difficult for her to read or write. After waiting months for a reply, Alice wrote again, urging on Octavia the need to compile the list of men who should be present at the Trial and to make other arrangements in case (as was most likely) the bishops called for the Box suddenly.[6] This time Octavia replied with profuse apologies and almost by return of post. She explained that arrangements were well in hand.

> I think that I have told you that the six Jews are quite ready to come, and we have bought the six extra chairs for them, in addition to the 48 chairs for the 24 Bishops and the 24 believers – making, in all, 54 very nice chairs, all alike and costing 25/- each!!
>
> I did not know that only men were to be present. However, amongst the 24 persons I have thought of, half this number can easily be made up with men. Next I can tell you we have

*One of the 54 special chairs purchased by the Panacea Society for the 24 bishops, 24 believers, and 6 Jews who would be invited to attend the 'Trial' of Joanna Southcott's Writings. The chairs were bought in 1934 at a cost of 25 shillings each.*

all the glass, silver, china, etc. etc. for 30 persons, and perhaps 18-20 bedrooms ready, even to the hot-water bottles and soap! Arrangements can, of course, be made at hotels for anyone else. All the catering would be done by an hotel here – we could not possibly have the worry of that. It may interest you to hear that, as an experiment, we have had all the tables laid, and we can give breakfast, luncheon, tea, and dinner, to 30 persons. All we had to provide extra were porridge-plates, and I may buy a large breakfast service, as I do not like one made up of different patterns. We are even laying down some wine. Personally, I do not think there is anything that could not be arranged for in one day.

A stand has been made (of exactly the right size) on which to place the Box, and it is in itself a Chest in which the Writings could be put, should the old Box fall to pieces.

My own view is that it would be necessary for you to come down immediately any real move is made, so that you could superintend the arrangements. Anyway, our invitation to you and Miss Robertson stands, and we could receive you any time between June 13th and 24th, or between July 17th and August 17th. Servants' holidays and other matters make it difficult for me to say 'Come at any time', as I should like to do. Please use your own judgment about telling Miss Robertson.[7]

Alice was in a dilemma. She wanted to visit Bedford, but found it impossible to leave Rock Cottage and all the treasures that she had collected over the years – the magnificent gold and jewel-encrusted banner made in 1917 to be used on the occasion of the opening of the Box; patchwork quilts sewn by Joanna; engraved glass communion beakers; original letters and manuscripts written by First Believers. On the other hand, if 'it were something very important – like the opening of the Box of Sealed Writings – then I hope our treasures will travel with us', she told Octavia.

> I had heard before that you had prepared a house for the reception of the bishops and holding the trial – I was told it was in Bedford, and another told me it was in London. Perhaps you will kindly tell me in your next where you have made these preparations?

Her question stemmed not from mere curiosity. Alice was convinced that, since the opening of the Box must take place in London, any arrangements made in Bedford would prove a waste of time.[8] Such an opinion was unwelcome to those who had poured love, energy, and personal fortunes into creating the kind of accommodation necessary for holding the Trial of Joanna's writings. Nevertheless, Octavia replied with another friendly letter:

> Just a line, in answer to your question, to say that the house we have prepared is here in Bedford. You will remember my house – well, I can now go through my own garden into the gardens of four other houses, one of which is the one I speak of. So it is all very convenient and very pretty. Thank you very much for your nice letter. I promise to write to you first of all, if anything should occur.[9]

What Octavia really thought of Alice's notions was expressed in a document addressed to Cecil K. Jowett on 8 October, 1934, entitled *Information & Suggestions in Preparation for the Opening of the Box*:

> In this Divine work we must recognise that the material arrangements must play a great part. To such a person as Miss Seymour, for instance, who supposes that Joanna herself will rise out of the tomb with the child in her arms, arriving at some house in Paddington where the Box will be found – no one having the smallest idea of how the Box got there or she got there – is very different indeed to your idea and ours. It seems time, therefore, for us to let you know one or two matters.
> 1. That the Hall you saw is completely ready; the chairs bought for the 24 Bishops, for the 24 Believers, for the 6 Jews, and any other persons, like yourself and your family and the Lawyer, the clergy who are interested, and so on.
> 2. Twenty bedrooms are practically ready for the Bishops, and the other four are being arranged for.
> 3. A scheme of having a large marquee for luncheons etc between *Castleside* & *The Haven* is on paper.
> 4. An oak stand has been made for the Box.
>
> Now comes the most interesting point: that the Jews are getting very interested in the fact that Joanna addressed many of her

*12 Albany Road, Bedford, photographed in the 1920s when it was the home of Octavia. The gardens behind this and four other houses owned by the Panacea Society were combined so that members could enjoy the beautiful grounds created.*

writings to the Hebrews, and about 3,000 of them have sent a Petition to the Bishops to open the Box. It is beautifully set out and printed by Raphael Tuck & Co; they have sent us some copies and we are sending one to you. Up to the present, the replies from the Bishops have annoyed the Jews very much, as naturally they think that the awful sufferings of the Jews in Germany, etc. should make any claim on their part for the possible relief of some Divine instructions arouse the Bishops' interest and sympathy. . . .

Joanna said the 'dangers to London will be overhead' and, of course, the same applies to England generally. The terrible possibilities which the German menace in the air would bring about makes this even more important.

We, ourselves, have yet to send one more Petition to the Bishops, signed by some 25,000 people, and then the way will be made for the Divine Powers to bring them to act through fear, seeing they will not act through entreaty. It is, however, very sad to think that the fear ordained *for them* will fall on Europe generally – the horrible forms of death that are being arranged for make us all feel rather sad, and we here, are all the more anxious to have everything in order and in readiness for the only help that there can be in Heaven or Earth.

Our Lawyer recommends that the Bishops should be required to sign something in the nature of . . . [a] form of application *to you* for the Box. . . .[10]

The lists of notes appended to this document reveal Octavia's incredible attention to detail. Would the Community need a new set of Prayer and Hymn Books for the Chapel? Would they need microphones? Should they buy or hire a harmonium? What visitors would be allowed to attend? They must ensure that all of Joanna's books were available. Someone must enquire of Cecil Jowett what legal form the application for the Box

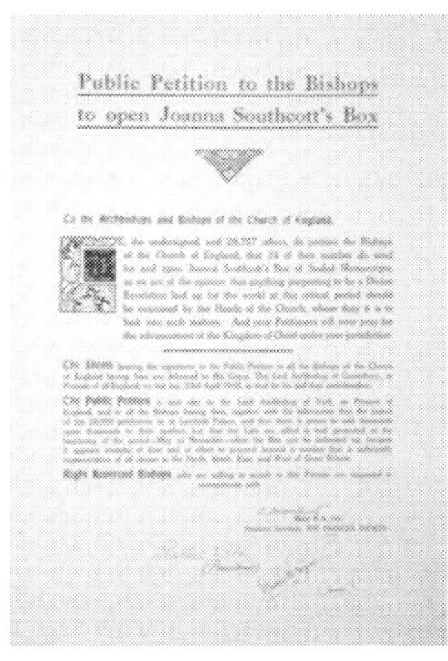

Public Petition to the Bishops to open Joanna Southcott's Box

To the Archbishops and Bishops of the Church of England.

*The Public Petition delivered to Archbishop Lang on 23 April, 1935, accompanied by the signatures of more than 28,000 people urging the Bishops to open Joanna Southcott's Box. It was signed on behalf of the Panacea Society by Major Carew-Hunt, Rachel J. Fox, and Canon Payne. The vast archive of the Society includes several brown paper packages containing thousands of the original signatures.*

should take. What would he require before giving it up? They needed an itinerary showing how to reach Cecil Jowett's home by road and rail; and red exercise books with the bishops' and suffragans' addresses. They drew up plans to turn *Castleside* into a small hotel with *The Haven* as an annexe and a marquee between. A Hotel would do all the catering, but they must remember to consult Mr Mazin about kosher food.[11]

The endless discussions must have been exhausting and inevitably took their toll. The people who worked with Octavia were full of admiration for her energy. Alice Seymour wrote on 24 October, 1934, to Miss Gillett, a member of the Panacea Society:

> It is wonderful how Mrs Barltrop has been preserved to work so hard all these years, and that I am also; I so often marvel at it all. And now the Great Box, in spite of all these preparations, may not be opened at Bedford, as it distinctly states it has to be taken wherever the Bishops may direct: so it would probably be Westminster again. That has an immense open space in front, also at the Houses of Parliament, as all believers are to gather in this open space on the fourth day. Trusting you are all well, also Mrs Barltrop. . . .[12]

Her trust was misplaced. In fact, Mabel Barltrop (Octavia) had died peacefully in her sleep eight days before. Alice Seymour was doubly shocked when she heard the news, because Octavia's death signified not just the passing of a friend, but a setback in arrangements for the Trial. She quickly sent a letter to Hilda Green, Secretary of the Society, stressing that she had been in correspondence with Octavia about the Box of Sealed Writings, but then immediately betrayed her ignorance by declaring that she knew that the Box had been transferred to Bedford the previous summer. She continued,

> Of course, it was a shock to us, as it was left in writing that it was not to be moved without consultation with the old Southcottian believers. Therefore, it could not be willed by Mr

> Jowett to his son in that way. However, we have kept it quiet for your sakes, as well as our own, and also for the safety of the Box itself, as I fear if our people knew it was there, they would come in a body to demand by what right you held it? But I know you are honourable women and will try to carry out the instructions for the Trial, as laid down in the Writings. Therefore, I felt it wiser not to acquaint our people with its removal.

If Alice Seymour was trying to flush out her opponents' cards, she had overplayed her hand. Emily Goodwin, a guiding spirit in the Panacea Society who came to the fore after Octavia's death, never trusted Alice Seymour after this, and warned other members to be on their guard against her wiles.[13] Accordingly, Hilda Green wrote a sharp note to Alice stating:

> I handed over to Mrs Goodwin the letter I received from you yesterday morning (Jan 30th) As she is the legal Representative of The Panacea Society (now that our Leader has passed over) and also 'The Instrument of the Divine Mother Jerusalem', if there is anything, at any time, you wish to know concerning our Society or its movements, will you correspond with her on the subject at the Society's address. . . . She is fully aware of the work you take so much interest in (The Box), as she has all your correspondence with our late Leader in her possession. With kind regards, Yours sincerely, Hilda Green.[14]

Alice realised that she had made a mistake in not going straight to the top, and quickly tried to put the matter right by writing to Emily Goodwin:

> I am sorry I addressed my letter to Miss Green instead of to you, but I did so as I had known her personally. As you have my letters to Mrs Barltrop, you will see how anxious I am to hear from you about the Box of Sealed Writings, and to know your plans with regard to the Trial of their Truth before the Bishops; so perhaps you will kindly answer my questions respecting it. I have never lost my love for those who have sealed – it is a strong, unbreakable bond – although we may subsequently differ on some points; we have each tried to carry on a difficult work for the Lord in the way we thought best.[15]

Mrs Goodwin's reply comprised a number of bland assurances:

> Octavia left everything in order under The Divine Mother's direction before she passed over, and all that is necessary now is to wait with patience until the Bishops are made, by circumstances, to call for the opening of the Box. They have

had Petitions from both Jews and Gentiles, also the last message has been sent to them from here. As usual, they refuse to have anything to do with the opening of the Box; they forget the time is very near when the Lord Himself will rise up in anger (because of their refusal) and terribly shake the earth, both animate and inanimate, then they will have to comply.

You may rest assured when I have any news from the Bishops I will let you know, and as you promised Octavia, if you should hear you would let us know. There must not be any diversity of opinions about this part of the work; we must be led entirely by The Divine Mother – then there are no mistakes or feelings about what we do, but perfect unity. I know that your work is in another channel but it is for the same object – viz the furtherance and bringing into being of 'The Kingdom of God on Earth' and the Opening of the Box of Sealed Writings.[16]

Such sentiments failed to satisfy Alice Seymour. Whilst thanking Mrs Goodwin 'for trying to smooth away any difficulties that may be between us in the very difficult work that lies ahead', she returned to the issue of where the Box was to be opened:

As I personally know some of the Bishops, and have been sending to them each year for so long, they are well acquainted with my efforts in this Cause, I am willing, as you have made such preparations [at Bedford], to suggest to them that it be held there, but *if they refuse*, I wish to *know definitely*, if you would send it where they desire? . . . I have not told our people that you have the Box of Sealed Writings; I think it is wiser and safer for as few as possible to know it in these strange times. I am willing to still keep it private if you will clearly state that you intend to carry out the Lord's directions for the Trial. If not, I feel I must call a Meeting of all the Believers, and consult them what they wish to do in the matter.[17]

The threat was clear, but it did not frighten Emily Goodwin. The Box was not at Bedford, but she knew where it was, and that gave her a psychological advantage over Alice Seymour. It meant that she could remain serenely uninvolved while Alice turned intellectual somersaults trying to work out how to safeguard the future of the Box. On 12 April, 1935, Alice wrote to her:

For some time I have been thinking what would be the wisest thing to do in regard to the Box of Sealed Writings so as to satisfy the old Southcottians or their descendants to whom the Box was entrusted.

> I consider that it is in safe keeping, but I do not feel that it is safe that it should be in the keeping, as it were, of one woman, however worthy she may be. Since Octavia's passing I see clearly that you should give me the names and addresses of two men (or a man and a woman) who would act for you in the case of illness or otherwise. I too would give you the names and addresses of two of our Southcottians to whom you could apply to know the wishes of the Bishops, should they suddenly apply for the Box as it foretells they will. These two men would then apply to you if I had passed on.
>
> We should then have a Committee of four custodians to act with us if we are still alive, and would sound reasonable to the Bishops if put before them, they would feel they were not to be made a laughing stock, which they greatly fear and which holds them back from demanding it.
>
> I also think the place of the custody of the Box should be kept as private as possible. I have not told even these two gentlemen yet about it, but I am waiting until I hear from you. . . .
>
> Mrs Barltrop kindly asked me to visit Bedford last summer and the summer before, but I was unable to come. Under these altered circumstances I will come this summer to see you and talk things over about the procedure of the Great Trial. I never for one moment thought I should not meet her there in love and harmony. It just shows how we must do our part now before too late.[18]

Sadly, it was already too late as far as Emily Goodwin was concerned, for she had never trusted Alice Seymour and there was nothing that Alice, in her ignorance of the Box's whereabouts, could do to improve the situation, so she continued in vain until she decided to approach Rachel Fox, President of the Panacea Society. She wrote a plaintive letter:

> Dear Mrs Fox, I was glad to hear that you were at Bedford as I cannot get a satisfactory reply from Mrs Goodwin with regard to the Box of Sealed Writings. In past years I have always known where it was and have seen it. Since it went to Bedford, I have corresponded with Mrs Barltrop about it and she told me she had had another Case made for it to ensure its safe removal. She had made great preparations for the Trial to be held at Bedford, but I told her we were commanded to have the Box taken to wherever the Bishops direct. . . .
>
> If you are ready to produce the Box when the Bishops send I shall be satisfied. I do not think Mrs Goodwin is quite suitable.

*Emily Goodwin (1858-1943), who moved to 12 Albany Road in 1921 to help nurse Octavia's elderly aunt. She soon began to channel instruction to Octavia from the Divine Mother. After Octavia's death in 1934, Emily took over direction of the Society and organised the Petition to the Bishops in 1935. She died at Bedford on 22 January, 1943.*

I arranged with Mrs Barltrop that if the Bishops sent to me for it, I would let her know at once and would go over to her as quickly as possible. She also arranged that if the Box were demanded of her, she would let me know at once. Of course Mr Jowett had no right to part with it without consulting the Southcott Friends. But I think things can be satisfactorily arranged if a small Committee of us knows how carefully it is kept and the names of two or three who are in actual charge of it. I have no objection to Mrs Goodwin being one of them, but I should be satisfied if you and two others were responsible for it. That is the only way your duty can be fulfilled to us; you will see this is only just, if you put yourself in our place. It is a sacred and solemn charge.[19]

Rachel Fox, who needed no prompting from Miss Seymour to know where her duty lay, passed the letter to Mrs Goodwin who, speaking for the Divine Mother, dictated a suitable reply:[20]

I am not surprised that you and Miss Midgley are uneasy about the future management of Joanna's Box, for neither of you comprehend that God has the matter in perfect control, and therefore it behoves us all to wait His direct Guidance. . . . Bedford is 'the place of My Glory', and it is sure to be the place of His Manifestation. We are all of one mind in the Centre as to it being only safe to follow the Divine directions which come through E.G. (Mrs Goodwin), as they came through Joanna, and which are equally unaffected by her mind.

Thanks to Octavia, from 1923 (and before) the Divine Mother's Guidance has been vouchsafed to us and we have walked by it; and as since Mrs B's deliverance it has been

> *continued*, you may rest assured that all will be ready for any sudden demand which the Bishops may make to The Society. They are aware of only one authority over the custody of the Box, and it could only confuse the issues if you or any Committee were involved.
>
> May I advise you as a friend, to lay down all hopes of and efforts for organising any human arrangements. The Bishops are not in the least likely to apply to you. Personally I do not know where the Box is, nor do I wish to know. From your point of view, it is a great pity that you would not come to see Octavia at the Centre when she asked, and when she would have been able to convince you that the Divine Guidance was the only safe one for the Divinely prepared Ark. You can see why I cannot take your point of view that you have any sacred and solemn task except that of being present, if permitted by health and strength.[21]

Still no one had enlightened Alice as to the true whereabouts of the Box, and to be told that her only role in the Trial was – if health and strength permitted – simply to be present, must have been taken as a snub. It was well over a year before she contacted Mrs Goodwin again. The charge that she should have visited Bedford when invited by Octavia rankled with Alice so, when she did write again, it was to explain that Joanna Southcott's writings contained specific commands not to meet those who held different beliefs until the Trial before the bishops had made all things plain.

> So you see although I never lost my love for Mrs Barltrop, and should like to have seen her, also Mrs Fox, I could not do so. Now I think the Great Trial is looming near, I feel we could come over in the early summer and talk over the various arrangements for it together, if you care for us to do so. But we *must* keep it private that we think it near, lest the newspapers get hold of it.[22]

Emily Goodwin welcomed the renewed contact and repeated the invitation for Alice to visit Bedford, urging her to come sooner rather than later,[23] but Alice, who had celebrated her eightieth birthday that January, was finding it ever more difficult to leave home. Firstly there was the Coronation of George VI, for which she had to prepare a special issue of her periodical (which since 1935 had been published under another new name: '*Watch*'). Then Mary Robertson fell ill, so Alice had to find another friend to accompany her to Bedford. Once it was arranged for a weekend visit in June, Alice began to have other misgivings. She now demanded to know the Panacea Society's intentions with regard to the opening of the Box and whether they were willing to send it to whatever place the bishops required. As far as she was concerned, this was not a matter for discussion, but something that she needed to have confirmed before she set foot in their Centre.[24]

Emily wrote back a long, inspirational letter, explaining that, just as Joanna wrote by the Spirit, so life at the Centre was founded on that same Spirit. 'We are a people that not only believe in Joanna's Writings but have the Power given to us by the Water and the Spirit which Joanna prophesied would come to enable man and woman to overcome the evil of mind and body and to be made ready to meet the Bride and the Bridegroom when They come to establish Their reign on the earth', she wrote. She also pointed out the difference between Alice's work which, valuable though it was, was limited to publicising Joanna Southcott's Mission, and the work of the Panacea Society, which was a further development of that Mission.[25]

This was not what Alice Seymour wanted to hear. She wanted to make her point that the Box must be taken to wherever the bishops required and that she could not come to Bedford unless she had this guarantee. In the ensuing battle of wills, Alice resorted to playing off the dead against the living. On 18 July, 1937, she wrote:

> Mrs Barltrop in her letters to me was clearly willing that the Box should be taken wherever the Bishops desired. . . . Knowing she was thus willing I did not tell her that she had no right to receive the Box from Eric [sic] Jowett, as I have seen the solemn written promises of the Jowetts, that they would part with it to no one but the Bishops. As she had it, I thought it safer in her hands than with Eric Jowett, so said nothing against her holding it.[26]

Mrs Goodwin could not give the kind of promise that was being demanded, because that would be to pre-empt the Will of God. She wrote back, 'Whatever leaning you have towards the Bishops it does not matter, you may be very certain that The Will of the Lord will be done about the Box of Sealed Writings and the Bishops in every particular, but first the Lord will have them in derision and this has begun if you see how the Church is falling, having no power to hold it up'.[27] Although she repeated her invitation for Alice to come to Bedford, the situation remained at stalemate, and Alice was never corrected of her belief that the Box had passed into the safe-keeping of the Society, when it was, of course, still at Gatley.

After the death of Emily Jowett in 1934, her daughter and son-in-law, Ursula and Thomas Burrow, continued to live at 'Southcot' in

Morecambe. When Ursula died after giving birth to a daughter in October, 1935, her husband occupied the bungalow on his own, while the baby was brought up by his sister-in-law. The family, however, was never forgotten by Octavia while she was still alive, and Emily Goodwin continued to send them gifts and greetings every Christmas, just as she sent to Cecil and Maud Jowett at Gatley in Cheshire. Her gifts were especially appreciated during the austerities of wartime. On 7 January, 1942, Cecil apologised for taking so long to write and thank her,

> The reason being that we have been up to Morecambe for Christmas and whilst there I worked my northern journey so was away from home for a fortnight. I had to work it this way to save petrol. On arrival home your letter was awaiting us. . . . thank you sincerely for your kindness in sending the notes. . . . I gave little Ursula hers, and now she is six years old she is going to write a little note to you herself . . . . This war is upsetting everything. I never thought you would be called upon to provide housing and billets for troops. This will have caused you much trouble. . . . I think in spite of all these setbacks your work will go on apace, and bring the day you all so desire. I am pleased to inform you that the 'treasure' is still inviolate and secure, and waiting for the time when the Bishops will assemble to witness the opening.[28]

The following December he wrote to acknowledge further gifts from Emily Goodwin:

> As you say it is a long time since you heard from me but even though I may not write it does not mean that all you kind friends have been out of our thoughts for we often talk about the events and wonder when the day will dawn when the Bishops will agree to present themselves for the opening of the 'Treasure'. This I may say is quite safe.[29]

That winter Emily Goodwin was in good health. She was eighty-five and only mildly set back by the brief spells of bronchitis that kept her in bed for several days. Her friends were, therefore, unprepared for the shock of finding her dead on Friday, 22 January, 1943, having passed away in her sleep. It fell to Robert Temple, as Honorary Secretary of the Panacea Society, to inform Cecil Jowett of the sad news. He wrote,

> You can imagine that her passing was a great shock and is a very great loss to us in Bedford. We can only try to continue our work on the same lines as before. Some of it, with which

*Robert Temple (1886-1967). As Honorary Secretary of the Panacea Society from 1935 until 1967, it fell to Temple to arrange for the collection of Joanna Southcott's Box from Gatley and its safe transport to Bedford after the death of Cecil Jowett in 1957.*

> Mrs Goodwin dealt personally, must of course cease, but we are established as a Society and must go on, hoping for some development which will bring matters to a head and see the fulfilment of our hopes and expectations. Your relations with Mrs Goodwin were of course largely personal, but you have paid visits to us and met some of our members and we hope the pleasant relations existing between yourself and The Society will always continue. On our part we shall always be pleased, as in the past, to receive a visit from you should you at any time be in the neighbourhood.[30]

Mr Temple did not betray any sign that he was addressing the Custodian of the Box. In his acknowledgement, Cecil Jowett was equally discreet: 'Although not a "sealed" believer, I have interests with the Society and will always fulfil my obligations to the new leader, whoever she may be', he wrote.[31] In fact, there was no obvious new leader for the Society. Emily Goodwin had been recognised by the Community as a true channel for spiritual guidance and she was sorely missed. For a while the Society ceased writing to the bishops even though their mission to spread the word continued unabated in the Press and the healing continued as before. Then, in November, 1944, Robert Temple was approached by a journalist who asked why the Panacea Society did not open the Box themselves. The brief resurgence of interest did not last longer than the explanation – that the matter could only be resolved by the bishops. However, it caused members of the Society to address the question, what would happen if the bishops suddenly asked for the Box? How should they respond? Dismayed that so little had been written down, Robert Temple wrote to Cecil Jowett:

> You are the Custodian of the Box and you alone can produce it; I think, however, in the circumstances, and I hope you will agree, that it is desirable that we should know exactly what are the requisite conditions on which you will do so. For instance, I believe it is not essential that the Bishops should attend in person but each must send a representative, e.g. a Bishop might send his

> Suffragan, or his chaplain? Would this be acceptable to you? I believe that at one time you did make all arrangements with Octavia but I am unable to find that anything is on record. If it is not asking too much I should be very grateful if you would let us have a short letter setting out the exact conditions on which you hold the Box and would be prepared to produce it.[32]

Receiving no immediate reply, Temple grew alarmed. He realised that anything could have happened to the Custodian without the Society knowing. After three weeks he wrote again, apologising for any offence his previous letter might have caused .[33] Cecil Jowett answered by return:

> I have received both your letters and with reference to your remarks re the 'box' I certainly am the custodian and if you look carefully through your records you will find a document made by 'Octavia'. The conditions of that document remain the same. The 'box' will be produced when the Bishops agree to be present at the opening. In my extract substitutes will not meet the case so I cannot agree to Suffragans or Chaplains. When the time comes the Bishops will be there, and the box also, but not before. If my remarks seem curt it does not mean that my manner is the same; it is not, and I wish the Society continued success.[34]

Reassured, Robert Temple unearthed Octavia's letter to Counsel and extracted from it the following:

> The history shows that no person could justly suppose that the devotion and care expended upon the Box could have any relation to vulgar fraud. All who have had to do with it have regarded it with deepest veneration and full recognition of its Divine character as being the Ark of the Testament or Will mentioned in Revelation XI, accepted as a sacred charge under declaration of the nature of an oath before Almighty God, e.g. 'As long as I hold the Sealed Writings they shall remain intact and uninjured. No person whatever, professing to be a believer or not, shall obtain them from my possession, save and except they are demanded by the proper Authority in the Nation, which shall make the surrender imperative.'[35]

In the difficult post-war years, crippled by food and fuel shortages, rationing and strikes, it was easy to draw people's attention to the cure for all ills that was the promise sealed in Joanna's Box. As regular advertisments urging the bishops to open Joanna Southcott's Box appeared in newspapers over the name and address of the Panacea Society, people naturally assumed that the Box was at their headquarters in Bedford, and from time to time articles announced this as a fact.

On 31 December, 1946, the *Bedford Record* proclaimed:

> 'Our nation's greatest treasure' is lying, Bedfordians will be surprised to learn, within two hundred yards of Castle Close. It is the famous Joanna Southcott Box, valued at something more than the Crown Jewels or the Koh-I-Noor by its present guardian and secretary of the Panacea Society, Mr Temple. The location of the 156 lb. box, which has awaited the assembly of 24 Bishops before its opening, has always been a closely guarded secret, but I can reveal that it lies within the shuttered and locked room of a three-storied house in Newnham Road.[36]

The people who came hunting for information tried to flush the Box out of hiding, suggesting it had never existed. *The People* in August, 1947, reported, 'I asked Mr Temple if he knew where the box is, and he pointed out that this was the kind of question the Society really didn't like answering. But he assured me that it would quite definitely be produced if the Bishops did their part'.[37] Over the next decade Robert Temple became used to such enquiries, and the retired banker who had spent years working for trading firms in South America and the Gold Coast was often glimpsed greeting journalists at the grey two-storey house in Albany Road that served as the Society's office. In September, 1947, he was clearly growing impatient at hearing the same question over and over again:

> When asked where the real box is now Mr Temple snaps his thin lips shut. He admits, however, that the Society has rather given up trying to get the Bishops to open the box and is concentrating upon healing through water and spirit cures based upon Joanna's writings.[38]

In Blockley Alice Seymour's fortunes had suffered during the war when Headland College, and the associated property that she still leased in Plymouth, was destroyed by bombing, and compensation went to the owner, the Earl of St Aldwyn. Her reduced circumstances forced her to accept a pension of ten shillings a week from a parish charity. What was worse, she also lost her stalwart friend and helper, Mary Robertson, who died in 1943 after a breakdown caused her to move into a nursing home in Edinburgh. Nor was Alice's home any longer her own. The Coach House, which was used as a book store in the grounds of Rock Cottage, had been badly damaged in the early part of the war and had to be repaired at the expense of Annie Vesey (later Stitt), who then purchased the whole property for the modest sum of £500. On the surface life at Rock Cottage continued as before, with Annie and Alice's nephew, Dr Seymour, keeping from her any details that might cause her anxiety. She died on 24 October, 1947, aged 90 years, and was buried in Blockley cemetery. Engraved on her headstone is a quotation from Habakkuk 2:3:

*The vision is yet for an appointed time*
*In the end it shall speak and not lie*
*Though it tarry – wait for it*

Meanwhile Cecil Jowett was carrying on his daily business from 3 Mount Grove, Gatley, apparently paying little attention to the Box that stood under a window in an upstairs bedroom. Even the Panaceans had to admit that it was difficult to keep Joanna Southcott's Box of Sealed Prophecies in the public consciousness. Paper shortage meant that newspapers were reluctant to afford space to the subject, and of the London daily papers only the *News Chronicle* accepted the occasional article. Yet the Society continued to advertise, and Robert Temple, their secretary and chief spokesman since 1935, believed that whatever they did was over-ruled for a divine purpose. He wrote twice to Cecil Jowett in 1949 and again in 1950 in an attempt to keep in touch, but received no replies.[39] Interviewed by the *Evening Standard* on 20 April, 1950, he talked freely about the Society's beliefs explaining how Joanna Southcott's Box had been handed down from guardian to guardian since her death. When asked where it was, Mr Temple said that he did not know; he did know, but refused to say, the name of the present guardian. When asked if he had seen the Box, he replied, 'No, I have taken it entirely on trust'.

If contact with Cecil Jowett had worn thin, it was a different story with Annie Veysey Stitt who increasingly turned to Robert Temple for help and advice after her husband's death in January, 1950. When she confided that she might sell Rock Cottage, she gave heavy hints that, as this would mean destroying valuable manuscripts, it might be desirable for the Panacea Society to purchase the property.[40] Mr Temple replied with a suggestion that, rather than see any relics destroyed, they could offer space and safe custody at Bedford to anything of value or interest connected with Joanna.[41] Annie wrote back a long letter by return:

> Yes! Indeed it would be a sad thing for this property to pass from the Work. I have had so many improvements done & also bought more Freehold land from the Churchill Estate, that it is now quite private. The Book Store is now a nice red tiled Hall & would be suitable for meetings etc. No doubt if a brewer bought it he would use it as a Store Cellar, to me quite a desecration!

She then listed the relics in her possession: engraved glass Communion goblets, a patchwork quilt, a cradle cover and robe and the original copper plate by William Sharp of Joanna's portrait. There was the splendid banner in safe storage she could retrieve within two hours, and the white silk dress that Alice Seymour had worn at St Paul's Cathedral for her confirmation by the late Bishop of London, Dr Arthur Foley Winnington Ingram. Alice had left it for Annie to wear on the occasion of the opening

*Annie Veysey Stitt (1884-1971), leader of the Southcott Society after Alice Seymour's death. This was taken by Annie's paralysed brother, as she came onto the terrace at Rock Cottage for tea with him.*

of the Box. Describing all this to Mr Temple left Annie quite overwhelmed; she confessed that in writing to him she had gone against the wishes of her late husband who used to caution her against making any enquiries through what he termed 'Bedford'.[42]

She wrote again the following year to compliment the Society for placing a notice in the *Daily Sketch:* 'I am thankful you have the power & means to make it known. God will richly bless your efforts!'.[43]

There was then a flurry of correspondence between them, as Mr Temple forwarded enquiries that he had received for Alice Seymour's publications and Annie explained that many were now out of print and there were no funds to reprint them. On Coronation Day, 1953, she proudly sent him a leaflet that she had produced for her local Coronation Committee, after they had asked for details about the movement. After repeating Alice Seymour's mistaken idea that the Box had to be opened within three miles of the City of London, Annie concluded her letter with the words, 'We must possess our Faith. Do you know who is the present Custodian? Since Mr Galpin died.'[44]

Mr Temple congratulated her on the leaflet and answered her questions:

> Wherever the opening will take place I hope it may be on this side of London. Indeed, we here have even hoped it might be in Bedford, but of course that conflicts with the limit of three miles from the heart of London. However, I suppose the last word on final arrangements would rest with the Custodian? With regard to the Custodian, I much regret that I cannot give you any information and, personally, I never heard of Mr Galpin; I have always thought the Custodian would be known to you. We continue to advertise from time to time, urging that the Bishops should open The Box as we firmly believe that they should, but I have often wondered how it would come about. As you say, we must keep the Faith and it seems right to do what we can to keep the matter in the public view.[45]

By return of post Annie wrote back to explain who Mr Galpin was and to say, 'Yes! She [Alice Seymour] did tell me where the Box is! But I have never yet confirmed it myself. She had *seen it*! . . . I did attend the opening of that American faked Box in 1926 [sic] at Church House, Westminster. My Godfather the late Bishop of Crediton, Dr R E Trefusis, also was represented by his Chaplain. Of course it proved to be a "Publicity Stunt", but it did not hasten the opening of the Real Box.'[46]

The following year the American evangelist, Billy Graham, set the country alight. Annie Stitt wrote to ask Mr Temple if the Panacea Society would collaborate with the Southcott Society in a campaign to draw attention to their own prophetess.[47] After discussion the idea was rejected by the Council at Bedford and Temple admitted sadly: 'The fact is, it seems to us, that "Billy Graham" is NEWS in a way in which, unfortunately, Joanna Southcott is not'.[48] The Panacea also pointed out that they regarded the Society as a separate entity, with objectives other than its strong advocacy of Joanna Southcott and the opening of the Box, so they felt they must continue to work on an entirely independent basis. Happily, this stance did nothing to spoil the relationship that had developed between Mr Temple and Annie Stitt, who wrote appreciatively each time she saw one of the notices in the paper. Mr Temple told her in September, 1956:

> We like to keep the subject in view by getting one in when we can but it does seem to grow more difficult to get space and of course the cost has risen very considerably since the war. It was indeed interesting to learn that you had a visit from a representative of the British Israel Federation; this would seem to be quite a new development on their part and we are very glad that you were able to re-assure him with regard to your financial position. We sincerely trust that there will never be any difficulty about this, and that your conviction that our 'Watch' is nearly ended may soon be proved true. Certainly all the appearances seem to show that the Opening of The Box cannot be very much longer deferred.[49]

Robert Temple's words may have given him pause to wonder, and perhaps worry, about the present custodian of the Box; despite his letters with enclosed stamped addressed envelopes he had heard nothing from Cecil Jowett since the war. Nor was he to hear anything until suddenly, on 12 May, 1957, a brief note arrived from 3 Mount Grove, Gatley:

> Dear Sir or Madam
> I am writing to inform you I have some information which I am sure will be of great interest to you so would be pleased if you will get in touch with me as soon as possible.
> Yours sincerely,
> Maud Jowett.[50]

This note would open a new chapter in the history of Joanna Southcott's Box of Sealed Prophecies.

# 12

# Coming to the Centre, 1957-2003

Robert Temple, realising that something must have happened to her husband, lost no time in contacting Maud Jowett to express a hope that all was well at 3 Mount Grove, Gatley.[1] When she wrote again, it was to confirm his sad suspicion:

> Dear Mr Temple
> Your letter dated 14th May safely to hand. The reason for my writing to you is my dear husband Cecil Kaye Jowett has passed away. In his safe keeping was a large box bequeathed to him by his Father Mr Edwin A Jowett, late of Morecambe which after my husband's death had to be handed over to the Panacea Society. Would you please make a date when *you personally* can call and collect the same. This being my husband's request. On no account will I hand it over to anybody else. Awaiting your reply
> Yours sincerely,
> Maud Jowett.[2]

After expressing his sorrow at the news and a wish that Cecil Jowett had been spared to keep the Box in safe custody for as long as might be necessary, Mr Temple assured Maud that the Panacea Society would faithfully continue the trust.

> I shall, as you suggest, appoint a day as soon as possible to collect the box but this will take a little time and it may not be until next week; I hope this may not be in any way inconvenient to you. I shall write again as soon as arrangements are settled and should be very grateful if you could let us have a note of any message or instruction about the box, if any, which may have been left by Mr Jowett in his Will or otherwise.[3]

On the same day he wrote in confidence to Mr G. Reinli, a member of the Society who lived at Stone, Staffordshire, and asked for his help. 'We wish to have a wooden box transported from a place called Gatley, in Cheshire, to Bedford; and do not care to entrust this to the Railway or to any Road Transport of a public nature. The box weighs well over 1 cwt but I do not know the dimensions. Could you convey

*R. F. Graham, a member of the Panacea Society who accompanied Robert Temple to Gatley to collect the Box from Maud Jowett on 27 May 1957. Travelling by train, they arrived back in Bedford that same night.*

this for us on your car? Nobody here now owns one!'[4]

Mr Reinli, who realised precisely what was being asked of him, replied: 'Many thanks for your letter. If it is Joanna's Box I doubt if my car is big enough. . . . However there is a Panacea publication either in leaflet or booklet form giving an illustration of the box with its exact dimensions. If you can get hold of it and give me the details it will help.'[5] Mr Reinli need not have worried. Robert Temple had already had second thoughts about carrying such a large, heavy box in a private car over such a distance, and decided to fetch it down by train. Together with Mr R.F. Graham, another member of the Society from Bedford, he travelled to Gatley where the Box was officially handed over to them. An official receipt was made out:

> May 27th 1957
>
> I hereby acknowledge to have received, on behalf of The Panacea Society, The Box bequeathed to The Society by the late Mr Cecil Kaye Jowett in whose care it has been since the death of his Father, Mr E.A. Jowett in 1926.
>
> R.T. Hon. Secretary, The Panacea Society.
>
> To Mrs Maud Jowett, 3 Mount Grove, Gatley, Cheadle, Cheshire.[6]

Temple and Graham arrived safely back in Bedford with the Box that night, and some time later put their signatures to the following affidavit:

> We, the undersigned, hereby certify that, on Monday, May 27th, 1957, we received from Mrs Maud Jowett at 3 Mount Grove, Gatley, Cheshire, a box which had been bequeathed to her late husband, Cecil Kaye Jowett, by his Father, Edwin A. Jowett, late of Morecambe, and left by Cecil Kaye Jowett to The Panacea Society, Bedford; which Box we positively believe

> to be the Box of Sealed Writings of Joanna Southcott. We brought the Box to Bedford where it has been placed in a locked Chest at 'Castleside', 9 Newnham Road, the key to be kept in the care of the Secretary, jointly with Mr P. Rasmussen, pending any further decision by The Panacea Society. R.F. Graham. R. Temple (Hon. Secretary)[7]

Although Robert Temple, now in his seventies, must have been exhausted after the journey, he found time to write to Maud Jowett the next day to apologise for the fact that they had not had time to chat the previous day, and to extend a warm welcome to Bedford should she ever think of coming south. His letter concluded: 'If there were anything we could do to help you; indeed, if we could be of service to you in any way at any time; I am sure we should be only too pleased to do anything we possibly could'.[8]

Few people beyond the Society knew that the Panacea was now the custodian of Joanna Southcott's Box of Sealed Prophecies. Outwardly things stayed the same. The same advertisements urging the bishops to open the Box appeared regularly in national newspapers. 'I was pleased to see your notice re. Joanna Southcott's Box in the *Daily Sketch* this week', Annie Stitt wrote to Mr Temple on Boxing Day that year, enclosing a cutting from a Cheltenham paper that contained an interview of herself and a photo of Rock Cottage. She had also worked out that Group Captain Peter Townsend was descended from the Southcott family, because in the reign of Henry VIII the niece of Lady Jane Seymour had married a George Southcott.[9] She wrote again the following year to thank the Panacea for placing another notice in the *Daily Sketch*, this time enclosing references to believers in New Zealand and California.[10] After this, several letters followed, with Annie often repeating herself and apologising for being in haste. She had obtained an old wooden chest from a retired postman and it bore the initials 'IC' – like Joanna's seal – so she had packed the Pascoe collection of manuscripts in it. She had also had George Troup's gravestone in Blockley churchyard repaired.[11]

In September, 1959, a letter was delivered to the office of the Panacea Society from Winifred Greenroyd, the widowed daughter of Edwin and Emily Jowett. Winifred, who lived in Morecambe, wondered whether the Society would like to buy a beautiful book of visions that she had inherited from her father.[12] After a brief exchange of letters in which it transpired that the money was needed for the forthcoming wedding of Winifred's daughter, Mr Temple sent her £100 for the book and in friendly memory of her father and his interest in the Society.[13] When she replied, Winifred could not thank him enough.

> With what appreciation I opened your letter this morning and read the contents. I first of all knelt down to thank our God for his goodness when I so much needed it. You have no idea what it means to my Daughter Emily and myself. She is being married on Dec.27th 1958. Now things will be as she had always wished, only her Dad won't be there, at least *not in Body*. . . . The offer was great and to thank you all I just don't know how.[14]

The correspondence obviously set minds wondering whether there were any more papers from earlier days of the movement that should be collected before they disappeared, and on 17 October, 1958, Mr Temple approached Maud Jowett at Gatley.

> I hope you will not mind my writing to you again about the Box we received from you in May last year, and which of course remains in our very sure keeping. It was perhaps remiss of me but it did not occur to me at the time to ask you whether Mr Jowett had left any message for us in connection with the Box, other than the simple mention of his desire that it should come to us; nor any papers which it would be of interest to have in connection with the Box?[15]

Maud, who had heard about the money paid to her sister-in-law, wrote back:

> I received your letter asking me if my dear husband had left any message for you as regards the box, which had been safely kept by us for many years. The only thing he told me was to see you got the box safe which I did and he said once when he visited Octavia that she said some gift would be given to me. So I was rather surprised at the way you took it after we had kept it secret for so long. But at the time I was too upset to say anything to you having lost my mother & father and then my dear husband all in three months.[16]

Robert Temple, clearly at a loss, replied as follows:

> Thank you for your letter . . . which occasioned me some surprise. The Box we received from you had of course, as no doubt you know, been handed down from one to another and regarded as a sacred trust until custody was accepted by Mr E.A. Jowett, and then by your husband Mr Cecil Jowett who, I am sure, regarded it in that light; in which spirit we also accepted it in our turn.

It never occurred to us that you might expect some material reward for the care bestowed upon it, or carrying out your husband's wishes. Of course Mr Jowett's association with Octavia in the matter was long before my connection with The Panacea Society and I had never heard of any promise such as you mention. But we naturally hold Octavia in the highest esteem as the founder of The Society, and for other reasons, and we should certainly wish to give effect to any desire or promise expressed by her. At the same time it is a little difficult to know just what was intended or might be expected. However, I enclose our cheque for £50 herewith, together with many thanks for your trouble in the matter, and trust you will feel that this adequately fulfils Octavia's intention.[17]

Maud was grateful for the cheque but took offence at Mr Temple's remarks. She wrote back angrily:

I am quite aware the box was a sacred trust and my dear husband and myself have always kept it as such. . . . When Octavia was alive she always kept in touch with my husband's parents when they were alive and after their death with my husband and myself. Each Christmas she sent us a small give [gift?] we always thought of her as a friend. By the tone of your letter you seem to think I am trying to exploit you in some way. Believe me that was not so. You wrote to me asking if I could tell you anything and I did so.[18]

Mr Temple sent another temperate reply:

I am quite sure that anyone who knew Octavia could not but have the happiest and kindest recollection of her; and I am glad that you will now have some permanent remembrance of your association with her. I am sorry if anything I wrote should have occasioned you any distress. Believe me, I certainly had no such intention but I merely had no knowledge of any arrangement; and I am glad to have been able to give effect to any intention Octavia had in mind.[19]

With this reply their correspondence ceased for some time.

On the last day of April, 1959, the secretary of the Panacea Society was interviewed for an article in the *Manchester Guardian*. 'In Bedford there lives a retired banker who believes that the key to the universe is contained in a sealed box weighing 156 lb and nailed with copper nails', it read. After outlining the theology of the Society and describing Robert Temple's background, the reporter asked him the usual question:

Where was the box at present? Temple replied, 'I'm afraid we couldn't reveal that sort of thing. But we can guarantee that it's ready for production if the bishops condescend to play their part'. When the next question came – Had he seen the box himself? – Temple 'paused for some time before grudgingly conceding that he had'.

Annie Stitt and members of the Southcott Society were hopeful of great things in 1960 because it marked fifty years since Alice Seymour had been called to publish her books on Joanna. Whilst politicians and diplomats looked to the United Nations to stop the world toppling into chaos, Robert Musel of *The Independence Examiner*, published in Missouri, proclaimed:

> BOX HOLDS PRESCRIPTION FOR ALL WORLD'S ILLS. The world is in such a parlous state that I got in touch with Robert Temple today and urged him to "open the box" right away.'I'd like to,' said the 74-year old secretary of the Panacea Society, but we cannot open the box unless there are 24 bishops of the Church of England present. And although we've been trying with newspaper advertisements, petitions and other forms of pressure for 44 years, we still cannot persuade enough bishops to gather at the same time.
>
> Temple is one of the guardians of what his Society calls 'Joanna Southcott's Box'. . . . Temple explained that since only Joanna Southcott had the revelation for peaceful existence it was natural that the summit and all other international conferences were foredoomed. His advice to Eisenhower, Khruschev, Macmillan and company is to save their time and convene the bishops instead.
>
> 'To open the box?'
>
> 'Certainly,' said Temple.
>
> 'Where is the box?'
>
> 'In safe hands.'
>
> 'Can I see it?'
>
> 'Alas, no – not until the bishops gather.'[20]

As the year progressed there were signs of imminent doom at home and abroad in the form of floods, earthquakes, and the build-up of nuclear weapons. 'How can anyone doubt the importance of the "Box of Sealed Writings"?' Annie Stitt asked Robert Temple, when writing to thank the Panacea Society for their notice on the front page of the *Daily Sketch* on 17 December, 1960. She also raised the spectre of selling Rock Cottage again, citing her age (she was seventy-six) and the difficulty of finding help as reasons.[21] Robert Temple suggested that she might try approaching the National Trust to see if they might take it on.

> We should be very sorry indeed if Rock Cottage passed out of your hands, but you say you are getting old and labour is difficult to get; and indeed we here begin to feel very much in the same position. It does grow more and more difficult to find persons who will come forward and carry on the work. . . . The way everything is going all over the world, in addition to the disasters in this country, which you so aptly mention as fulfilling Joanna's word, does seem to show that that time cannot be far off now, but it will of course take a lot to bring the Bishops to their knees; they are very stubborn. Meantime, as you say, we can only try to go on in Faith and Hope.[22]

The crux of the problem was finding persons who would come forward to carry on the work. The Box of Sealed Prophecies was safe, and as far as the Box was concerned there was little to do beyond keeping it safe and regularly reminding the world (especially the bishops) of its existence.

Perhaps it was one of the advertisements about the Box that drew the attention of Ursula Jowett Bowden, a granddaughter of Edwin Armstrong Jowett, who wrote from Plymouth in September 1961 offering to sell to the Panacea Society a large collection of letters that had been left at 'Southcot', Hawarden Avenue, Morecambe, after the death of her father.

> I would inform you that these have come into my possession through my family, the Jowetts until the death of my Grandfather – before my birth – he had in his trust the Johanna Southcott box – this was then taken into the care of my Uncle – Mr Cecil Kaye Jowett who resided until his death 3-4 yrs ago at 3, Mount Grove, Gatley. From this address the box was taken into the custody of the Society in Bedford.[23]

A similar account of the Box's recent history came from Emily Nicholson, another of Edwin Jowett's granddaughters, who wrote to the Panacea Society that same month. 'Please find enclosed an item which I suppose is connected with the writings of Johanna Southcot', she wrote. 'It has come to light among some odds & ends which I got from the bungalow 'Southcot' when my Uncle Tom (Burrow) died at Christmas. I know my Uncle Cecil (Jowett) of Gatley had the 'box' & when he died Auntie Maud arranged with you to take it all away to Bedford, so as this appears to be connected with that, I am sending it on herewith & trust it will be of interest to you'.[24]

Towards the end of 1961 Annie Stitt wrote to Robert Temple to thank him for the Panacea Society's recent notices in national newspapers. Because she had been ill earlier in the year, she had done nothing about Rock Cottage, where the administration of the Southcott Society was falling into neglect. Many of Joanna's books were now out of print and there was no secretary or subscription list. Annie struggled on, but found it increasingly difficult to cope with enquiries: 'If I feel it is a genuine old Believer who wants a certain book I just try to find one & send it', she admitted. She also revealed both anxiety and excitement at the prospect of a grand conjunction of planets the following year:

> I feel if we can safely get to Feb 1962 without any major trouble, the danger will be lessened. There will be 7 Planets round the sign Aquarius in the Heavens then, it could only happen once in 20,000 years & a Sect in India said, 'The World will be destroyed then.' Now they have altered their minds & I believe it will [be] the time of the 'Conquest of Evil' in this World, & Peace will reign. May God grant our prayers will be answered.[25]

Mr Temple, naturally sympathetic, wrote:

> You say that there is now no Secretary or Subscription List; we here are a rather dwindling community and find ourselves in a somewhat similar position. But is there now no other body representing a Southcott Movement or Connection? We have never been in touch with any other than yourself since the deaths of two of our great Founders and Leaders. I read about the prediction of the Indian Sect, and whatever may be the truth about that I hope that your own feeling about February 1962 may be true and that the answer to our hopes and prayers may be given very soon. It does indeed grow ever more difficult to carry on, but I do trust that you as well as myself and others here may see their fulfilment.[26]

The prospect of the grand conjunction focused Mr Temple's mind. If it presaged the long-expected request from the bishops to open the Box, then all must be made ready. Perhaps whilst rehearsing the event in his mind he remembered a vital detail. They would need a key, but no keys had been handed over with the Box. On 16 November he wrote to Maud Jowett:

> Dear Mrs Jowett
> It is just over two years since I last had occasion to write to you, and I hope you will not mind my approaching you again in the hope that you may be able to help us. You may perhaps know that we have recently acquired from your niece, Mrs Bowden, a very interesting collection of letters written to followers, and by followers, of Joanna Southcott, from the earliest days until now. Among these we found a transcript by Mrs E.A. Jowett of a Special Note left by her husband to the effect that: 'in case Cecil does not care to have the responsibility, I desire the Box and two keys shall be forwarded to Mrs Barltrop, 12 Albany Rd, Bedford.' At the death of your husband we duly received the Box at your hands, but no keys, and I am unable to find that any keys were sent at any time to Mrs Barltrop (Octavia) and we should be very grateful if you could throw any light on the matter of their disposal, or give us any information at all about the keys.[27]

When, after nearly three weeks, he had received no reply, he wrote again.[28] He received a prickly response. Maud knew all about what her sisters-in-law had sent him, but was offended by what she thought was Mr Temple's insinuation that her husband had not wanted to care of the Box. She expostulated:

> Well, I would not think we would guard it for over thirty years if this had been so. Well I have got the keys you mentioned which I did not know about when you took the box I found them amongst my husband['s] belonging[s]. There are two keys in a case also one of the writing. Now I shall expect you to send me some recompense for these And when you have done so I will register the same to you. I can very well do with this with Christmas coming along.[29]

Mr Temple politely explained that he had said nothing about Maud's husband but had merely quoted a Special Note left by her father-in-law. He pointed out that the Box had been handed down since 1814; its custody had always been accepted as an honour and a privilege, and never had the new Custodian been expected to recompense the previous one for his care. He concluded:

> The keys have always been handed on with the Box and we are confident that it would be your husband's wish that this should be done. The Box could certainly be opened without the keys, but it will be sad to record, when the time comes . . .

> that the keys were not faithfully passed on, as they had been thitherto, at the death of Mr Cecil Jowett. We would ask you to give serious consideration to the nature of such dereliction. We find it quite impossible to say what recompense we should offer for the carrying out of such a duty and perhaps you will advise us what you would consider adequate; we would then consider the matter.[30]

Maud did not like this reply. She wrote:

> I notice your remarks to me. Now I don't feel like being worried any more about this matter I have had enough worry in the last few years when one has to get along alone. As you say you can open the box without keys. Well if that is so you need not bother any more.[31]

Mr Temple waited until after Christmas before pursuing the matter further. He then trod delicately.

> We thank you for your letter of December 13th but have delayed to reply as we have certainly no wish to trouble you unduly. At the same time, may I point out that the surest way to avoid any further trouble in the matter would be to carry out the charge which has been handed down so faithfully, for so many generations, and send us the keys of The Box, which should have accompanied it. . . . We should, of course willingly repay your costs in the matter and, if it is a question of price, as we said in conclusion of our last letter, if you will let us know what you would consider an adequate remuneration we would give the matter our serious consideration.[32]

Maud, still riled, replied:

> I did my duty in sending you word about the box as soon as my dear husband passed away. So I have in no way not filled my trust. The keys I found afterwards and which you did not know anything about till you got the things from Morecambe. So I resent your remarks. Now as you say an adequate remuneration will be sent to me. Well I shall just leave this matter with you and as soon as I receive the same I will send the key.[33]

After a further spiky exchange, Maud sent off the keys by registered post and received by return a cheque and accompanying note:

> Dear Mrs Jowett, We have today received your Registered Packet containing the keys and, as promised, send you herewith our cheque for £50, to which we have added the sum of 5/- to

*The keys to Joanna Southcott's Box of Sealed Prophecies that were passed on to the Panacea Society by Maud Jowett in February, 1962. The larger key is labelled 'S.W.' [='Sealed Writings] followed by J.S. This key turns in the lock of the outer box, the lid of which is nailed shut. The smaller key should open the inner box.*

cover the cost of packing and postage.[34]

Although Mr Temple heard no more from Maud Jowett he was still regularly approached by journalists repeating the same questions about the Box. When Annie Stitt[35] commended him on the way he dealt with questions posed out of idle curiosity, he explained, 'I always hope that I am guided to say the right thing for it would not do to refuse an interview, and it always helps to make Joanna's name known and keeps the matter of the Box in the public mind'.[36]

Annie Stitt, now in her eighties, had all but given up the struggle to cope with her responsibilities. When people enquired for Joanna Southcott's books, she directed them to the public libraries or the British Museum, but it weighed on her conscience that there was still a stock of copies in the Book Store at Rock Cottage being kept ready for the opening of the Box.[37] Mr Temple, after asking whether it would be better if he did not direct any future enquiries for Joanna's books to Annie, explained: 'We have never kept a stock of these and of course printing costs are several times greater than they were in Miss Seymour's day. While it may well be that people sometimes enquire from curiosity, they cannot become genuine Believers until that curiosity has been satisfied!' She had invited him to visit Blockley, but he could not accept because he had given up his car and no longer left Bedford. He did, however, arrange for Mrs Sybil Cuthbertson, the President of the Panacea Society, to visit Annie later in the year for a chat and to see the cottage.[38]

Mr Temple's reference to the high costs of reprinting Alice Seymour's books must have sent alarm bells ringing in Annie's head. In a letter marked 'Private & Personal' she wrote back quickly to say:

> The Books written by Miss Seymour are copyright and from MSS [manuscripts] left her by her parents & Grandparents. When she passed over, the British Museum sent a Barister

*Sybil Cuthbertson, President of the Panacea Society, 1964-78.*

[sic] here at my request, & he selected what he felt was of value from the MSS. He wished them to be brought to London by ourselves. So I took the woman who worked here with me for safety. We packed it in two large *Brown Paper parcels. Not* Deed Boxes. At Paddington I quickly called a Taxi & arrived at the Museum & were in his room when the Phone rang. After a short time he said 'You have missed the ladies they are safely in my room, please return here now.' He then told me, 'I sent 2 Detectives to meet your train & bring you back here in my car. They now tell me you were *not on the train*.' I quite understood. As we were plainly dressed & carrying *Brown Paper Parcels*. It was rather a thrill to think we were *not* observed. I was so many years in a large West End of London Bank, I knew it was safer not to attract any attention, & no doubt were mistaken for Dressmakers parcels! And not valuable MSS. At the museum the keeper remarked 'We have not received such a gift of MSS Southcott interest since 1875.'[39]

This account of how she had deposited Alice Seymour's collection of manuscripts in the British Museum after 1947 prompted Mr Temple to ask Annie whether she could tell him where in Joanna's Writings were to be found the conditions attached to the opening of the Box.[40] His question put Annie on the spot and she admitted:

> The real Box, as far as I know has never been opened. I do not know of the conditions of the opening in due course. I understood from Miss Seymour it would be within 3 miles of the City of London & may be at the Brit Museum in the King's Library *by* the *24 Bishops* **or** *their Representatives*. In a time of 'National Danger'. This may even mean Financial Danger & surely we are getting into a disturbed period even at this moment with strikes, prices, & dissatisfaction everywhere. . . . I believe *no women* will attend the day of opening. But *when asked must* go *clad* all in *white*! Miss S. told me the Clergy will find that therein to cause them to *'weep on their knees'* . . . . *I* have never *seen* the Box, but it may even enclose

> 'Ancient Deeds' as Joanna's Family formerly held large estates in Herts. The people who have the Box must surely know what the conditions are! I believe the Jowett Family held it at one time. I must cease, but feel I can not give any definite opinion of its 'Contents'. . . . I am now 81 years, so I am no longer an expert at expressing my own ideas![41]

When Mrs Cuthbertson and a friend called at Rock Cottage on Tuesday, 25 May, 1965, for their brief visit to Annie, they found her living like a recluse. She seldom left the house and normally refused to let anyone in. She only welcomed Mrs Cuthbertson because she had been sent by Mr Temple. An American caller had recently begged her to let him in, but she had refused.[42] By 1970, however, Annie was forced to accept help from the village postmaster's wife, who came each morning to dress her arthritic legs and bring her food, an arrangement that worked well for eighteen months before tragedy struck. The occupant of a house across the road looked out from her bedroom in the early hours of 26 July, 1971, to see Rock Cottage in flames. She raised the alarm, but by the time anyone reached the cottage it was an inferno. 'No-one could have saved Mrs Stitt,' the neighbour said, after Annie's body was found, badly burned, on the ground floor. Another remarked, 'Mrs Stitt was an old lady with no relations, who lived for yesterday all the time. It was terribly sad because she was a wonderful woman in her day.'[43]

The Executors of Annie Stitt's Will were left to sort out the problem of what to do with the Southcott relics that survived the fire. Some, including the banner, patchworks, and costly gifts made for Shiloh, had been sent by Annie to a local bank for safe-keeping. Before deciding where to send them, the Executors contacted the Panacea Society to say:

> We are not quite certain as to the connection between your Society and the Joanna Southcott Movement, but we would however appreciate any information you can give us as to whether or not there are any authorised officers, i.e. Treasurer, Secretary, etc. of the Joanna Southcott Movement and if so, we would be grateful if you could supply us with their addresses. We also understand that the Southcott Box is held by your Society and perhaps you would be kind enough to confirm this for us.[44]

Mrs Cuthbertson explained:

> Early members of The Panacea Society belonged to the Joanna Southcott Movement, which was then under the auspices of

*Details of cords around the box with a label addressed to Robert Stuckey, the eighth Custodian. The letters 'S.W.' [Sealed Writings] have been carved into the lid and are visible at the lower right.*

> Miss Alice Seymour. When some members decided the time had come to write to the Bishops requesting them to open Joanna Southcott's Box of Sealed Writings, Miss Seymour disagreed, and this was the beginning of the breaking away of the Society from Miss Seymour.
>
> We are sorry we cannot give you the names of any authorised officers of the Southcott Movement at present as members are scattered, but we consider our Society (registered with the Charity Commissioners since 1926) the responsible body for any future developments. The Society knows the whereabouts of the Box and it will be produced when the Bishops comply with the conditions laid down.[45]

In the absence of officials or even a subscription list of members, the Executors had to decide who should operate the bank accounts opened years before in the name of The Southcott Fund.[46] No one had been appointed officially at Mrs Stitt's death to take over her office, but two long-standing members (Mr Michael Nicholas and Lily Duckett) managed to trace the address of Frederick O. Mills, an 'old believer' who lived in London. Mr Mills said that he had been appointed a Trustee and signed to that effect, but there was no document to prove

*Joanna Southcott's Box, photographed in 2001.*

it. When he mentioned that he had given £100 to the cause and now regretted it, Lily asked if he could prove that he had made the gift. He found the counter-foil of his cheque, sent in the number, and it cleared the way. They were accepted as administrators, and the Southcott Fund, said to be less than £2000, was transferred to Lily Duckett's address in Sunderland.[47]

Lily Duckett, working from home at 22 Frederick Street, Sunderland, became the new head of the Southcott Society. One of her first tasks was to collect a lorry-load of books from Rock Cottage. She later reported that they had been sadly neglected, and those that could not be cleaned were destroyed. The Charity Commissioners insisted that the magnificent banner and all other relics had to go to a museum and they were duly sent to the Royal Albert Museum in Exeter where they remain to this day.[48]

As head of the Southcott Society it fell to Lily Duckett to answer enquiries about Joanna's writings, especially from members visiting from abroad. In May, 1974, she wrote to tell Mrs Cuthbertson that she had been entertaining Mr Aubrey Glover, President of the Southcott Society of Australia.

> The two Mr Glovers have been here for a few days – They thank

*The author and two of the Trustees of the Panacea Society, Mrs Ruth Klein and Mr John Coghill, examining the label on the Box.*

> you for your kindness in sending them the leaflets – They have gone to tour Scotland and will be back in a week I expect – They are most anxious that the Box is in safe keeping and were pleased to know you had it at Bedford – There was a rumour it was in London. So that puts that right. That is of course if it is true you have it. I think the time is getting near for the opening. . . . I will be very pleased if you will kindly confirm that you have it.

Mrs Cuthbertson immediately replied, saying that the whereabouts of the Box of Sealed Writings was to be kept secret until twenty-four bishops asked to have it produced.[49]

By May, 1976, Lily Duckett had moved, taking all the leaflets, books and letters belonging to the Southcott Society to her new home, a semi-derelict former Masonic Hall at 14 Toward Road in Sunderland. The building was far too big for her to maintain, but she used some of the spaces between pews and on the platforms to store piles of old books and the new leaflets she had reprinted from Alice Seymour's work. The main focus for both the Southcott Society and the Panacea Society was, as always, the opening of Joanna Southcott's Box of Sealed Prophecies. On 24 May, 1976, Lily Duckett wrote to Sybil Cuthbertson:

> The opening of the great Box is the great event to establish the honour of God & the good of mankind to make good all that the Devil made bad & give us all greater blessings than we ever had – God says He has never proved the truth yet but He will at the opening – Then we will have no excuse if we do not obey – Satan will be cast out. . . .[50]

Lily maintained a friendly correspondence with the head of the Panacea Society despite a hint of resentment that the latter had become official custodians of Joanna's Box. Writing to 'Dear Sybil' on 6 July, 1976, Lily said, 'We know the history of the Banner – Also how you got the Box – I leave all this with the Almighty who is a God of Truth. . . . This letter is sent in love to you all. God Bless you, Lily'.[51]

For the rest of the century advertisements urging the bishops to open Joanna Southcott's Box continued to appear in national newspapers regularly twice a year, May and November. There were also occasional attempts to put pressure on the bishops. When Aubrey Glover came on a visit from Australia in 1977, he wrote to the Archbishop of Canterbury and was shocked to receive a reply from the latter's office stating: 'Regarding Joanna Southcott's Box the truth is that this was opened about fifty years ago and was found to contain nothing but a woman's nightcap and a lottery ticket'.[52] Glover asked the Panacea Society, as Custodians of the Box, to help him to confirm its existence beyond doubt, so that neither the bishops nor the general public would be able to draw on this excuse any longer. He wrote:

> You must realise that this ridiculous situation is quite unnecessary when you could so easily put it right. You must also realise that the longer the Box remains closed the greater the judgements will be which will fall upon this nation. All other groups engaged in this work are prepared to put forward a united effort to push on with God's work which He has stated neither men nor devils will prevent. Once again I write to ask you if you are prepared to come forward to assist with this work. I sincerely hope you will at this time join us and would ask you to please direct your reply to our Secretary Miss L. Duckett as to your intentions.[53]

In her reply, Mrs Cuthbertson, President of the Panacea Society, pointed to a publication entitled, *Transactions of the Panacea Society with the Archbishops and Bishops of the Church of England*, which contained a detailed record of their campaign to gain the bishops' co-operation. She explained that, since the end of this formidable campaign, the Lord had commanded that the Church should be left to itself, and that there would be no more divine directions until, in a grave national crisis, the bishops would be compelled by the people to ask for the Box to be opened.[54]

Mrs Cuthbertson was expressing one side of a dichotomy that had polarized the Southcott movement ever since Joanna's death. There had always been tension between a pro-active group, comprising those who wanted to force the bishops to call for the opening of the Box, and a passive group, composed of those who insisted that there was nothing to do but wait patiently on the Lord, Who would accomplish all in His own good time. The Panacea Society has at different times embraced both points of view: pro-active during Octavia's lifetime, they adopted a more passive approach during the second half of the twentieth century. With the dawn of a new millennium, however, and the unprecedented threat facing humanity, the current Custodians have become more dynamic in promoting awareness of the Box which they claim is 'this country's greatest treasure'.

In August, 2002, two of the Trustees of the Panacea Society were asked to explain the significance of Joanna Southcott's Box. They said,

> It has been prophesied, that, when the Box is opened in the right conditions, it will bring relief from all immediate danger and show us how to seize our spiritual destiny. Prophets have told us that the Box will be sent for suddenly and unawares – in fear – in every kind of fear, physical, religious, political and social.
>
> But, afterwards – then there will be a time of such revival as has never been seen before.

*Semper redivivus* – the promise of spiritual renewal and the great return – if this is the promise locked up in Joanna Southcott's Box of Sealed Prophecies, it explains why, for over two hundred years, believers have held it in such reverence and continue to view it with awe. It also explains why, for more than two centuries, a succession of custodians and hundreds of believers have made it the central task of their lives to safeguard the Box and mounted such exhaustive campaigns to persuade the bishops to have it opened.

# Notes

Note on Calendar: There are frequent references to 'Old Style' and 'New Style' dates in Southcottian writings. These refer to the transition from the Gregorian (O.S.) to the Julian (N.S.) that took place in England in 1752, when the calendar was moved forward eleven days. Although Joanna claimed that the Spirit had instructed her to use 'Old Style' dates, she did not invariably do this.

CHAPTER 1

1. LMA Acc. 1040/187, p.1376.
2. Southcott, *Strange Effects of Faith, With Remarkable Prophecies* [Book 1], Exeter, 1801, p.19.
3. Southcott, *Strange Effects of Faith, With Remarkable Prophecies* [Book 1], Exeter, 1801, p.21.
4. Blockley Coll. 577/3.
5. BL Add. MS 32634, f.156.
6. BL Add. MS 32635, f.175.
7. Southcott, *Divine & Spiritual Letters of Prophecies* [Book 9], London, nd. p.9.
8. Jones, L.E.C.[ed.] *The Time for Worshipping in the Spirit illucidated from the Visitation of Prophecy to J.S. 1792-1814*. Bradford-on-Avon, 1853, p.8.
9. LMA Acc. 1040/213.
10. BL Add. MS 47794, f.1.
11. Southcott, *Trial of Joanna Southcott during Seven Days* [Book 25], p. 43.
12. Southcott, *Trial of Joanna Southcott during Seven Days* [Book 25], p. 74-5
13. Blockley Coll. 596/15.

CHAPTER 2

1. *An Answer to the World,* [Book 43], London, 1806, pp.4-5.
2. A full account of this 'Trial' of Joanna's Writings may be read in Brown, *Joanna Southcott: The Woman Clothed With the Sun*, Lutterworth, 2002, pp.124-6.
3. Quoted in Exell, *Joanna Southcott at Blockley*, p.22.
4. Foley's Diary, Blockley 515, pp.28, 30, 32.
5. PS Sotheran Collection, Item 80, p.114.
6. *An Answer to the World,* [Book 43], London, 1806, p.5.
7. PS [3-1-1] n/d MS letter.
8. PS Sotheran Collection, Field to Ingall, 9/5/1803.
9. BL Add. MS 47799, f.86.
10. Southcott, *Trial of Joanna Southcott during Seven Days* [Book 25], p.55.
11. Southcott, *Trial of Joanna Southcott during Seven Days* [Book 25], pp.55-6.

12. Southcott, *Trial of Joanna Southcott during Seven Days* [Book 25], pp.91-2.
13. Southcott, *Trial of Joanna Southcott during Seven Days* [Book 25], pp.103.
14. Southcott, *Trial of Joanna Southcott during Seven Days* [Book 25], p.133.
15. *An Answer to the World* [Book 43], London, 1806, p.62.
16. BL Add. MS 26038, f.61.
17. BL Add. MS 47795, ff.65-68.
18. Balleine, *Past Finding Out,* p.68.
19. Townley, *Letter to the Editor of the Council of Ten*, p.9.
20. Balleine, *Past Finding Out,* p.69.
21. Letter, 25/12/1815, in BL Add. MS 47800.
22. Balleine, *Past Finding Out,* p.75.
23. Letter, 21/6/1815, in BL Add. MS 47795, f.69.
24. PS Sotheran Collection, Baker to Tolhurst, 31/1/1815.
25. PS Sotheran Collection, 48/225, Underwood to Hirst, 15/4/1815.
26. BL Add. MS 47794, f.136.
27. PS Sotheran Collection, Foley to Eyre, 27/8/1817.
28. BL Add. MS 47795, f.77.
29. DRO 3703Z/Z23, p. 1137.
30. PS [3-1-1], Jowett to Kidd, 19/5/1818.
31. BL Add. MS 47795, f.79.
32. BL Add. MS 47795, ff.81-2.
33. PS [3-1-1], Jowett to Kidd, 21/11/1818.
34. PS [3-1-1], Jowett to Kidd, 3/12/1818.
35. BL Add. MS 47795, f.84.
36. PS [3-1-1], Underwood's letter, 16/6/1819.
37. BL Add. MS 47794, f.136.
38. PS [3-1-1], Jowett to Kidd, 12/12/1819.
39. BL Add. MS 47794, f.140.
40. BL Add MS 47795, f.98.
41. Will of William Sharp, proved 30 September 1824 – PROB 11/1690.
42. BL Add. MS 47798, f.110.
43. BL Add. MS 47798, f.110.
44. Gent. Mag. 1824, ii, 469.
45. BL Add. MS 33404, f.210.

## CHAPTER 3

1. *The Rochdale Monthly*, Nov 1904.
2. Townley, *Letter to the Editor of the Council of Ten*, p.33.
3. Townley, *Letter to the Editor of the Council of Ten*, p.10.
4. BL Add. MS 47796, f.1.
5. BL Add. MS 47796, f.5.
6. BL Add. MS 47796, f.8.
7, BL Add. MS 47796, f.10.
8. BL Add. MS 47796, f.12.
9. BL Add. MS 47796, f.14.
10. BL Add. MS 47796, f.16.

11. BL Add. MS 47794, ff.136-7.
12. BL Add. MS 47796, f.22.
13. BL Add. MS 47796, f.24.
14. BL Add. MS 47796, f.54.
15. BL Add. MS 47796, f.58.
16. BL Add. MS 47796, f.64.
17. BL Add. MS 47794, ff.138-9.
18. PS [3-1-1] Jowett to Kidd, 12/12/1819.
19. BL Add. MS 47795, f.88.
20. PS [3-1-1] Jowett to Kidd, 2/2/1820.
21. BL Add. MS 47794, f.140.
22. Balleine, *Past Finding Out,* pp.80-82.
23. BL Add. MS 47795, ff.98-9.
24. Townley, *Letter to the Editor of the Council of Ten*, p.11.
25. Townley, *Letter to the Editor of the Council of Ten*, pp.12-13.
26. BL Add. MS 47798, f.94.
27. Townley, *Letter to the Editor of the Council of Ten*, p.13.
28. BL Add. MS 47795, ff.104-5.
29. BL Add. MS 47798, f.94.
30. BL Add. MS 47794, f.142.
31. Balleine, *Past Finding Out,* p.69.
32. Townley, *Letter to the Editor of the Council of Ten*, p.9.
33. BL Add. MS 47795, ff.106-7.
34. BL Add. MS 47798, f.92.
35. PS Sotheran Collection, Baylis to Gompertz, 8/7/1822.
36. BL Add. MS 47798, f.97.
37. BL Add. MS 47798, f.99.
38. PS Sotheran Collection, Kidd to Townley, 31/10/1822.
39. BL Add. MS 47798, f.101.
40. BL Add. MS 47802, f.25.
41. BL Add. MS 47794, f.144.
42. Townley, *Letter to the Editor of the Council of Ten*, p.26.
43. BL Add. MS 47795, f.110.
44. PS Sotheran Collection, Communication to Townley, 25/7/1824.
45. PC, Communication to Townley, 6/8/1824.
46. BL Add. MS 70933, f.39.
47. BL Add. MS 47798, f.111.
48. PC, Communication to Townley, 12/9/1924.
49. PS Sotheran Collection, Sankey to Thompson, 19/9/1824.
50. PC, Pughe to Pye, 13/10/1824.
51. BL Add. MS 70933, Communication to Townley, 21/10/1824.
52. LMA Acc No. 1040/209.
53. WRO; Foley's Diary; H.E.P. transcript.
54. LMA Acc No. 1040/209.
55. PS [3-1-1] Pughe to Friends, 5/5/1825.
56. LMA Acc No. 1040/209.
57. LMA Acc No. 1040/206.
58. DRO 3703Z/Z23, p. 1137.

## CHAPTER 4

1. BL Add. MS 47795, f.102.
2. BL Add. MS 47795, ff.104-5.
3. BL Add. MS 47795, ff.108-9.
4. H.J.Haden in N&Q, 5/7/1952.
5. PS [3-1-1] Pughe to Friends, 5/5/1825.
6. DRO 3703Z/Z23.
7. WRO; Foley's Diary; H.E.P. transcript.
8. PS [3-4-16] Foley to Pughe, 1825 [extract]
9. WRO; Foley's Diary; H.E.P. transcript.
10. BL Add. MS 47800, Foley to Pughe, 29/8/1825.
11. PS Archives, T.P.Foley to J.Crossley, 22/9/1825.
12. BL Add. MS 70933, f.45.
13. BL Add. MS 47795, f.116.
14. BL Add. MS 47795, f.118.
15. PS [3-1-1] included in 4/11/1826.
16. BL Add. MS 47795, f.118.
17. *On the Prayers for the Fast Day,* [Book 21], London, 1804, p.11; also, *The Strange Effects of Faith,* [Book 2], Exeter, 1801, pp.81-2.
18. PS Sotheran Collection, Foley to friend, 8/11/1826.
19. PS [3-1-1] Jowett to Kidd, 31/5/1828.
20. PS [3-1-1] Foley to Crossley, 2/10/1828.
21. PS [3-4-16] Foley to a friend, March 1829. [extract]
22. PS [3-1-1] Jowett to Kidd, 14/3/1829.
23. BL Add. MS 47795, f.123.
24. BL Add. MS 47795, ff.124v-125r.
25. BL Add. MS 47795, f.127.
26. BL Add. MS 57860, f.241. Rockett to Foley, August 1830.
27. BL Add. MS 57860, f.237. Taylor to Foley, 30/5/1830.
28. BL Add. MS 47795, f.128.
29. PS [3-1-1] Jowett to Kidd, 24/2/1831.
30. PS [3-1-1] M. Crossley to J. Jowett, 11/12/1833.
31. PS [3-1-1] J. Jowett to S. Jowett, 13/9/1835.
32. PS [1-1-01] J. Jowett to Kidd, 13/9/1835.
33. PS [3-1-1] Eyre's Circular to Believers, 7/10/1835.
34. PS [3-1-1] quoted in 7/10/1835.
35. PS [3-1-1] Eyre to J. Jowett, 7/10/1835.
36. PS [3-1-1] J. Jowett to Kidd, 11/10/1835.

## CHAPTER 5

1. LMA Acc No. 1040/127.
2. BL Add. MS 70933, f.45.
3. PS [3-1-1] L.E.C. Jones to friends, n/d.
4. PS [3-1-1] J. Jowett to Kidd, 24/2/1831.
5. PS [3-1-1] Hagger to J. Jowett, 28/3/1832.
6. PS [3-1-1] J. Jowett to Kidd, 30/6/1832.

7. PS [3-1-1] Harrison to S. Jowett, 22/12/1832; 3/1/1833.
8. PS [3-1-1] M.A. Jowett to Kidd, 9/10/1835.
9. PS Sotheran Collection, D. Jones to Pomeroy, 21/12/1835.
10. PS [3-1-1] J. Jowett to Kidd, 31/12/1835.
11. PS [3-1-1] R. Foley to J. Jowett, 26/2/1836.
12. PS [3-1-1] R. Foley to J. Jowett, 13/4/1836.
13. PC, vellum given to L.E.C. Jones by Stephens, November 1836.
14. PS Sotheran Collection, Underwood to Hirst, 15/4/1815, with note, 22/10/1837.
15. LMA Acc. 1040/92.
16. PS [3-1-1] S. Jowett to friend, 2/11/1838.
17. PS [3-1-1] Harrison to Jowett, 14/5/1839.
18. PS [3-1-1] report by W.B. Harrison of visit to R. Foley, 8/6/1840.
19. PS [3-1-1] report by W.B. Harrison of visit to R. Foley, 8/6/1840.
20. PS [3-1-1] L.E.C. Jones, Circular, March 1840.
21. PS [3-1-1] L.E.C. Jones to Mr Kidd, 25/5/1840.
22. PS [3-1-1] S. Jowett to Harrison, 28/5/1840.
23. PS [3-1-1] R. Foley to Harrison, 29/5/1840.
24. PS [3-1-1] Harrison, to J. Jowett, 30/5/1840.
25. PS [3-1-1] R. Foley to Harrison, 18/6/1840.
26. PS [3-1-1] Kidd to J. Jowett, 8/6/1840.
27. PS [3-1-1] Kidd to Jowett, 8/6/1840.
28. PS [3-1-1] S. Jowett to friend, 5/6/1840.
29. PS [3-1-1] J. Crossley to friend, 22/6/1840.
30. PS [3-1-1] Samuel Jowett to friend, 22/7/1840.
31. PS [3-1-1] & [3-4-16] R. Foley to Gentlemen, 21/7/1840.
32. PS [3-1-1] S. Jowett to R. Foley, 23/7/1840.
33. PS [3-1-1] Harrison to S. Jowett, 24/12/1840.
34. PS [3-1-1] S. Jowett to London Friends, 16/5/1841.
35. PS [3-1-1] M. Crossley to J. Jowett, 5/9/1841.
36. PS [pamphlet] *A Copy of a Letter Addressed to the London Friends*, Leeds, 5/10/1841.
37. PS [3-1-1] J. Jowett to friend, 31/1/1842.
38. PS [3-1-1] J. Jowett to Harrison, 19/3/1842.
39. PS [3-1-1] J. Harrison to J. Jowett, 27/3/1842.
40. PS [3-1-1] J. Jowett to Harrison, 2/4/1842.
41. PS [3-1-1] correspondence between S. Jowett & S. Sibley, 7/11/1842; 29/11/1842; December 1842.
42. *The Castle Cary Visitor*, 1901, p.118.

## CHAPTER 6

1. LMA Acc No. 1040/45.
2. PS [pamphlet bound in *Southcott's Prophecies*] *An Invitation to the Southcottian Churches in London, Birmingham, Manchester, Stockport, Warrington, Ashton, Worcester, and all other parts of England,* 25/5/1843.
3. LMA Acc No. 1040/79.
4. *The Times*, 30/5/1862.

5. PS [pamphlet bound in *Southcott's Prophecies*] *An Address to the Protestants of England especially the Queen, the Archbishops, Bishops and Clergy, to every sect of professing Christians and every one who believes the Bible to be the True Word of God*. 1844.
6. PS [pamphlet] *To the Believers in Joanna Southcott's Visitation*, Samuel Jowett, Leeds, September 1844.
7. PS [3-1-1] London Southcottian Church to Churches in Same Faith, 15/10/1844.
8. PC, *Indictment against Satan*, 25/11/1844.
9. PS [pamphlet] *The Indictment against that tyrannical, cruel, and bloody monarch, Satan, etc*. London, 20/1/1845.
10. LMA Acc No. 1040/77.
11. PS [3-1-1] Harrison to Friend, 9/5/1845.
12. LMA Acc No. 1040/46.
13. LMA Acc No. 1040/7.
14. PS [3-1-1] Harrison to S. Jowett, 4/6/1852.
15. PS [3-1-1] D. Skinn to S. Jowett, 29/4/1852.
16. PS [3-1-1] D. Jones to T.P. Hudson, 28/4/1852.
17. PS [3-1-1] S. Jowett, etc. to R. Foley, 7/4/1852.
18. PS [3-1-1] R. Foley to D. Jones, 1/5/1852.
19. PS [3-1-1] Harrison to Eyre, 9/5/1852.
20. PS [3-1-1] Harrison to Foley, 9/5/1852.
21. PS [3-1-1] Foley to Harrison, 15/5/1852.
22. Southcott, *The Second Book of Wonders, More Marvellous Than the First*, [Book 58] London, 1813, p.4.
23. PS [3-1-1] Harrison to S. Jowett, 6/5/1852.
24. PS [3-1-1] Harrison to S. Jowett, 8/5/1852.
25. PS [3-1-1] Harrison to D. Jones, 9/5/1852.
26. PS [3-1-1] D. Jones to Miller & Norris, 23/5/1852.
27. PS [3-1-1] Harrison to a friend, 27/5/1852.
28. PS [3-1-1] Harrison to R. Foley, 30/5/1852.
29. PS [3-1-1] Norris & Miller to D. Jones, 2/6/1852.
30. PS [3-1-1] Harrison to S. Jowett, 4/6/1852.
31. PS [3-1-1] S. Jowett to Kidd, 23/6/1852.
32. PS [3-1-1] S. Jowett to Kidd, 13/7/1852.
33. PS [pamphlet] Jones, *To the Believers in the Cause of Joanna Southcott*, Bradford, Wilts, September 1852.
34. PS [3-1-1] D. Jones to Harrison, 26/9/1852.
35. PS [3-1-1] D. Jones to Harrison, 26/10/1852.
36. PS [3-1-1] Harrison to Kidd, 29/10/1852.
37. PS [3-1-1] Harrison to Kidd, 7/11/1852.
38. PS [3-1-1] Harrison to S. Jowett, 10/11/1852.
39. PS [3-1-1] S. Jowett to Kidd, 9/11/1852.
40. PS [3-1-1] Harrison to Kidd, 21/12/1852.
41. PS [3-1-1] D. Jones to R. Foley, 12/3/1854.
42. PS [3-1-1] R. Foley to Harrison, 14/3/1854.
43. PS [3-1-1] R. Foley to Harrison, 28/9/1854.
44. PS [3-1-1] Harrison to S. Jowett, 30/9/1854.

45. PS [3-1-1] S. Jowett to Harrison, 9/10/1854.
46. PS [3-1-1] R. Foley to Harrison, 23/12/1854.
47. PS [3-1-1] Harrison to Kidd, 2/1/1855.
48. PS [3-1-1] S. Jowett to Mrs Mallinson, 12/12/1855.
49. PS [3-1-1] L.E.C. Jones to R. Foley, 6/2/1856.
50. PS [3-1-1] R. Foley to Harrison, 7/2/1856.
51. PS [3-1-1] S.Jowett to Harrison, 11/2/1856.
52. PS [3-1-1] Harrison to R. Foley, 23/2/1856.
53. PS [3-1-1] M. Crossley to Kidd, 2/3/1856.
54. PS [3-1-1] R. Foley to Harrison, 24/9/1857.
55. PS [3-1-1] D. Jones to F. Foley, 28/12/1858.
56. PS [3-1-1] R. Foley to Harrison, 1/1/1859.
57. PS [3-1-1] M. Crossley to Kidd, 26/1/1860.
58. PS [3-1-1] M. Crossley to S. Jowett, 30/3/1860
59. PS [3-1-1] M. Crossley to S. Jowett, 8/4/1860.
60. PS [3-1-1] S. Jowett to Mrs Mallinson, 16/6/1860.
61. PS Sotheran Collection, L.E.C. Jones to D. Wells, 20/1/1861.
62. PS [3-1-1] S. Stuckey to J.M. Jowett, 9/4/1861.
63. PS [3-1-1] Crocker to J.M. Jowett, 2/6/1861.

## CHAPTER 7

1. PS [1-101] S. Jowett to F. Foley, n/d.
2. PS [3-1-1] E. Pickthorn to S. Jowett, 1/6/1861, quoted in printed letter, 4/6/1861.
3. PS [3-1-1] printed letter, J.M. Jowett to Friends, 4/6/1861.
4. PS [3-1-1] Graystock to J.M. Jowett, 6/6/1861.
5. PS [3-1-1] S. Galpin to J.M. Jowett, 9/6/1861.
6. PS [3-1-1] Crocker to J.M. Jowett, 10/6/1861.
7. PS [3-1-1] S. Galpin to J.M. Jowett, 12/6/1861.
8. PS [3-1-1] Crocker to J.M. Jowett, 12/6/1861.
9. PS [3-1-1] Graystock to J.M. Jowett, 13/6/1861.
10. PS [1-1-01] S. Jowett to J.M. Jowett, 18/6/1861.
11. PS [3-1-1] Molineaux to J.M. Jowett, 22/6/1861.
12. PS [3-1-1] M. Crossley to J.M. Jowett, 24/6/1861.
13. PS [3-1-1] M. Crossley to Kidd, 14/7/1861.
14. PS [3-1-1] Norris to J.M. Jowett, 25/6/1861.
15. PS [3-1-1] L.E.C. Jones to Hayward, 28/6/1861.
16. PS [3-1-1] Mallinson to J.M. Jowett, n/d.
17. PS Sotheran Collection, L.E.C. Jones to D. Wells, 11/7/1861.
18. PS Sotheran Collection, D. Jones to D. Wells, 11/8/1861.
19. PS [3-1-1] M. Crossley to Kidd, 8/9/1861.
20. PS [1-2-8] S. Jowett to Friends [printed circular], 3/10/1861.
21. PS [3-1-1] C. Hill to Romilly, n/d.
22. LMA Acc. 1040/173.
23. LMA Acc. 1040/157; 109; 173.
24. LMA Acc. 1040/173.
25. LMA Acc. 1040/104.

26. PS [3-1-1] Molineaux to Bennett, 17/8/1863.
27. PS [3-1-1] D. Jones to J.M. Jowett, 16/8/1864.
28. LMA Acc. 1040/198.
29. PS [1-2-8] D. Jones, Bradford-on-Avon, Printed Circular, February 1865.
30. PS [1-1-01] S. Jowett, n/d. See also, PS [1-2-19]
31. PS [1-1-01] S. Jowett, 'Disposition of the Box of Sealed Writings', 23/9/1866.
32. LMA Acc. 1040/115.
33. LMA Acc. 1040/129a.
34. PS [3-1-1] S. Jowett to Mrs Mallinson, 19/3/1867.
35. PS [3-1-1] S. Jowett to G. Churchill, 6/9/1867.
36. PS [3-1-1] Memorial Card for James Kidd, died 30/1/1868.
37. LMA Acc. 1040/121.
38. LMA Acc. 1040/127.
39. LMA Acc. 1040/128.
40. LMA Acc. 1040/121.
41. LMA Acc. 1040/129a.
42. LMA Acc. 1040/131.
43. LMA Acc. 1040/133a.
44. LMA Acc. 1040/134.
45. LMA Acc. 1040/133a.
46. LMA Acc. 1040/123.
47. LMA Acc. 1040/124a.
48. PS [3-1-1] Rowland Hill to J.M. Jowett, 1870.
49. LMA Acc. 1040/199-205.
50. PS Sotheran Collection, Thornton to L.E.C. Jones, 9/1/1873.
51. LMA Acc. 1040/159.
52. LMA Acc. 1040/160.
53. LMA Acc. 1040/146.
54. LMA Acc. 1040/162.
55. LMA Acc. 1040/163.
56. LMA Acc. 1040/186.

## CHAPTER 8

1. LMA Acc. 1040/147.
2. PS [3-1-1] M. Brownell to J.M. Jowett, 10/1/1888.
3. PS [3-1-1] Jubal Sagar to S. Jowett, 1/8/1869.
4. Robertson, *Authentic History of the Great Box of Sealed Writings left by Joanna Southcott.* Plymouth, 2nd Edition, 1929, p.6.
5. PS [3-1-1] Legg to J.M. Jowett, 15/10/1887.
6. PS [3-1-1] Legg to J.M. Jowett, 14/11/1887.
7. PS [3-1-1] S. Stuckey to J.M. Jowett, 21/11/1887.
8. PS [3-1-1] Begley to J.M. Jowett, 12/12/1887.
9. PS [3-1-1] J.M. Jowett to Begley, 18/12/1887.
10. PS [3-1-1] Begley to J.M. Jowett, 23/12/1887.
11. PS [3-1-1] M. Brownell to J.M. Jowett, 10/1/1888.
12. PS [3-1-1] Scott [MacLaughlin] to J.M. Jowett, 5/5/1892.
13. LMA Acc. 1040/149.

14. DRO 3703Z/Z3, loose letter, S. Stuckey to Hayward, 21/2/1890.
15. LMA Acc. 1040/164.
16. PS [3-1-1] J. Harrison to J.M. Jowett, 29/3/1894.
17. PC, Bennett to Mrs Pye, 21/12/1895.
18. PS [1-1-01] Sealy Stuckey to Edwin Jowett, 8/4/1898.
19. PS [1-2-21] Edwin Jowett to Alice Seymour, 22/2/1915.
20. PS [3-1-1] J. Harrison to J.M. Jowett, 13/5/1898.
21. PS [1-1-01] L. Oldfield to S. Stuckey, 28/5/1898.
22. Robertson, *Authentic History of the Great Box of Sealed Writings left by Joanna Southcott.* Plymouth, 2nd Edition, 1929, p.6.
23. PS [1-1-01] R. Stuckey to Edwin Jowett, 1/10/1918.
24. *Southcott Express*, No.3, September 1926, p.70.
25. *Express Leaflet*; February 1912, pp.2-3.
26. *Daily Mail*, 11/02/1915.
27. PS [1-2-21] Edwin Jowett to Alice Seymour, 14/2/1915.
28. PS [1-2-21] Alice Seymour to Edwin Jowett, 17/2/1915.
29. PS [1-2-21] Edwin Jowett to Alice Seymour, 22/2/1915.
30. *Two Witnesses*, No.13, March 1916, pp.4-5.
31. PS [1-1-01] R. Stuckey to Edwin Jowett, 1/10/1918.
32. *Burnham Gazette*, 19/5/1917, p.5.
33. *Two Witnesses*, No.31, October 1917, p.11.
34. Longford, *Victoria R.I.,* London, 1964, p.423.
35. *Southcott Despatch;* March 1919.
36. PS [3-4-16] Lady Paget to R. Fox, April, 1918.
37. PS [3-4-16] Lady Paget to R. Fox, 20/4/1918.
38. PS [3-4-16] Lady Paget to R. Fox, 28/4/1918.
39. PS [3-4-16] R. Fox to Lady Paget, 29/4/1918.
40. PS [3-4-16] R. Fox to Boyd-Carpenter, 1/5/1918.
41. PS [3-4-16] Boyd-Carpenter to R. Fox, 2/5/1918.
42. PS [1-1-17] Princess Louise to Boyd-Carpenter, 27/5/1918.
43. PS [3-4-16] R. Fox to King George V, 22/9/1920.
44. PS [1-1-01] R. Stuckey to Edwin Jowett, 1/10/1918.

## CHAPTER 9

1. *Southcott Despatch*, 34, December1921, pp.2-3.
2. *Southcott Despatch*, 36, February 1922, pp.2-3.
3. *Southcott Express,* 3, September 1926, pp.70-1.
4. *Daily News,* 4/8/1923; *Southcott Express* 4, p.93.
5. PS [1-2-14] Edwin Jowett to *Daily News*, 22/8/1923.
6. PS [1-1-01] R. Stuckey to Edwin Jowett, 5/9/1923.
7. *Cassell's Weekly*, 5/9/1923; 12/9/1923.
8. PS [1-2-20] Edwin Jowett to H. Green, 12/11/1923.
9. PS [1-2-20] correspondence between H. Green and Edwin Jowett, 17/11 & 19/11/1923.
10. PS [1-2-20] A. Midgley to Edwin Jowett, 12/12/1923.
11. PS [1-2-20] Octavia to Edwin Jowett, 12/12/1923.
12. PS [1-2-20] Edwin Jowett to Octavia, 13/12/1923.

13. Rougemont Museum (Exeter), Firth to Mullen, Salford Museum, 4/3/1924.
14. PS [1-2-20] Octavia to Edwin Jowett, 25/5/1924.
15. PS [1-2-20] Edwin Jowett to R. Stuckey, 26/5/1924.
16. PS [1-2-21] R. Stuckey to Edwin Jowett, 27/5/1924.
17. PS [Events and Dates], 17/6/1924.
18. PS [1-2-21] Edwin Jowett to M. Robertson, 27/11/1924.
19. PS [1-2-21] Edwin Jowett to M. Robertson, 29/12/1924.
20. *Southcott Express* 4, p.93.
21. PS [1-2-21] M. Robertson to Edwin Jowett, 20/7/1925.
22. PS [1-2-14] R. Stuckey to Edwin Jowett, 23/7/1923.
23. PS [1-2-14] Edwin Jowett to R. Stuckey, 25/7/1925.
24. PS [1-1-01] R. Stuckey to Edwin Jowett, 31/7/1925.
25. PS [1-2-14] R. Stuckey to Edwin Jowett, 17/9/1925.
26. PS [1-1-01] R. Stuckey to Edwin Jowett, 25/9/1925.
27. PS [1-1-01] Edwin Jowett to R. Stuckey, 25/9/1925.
28. PS [1-2-14] R. Stuckey to Edwin Jowett, 2/10/1925, also n/d letter.
29. PS [1-1-01] R. Stuckey to Edwin Jowett, 14/1/1926.
30. PS [1-1-01] R. Stuckey to Edwin Jowett, 22/5/1926.
31. PS [1-1-01] R. Stuckey to Edwin Jowett, 4/6/1926.
32. PS Note attached to framed portraits of S. Jowett and J.M. Jowett, marked: 'E. Jowett's letter accepting his seal,' 26/5/1926.
33. PS [1-1-01] R. Stuckey to Edwin Jowett, 22/6/1926.
34. PS [1-1-01] Edwin Jowett – Special Note, 16/7/1926.

## CHAPTER 10

1. PS [1-2-16] Emily Jowett to Octavia, 15/11/1926.
2. PS [1-1-16] Octavia to Emily Jowett, 18/11/1926.
3. *Daily Mail,* 19/4/1927.
4. PS [1-2-16] R. Stuckey to Emily Jowett, 4/5/1927.
5. PS [1-2-16] Emily Goodwin to Emily Jowett, 29/4/1927.
6. PS [3-4-16] Harry Price to R. Fox, 28/6/1927.
7. *Western Mail,* 6/5/1927.
8. PS [1-2-16] Emily Jowett to Octavia, 6/7/1927.
9. *Daily News,* 12/7/1927.
10. PS [1-2-16] Octavia to Goodhall, 28/7/1927.
11. PS [1-2-16] Goodhall to Octavia, 8/9/1927.
12. PS [1-2-15] Emily Jowett to R. Stuckey, 2/9/1927.
13. PS [1-2-15] R. Stuckey to Emily Jowett, 20/9/1927.
14. PS [1-2-15] Emily Jowett to Octavia, 1/11/1927.
15. PS [1-2-15] Emily Jowett to R. Stuckey, 2/11/1927.
16. PS [1-2-15] R. Stuckey to Emily Jowett, 14/11/1927.
17. PS [1-2-15] S. Galpin to Emily Jowett, 15/11/1927.
18. PS [1-2-15] Emily Jowett to S. Galpin, November 1927.
19. PS [1-2-16] Goodhall to Octavia, 19/5/1928.
20. PS [1-2-16] Octavia to Emily Jowett, 21/5/1928.
21. *Southcott Express* 11, p.66.

22. PS [1-2-16] Jowetts to Miss Green, 26/2; 4/3/1929.
23. PS [1-2-16] M. Barltrop to Cecil Jowett, 6/3/1929.
24. PS [1-2-16] Cecil Jowett to M. Barltrop, 8/3/1929.
25. PS [1-2-16] Goodhall to M. Barltrop, 18/3/1929.
26. PS [1-2-16] M. Barltrop to Goodhall, 21/3/1929.
27. PS [1-2-16] Octavia to Goodhall, 30/6/1928.
28. PS [1-2-16] M. Barltrop to Goodhall, 31/3/1929.
29. PS [1-2-16] Goodhall to Miss Green, 12/4/1929.
30. PS [1-2-16] Octavia to Goodhall, 27/4/1929.
31. PS [1-2-16] Goodhall to Carew-Hunt, 8/5/1929.
32. PS [1-2-15] Galpin to Emily Jowett, 7/5/1929; Emily Jowett to Octavia, 10/5/1929.
33. PS [1-2-16] Carew-Hunt to Goodhall, 22/5/1929.
34. PS [1-2-16] Goodhall to Carew-Hunt, 25/5/1929.
35. PS [1-2-16] M. & C. Jowett to Octavia, 27/5/1929.
36. PS [1-2-16] Goodhall to Carew-Hunt, 25/5/1929.
37. PS [1-2-16] Carew-Hunt to Goodhall, 1/6/1929.
38. PS [1-2-16] C. Jowett to Carew-Hunt, 2/6/1929.
39. PS [1-2-16] Emily Jowett, Memorandum, 5/6/1929.
40. PS [1-2-16] Carew-Hunt to C. Jowett, 15/6/1929.
41. PS [1-2-16] Octavia to C. Jowett, 17/6/1929.
42. PS [1-2-16] C. Jowett to Octavia, 30/6/1929.
43. PS [1-2-16] Carew-Hunt to C. Jowett, 2/7/1929.
44. PS [1-2-16] Carew-Hunt to C. Jowett, 4/7/1929.
45. PS [1-2-16] M. Barltrop to Goodhall, 4/7/1929.
46. PS [1-2-16] Carew-Hunt to Goodhall, 13/7/1929.
47. PS [1-2-16] Telegram to Archbishop of Canterbury, 12/7/1929.
48. PS [1-2-16] Goodhall to Carew-Hunt, 19/7/1929.
49. PS [1-2-16] Carew-Hunt to Goodhall, 5/8/1929.
50. PS [1-2-16] Goodhall to Carew-Hunt, 13/8/1929.
51. PS [1-2-16] Goodhall to Carew-Hunt, 14/9/1929.
52. PS [1-2-16] Carew-Hunt to Goodhall, 4/10/1929.
53. PS [1-2-16] Goodhall to Carew-Hunt, 7/10/1929.
54. PS [1-2-16] Carew-Hunt to C. Jowett, 22/10/1929.
55. PS [1-2-16] Carew-Hunt to Trotter, 28/10/1929.
56. PS [1-2-16] Trotter to Carew-Hunt, 29/10/1929.
57. PS [1-2-16] Carew-Hunt to Trotter, 29/10/1929.
58. PS [3-4-16] Carew-Hunt to Archbishop of Canterbury, 14/11/1929.
59. PS [3-4-16] Carew-Hunt to Bishops, 25/3/1930.
60. PS [3-4-16] Carew-Hunt to Archbishop of Canterbury, 14/4/1930.
61. PS [3-4-16] Carew-Hunt to Archbishops and Bishops, 18/6/1931.
62. PS [1-2-28] Don to Carew-Hunt, 15/7/1931.
63. PS [1-2-11] C. Jowett to Octavia, 28/8/1931.
64. PS [1-2-11] C. Jowett to the Divine Mother, 1/6/1932.
65. PS [1-2-28] Clements to Carew-Hunt, 30/12/1933.
66. PS [1-2-11] C. Jowett to the Divine Mother, 17/1/1934.

CHAPTER 11

1. PS [1-4-3] A. Seymour to M. Barltrop, 16/1/1934.
2. PS [1-4-3] M. Barltrop to A. Seymour, 19/1/1934.
3. PS [1-4-3] A. Seymour to M. Barltrop, 26/1/1934.
4. PS [1-4-3] M. Barltrop to A. Seymour, 29/1/1934.
5. PS [1-4-3] A. Seymour to M. Barltrop, 4/2/1934.
6. PS [1-4-3] A. Seymour to M. Barltrop, 4/6/1934.
7. PS [1-4-3] M. Barltrop to A. Seymour, 6/6/1934.
8. PS [1-4-3] A. Seymour to M. Barltrop, 16/6/1934.
9. PS [1-4-3] M. Barltrop to A. Seymour, 20/6/1934.
10. PS [1-2-17] *Information & Suggestions*, 8/10/1934.
11. PS [1-2-17] *Needful Information*, 8/10/1934.
12. PS [1-4-3] A. Seymour to Miss Gillett, 24/10/1934.
13. PS [1-2-40] A. Seymour to Miss Green, 29/1/1935.
14. PS [1-2-40] H. Green to A. Seymour, 31/1/1935.
15. PS [1-2-40] A. Seymour to E. Goodwin, 4/2/1935.
16. PS [1-2-40] E. Goodwin to A. Seymour, 5/2/1935.
17. PS [1-2-40] A. Seymour to E. Goodwin, 12/2/1935.
18. PS [1-2-40] A. Seymour to E. Goodwin, 12/4/1935.
19. PS [1-2-40] A. Seymour to R. Fox, 18/5/1935.
20. PS [1-2-40] E. Goodwin to R. Fox, 24/5/1935.
21. PS [1-2-40] R. Fox to A. Seymour, 25/5/1935.
22. PS [1-2-40] A. Seymour to E. Goodwin, 27/2/1937.
23. PS [1-2-40] E. Goodwin to A. Seymour, 13/3/1937.
24. PS [1-2-40] A. Seymour to E. Goodwin, 18/5/1937.
25. PS [1-2-40] E. Goodwin to A. Seymour, 27/5/1937.
26. PS [1-2-40] A. Seymour to E. Goodwin, 18/7/1937.
27. PS [1-2-40] E. Goodwin to A. Seymour, 31/7/1937.
28. PS [1-1-01] C. Jowett to E. Goodwin, 7/1/1942.
29. PS [1-1-01] C. Jowett to E. Goodwin, 19/12/1942.
30. PS [1-1-01] R. Temple to C. Jowett, 16/3/1943.
31. PS [1-1-01] C. Jowett to R. Temple, 17/3/1943.
32. PS [1-1-01] R. Temple to C. Jowett, 25/11/1944.
33. PS [1-1-01] R.Temple to C.Jowett, 16/12/1944.
34. PS [1-1-01] C. Jowett to R. Temple, 26/12/1944.
35. PS [1-1-01] R. Temple to C. Jowett, 30/12/1944.
36. *Bedford Record and Circular*, 31/12/1946.
37. *The People*, 31/8/1947.
38. *News Review*, 25/9/1947.
39. PS [1-1-01] R. Temple to C. Jowett, 22/3; 15/12/1949; 18/12/1950.
40. PS [1-2-22] A. Stitt to R. Temple, 22/1/1951.
41. PS [1-2-22] R. Temple to A. Stitt, 24/1/1951.
42. PS [1-2-22] A. Stitt to R. Temple, 25/1/1951.
43. PS [1-2-22] A. Stitt to R. Temple 12/9/1952.
44. PS [1-2-22] A. Stitt to R. Temple, 2/6/1953.
45. PS [1-2-22] R. Temple to A. Stitt, 5/6/1953.
46. PS [1-2-22] A. Stitt to R. Temple, 6/6/1953.

47. PS [1-2-22] A. Stitt to R. Temple, 5/4/1954.
48. PS [1-2-22] R. Temple to A. Stitt, 8/4/1954.
49. PS [1-2-22] R. Temple to A. Stitt, 25/9/1956.
50. PS [1-1-01] M. Jowett to Panacea Society, 12/5/1957.

## CHAPTER 12

1. PS [1-1-01] R. Temple to M. Jowett, 14/5/1957.
2. PS [1-1-01] M. Jowett to R. Temple, 16/5/1957.
3. PS [1-1-01] R. Temple to M. Jowett, 20/5/1957.
4. PS [1-1-01] R. Temple to G.Reinli, 20/5/1957.
5. PS [1-1-01] G. Reinli to R. Temple, 22/5/1957.
6. PS [1-1-01] R. Temple to M. Jowett, 27/5/1957.
7. PS [1-1-01] Affidavit, signed Graham & Temple, 27/5/1957.
8. PS [1-1-01] R. Temple to M. Jowett, 28/5/1957.
9. PS [1-2-22] A. Stitt to R. Temple, 26/12/1957.
10. PS [1-2-22] A. Stitt to R. Temple, 2/6/1958.
11. PS [1-2-22] A. Stitt to R. Temple, 12/6/1958.
12. PS [1-1-01] W. Greenroyd to E. Goodwin, 14/9/1958.
13. PS [1-1-01] R. Temple to W. Greenroyd, 22/10/1958.
14. PS [1-1-01] W. Greenroyd to R. Temple, 23/10/1958.
15. PS [1-1-01] R. Temple to M. Jowett, 17/10/1958.
16. PS [1-1-01] M. Jowett to R. Temple, 22/10/1958.
17. PS [1-1-01] R. Temple to M. Jowett, 25/10/1958.
18. PS [1-1-01] M. Jowett to R. Temple, 29/10/1958.
19. PS [1-1-01] R. Temple to M. Jowett, 5/11/1958.
20. *The Independence Examiner*; 18/2/1960.
21. PS [1-2-22] A. Stitt to R. Temple, 17/12/1960.
22. PS [1-2-22] R. Temple to A. Stitt, 22/12/1960.
23. PS [1-1-01] U. Bowden to Panacea Society, 5/9/1961.
24. PS [1-1-01] E. Nicholson to R. Temple, 21/9/1961.
25. PS [1-2-22] A. Stitt to R. Temple, 27/10/1961.
26. PS [1-2-22] R. Temple to A. Stitt, 10/11/1961.
27. PS [1-1-01] R. Temple to M. Jowett, 16/11/1961.
28. PS [1-1-01] R. Temple to M. Jowett, 5/12/1961.
29. PS [1-1-01] M. Jowett to R. Temple, 6/12/1961.
30. PS [1-1-01] R. Temple to M. Jowett, 11/12/1961.
31. PS [1-1-01] M. Jowett to R. Temple, 13/12/1961.
32. PS [1-1-01] R. Temple to M. Jowett, 22/1/1962.
33. PS [1-1-01] M. Jowett to R. Temple, 25/1/1962.
34. PS [1-1-01] R. Temple to M. Jowett, 27/2/1962.
35. PS [1-2-22] A. Stitt to R. Temple, 23/8/1964.
36. PS [1-2-22] R. Temple to A. Stitt, 1/9/1964.
37. PS [1-2-22] A. Stitt to R. Temple, 6/3/1965.
38. PS [1-2-22] R. Temple to A. Stitt, 10/3/1965.
39. PS [1-2-22] A. Stitt to R. Temple, 13/3/1965. This collection of Alice Seymour's manuscripts is available for study in the British Library. The conspiratorial way in which Annie Stitt delivered her 'two large Brown Paper parcels' is probably

responsible for a recent suggestion that they contained the sealed prophecies from Joanna Southcott's Great Box, but the above exchange of letters shows that this was certainly not so. Moreover, her correspondence with the Panacea Society makes it clear that Annie Stitt never had possession of the Box.

40. PS [1-2-22] R. Temple to A. Stitt, 15/4/1965.
41. PS [1-2-22] A. Stitt to R. Temple, 16/4/1965.
42. PS [1-2-22] A. Stitt to S. Cuthbertson, 17/6/1965.
43. *Echo*, 26/7/1971.
44. PS [1-4-8] National Westminster Bank to Panacea Society, 31/8/1971.
45. PS [1-4-8] Panacea Society to National Westminster Bank, 7/9/1971.
46. PS [1-4-8] Lloyds Bank to Panacea Society, 7/1/1972.
47. PS [1-4-8] L. Duckett to S. Cuthbertson, 24/5/1976.
48. PS [1-4-8] L. Duckett to S. Cuthbertson, 6/7/1976.
49. PS [1-4-8] L. Duckett to S. Cuthbertson, 20/5/1974.
50. PS [1-4-8] L. Duckett to S. Cuthbertson, 24/5/1976.
51. PS [1-4-8] L. Duckett to S. Cuthbertson, 6/7/1976.
52. PS [1-4-8] Archbishop of Canterbury's office to L. Duckett, 23/3/1977.
53. PS [1-4-8] A. Glover to Panacea Society, 8/5/1977.
54. PS [1-4-8] Panacea Society to L. Duckett, 20/5/1977.

# Appendix 1:
## Custodians of Joanna Southcott's Box

The Box originated at Exeter where for the first four years it was left in the care of various friends of Joanna, particularly the Symons Family in Gandy Lane. Early in 1802 it was delivered to William Sharp who became its first official Custodian.

| | | |
|---|---|---|
| First Custodian | 1802-1820 | William Sharp,<br>*Titchfield Street, London* |
| Second Custodian | 1820-1825 | Jane Townley,<br>*Weston Place,St Pancras,London* |
| Third Custodian | 1825-1835 | Thomas Foley,<br>*Old Swinford, Worcestershire* |
| Fourth Custodian | 1835-1861 | Richard Foley,<br>*Kingswinford (1835-42)*<br>*North Cadbury (1842-61)* |
| Fifth Custodian | 1861-1876 | Samuel Jowett,<br>*Leeds, Yorkshire* |
| Sixth Custodian | 1876-1898 | John Marshall Jowett,<br>*Bradford, Yorkshire* |
| Seventh Custodian | 1898 | Sealy Stuckey,<br>*Burnham, Somerset (died 1898)* |
| Eighth Custodian | 1898-1925 | Robert Stuckey,<br>*Burnham, Somerset* |
| Ninth Custodian | 1925-1926 | Edwin Armstrong Jowett,<br>*Morecambe, Lancs* |
| Tenth Custodian | 1926-1934 | Emily Jowett,<br>*Morecambe, Lancs.* |
| Eleventh Custodian | 1934-1957 | Cecil K. Jowett,<br>*Gatley, Cheshire* |
| Twelfth Custodian | 1957- | The Panacea Society,<br>*Bedford* |

# Appendix 2
# Biographical Notes

**Edmund Baker** (1766-1857)

Southcottian minister. Born 6 March, 1766, Edmund Baker led a Southcottian group in Teddington, Middlesex, until 1811 when Joanna sent him into Somerset where Mrs Jane Parke and her sister, Anne Gibson, provided him with a chapel at Parke House, Dowlish Wake. For many years he and his wife, Mary, lived in Langport Street, Ilminster, which became the centre for Southcottians in Somerset. He retired from preaching in 1851 and died 9 December, 1857.

**Mabel Barltrop** (Octavia) (1866-1934)

Founder of the Panacea Society. Born Mabel Andrews, at Peckham, Surrey, on 11 January, 1866. Her godfather was Coventry Patmore. She married Arthur Henry Barltrop (1856-1906), a schoolmaster, who was ordained in 1888 and became curate of St Augustine's, Croydon. They had three sons and one daughter. After reading one of Alice Seymour's pamphlets, Mabel campaigned vigorously for the bishops to open Joanna Southcott's Box. In *Keys to the Whole Body of Truth for the Whole Body of Believers*, she brought together the teachings of Southcott, Brothers, Turner, Wroe and Jezreel. Her own reputation drew many to Bedford where she became known as 'Octavia', the eighth prophet in the Book of Revelation, and was recognised as Shiloh. The discovery of healing powers in 1923 resulted in her community adopting the name of The Panacea Society. Octavia died in her sleep on 16 October, 1934.

**Revd. Walter Begley** (1846-1905)

Anglican clergyman and scholar. Born in Kings Lynn, Norfolk, and graduated from Corpus Christi, Cambridge, Begley was ordained in 1868. After serving as curate and vicar at East Hyde, Bedfordshire, he retired to 24 Greencroft Gardens, Hampstead, where he died on 3 December, 1905. Author of *Is it Shakespeare?; Biblia Cabalistica; Biblia Anagrammatica*; and editor of Milton's *Nova Solyma*. A great-grandson of Revd. Thomas Webster, one of Joanna Southcott's early supporters, Begley inspired and helped Alice Seymour to revive Joanna's cause in the twentieth century.

**Rt. Revd. George Kennedy Allen Bell** (1883-1958)
Bishop of Chichester. Born at Hayling Island, eldest child of Revd. James Allen Bell. Educated at Westminster School and Christ Church, Oxford. Ordained Priest at Ripon in 1908. Curate of Leeds, 1907-10. Lecturer and Tutor of Christ Church, Oxford, 1910-14; Resident Chaplain to Archbishop of Canterbury, 1914-24; Dean of Canterbury, 1924-29. Bishop of Chichester, 1929-1958. Chairman of the central committee of the World Council of Churches, 1948-54, and honorary president from 1954 until his death. Bell was devoted to Christian unity and a prolific author, whose books include: *The Modern Parson* (1928); *Life of Randall Davidson* (1935); *Christianity and World Order* (1940); *The Kingship of Christ* (1954).

**Rt. Revd. William Boyd Carpenter** (1841-1918)
Bishop of Ripon. Born at Liverpool on 26 March, 1841, son of Henry B. Carpenter, P.C. of St Michael's, Liverpool. Educated at Royal Institution, Liverpool, and St Catharine's, Cambridge. Chaplain of Queen Victoria, 1879-84. Bishop of Ripon, 1884-1911.Canon of Westminster, 1911; Sub-Dean. Clerk to the Closet to Edward VII and to George V, 1903-1918. Author of commentaries, reviews, books of devotion, religious poetry and popular expositions of the poets, especially Dante. A famous preacher, popularly known as the 'Silver tongued Bishop of Ripon'. He died 26 October, 1918, and was buried in the cloisters of Westminster Abbey.

**John Crossley** (1777-1852)
Loyal follower of Joanna. Born at Halifax in 1777, son of Eli Crossley, married Hannah, daughter of William Jowett. They had seven sons, including Barnabus (died 1840, Wakefield), Barak (died 1853, Derby), and Matthias (died 1867, Wakefield). John Crossley published several pamphlets in support of Joanna Southcott's mission.

**Most Revd. Randall Davidson** (1848-1930)
Archbishop of Canterbury, 1903-28. Born in Edinburgh, eldest child of Henry Davidson, merchant. Educated at Harrow and Trinity College, Oxford. Ordained Priest at Canterbury in 1875. Curate of Dartford, 1874-77. Resident Chaplain to Archbishop of Canterbury, 1877-83. Dean of Windsor and Domestic Chaplain to Queen Victoria, 1883-91. Clerk of the Closet, 1891-1903. Consecrated Lord Bishop of Rochester in 1891, translated to Winchester in 1895, and to Canterbury in 1903. Davidson took a deep interest in the Anglican Church abroad and was the first Archbishop of Canterbury to pay an official visit to Canada and U.S.A. .On his resignation in 1928 he was created Baron Davidson

of Lambeth. Author of *History of the Lambeth Conferences* (1896); *The Christian Opportunity* (1904); *Captains and Comrades in the Faith* (1911); *The Character and Call of the Church of England* (1912); *The Testing of a Nation* (1919); *Occasions* (1925).

**Very Revd. Alan Campbell Don** (1885-1966)
Dean of Westminster, 1946-59. Born at Broughty Ferry, Dundee, son of Alan Bogle Don and Lucy Flora Campbell. Educated at Rugby School and Magdalen College, Oxford. Ordained Priest at York in 1913, and the following year married Muriel McConnel. Curate of St Peter's, Redcar, 1912-16; Vicar of Norton, Yorks, 1916-21; Provost of St Paul's Cathedral, Dundee, 1921-31, and Hon. Canon, from 1949; Chaplain and Secretary to Archbishop of Canterbury, 1931-41; Chaplain to the King, 1934-46; Chaplain to the Speaker, House of Commons, 1936-46; Canon of Westminster and Rector of St Margaret's, Westminster, 1941-6; Sub-Dean, 1941-46; Sub-Prelate, St John of Jerusalem from 1948; K.C.V.O., 1948. Knight Commander, Order of the Phoenix, 1953.

**Helen Exeter** (1851-1918)
Follower of Joanna Southcott. Born in Cape of Good Hope, South Africa, daughter of an English general. At sixteen, married Sir Theophilus Shepstone, K.C.M.G., a distinguished lawyer, and gave birth to her first child the following year. After her husband's death, she developed an interest in spiritualism and felt impelled to come to England to persuade the Archbishop of Canterbury to open Joanna Southcott's Box. She joined forces with Rachel Fox and Mabel Barltrop, and was recognised as the 'Seventh Prophet' in the Visitation. She was drowned when the *Galway Castle* was torpedoed off Plymouth on 14 September, 1918.

**Rev. Samuel Eyre** (1776-1853)
Anglican clergyman and supporter of Joanna. Born in Wylye, Wiltshire, youngest son of Rev. John and Susanna Eyre. He heard of Joanna Southcott when he arrived in Bristol in 1804, immediately embraced her cause and remained faithful to his death. He died at his residence, Stoke's Croft, in Bristol and was buried in Arnos Vale cemetery.

**Rev Richard Foley** (1801-1861)
Custodian of Joanna Southcott's Box, 1835-1861. Born 18 July, 1801. Educated at Rugby school and Emmanuel College, Cambridge, 6th Wrangler in 1823. Ordained priest in 1830; Rector of Kingswinford, Staffs, 1836-46; Rector of North Cadbury, Somerset, 1842-61. Although not a believer, in 1835 he succeeded his father as custodian

of the Box. In 1850 he married a widow, Frances Essex Talbot (1803-66), daughter of Vincent Langworthy of Ilminster. Richard Foley died without issue at North Cadbury on 16 May, 1861.

**Rev. Thomas Philip Foley** (1758-1835)

Custodian of Joanna's Box, 1825-1835. Son of Rev. Philip Foley, Rector of Shelsley, Worcestershire, and kinsman of Thomas, Baron Foley. Educated at Repton School and Jesus College, Cambridge, he became Rector of Oldswinford, Worcestershire, in 1797, and married Elizabeth Bache on 6 October, 1801. An adherent of Richard Brothers, after meeting Joanna Southcott in 1801, he embraced her cause and maintained his belief in her mission to the end of his life. From the death of Jane Townley in 1825 he was Custodian of the Box. He became senile in his last years and died on 4 September, 1835. His widow, Elizabeth, died in 1854.

**Rachel Juliet Fox** (1858-1939)

First President of the Panacea Society. Born 11 January 1858, seventh of ten children born to Henry and Ann Ford Fowler, and a granddaughter of Elizabeth Gurney, a first cousin of Elizabeth Fry. In 1882 she married George Henry Fox of Falmouth, who, like her, came from a Quaker family. Rachel Fox joined the Church of England in 1919 and was indefatigable in her efforts to publicise the mission of Joanna Southcott. Author of numerous books. In 1936 she moved from Falmouth to Bedford where she died in August 1939, aged 81. Cousin of Beatrice Mary Pease (Lady Portsmouth).

**Emily Goodwin** (1858-1943)

Octavia's friend and supporter. Born 1857, daughter of William Beal, Emily married Henry Goodwin, a baker, in 1880. She moved into Octavia's home in 1921 to help nurse her elderly aunt. On 28 January, 1923, she began to channel the Voice of Jerusalem, the Divine Mother. She rejected Octavia's offer to hand over the leadership of the Panacea Society, stressing that she was merely the Instrument by which Octavia would be instructed. After Octavia's death, Emily Goodwin took over the direction of the Panacea Society and organised their Petition to the Archbishop of Canterbury in 1935. She died at Bedford on 23 January, 1943.

**William Bown Harrison** (1792-1860)

A loyal follower of Joanna Southcott and trusted friend of the Jowetts. Lived in Manchester and worked as an accountant, but fell into debt and lost his Assurance Agency in 1840. His belief in Joanna began in 1805 when he went to live with his grandfather, a devout Southcottian.

For years plagued by business and family worries. His first wife died in 1837 after a disastrous marriage. He provided a valuable means of communication between Richard Foley and the Old Southcottians and wrote a number of pamphlets explaining Joanna's mission.

**Rt Revd. John Edward Hine** (1857-1934)

Bishop Suffragan of Grantham. Second son of Benjamin Hine, Nottingham. Educated at University College School and University College, London. M.R.C.S. London, 1879. M.B. 1879; M.D. 1883. University of Oxford, B.A. 1885, M.A. 1890, Hon. D.D. 1896. Ordained at Rochester in 1887. Curate of Richmond, Surrey, 1886-88. Missionary at Likoma, Nyasa, 1889-90; Bishop of Likoma, 1896-1901; Bishop of Zanzibar, 1901-8; Chaplain, Tangier, 1908; Constantinople, 1909; Bishop of Northern Rhodesia, 1910-14; Vicar of Lastingham, 1916-18; Rector of Stoke, Grantham, 1918-25; Bishop Suffragan of Grantham, 1920-30; Archdeacon of Lincoln, 1925-33. Author of *Days Gone By*, 1924.

**Esther Jezreel** (1860-88)

Leader of the 'Jezreelites', 1885-1888. Daughter of Edward Rogers, a sawyer, of 11 Copenhagen Road, New Brompton, Kent. Esther joined the New & Latter House of Israel and made a preaching tour of the U.S.A. in 1878. The following year she married James Jezreel and assumed the name of Esther, Queen of Israel. Together they toured America and made many converts before returning to England and settling at Woodlands, Gillingham, which became their headquarters. After Jezreel's death, Esther succeeded to the leadership of the sect. In 1887 she started a monthly publication: *The Messenger of Wisdom & Israel's Guide*. She died at Woodlands on 30 June, 1888, and was buried in Gillingham cemetery. Her father then took over the leadership, but failed to hold the sect together and the building of their temple was suspended.

**James Jershom Jezreel** (1840-85)

Founder of 'The New & Latter House of Israel' (or 'Jezreelites'). Formerly known as James White. After joining The New House of Israel, a development of the Christian Israelite Church founded by John Wroe, Jezreel claimed to have received direct revelations that he published as *Extracts from The Flying Roll*. He established a religious and trading community at Gillingham (Kent) that flourished 1883-85. It built houses, shops, a college, and began building a temple planned to be 120 feet high, 120 feet square, and to hold 20,000 people. Jezreel died at Woodlands on 1 March 1885 and was buried in Gillingham cemetery. His wife succeeded to the leadership of the sect.

**Daniel Jones** (1796-1866)

Builder and Printer of Bradford-on-Avon, Wiltshire. Born 20 January, 1796, son of John Jones and Ann (formerly Beaven). Had a younger brother, Charles (1798-1852) with whom he worked in partnership as architect and builder, employing over thirty men. Daniel married Lavinia Elizabeth Chapman in 1821. From his private printing press he published more than twenty books and pamphlets to publicise Joanna Southcott's mission. He died of congestion of the liver at Torey, Bradford-on-Avon, on 27 November, 1866, and was buried in Christchurch graveyard.

**Lavinia Elizabeth Chapman Jones** (1801-79)

Ardent follower of Joanna Southcott. Born in Greenwich in 1801. Married Daniel Jones of Bradford-on-Avon, Wilts, in 1821. Scoured the country to collect unpublished manuscripts left by Joanna and resorted to desperate measures in trying to gain possession of the Box of Sealed Prophecies. Died 8 April, 1879, at the Brighton home of her sister, Abigail, widow of the Reverend William Edelman, and her body was taken to Merton, Surrey, for burial in the Edelman grave.

**Cecil Kaye Jowett** (1893-1957)

Custodian of Joanna's Box, 1934-1957. Only son of Edwin and Emily Jowett, and married to Maud (1895-1966). Worked as a Commercial Salesman for a Printing Inks firm. In 1933 moved from 38 Cross Street, Morecambe, to 3 Mount Grove, Gatley, Cheshire, where he received Joanna Southcott's Box and stored it in an upstairs bedroom.

**Edwin Armstrong Jowett** (1848-1926)

Custodian of Joanna's Box, 1925-1926. Born in Leeds, fourth son of John Marshall and Mary Jowett, and married to Emily (1856-1934). A bookseller, stationer and printer in Morecambe, where Joanna's Box was kept in a bungalow named 'Southcot', built by Edwin Jowett in 1925. He died 16 September, 1926.

**Emily Jowett** (1856-1934)

Custodian of Joanna's Box, 1926-1934. Born at Rastrick, York, daughter of Mary and John Aspinall Robinson, a prosperous stone merchant. Emily married Edwin Armstrong Jowett at St Matthews Church, Rastrick, in 1878. 'An ideal parent and mother' according to her son. She died on 11 January, 1934, at 'Southcot', Hawarden Avenue, Morecambe.

**John Marshall Jowett** (1816-1898)

Custodian of Joanna's Box, 1876-1898. Born in Leeds, York, son of Samuel Jowett. His wife, Mary, was born in Ireland in 1810. Settled in Bradford, where he introduced the first steam printing press and made his fortune as a publisher and builder. He advocated Temperance, and established Turkish baths in Leeds Road. He had four sons (William Henry, John Samuel, Joshua, Edwin Armstrong) and three daughters (Mary Jane, Sarah Proctor, Eva). He owned more than two dozen houses near his home, Apple Hall, Barkerend Road, where he spent his final years living as a recluse. He died on 23 March, 1898, and was buried at Undercliffe Cemetery, Bradford.

**Joseph Jowett** (1783-1848)

Ardent follower of Joanna Southcott. Son of William Jowett, one of Joanna's 'judges', and brother of Samuel. Joseph married Sarah Kidd and was survived by two daughters, Martha Ann and Sarah. A son, William, died in 1819. Joseph set up business as a coach-builder in Birmingham in 1823, later worked as an inn-keeper, travelling salesman, and brewer's clerk. He died of a fever on 7 February, 1848, at Redditch.

**Samuel Jowett** (1784-1876)

Custodian of Joanna's Box, 1861-1876. Born in Leeds, son of William Jowett, one of the judges at Joanna's 'Trials'. As printer and publisher, he produced many pamphlets for the movement, and as a preacher and prolific correspondent was regarded as the leader of Southcottians in the north.

**James Kidd** (1791-1868)

Ardent follower of Joanna Southcott. Born 29 October, 1791. James Kidd remained a bachelor, but after his sister married Joseph Jowett he enjoyed a close relationship with her family. A cloth manufacturer, he died at Binns Cottage, Southowram, on 30 January, 1868, leaving effects worth £3,000 to his two nieces, Martha Ann Jowett and Sarah Kidd Jowett. He was buried in the Borough Cemetery, Halifax.

**Most Revd. Cosmo Gordon Lang** (1864-1945)

Archbishop of Canterbury, 1928-42. Born at Fyvie Manse, Aberdeen, third son of Revd. John Marshall Lang. Educated at Park School, Glasgow, and Balliol College, Oxford. B.A. 1886, M.A. 1888, D.D. 1901. Ordained Priest at Oxford in 1891; Fellow of All Souls College, 1889-93 and 1897-1928, Fellow of Magdalen College, Oxford, 1893-97; Curate of Leeds 1890-93; Vicar of St Mary the Virgin, Oxford, 1894-96; Vicar of Portsea, 1896-1901. Honorary Chaplain to Queen Victoria 1899-1901. Canon and Treasurer of St Paul's Cathedral, 1901-08. Prelate, St John of Jerusalem from 1911. Consecrated Bishop

Suffragan of Stepney in 1901; translated to York in 1909, and to Canterbury in 1928. Soon after enthronement Lang was stricken by illness, but recovered in 1932 and worked tirelessly for the next decade. Member of the Privy Council. Lord High Almoner from 1933. Lang was regarded as a valued counsellor and friend by King George V. After his resignation in 1942, he was created Baron Lang of Lambeth. Author of *The Miracles of Jesus; The Parables of Jesus;* and *The Opportunity of the Church of England.*

**Princess Louise, Marchioness of Lorne, Duchess of Argyll** (1848-1939)

Sixth child of Queen Victoria. Born 18 March, 1848. Married Lord Lorne, who claimed clairvoyant vision. She was interested in spiritualism. In 1880 was badly injured in a sleigh accident. Soon afterwards her marriage broke down, but there was no formal separation.

**Walburga Ehrengarde Helena, Lady Paget** (1839-1929)

Member of the royal court. Eldest daughter of Charles Frederick Anthony de Hohenthal, Count of the Holy Roman Empire. She married in 1860 the Right Hon. Sir Augustus Berkeley Paget, (1823-1896), Ambassador at Rome and Vienna. Lady Paget was one of Queen Victoria's most trusted friends. She was interested in spiritualism, wrote on the reincarnation of souls in the bodies of animals, and used her influence to interest members of the royal family in Joanna Southcott's Box.

**Rev. Joseph Pomeroy** (1749-1837)

Anglican clergyman. Born at Lanton in Cornwall 6 November, 1749, son of John and Grace Pomeroy. Joseph married Melloney Scobell in 1778 at Madron. She died on 30 August, 1799, and his father died three days later. Persecuted by Southcottians for his alleged betrayal of Joanna. For over sixty years he was vicar of St Kew in Cornwall where he lies buried in a granite coffin specially prepared and laid in the ground during his lifetime.

**Beatrice Mary, Lady Portsmouth** (1866-1935)

Cousin of Rachel Fox and friend of Lady Paget. Born at Torquay, the only child of Edward Pease, of Darlington and Bewdley, and niece of Sir Joseph Whitwell Pease, 1st Baronet. On 17 February, 1885, married Newton, 6th Earl of Portsmouth (1856-1917) M.P. for Barnstaple, 1880-85, and North Devon, 1885-91. Under secretary of State for War 1905-8. He died without issue on 4 December, 1917. Lady Portsmouth urged the Archbishop of Canterbury to call for Joanna's Box. She died 13 December, 1935.

**William Owen Pughe** (1759-1835)

Welsh antiquary and lexicographer. Known in early life as William Owen. Born at Tynybryn in Merioneth, son of a skilled singer to the harp. Arrived in London in 1776 and after 1783 began to collect materials for his Welsh-English dictionary, published in 1803. Three years later he succeeded to a small estate at Nantglyn, near Denbigh, and assumed the surname of Pughe. He had married Sarah Elizabeth Harper in 1790 and they had a son, Aneurin Owen, and two daughters. Friend of William Blake, an adherent of Joanna Southcott, and for many years secretary/adviser to Jane Townley.

**Mary S. Robertson** (d.1943)

Author of *Authentic History of the Great Box of Sealed Writings left by Joanna Southcott* (1925). Born in Scotland and graduated from St Andrew's University. A member of Alice Seymour's teaching staff at Headland College. Joined her at Rock Cottage, Blockley, in 1919, to help in the work of publicising Joanna Southcott's mission. Formed the Olive Branch League, an international society for young Southcottians, in 1928. Lost her hearing and suffered a nervous breakdown in later years. Retired to a nursing home in Edinburgh, where she died of pneumonia on 17 December, 1943.

**Alice Seymour** (1857-1947)

Biographer of Joanna Southcott and founder of the Southcott Society. Born 10 January, 1857, at 16 Wyndham Square, Plymouth, daughter of James Seymour, a linen draper. Her aunt had married John Wroe's eldest son and Alice was confirmed by the Bishop of London, Dr Arthur Foley Winnington Ingram, a great-grandson of the Reverend T.P. Foley. Educated at Queen's College, London, she became owner and Principal of Headland College, a girls' school in Plymouth. In 1909 she published *The Express*, a life of Joanna Southcott in two volumes. Retired to Rock Cottage, Blockely, in 1919. After her fortunes suffered during the war, the cottage was sold to Annie Vesey-Stitt, but Alice stayed on at Rock Cottage till her death on 24 October, 1947.

**William Sharp** (1750-1824)

Eminent engraver and Custodian of Joanna's Box, 1802-1820. Born in the Minories, London, on 17 January, 1750, son of William and Sarah Sharp. Apprenticed to an engraver of firearms and from 1787 published his own work. Friend of Thomas Paine, at one time a believer in Swedenborg, afterwards in Richard Brothers. By 1814 Sharp had achieved international fame and was elected an honorary member of the Imperial Academy at Vienna and the Royal Academy at Munich.

Became a staunch supporter of Joanna Southcott whom he brought from Exeter and maintained at his own expense for a considerable time. The last of her followers to admit the reality of her death, Sharp never lost faith in her divine mission. He died of dropsy and was buried in Chiswick Churchyard, leaving what was left of his wealth to Hannah Eikenhead (1771-1838), his housekeeper for over twenty years.

**Annie Veysey Stitt** (1884-1971)

Leader of the Southcott Society after Alice Seymour's death. Daughter of Revd. James Veysey and goddaughter of Dr Robert Trefusis, Bishop of Crediton. Worked at Westminster Bank, Piccadilly for many years and was present at the opening of Harry Price's spurious Box at Westminster in 1927. After visiting Blockley most weekends to help Alice Seymour, in 1941 Annie bought Rock Cottage, to escape from London air-raids and to provide a home for her disabled brother. In 1942 she married John Muir Stitt, Printer and fellow Southcottian. In 1947 they took over leadership of the Southcott Society. John Stitt died in January, 1950. Annie died in a fire at Rock Cottage on 26 July, 1971.

**Robert Stuckey** (1843-1931)

Custodian of Joanna's Box, 1898-1925. Born at Montacute, Somerset, son of Sealy and Anna Stuckey. Ran a confectionery business in Bridgwater with his first wife, Albenia (1845-1883). Married Lily Kirby Herbert in 1886 and ran a restaurant in Bristol, where his son, Ralph (1888-1917) was born. Returned to live at Paradise Cottage, Burnham, after his father's death. A Director of Burnham Gas Company and served on Burnham Urban District Council. Politically he was an ardent Conservative and also a Freemason. A keen sportsman and staunch churchman. Buried in Burnham cemetery.

**Sarah Anne Stuckey** (1841-1918)

Devout follower of Joanna Southcott. Born at Montacute, Somerset, daughter of Sealy and Anna Stuckey. Her health collapsed after the death of her mother in 1883. She became a recluse and was incapable of managing on her own, but lived in the family home and took care of the Box from 1898 until her death on Good Friday, 29 March, 1918. Buried in Burnham cemetery.

**Sealy Stuckey** (1814-98)

Custodian of Joanna's Box, 1898. Born at Seavington, Somerset, son of Robert Stuckey, a baker. In 1831 he became acquainted with the Southcott movement. Married Anna Brian (1813-1883) at Langport.

In 1847 they moved from Oddcomb, Somerset, to Burnham-on-Sea, where Stuckey established a successful confectionery business in Regent Street. In 1849 he was chosen one of the seven elders of Edmund Baker's church in Ilminster. His wife lies buried in St Andrew's churchyard, Burnham, with an infant son, who died 1860, and her mother. By 1881 Sealy Stuckey had retired and moved to Paradise Cottage, in Mount Burnham, where he took custody of the Box shortly before his death on 25 May, 1898. Buried in Burnham cemetery.

**John Tremlett Symons** (c1783-1814)
Supporter of Joanna Southcott. Born in Exeter, son of William and Mary Symons. Took over his father's business as auctioneer and undertaker. In 1803 listed as Volunteer in the Exeter Militia. In 1808 married Sarah Melluish, who died in childbirth the following year. Served as Clerk of the Stores in the Field Train Department and died in Sicily in 1814.

**Mary Symons** (1747-1813)
Loyal friend and supporter of Joanna Southcott. Wife of William Symons and lived at 4 Gandy's Lane, Exeter, where Joanna rented accommodation and was occasionally employed. Mary Symons looked after the Box when Joanna worked elsewhere in the city. She died in June, 1813, and was buried at Allhallows, Goldsmith Street, Exeter.

**William Symons** (1749-1814)
Friend and supporter of Joanna Southcott. By 1796 had set up business as a furniture-broker at 4, Gandy's Lane, Exeter. In 1803 he was serving in the Cavalry. Died in December, 1814, and was buried at Allhallows, Goldsmith Street, Exeter, where he had been a churchwarden.

**Robert Temple** (1885-1967)
Honorary Secretary of the Panacea Society from 1935. A banker who had spent years working for trading firms in South America and the Gold Coast. In 1921 he joined the Panacea Society, and in 1933 retired and came to live in Bedford. In 1957 he journeyed to Gatley, Cheshire, to collect the Box on behalf of the Panacea Society who have been its Custodians ever since. He died 17 October, 1967.

**Jane Townley** (1761-1825)
Custodian of Joanna's Box, 1820-1825. Born at Belfield Hall, near Rochdale, daughter of Colonel Richard Townley, High Sheriff of Lancashire, and his first wife Ann (née Western) who died in 1761.

Christened at St Chad's parish church on 19 August, 1761, Jane was regarded as an invalid when she met Joanna in 1803 and became her life-long supporter. She provided Joanna with a home for ten years, acting as her amanuensis and close friend. After Joanna died, Jane became convinced that she herself was now recipient of divine communications. She died at 17 Weston Place, St Pancras, on 25 March, 1825, and was buried privately at St Martin's Burying Ground, Camden Town.

**George Turner** (d.1821)

Leeds merchant and disciple of Brothers. Turner was one of the Seven Stars who went to Exeter to judge Joanna's writings in 1801. He acted as a judge at her trials and was her host when she visited Yorkshire. Acknowledged as Joanna's successor by Southcottian groups in Yorkshire, Lancashire and the West Country, he was rebuffed by Sharp, Foley and Harwood. After his predictions grew increasingly wild he was committed to a Quaker asylum where he published fourteen books and gradually resumed the direction of the Movement. Turner regained his liberty in 1820 and promptly promised the appearance of Shiloh in London on 14th October. He died September 1821, bitterly disappointed.

**Anne Underwood** (1766-1825)

Devoted servant of Jane Townley and Joanna Southcott's chief amanuensis. Born 8 April, 1766. Widowed young, she had a daughter, Ann, who married Charles Vincent Barnard, another fervent Southcottian. She appeared genuinely fond of Joanna, whom she nursed to the bitter end. Then, after wearing herself out nursing Townley through her last illness, she herself died six weeks later and was buried at St Martin's Burying Ground, Camden Town, in the grave that already held her daughter. Her grandsons sold the box of manuscripts to Daniel Jones that was later published as *The Sixth Book of Wonders.*

**John Wroe** (1782-1863)

Founder of Christian Israelites. Born at Bowling, Bradford, eldest son of Joseph Roe, whom he joined in business as farmer, worsted manufacturer and collier. He set up independently c.1810 and came under the influence of George Turner, leader of Joanna Southcott's followers in the north. After Turner's death, Wroe claimed the succession. He travelled in many parts of Europe, his followers called themselves 'Christian Israelites' and divided into twelve tribes. Having set up his headquarters at Ashton, he opened a costly 'sanctuary' in Church Street, with four 'gates' on the outskirts of town marking a future temple area. A series of scandals forced Wroe to leave Ashton in 1831, after which date his followers separated from the main group of Southcottians. In his later years Wroe travelled in Australia, New Zealand, and America, making numerous converts wherever he went. He died on 5 February, 1863, at Melbourne.

# Appendix 3
# Conditions under which the Box may be Opened

I. Extracted from Ann Underwood to a friend in Leeds, 12 November, 1813:

In respect to the inquiry of the Whitby friends concerning the Trial she can give no answer for she know nothing about the manner of the Trial nor whether it may be in the Bishops Palace, the 24 of her friends that will be chosen for her must have admittance with the other 24 ministers, but whether any other person will have admittance she cannot tell, it is all concealed from her and as she will have nothing to do with giving directions any further than the Lord has given, that such a number must be present to try the Cause, she cannot give any herself, as this will be different to what was done at Paddington or at the Neckinger, therefore she don't know that any will be permitted to be present only those that are chosen – and this is all the information she can at present give about it, but when it is settled we may know more about it, and I shall give you all the information I can, but if it should be in the Bishops Palace, Joanna will have no authority there to admit anyone, but we may know more about it before it take place. [PS; 3-1-1]

II. Extracted from Alice Seymour, *Southcott Despatch*, 1919-22, page 3:

'The command is given, as we believe by the Lord, that the Great Trial is to be held some time between May and November, Old Style (i.e. between May 12th and December 12th). The twenty-four are to meet the twenty-four and form a double jury – the Bishops are to be the judges of this weighty Trial.'

III. Information upon the Approximate Conditions for the Opening of Joanna Southcott's Box of Sealed Writings – as supplied by the Panacea Society in 2002, based on Octavia, *Healing For All*, 1925, page 117.

1. The present custodian of the Box is The Panacea Society, Bedford. The Box is held at a secret location.
2. Portions from the Writings of Joanna Southcott, from the moment they were written, were commanded to be kept close till the Bishops should ask for them 'in a time of grave national danger'. The initiative must therefore be taken by the Bishops or by some authority in the land and not by believers in the Visitation. But, when the Bishops agree to send for the Box, 24 believers will come forward to form a Jury, to meet the 24 Bishops or their representatives.
3. The Book of the Trial of the claims of Joanna Southcott (1804) must be read by all those consenting to be present. It will be produced for the Bishops.
4. An Attorney must be present.
5. There are written instructions for the Judges and the Jury, which are to be kept sealed until the Assembly meets.
6. A suitable house must be lent or rented for the occasion. The Box of Writings must be previously placed for three days in the vault or cellar of the house.
7. The house must be close to a field or railed-in space.
8. The 65 Books and any original MSS. possessed by believers are to be exposed for investigation on the first three days of the Assembly.
9. On the *First Day* the double Jury of believers must meet the Bishops that they may discuss the problems at stake.
10. On the *Second Day* there will be a sign from the Lord of great importance.
11. On the *Third Day* the Sealed Writings are to be cut open and examined.
12. This Trial is the herald or precursor of the doom of Satan, as described in Rev.20. There will be no rest in the world until the opportunity be afforded of putting the assertion in Joanna's Writings to the proof.
13. If the verdict of the Bishops be against the Writings, they may be burnt.
14. It will be recognised, when the Box is opened, that the Trial compares for importance with the Trial of Christ before the Sanhedrin.
15. In the published Writings, the ceremony is also compared to the reading of a last Will or Testament.
16. It is also compared in the Writings to an inquest, the Box to be regarded as men regard a body which has been discovered.

17. On this occasion, the Church of England will stand her trial, to keep or lose her place among the Candlesticks.
18. Those calling the Trial must sustain the costs, i.e. the expenses of Jury and Witnesses, etc.
19. No sealed person is to be refused admission to the Trial.
20. 'As I made Myself known in the breaking of bread at Emmaus, so will I make Myself known in the breaking of the Seals of the Writings.'

# Appendix 4

## Schedule of Bishops from whom 24 may Gather

Bath and Wells
Birmingham
Blackburn
Bradford
Bristol
Canterbury
Carlisle
Chelmsford
Chester
Chichester
Coventry
Derby
Durham
Ely
Exeter
Gloucester
Guildford
Hereford
Leicester
Lichfield
Lincoln
Liverpool
London
Manchester
Newcastle
Norwich
Oxford
Peterborough
Portsmouth
Ripon and Leeds
Rochester
St Albans
St Edmundsbury and Ipswich
Salisbury
Sheffield
Sodor and Man
Southwark
Southwell
Truro
Wakefield
Winchester
Worcester
York

Total: 43, Information from: *The Church of England Year Book, 2002*

# Appendix 5

## Map showing Locations of the Box, 1798-2003

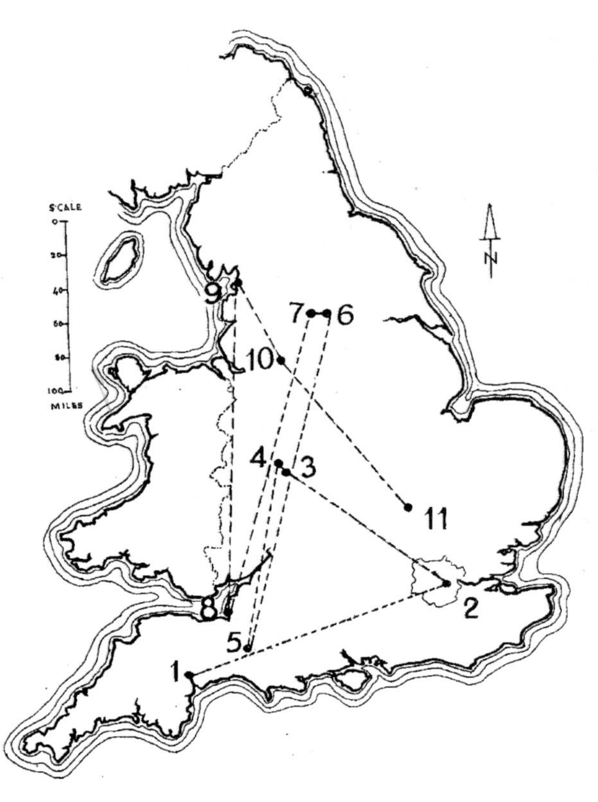


1. Exeter: 1798-1802
2. London: 1802-1825
3. Old Swinford: 1825-1835
4. Kingswinford: 1835-1842
5. North Cadbury: 1842-1861
6. Leeds: 1861-1876
7. Bradford: 1876-1989
8. Burnham on Sea: 1898-1925
9. Morecambe: 1925-1934
10. Gatley: 1934-1957
11. Bedford: 1957-

# Bibliography

## A Note on Sources

The main sources for Joanna Southcott's Box of Sealed Prophecies are the sixty-five works of her canon (originally indexed by Philip Pullen in 1815) and unpublished materials held in collections by the following:

1. Panacea Society, Bedford [PS]
2. British Library, London [BL]
3. London Metropolitan Archive [LMA]
4. Humanities Research Centre, University of Texas, Austin
5. West Country Studies Library, Exeter [WCSL]
6. Blockley Antiquarian Society, Blockley, Gloucestershire
7. Harry Price Library, University of London
8. John Rylands University Library, Manchester
9. Guildhall Library, London
10. Devon Record Office [DRO]
11. Gloucestershire Record Office [GRO]
12. Worcestershire Record Office [WRO]
13. Local Studies Library, Taunton
14. Private Collections [PC]

## Works by Joanna Southcott or Recognised as Part of her Canon:

*The Strange Effects of Faith, With Remarkable Prophecies (Made in 1792, etc) of Things Which Are to Come: Also, Some Account of My Life*. Exeter. Published in six parts. Parts 1-5, 1801; Part 6, 1802. [Books 1-6]

*A Continuation of Prophecies by Joanna Southcott from the year 1792 to the present time*. Exeter, 1802. [Book 7]

*The Strange Effects of Faith; being a Continuation of Joanna Southcott's Prophecies of Things Which Are to Come*. London, 1802. [Book 8]

*Divine & Spiritual Letters of Prophecies, Sent to Reverend Divines, etc*. London, nd. [Book 9]

*Second Book of Letters*. London, nd. [Book 10]

*A Dispute between the Woman & the Powers of Darkness*. London, 1802. [Book 11]

*The Answer of the Lord to the Powers of Darkness*. London, 1802. [Book 12]

*A Communication Given to Joanna, in Answer to Mr Brothers' Last Book,*

*Published the End of This Year*. London, 1802. [Book 13]

*Prophecies. A Warning to the Whole World, from the Sealed Prophecies of Joanna Southcott, and Other Communications, etc.* [also known as: The First Book of the Sealed Prophecies]. London, 1803. [Book 14]

*The Continuation of the Prophecies of Joanna Southcott. A Word in Season to a Sinking Kingdom*. London, 1803. [Book 15]

*The Second Book of Visions*. London, 1803. [Book 16]

*A Word to the Wise or a Call to the Nation, That They May Know the Days of Their Visitation, etc.* Stourbridge, 1803. [Book 17]

*Divine & Spiritual Communications, Written by Joanna Southcott On the Prayers of the Church of England, etc.* London, 1803. [Book 18]

*Sound an Alarm in My Holy Mountain*. Leeds, 1804. [Book 19]

*A Warning to the World. Joanna Southcott's Prophecies*. London, 1804. [Book 20]

*On the Prayers for the Fast Day, May 1804. Letters on Various Subjects from Mrs Joanna Southcott to Miss Townley*. London, 1804. [Book 21]

*Copies & Parts of Copies of Letters & Communications, Written from Joanna Southcott and Transmitted by Miss Townley to Mr W. Sharp in London*. London, 1804. [Book 22]

*Mr Joseph Southcott, the Brother of Joanna Southcott, Will Now Come Forward as Dinah's Brethren Did, etc.* London, 1804. [Book 23]

*Letters & Communications of Joanna Southcott, the Prophetess of Exeter, Lately Written to Jane Townley*. Stourbridge, 1804. [Book 24]

*The Trial of Joanna Southcott, during Seven Days, Which Commenced on the Fifth, and Ended on the Eleventh of December, 1804. At Neckinger House, Bermondsey, Near London*. London, 1804. [Book 25]

*Joanna Southcott's Answer to Garrett's Book, Entitled, 'Demonocracy Detected', etc.* London, 1805. [Book 26]

*Joanna Southcott's Answer to Five Charges in the Leeds Mercury, etc.* London, 1805. [Book 27]

*The True Explanation of the Bible, Revealed by Divine Communications to Joanna Southcott, etc.* Published in six parts. London, 1804-5. [Books 28-33]

*An Explanation of the Parables Published in 1804 by Joanna Southcott; Also an Answer to a Book by L.Mayer, etc.* London, 1806. [Book 34]

*The Kingdom of Christ is at Hand etc.* London, 1805. [Book 35]

*The Second Book of the Sealed Prophecies*. London, 1805. [Book 36]

*The Answer of the Rev. Thomas P. Foley, to the World, Who Hath Blamed His Faith, etc. Stourbridge, 1805* [by Thomas Foley]. [Book 37]

*The Controversy between Joanna Southcott and Elias Carpenter, One of Her Judges, Made Public*. Published in five parts. London, 1805. [Books 38-42]

*An Answer to the World for Putting in Print a Book in 1804 Called Copies & Parts of Copies, etc.* London, 1806 [by William Sharp]. [Book 43]

*The Full Assurance That the Kingdom of Christ Is at Hand, from the Signs of the Times*. London, 1806. [Book 44]

*A Few Remarks & Inquiries on a Sermon Preached by the Rev. Joseph Cockin, Independent Minister at Halifax, Being the Contents of a Letter, etc.*

Leeds, 1806. [Book 45]

*The Long-Wished-For Revolution, Announced to Be at Hand in a Book Lately Published by L. Mayer . . . Explained by Joanna Southcott, etc*. London, 1806. [Book 46]

*Answer to Mr Brothers' Book, Published in September, 1806 . . . Also a Letter Sent to Mr Huntingdon, etc*. London, 1806. [Book 47]

*A Caution & Instruction to the Sealed, That They May Know for What They Are Sealed*. London, 1807. [Book 48]

*An Account of the Trials on Bills of Exchange, Wherein the Deceit of Mr John King and His Confederates . . . Is Exposed, etc*. London, 1807. [Book 49]

*An Answer to a Sermon Published & Preached by Mr Smith . . . at Beersheba Chapel, etc*. London, 1808. [Book 50]

No Title [known as: *Answer to False Doctrine & the Crying Sins of the Nation*] London, 1808. [Book 51]

*A True Picture of the World & A Looking-Glass for All Men*. London, nd, ?1809. [Book 52]

*True Explanations of the Bible* – 7th Part. London, 1810. [Book 53]

*The Controversy of the Spirit with the Worldly Wise, As Given through Joanna Southcott*. London, 1811. [Book 54]

*A Continuation of the Controversy with the Worldly Wise*. London, 1811. [Book 55]

*An Answer to Thomas Paine's Third Part of the Age of Reason . . . Likewise to S. Lane . . . & to Hewson Clarke, etc*. London, 1812. [Book 56]

*The Book of Wonders, Marvellous & True*. London, 1813. [Book 57]

*The Second Book of Wonders, More Marvellous Than the First*. London, 1813. [Book 58]

*Copies of Letters Sent to the Clergy of Exeter from 1796 to 1800, with Communications & Prophecies Put in the Newspapers in 1813*. London, 1813. [Book 59]

*Wisdom Excelleth the Weapons of War . . . Judgments Are the Strange Works of the Lord, But Mercy His Darling Attribute*. London, 1814. [Book 60]

*The Third Book of Wonders, Announcing the Coming of Shiloh; With a Call to the Hebrews, etc*. London, 1814. [Book 61]

*The Fourth Book of Wonders, Being the Answer of the Lord to the Hebrews*. London, 1814. [Book 62]

*The Fifth Book of Wonders, Announcing the Event Having Taken Place Which Was Promised in the Fourth Book Should Be in May . . . Also an Answer to the Address of the Rev. James Hearn, etc*. London, 1814. [Book 63]

*A Communication Sent in a Letter to the Reverend Mr P. in 1797, with an Explanation Thereon Now Given*. London, 1814. [Book 64]

*Prophecies Announcing the Birth of the Prince of Peace, Extracted from the Works of Joanna Southcott, etc*. London, 1814. [Book 65]

## Primary Works


Allman, Joseph. *Truth Defended, or Christ's Glorious and Peaceable Reign is at Hand*. London, 1810.

Anon. *Observations relating to the Divine Mission of Joanna Southcott*, London, 1807.

*Memoirs of the Life & Mission of Joanna Southcott etc. to which is added a Sketch of the Rev. W. Tozer.* London, 1814.

*The Life and Prophecies of Joanna Southcott from her infancy to the present time*, London, 1815.

*Sermons abstracted from the Prophetic and inspired Writings of Joanna Southcott, etc.* London, 1817.

Bennett, George. *A Warning to the Nation, from the Prophecies of Joanna Southcott*. London, nd.

Blunt, Christiana. *A Midnight Dialogue between Joanna Southcott and Satan, Translated from a Luciferian Manuscript*. 2nd Ed. London, 1814.

Bramall, James. *A Review of the Prophecies of Mrs Joanna Southcott taken by James Bramall, late Secretary to St Ann's Sunday School.* Manchester, nd.

Brooks, Joshua, comp. *A Dictionary of Writers on the Prophecies*. London, 1835.

Brothers, Richard. *An Exposition of the Trinity*, London, 1795.

*A Letter from Mr Brothers to Miss Cott*, London, 1798.

*A Poem on the Creation*, London, 1806.

*A Revealed Knowledge of the Prophecies and Times*, Book I. London, 1794.

*A Revealed Knowledge of the Prophecies and Times*, Book II, London, 1794.

*Wisdom and Duty*, London, 1805.

*Wonderful Prophecies*, London, 1795.

Burns, Revd. J. *Evans' Sketch of the Denominations of the Christian World, etc*. London, 1839.

Carpenter, Elias. *Nocturnal Alarm, being an Essay on Prophecy and Vision, etc*. London, 1803.

*Modern Realities. . . . A Reply to 'Modern Visionaries,' by J.T., etc.* London, 1805.

*Who are the Deluded? Or Mystery Unmasked, being a few Extracts from . . . Revelations and Visions communicated to a Deceased Character, etc.* London, 1805.

*An Apology for Faith, and Detection of Existing Errors Subversive of the Truth, etc.* 2 parts. London, 1814.

*The Extraordinary Case of a Piccadilly patient or Dr Reece physick'd by six female Physicians*. London, 1815.

Carpenter, S. Catherine. *Are These Things So? Being Remarks on 'Demonocracy Detected,' etc*. London, 1805.

Copas,Thomas. *An Address to the Believers in Joanna Southcott's Mission, partly in Answer to Mr Samuel Jowett of Leeds.* London, 1843.

Crossley, John. *The Master and Scholar Refuted*, London, 1810.

*Letters and Observations to Ministers*, Bradford, 1814

*The Old Religion, extracted from the Halifax Journal, Aug.4th, 1810, with additions*

Crossley, John, and Jowett, William. *A Vindication of Joanna Southcott's Writings; Being a Reply to an Anonymous Pamphlet Published against Her at Halifax,* Leeds, 1805.

Cumming, James. *The Scripture Looking-Glass: wherein Any Person May See What They Are*. Glasgow, 1878.

Denham, G. *Remarks on the Writings and Prophecies of Joanna Southcott.* London, 1814.

Fairburn, J.F. *The Life of Joanna Southcott, the Prophetess*. London, 1814.

Fielden, Thomas. *An Exposition of the Fallacies and Absurdities of that Deluded Church Generally Known as Christian Israelites, or 'Johannas.'* Rawtenstall, 1850.

Finlayson, John. *An Essay on the Latter Part of Verse 7th and 11th and 12th Verses, of the Twelfth Chapter of Daniel* . . . London, 1798.

*An Essay on the First Resurrection, and on the Commencement of the Blessed Thousand Years*. London, 1798.

Foley, T.P. *An Epistle to the Revd. The Vice-Chancellors of Cambridge and Oxford, etc.*, Stourbridge, 1803.

Fox, Rachel. *The Finding of Shiloh*, London, 1921.

*Joanna Southcott's Place in History: A Forecast*. Plymouth, 1925.

*The Sufferings and Acts of Shiloh-Jerusalem*, London, 1927.

*How We Built Jerusalem in England's Green & Pleasant Land*. 2 vols. Bedford, 1931.

Fox, John Enochiah V.N. *Remarkable Revelations and Prophecies from Heaven by the Virgin Joanna . . . and various other Prophets.* Newcastle-on-Tyne, 1840.

Glover, Aubrey E. *The Mystery of God*, 2nd Ed. Australian Branch of Southcott Society, 1982.

Hagger, John, and others. *A Circular addressed to All the Believers in the Divine Mission of the Lord to Joanna Southcott.* London, 1841.

*Letters to the Believers in the Divine Mission to Joanna Southcott, etc.* London, 1842.

*Copy of Address to the Chairman of the Anti-Corn Law Conference in London . . . Remedy for present evils . . . from the Prophetic Writings of Joanna Southcott*. London, 1842.

*A Call to the Believers in the Divine Mission of the Lord to Joanna Southcott, etc.* London, 1843.

*An Address to the Protestants of England, especially the Queen, the Archbishops, etc.* London, 1844.

*A Call from the Most High God . . . to His Ancient People, the Jews, etc.* London, 1845.

Halhed, Nathaniel Brassey. *The Second Speech of Nathaniel Brassey Halhed Esq.* London, 1795.

*Two Letters to the Right Hon. Lord Loughborough, Lord High Chancellor of England, on the Present Confinement of Richard Brothers, in a Private Mad-House*. London, 1795.

*The Whole of the Testimonies to the Authenticity of the Prophecies and Mission of Richard Brothers, as Prince and Prophet of the Hebrews.* London, 1795.

Hann, R. *Charges against Joanna Southcott and her twelve Judges, the Jury, and four-and-twenty Elders, etc.* London, nd.

*The Remarkable Life, Entertaining History, and Surprising Adventures of Joanna Southcott, etc. also an Account of the Seal.* London, nd.

*The Prophecies of Joanna Southcott, of Dreadful Judgments that are to fall on this Nation in the Year 1810 . . . and also of the Millennium* . . .London, nd.

*A Letter to the Right Reverend the Lord Bishop of London, concerning the Heresy and Imposture of Joanna the Prophetess*, London, 1810.

Harrison, W.B. *A Letter addressed to a Friend explanatory of the Object and Manner of Christ's Second Coming, etc.* Leeds, 1834.

*Letter addressed to an Eminent Clergyman. . .explaining the nature and object of the Divine Mission of the late Joanna Southcott.* Leeds, 1842.

Harrison & others. *Correspondence of the Southcottian Church*. London, 1843.

Hodgkins, B. *A few plain Remarks on the pretended prophecies and delusions of a Modern Prophetess.* Birmingham, 1813.

Hudson, T.P. *Copies of Deep and Important Letters, addressed to the Queen, Prince Albert, etc.* London, 1843.

*The Royal Proclamation for the Crowning of the Lord Jesus Christ. . .Decem. 26, 1847 in all the Churches of the True Israel, in England* . . . London, 1847.

Hughson, D. *The Life of Joanna Southcott.* London, 1814.

Jezreel, Esther. *The Messenger of Wisdom & Israel's Guide,* New Brompton (Kent), 1887 (monthly).

Jezreel, J.J. *Extracts from the Flying Roll*, New Brompton (Kent), 1879.

Jones, D. *A Letter addressed to the Believers in the Everlasting Covenant.* Bradford (Wilts), 1835. *A Second Letter to the Believers in the New Covenant,* Brighton, 1835.

*A Scriptural Treatise upon the Fall of Man, and also upon the Second Coming of Christ, etc.* London, 1835.

*A Letter of Warning to the Whole World; from the Signs of the Seven Days, compared with Seven Thousand Years*. Bradford (Wilts), 1836.

*Table of the Kingdoms of Men and the Kingdom of God.* London, 1839.

*A Letter Addressed to the Lords Spiritual and Temporal of Great Britain* . . . London, nd.

*Scriptural Evidences on the Day of Judgment, and the Ten Last Kingdoms preceding the Millenium*, London and Bradford (Wilts), 1843.

*An Offering from the Seven Spirits which are before the Throne, etc*. London and Bradford (Wilts), 1847.

*To the Believers in the Cause of Joanna Southcott*, Bath, 1852.

*The Sixth Book of Wonders, being a verbatim copy of the Six Sealed Letters dated September 1813 announcing 'This Day the Rev. Joseph Pomeroy married to Joanna Southcott, the Great Prophetess, and the Wonder of the World.'* Bath, 1852. [comp.]

*An Essay with the Assistance of Divine Revelation, on the Restoration of the Lost Creation.* Bradford-on-Avon, 1853.

*An Answer to a Pamphlet called 'The Coming Struggle among the Nations of the Earth.'* Bradford (Wilts), 1853.

*Book of Letters, Joanna Southcott and others,* 1803-1853. [comp.]

*Southcott's Prophecies*, Bradford-on-Avon, 1853-1860. [comp.]

*A Letter to the Believers in the Mission of Joanna Southcott, upon 'The Sixth and Seventh Books of Wonders.'* Bradford (Wilts), 1859.

*Texts of Scripture relating to the Kingdom of God on Earth*. Bradford (Wilts), 1859.

*The Everlasting Gospel. Shiloh's Ten Days' Warning to the Churches*. Bradford (Wilts), 1864.

*The Everlasting Gospel. Shiloh's Seven Seals*. Bradford (Wilts), 1864.

Jones, L.E.C. [Ed.] *Songs of Faith, Hope and Joy, founded on the Prophecies given from 1792 by Joanna Southcott.* Brighton, 1835.

*The True Explanation of the Bible revealed by Divine Communications to Joanna Southcott*. Brighton, 1835.

*Scriptures of the Revelation of the Most High, etc*. London, 1843.

*The Time for Worshipping in the Spirit, Illucidated from the Visitation of Prophecy to Joanna Southcott during the years 1792-1814*. Bath, 1853.

*The Small Still Voice in London: Explaining Mysteries hitherto unknown*. Bradford, Wilts, 1856.

*Commentary upon the Prayers and Ordinances of the English Protestant Church, etc*. Bradford (Wilts), 1863.

*The Scriptures of the Holy Trinity. The New Testament explained in England by the Voice of the Spirit of Christ.* Parts 1-4. London, 1865.

Jowett, Joseph. *An Address to the Believers in the Divine Mission of Joanna Southcott*. Leeds, 1841.

Jowett, Samuel. *To Messrs Hagger, Copas, Pye, and Malby, etc*. Leeds, 1842.

*An Address to the Believers . . . being a reply to the Appeal of Mr Copas*. Leeds, 1842.

*To the Believers in Joanna Southcott's Visitation*. Leeds, 1844.

Kirby, R.S. *Kirby's Wonderful and Eccentric Museum; Or Magazine of Remarkable Characters, Including All the Curiosities of Nature and Art, from the Remotest Period to the Present Time*. London, 1820.

Lane, S. *Joanna Southcott, M.A., Detected, etc*. Yeovil, 1811.

Law, Richard. *Copy of an Epistle of the Most Extraordinary Nature; Sent to the Right Hon. Henry Addington, etc. July 19th, 1803*. London, nd.

Lewis, F. *An Address to the Clergy, Particularly the Bench of Bishops, etc*. London, 1803.

Malby, Thomas. *Letters to the Believers in the Divine Mission to Joanna Southcott. In Reply to the Various Letters Received in Connection with their Second Circular*. nd.

*The Testimony of the Southcottian Church in London on the Late Visitation of Joanna Southcott, that the Child was Born on the 16th December, 1814, etc*. London, 1843.

*An Appeal to the Believers in the Divine Mission of Joanna Southcott*. London, nd.

Mathias, P. *The Case of Joanna Southcott*. London, 1815.

Mayer, Lewis. *The Woman in the Wilderness, or the Wonderful Woman with her Wonderful Seal, etc*. London, 1806.

Panacea Society Publications:

*Keys to the Whole Body of Truth for the Whole Body of Believers*, Bedford, 1918.

*Brushes with the Bishops,* (Besma), London, 1919.

*Early Dawn of the Great Prophetical Visitation to England*, London, 1922.

*Healing for All*, (Octavia), London, 1925.

*A Petition to the Episcopate*, [pamphlet] Bedford, 1930.

*England Awake!,* Bedford, 1935.

*Transactions of the Panacea Society with the Archbishops and Bishops of the Church of England*, London, 1935.

*The Panacea* [Magazine, bound in 11 vols] Bedford, nd.

*The Writings of the Holy Ghost* [16 vols] Bedford, 1919-34.

Peacock, Elizabeth Fairlight Argus. *A Warning to the Whole World being a Letter sent March 10th, 1853, to the Bishops* . . . London, 1853.

*Proclamation to the Believers in the Divine Mission of Joanna Southcott*, Walworth Common, 1864.

Priestley, Joseph. *The Present State of Europe Compared with Ancient Prophecies,* London, 1794.

Pullen, P. *Songs of Moses and the Lamb. An Hymn Book for the Sealed number, of the Millennium Church, collected from the writings of Joanna Southcott, etc*. London, 1804.

*Hymns or Spiritual Songs, composed from the Prophetic Writings of Joanna Southcott,* London, 1814.

*Index to the Divine & Spiritual Writings of Joanna Southcott*. London, 1815.

*Triumphal Ode and Songs of Praise and Thanksgiving on Shiloh*. London, 1815.

*A Complete Refutation of the Statement and Remarks published by Dr Reece relative to Mrs Southcott, etc*. London, 1815.

Reece, Richard. *A Correct Statement of . . . the Last Illness and Death of Mrs. Southcott.*. London, 1815.

Roberts, D. *Observations relative to the Divine Mission of Joanna Southcott*. London, 1807.

Robertson, Mary S. *The Way to God*, Ashford, 1935.

Seymour, Alice. *Radia*. 1906; Ashford, 1919.

*The Express*. 2 vols. London, 1909. [comp.]

*The Voice in the Wilderness*. Ashford, 1933.

*Order of Service for January 12th. The Uplifting of Hands. According to the Command Given to Joanna Southcott.* Plymouth, 1913.

Seymour, Alice [ed.]. *Express Leaflets* [1911-1914]

*The Two Witnesses* [1915-1918]

*The Southcott Despatch* [1919-1922]

*The Southcott Express* [1926-1929]

*Watch* [1935-1938]

Sibley, Samuel. *A Copy of the Articles of Faith, as Acknowledged and Believed by the Children of the Faithful, Belonging to the House of faith, Or Philadelphian Church; Well Known by the Name of the Followers of the Divine Mission on Joanna Southcott,* London, 1819.

Southcottian Friends. *Truth Defended: or, Christ's Glorious and Peaceable Reign is At Hand*. London, 1840.

*An Invitation to the Southcottian Churches, etc*. 1843.

*The Indictment against that Tyrannical, Cruel, and Bloody Monarch, Satan,. . . Also, the Minutes of the Conference of the Members of the Southcottian Churches in London, for Seven Days, from the 19th to the 25th of November, 1844*. London, 1845.

*The Trial, Casting, and Condemnation of the Prince of this World, . . . at the Court of Equity, Little James Street, Gray's Inn Lane, London, from the 25th to the 31st of December, 1846*. London, 1847.

Southey, Robert. *Letters from England by Don Manuel Alvarez Espriella*, London, 1807.

Spencer, John, & Others. *A Circular addressed to all the Believers in the Divine Mission of the Lord to Joanna Southcott*, London, nd.

*Second Circular. To the Believers in the Divine Mission to Joanna Southcott*, London, 1841.

Townley, Jane. *A Letter from Mrs Jane Townley to the Editor of the Council of Ten in Answer to His Remarks and Misrepresentations Respecting the Mission of Joanna Southcott*. London, 1823.

*Communications & Directions given to Mrs Jane Townley, after the publication of her Answer to the Editor of the Council of Ten*. London, 1824.

Townley, Richard. *A Journal Kept in the Isle of Man*. 1791.

Turnbull, Joseph. *Unbelief and Credulity. A Sermon Occasioned by the Death of Mrs Joanna Southcott, preached at her Native Place, Ottery Saint Mary, Devon, on the Lord's Day Evening, the 8th of January, 1815*. Chard, 1815.

Turner, George. *Communications of the Holy Spirit of God, given at different times to George Turner of Leeds*. Leeds, 1805.

*A Vindication for the Honour of God in answer to J.Aked, Halifax*. Leeds, 1807.

*The Cheat Detected*. Leeds, 1810.

*A Book of Wonders*, 1817.

*Wonderful Prophecies . . . being a Call to the Jews to Return*. London, 1818.

*Second Part of Wonderful Prophecies*, London, 1819.

*The Assurance of the Kingdom*, London, 1819.

*The Assurance of the Kingdom*, Part II. London, 1820.

Turpin, Theodore. *Extracts from Sermons preached at different Chapels in the Years 1812, 1813, and 1814*. London, 1825.

Twort, C.W. [publisher for John Ward] *The Vision of Judgment, or, the Return of Joanna from Her Trance*. London, 1829.

*The Vision of Judgment,(continued) or the Trial and Reward of Faith, etc.*. London, 1829

*The Living Oracle or, the Star of Bethlehem: written in answer to a letter of the Rev. T.P.Foley . . . addressed to Mr T.Pierce, of Nottingham*, Nottingham, 1830.

Wardle, I.P. *Questions Proposed to the Preachers of the Gospel, on Things Which Are To Come*, Stockport, nd.

Webster, Revd. Thomas. *Reasons for the Fall of Man*. London, 1804.

Wetherell, William Roundell. *A Testimony of Joanna Southcott, the Prophetess;*

*Sent by the Lord, to Warn the People of His Coming*, London, 1804.

Wilson, H., and J. Caulfield. *The Book of Wonderful Characters: Memoirs and Anecdotes of Remarkable and Eccentric Persons in All Ages and Countries*. London, 1870.

Wroe, John. *Sermons selected from the Scriptures . . . being a guide to the people surnamed Israelites to preach the everlasting Gospel*. 1846.

*Extracts from the teachings of John Wroe, Prophet-Missionary, 1853-1854*. nd.

Zimpel, C.F. *Joanna Southcott, Das Sonnenweib nebst einen Schlussel zum richtigen verstandniss der Bibel,* 1861.

## SECONDARY WORKS

*Alumni Cantabrigienses*, compiled by John Venn & J.A.Venn. Cambridge, 1922.

*Alumni Oxonienses*, compiled by Joseph Foster. London, 1888.

Armytage, W.H.G. *Heavens Below: Utopian Experiments in England, 1560-1960*. Toronto, 1961.

Ashton, John. *The Dawn of the XIXth Century in England*. London, 1906.

Baker, W.S. *William Sharp*. Philadelphia, 1875.

Balleine, G.R. *Past Finding Out: The Tragic Story of Joanna Southcott & Her Successors*. London, 1956.

Baring-Gould, S. *Devonshire Characters & Strange Events*. London, 1908.

Booth, Frank. *Robert Raikes of Gloucester*. Redhill, 1980.

Brockett, A. *Nonconformity in Exeter, 1650-1875*. Manchester, 1962.

Brown, Frances. *Joanna Southcott, the Woman Clothed with the Sun*, Cambridge, 2002.

Carpenter, S.C. *Eighteenth Century Church & People*. London, 1959.

Carr, Glenda. *William Owen-Pughe*. Cardiff, 1983.

Chick, Elijah. *A History of Methodism in Exeter & the Neighbourhood from the year 1739 until 1907*. Exeter, 1907.

Cohn, Norman. *The Pursuit of the Millennium*. London, 1970.

Cole, G.D.H. & Raymond Postgate. *The Common People*. London, 1956.

Derrett, J.D.M. *Prophecy in the Cotswolds, 1803-1947*. Shipston-on-Stour, 1994.

Exell, A.W. *Joanna Southcott at Blockley & The Rock Cottage Relics*. Shipston-on-Stour, 1977.

Forth, Brent. *And the Lord Spake unto Joanna Southcott*. London, 1937.

Fox, Rachel. *Joanna Southcott's Place in History: A Forecast*. Plymouth, 1925.

Gratus, Jack. *The False Messiahs*. London, 1975

Haden, J.M. *The Priest and the Prophetess*, (cyclostyled) Dudley Teachers' Centre, 1981

Harrison, J.F.C. *The Second Coming*. London, 1979.

Hopkins, J.K. *A Woman to Deliver Her People*. Austin, 1982.

Hoskins, W.G. *Industry, Trade & People in Exeter, 1688-1800*. Exeter, 1968.

James, William. *The Varieties of Religious Experience*. London, 1985.

Lamont, William. *Godly Rule: Politics & Religion, 1603-1660*. London, 1969.

Lane, C. *Life of Joanna Southcott & Bibliography of Joanna Southcott*. Reprint. Exeter, 1912.

Lewis, Val. *Satan's Mistress: The Extraordinary Story of the Eighteenth Century Fanatic Joanna Southcott and her Lifelong Battle with the Devil*, London, 1997.

Longford, Elizabeth. *Victoria R.I.* London, 1964.

Margary, Harry. *A to Z of Regency London*. London, 1985.

Matthews, Ronald. *English Messiahs*. London, 1936.

Perry, N. *The Story of St Mary's Church and the Parish of Oldswinford,* Oldswinford, 1989.

Robertson, Mary S.

*The True Story of Joanna Southcott*. Ashford, 1923.

*Authentic History of the Great Box of Sealed Writings left by Joanna Southcott.* Plymouth, 1925 (2nd ed.1929).

Thomas, Keith. *Religion & the Decline of Magic*. London, 1971.

Tobin, P.J. *The Southcottians in England* – unpublished M.A. thesis, University of Manchester, 1978.

Warne, Arthur. *Church & Society in Eighteenth Century Devon*. Newton Abbot, 1969.

Wright, E.P. *A Catalogue of the Joanna Southcott Collection at the University of Texas*. Austin, 1968.

'Xenes'. *Joanna Southcott and Her Box*. London, nd.

# Index

If you have enjoyed this book you will also be interested by:

# Joanna Southcott:
## The Woman Clothed with the Sun

### Frances Brown

A major biography of the visionary and prophet, Joanna Southcott, describing Joanna's life from her humble upbringing in rural Devon, to her death in fashionable London. Her early nature prophecies, based on the 'still, small voice' that was to guide her for two decades, brought her a reputation, initially locally. Her claims that the voice was that of God were rejected by the Church authorities, but her reputation grew as her prophecies became broader, and tens of thousands were 'sealed' as believers, while her writings were best-sellers.

The whole nation looked on in wonder in 1814 when Joanna – at the age of sixty-four – announced the forthcoming birth of 'Shiloh', which she saw as the second coming of Jesus. The pregnancy was confirmed by the leading doctors of the day, but Joanna died, and no trace of Shiloh could be found.

Frances Brown has used not only Joanna's sixty-five published works and many unpublished manuscripts, but also contemporary letters, newspapers, local histories and parish records to produce a rounded picture of a woman who was an extraordinary phenomenon in her own time and who has continued to intrigue later generations.

ISBN 0 7188 3018 0 360 pages 50 coloured and monochrome pictures